HONOR, SHAME, AND THE RHETORIC OF 1 PETER

SOCIETY
OF BIBLICAL
LITERATURE

DISSERTATION SERIES
Michael V. Fox, Old Testament Editor
E. Elizabeth Johnson, New Testament Editor

Number 160

HONOR, SHAME, AND THE RHETORIC OF 1 PETER

by
Barth L. Campbell

Barth L. Campbell

HONOR, SHAME, AND THE RHETORIC OF 1 PETER

Society of Biblical Literature
Dissertation Series

Scholars Press
Atlanta, Georgia

HONOR, SHAME, AND THE RHETORIC OF 1 PETER

by
Barth L. Campbell

Ph.D., 1995
Fuller Theological Seminary

Advisor:
Dr. Donald A. Hagner

Library of Congress Cataloging in Publication Data
Campbell, Barth L., 1952–
    Honor, shame, and the rhetoric of 1 Peter / Barth L. Campbell.
        p.   cm. — (Dissertation series / Society of Biblical Literature ; no. 160)
    Includes bibliographical references.
    ISBN 0-7885-0510-6 (alk. paper) — ISBN 978-1-58983-539-9 (paper : alk. paper)
    1. Bible. N.T. Peter, 1st—Socio-rhetorical criticism. 2. Honor in the Bible. 3. Shame in the Bible. I. Title. II. Series: Dissertation series (Society of Biblical Literature) ; no. 160.
BS2795.2.C35   1998
227'.92066—dc21   98-42330
                  CIP

Printed in the United States of America
on acid-free paper

TABLE OF CONTENTS

LIST OF FIGURES

ACKNOWLEDGEMENTS

I would like to express appreciation for the invaluable assistance by the following people in the production of this dissertation: the late Robert A. Guelich, who first suggested 1 Peter to me as a dissertation topic and guided me on my initial research of the letter; Leonard S. Wallmark, who encouraged me to pursue doctoral studies at Fuller Theological Seminary; Ralph P. Martin, who provided encouragement on my dissertation topic when the project was in its formative stages; John H. Elliott, who gave criticism and comment of inestimable worth for the research which served as a foundation to the dissertation. I am grateful for the many enjoyable hours he and I spent discussing 1 Peter in his home.

First Baptist Church, Modesto, California, helped with love, prayers, flexible employment, and insurance benefits throughout my years of study. I am most grateful to my church family for these kindnesses.

For my mother and late father I express gratitude for their substantial financial support and constant encouragement. My parents-in-law, Mr. and Mrs. Charles J. Bell, consistently provided generous monetary assistance to me and my family throughout the doctoral program. To them I give heartfelt thanks.

To my marvelous wife, Sandi, and precious daughter, Katie, I give my deepest thanks and affection. Their ceaseless sacrifice, understanding, and patience enabled me to persevere with joy and hope during my days of study, research, and writing. To them I dedicate this work with love.

LIST OF ABBREVIATIONS

Ar. *Frag.*	Aristophanes, *Fragments*
Arist. *Poet.*	Aristotle, "On the Art of Poetry"
Arist. *Rh.*	Aristotle, *The "Art" of Rhetoric*
AV	Authorized (King James) Version
BFC	La Bible en français courant
bis	twice
Brenton	English translation of the Septuagint by Lancelot C. L. Brenton
Cic. *Att.*	Cicero, Letters to Atticus
Cic. *De Or.*	Cicero, *De Oratore*
Cic. *Inv.*	Cicero, *De Inventione*
Cic. *Or.*	Cicero, *Orator*
Cic. *Part. Or.*	Cicero, *De Partitione Oratoria*
Cic. *Top.*	Cicero, *Topica*
Demet. *Eloc.*	Demetrius, *On Style* (*Elocutione*)
DSS	Dead Sea Scrolls
Goodspeed	*The New Testament: An American Translation*, by Edgar J. Goodspeed
Her.	*Rhetorica ad Herennium*
Hom. *Od.*	Homer, *The Odyssey*
JB	Jerusalem Bible
Long. *Subl.*	Longinus, *On the Sublime*
Luther	Das neue Testament, by Martin Luther
LXX	The Septuagint
Moffatt	The New Testament: A New Translation, by James Moffatt
NAB	New American Bible
NAS	New American Standard Bible
NEB	New English Bible (1961)
Nestle-Aland[26]	The Greek New Testament, ed. Eberhard Nestle, Erwin Nestle, Kurt Aland, et al.
NIV	New International Version
NJB	New Jerusalem Bible
NRSV	New Revised Standard Version

NTHD	Das neue Testament in heutigem Deutsch
pc	*pauci* (a few)
Phillips	The New Testament in Modern English, by J. B. Phillips
Plut. *Marcel.*	Plutarch, Marcellus (from *Plutarch's Lives*)
Plut. *Tib. Grac.*	Plutarch, Tiberius Gracchus from *Plutarch's Lives*)
Quint. *Inst. Or.*	Quintilian, *The Institutio Oratoria*
REB	Revised English Bible
Rh. Al.	*Rhetorica ad Alexandrum*
RV	Revised Version
Suet. *Nero*	Suetonius, Nero (from *The Twelve Caesars*)
Tacitus *Ann.*	Tacitus, *The Annals of Imperial Rome*
TEV	The New Testament in Today's English Version
t.t	technical term
UBS^3	The Greek New Testament, United Bible Societies, 3rd ed.
Vg	Latin Vulgate (New Testament, ed. H. J. White)
Weymouth	New Testament in Modern Speech, by Richard Francis Weymouth
WH	The Greek New Testament, ed. B. F. Westcott and F. J. A. Hort
ZB	Zürich Bible

CHAPTER ONE

Introduction

Classical-Rhetorical Criticism of the New Testament

Definition

In his presidential address to the Society of Biblical Literature in 1968, James Muilenburg[1] urged biblical scholars to focus on the rhetorical aspects of scriptural texts. His summons was for interpreters to go beyond form criticism, a method that generalizes features of texts, toward interpretations that consider traditional forms as shaped by contingency. The "rhetorical criticism" that Muilenburg advocated transcends stylistics. It identifies literary composition, structural patterns, and the myriad devices by which "predications are formulated and ordered into a unified whole."[2]

Muilenburg directed his summons toward those who engage in Old Testament criticism and they have answered with a growing collection of inquiries into the rhetorical features of Old Testament literature.[3]

In hindsight, Muilenburg's address appears to have been the clarion call to a New Testament rhetorical criticism as well.[4] Rhetorical studies of the Bible were sparse between the late 1700's and the 1950's. W. Wuellner recently exclaimed, however, that

---

[1] James Muilenburg, "Form Criticism and Beyond," *Journal of Biblical Literature* 88 (1969): 1–18.

[2] Ibid., 8.

[3] Recent surveys of OT rhetorical criticism are C. Clifton Black II, "Keeping up with Recent Studies XVI: Rhetorical Criticism and Biblical Interpretation," *The Expository Times* 100 (April 1989): 252–58; D. F. Watson, "Rhetorical Criticism," in *The International Standard Bible Encyclopedia* [hereafter *ISBE*], ed. Geoffrey Bromiley, et al. (Grand Rapids: William B. Eerdmans, 1988), 4:181 82.

[4] Duane F. Watson, "The New Testament and Greco-Roman Rhetoric: A Bibliography," *Journal of the Evangelical Theological Society* 31 (December 1988): 465.

"there have been more books, dissertations, and essays published related to rhetorical criticism of biblical texts in the decade of the 1980's than in several centuries prior to this!"[5]

In this dissertation, I use a specific kind of rhetorical criticism[6] which is a classical-rhetorical criticism of the New Testament (CRCNT). The method is based on the standards of Greco-Roman rhetoric found in the ancient Greek and Latin handbooks on the subject. According to C. Clifton Black II, much of what is labeled as rhetorical criticism in biblical studies refers to a literary criticism (particularly of style) in scriptural texts.[7] Narrative criticism and compositional criticism are varieties of literary criticism.[8]

CRCNT Explained

In 1975, Hans Dieter Betz's study[9] utilizing CRCNT appeared, an article that likely represents the first application of the approach to a portion of the New Testament.[10] Betz followed the

---

[5] W. Wuellner, "Rhetorical Criticism and Its Theory in Culture-Critical Perspective: The Narrative Rhetoric of John 11," in *Text and Interpretation: New Approaches in the Criticism of the New Testament,* ed. P. J. Hartin and J. H. Petzer, New Testament Tools and Studies 15 (Leiden: E. J. Brill, 1991), 175.

[6] I do not differentiate between "rhetorical analysis" and "rhetorical criticism" of the NT in my study as does Richard N. Soulen, *Handbook of Biblical Criticism,* 2nd ed. (Atlanta: John Knox Press, 1981), 168–70. Under the former term he refers to the parts of a classical rhetorical address. The latter term denotes for him Muilenburg's approach to structure and literary device as constituent parts of a whole. See Muilenburg, "Form Criticism," 18.

[7] C. Clifton Black II, "Rhetorical Questions: The New Testament, Classical Rhetoric, and Current Interpretation," *Dialog* 29 (Winter 1990): 69.

[8] David S. Dockery, "New Testament Interpretation: A Historical Survey," in *New Testament Criticism and Interpretation,* ed. David Alan Black and David S. Dockery (Grand Rapids: Zondervan, 1991), 61–62. An example of a literary criticism with narrative and compositional concerns is R. Alan Culpepper, *Anatomy of the Fourth Gospel: A Study in Literary Design,* New Testament Foundations and Facets (Philadelphia: Fortress Press, 1983).

[9] Hans Dieter Betz, "The Literary Composition and Function of Paul's Letter to the Galatians," *New Testament Studies* 21 (1975): 353–79.

[10] "In 1975, Hans Dieter Betz produced [see n. 9 above] what to my knowledge is the first rhetorical analysis of a portion of the New Testament using Greco-Roman rhetoric," says Duane Frederick Watson, *Invention,*

article with a major commentary on Galatians in 1979.[11] Definitive introductions to CRCNT have been penned by George A. Kennedy,[12] and Burton L. Mack.[13] Their works define CRCNT as the study of the New Testament according to the standards of Greco-Roman rhetoric.[14] Their analyses are of the various persuasive means from classical rhetoric that a New Testament

---

Arrangement, and Style: Rhetorical Criticism of Jude and 2 Peter, Society of Biblical Literature Dissertation Series 104 (Atlanta: Scholars Press, 1988), 6.

[11] Hans Dieter Betz, *Galatians: A Commentary on Paul's Letter to the Churches in Galatia*, Hermeneia—A Critical and Historical Commentary on the Bible (Philadelphia: Fortress Press, 1979). About this work Black, "Rhetorical Questions," 63, claims: "probably no work has spurred more interest in New Testament rhetoric than the Hermeneia commentary on Galatians."

[12] George A. Kennedy, *New Testament Interpretation through Rhetorical Criticism* (Chapel Hill: University of North Carolina Press, 1984).

[13] Burton L. Mack, *Rhetoric and the New Testament*, Guides to Biblical Scholarship, New Testament Series, ed. Dan O. Via, Jr. (Minneapolis: Fortress Press, 1990).

[14] General orientations to the subject of classical rhetoric are: Charles Sears Baldwin, *Ancient Rhetoric and Poetic: Interpreted from Representative Works* (n.p.: Macmillan Co., 1924; repr., Gloucester, MA: Peter Smith, 1959); idem, *Medieval Rhetoric and Poetic (to 1400): Interpreted from Representative Works* (n.p.: Macmillan Co., 1928; repr., Gloucester, MA: Peter Smith, 1959); Donald Lemen Clark, *Rhetoric in Greco-Roman Education* (Morningside Heights, NY: Columbia University Press, 1957); Thomas Cole, *The Origins of Rhetoric in Ancient Greece*, Ancient Society and History (Baltimore and London: Johns Hopkins University Press, 1991); G. Fesenmayer, "Rhetorik," *Lexikon für Theologie und Kirche*, 2nd ed., ed. Josef Höfer and Karl Rahner (Freiburg: Herder, 1963), 8:1276–78; Gilbert Highet, *The Classical Tradition: Greek and Roman Influences on Western Literature* (New York and London: Oxford University Press, 1949); Ronald F. Hock and Edward N. O'Neil, *The Chreia in Ancient Rhetoric: Volume I. The Progymnasmata*, Texts and Translations 27, Graeco-Roman Religion Series, ed. Hans Dieter Betz and Edward N. O'Neil, no. 9 (Atlanta: Scholars Press, 1986); George A. Kennedy, *The Art of Rhetoric in the Roman World 300 B.C.-A.D. 300* (Princeton: Princeton University Press, 1972); idem, *Classical Rhetoric and Its Christian and Secular Tradition from Ancient to Modern Times* (Chapel Hill: University of North Carolina Press, 1980); Wilhelm Kroll, "Rhetorik," in *Paulys Realencyclopädie des classischen Altertumswissenschaft*, ed. Wilhelm Kroll et al., supplemental vol. 7 (Stuttgart: J. B. Metzler, 1940), cols. 1039–138; Heinrich Lausberg, *Handbuch der literarischen Rhetorik: Eine Grundlegung der Literaturwissenschaft*, 2 vols. (Munich: Max Hueber, 1960) [refs. in my diss. are to sections]; Josef Martin, *Antike Rhetorik: Technik und Methode*, Handbuch der Altertumswissenschaft 2.3 (Munich: C. H. Beck, 1974).

author/redactor utilizes in written discourse. How the
readers/hearers may likely understand and respond to the
content of the author's rhetoric is also of concern to these and
other practitioners of CRCNT.[15]

---

[15] Orientations to CRCNT are Klaus Berger, "Hellenistische Gattungen im
neuen Testament," in *Aufstieg und Niedergang der römischen Welt*, ed. Hildegard
Temporini, Wolfgang Haase, and W. Haace (Berlin and New York: Walter De
Gruyter, 1984), 2.25.2: 1031–1432, 1831–85; idem, *Formgeschichte des neuen
Testaments* (Heidelberg: Quelle & Meyer, 1984); Black, "Recent Studies,"
254–58; idem, "Rhetorical Questions," 62–70; G. Walter Hansen, "Rhetorical
Criticism," in *Dictionary of Paul and His Letters*, ed. Gerald F. Hawthorne,
Ralph P. Martin, and Daniel G. Reid (Downers Grove, IL, and Leicester:
InterVarsity Press, 1993), 622–26; Kennedy, *NT Interpretation*; idem, "'Truth'
and 'Rhetoric' in the Pauline Epistles," in *The Bible as Rhetoric: Studies in
Biblical Persuasion and Credibility*, ed. Martin Warner, 195–202 (London and
New York: Routledge, 1990); Mack, *Rhetoric and the NT*; Ruth Majercik,
Thomas B. Dozeman, and Benjamin Fiore, "Rhetoric and Rhetorical
Criticism," in *The Anchor Bible Dictionary* [hereafter *ABD*], ed. David Noel
Freedman, et al. (New York: Doubleday, 1992), 5:717–19; Watson, "Bibliogra-
phy," 465–72; idem, *Invention*, 1–28; idem, "The New Testament and
Greco-Roman Rhetoric: A Bibliographical Update," *Journal of the Evangelical
Theological Society* 33 (December 1990): 513–24; idem, ed., *Persuasive Artistry:
Studies in New Testament Rhetoric in Honor of George A. Kennedy*, JSNT
Supplement 50 (Sheffield: JSOT Press, 1991); idem, "Rhetorical Criticism,"
in *Dictionary of Jesus and the Gospels*, ed. Joel B. Green, Scot McKnight, I.
Howard Marshall (Downers Grove, IL, and Leicester: InterVarsity Press,
1992), 698–701; idem, "Rhetorical Criticism [*ISBE*]," 181–82.
    Watson's "Bibliography" (1988) and "Bibliographical Update" (1990) are
excellent guides to the literature of CRCNT. Since the latter bibliography,
some works featuring elements of CRCNT that have appeared are:
    Gospels and Acts: Eckard Rau, *Reden in Vollmacht: Hintergrund, Form, und
Anliegen der Gleichnisse Jesu*, Forschungen zum Religion und Literatur des
alten und neuen Testaments 149 (Göttingen: Vandenhoeck & Ruprecht,
1990); Vernon K. Robbins, "Writing as a Rhetorical Act in Plutarch and the
Gospels," in *Persuasive Artistry*, ed. Duane F. Watson, 142–68 [1991]; Duane F.
Watson, "Paul's Speech to the Ephesian Elders (Acts 20:17–38): Epideictic
Rhetoric of Farewell," in *Persuasive Artistry*, ed. Duane F. Watson, 184–208
[1991]. **Paul/Deutero-Paul:** *Romans:* Douglas A. Campbell, *The Rhetoric of
Righteousness in Romans 3:21–26*, JSNT Supplement Series 65 (Sheffield: JSOT
Press, 1992); Karl P. Donfried, *The Romans Debate: Revised and Expanded
Edition* (Peabody, MA: Hendrickson, 1991 [revision of *The Romans Debate*
(Minneapolis: Augsburg Publishing House, 1977)]); Neil Elliott, *The Rhetoric
of Romans: Argumentative Constraint and Strategy and Paul's Dialogue with
Judaism*, JSNT Supplement Series 45 (Sheffield: JSOT Press, 1990); Charles
D. Myers, Jr., "Chiastic Inversion in the Argument of Romans 3–8," *Novum

CRCNT: Five Steps

Generally, five steps comprise the classical-rhetorical analysis of a New Testament text.[16]

1. Determine the rhetorical unit. The interpreter utilizing CRCNT must determine the rhetorical unit to be studied, that is, a passage with a discernible beginning, middle, and end. Proem, epilogue, and inclusion assist one in identifying a distinct rhetorical unit that may be from five or six verses to several chapters in length.

2. Determine the rhetorical situation. The rhetorical critic must ask what situation has demanded a rhetorical response, who are those being addressed, and what means are effective in helping them in their circumstances. Lloyd F. Bitzer has defined the rhetorical situation in the following way:

> Rhetorical situation may be defined as a complex of persons, events, objects, and relations presenting an actual or potential exigence which

---

Testamentum 35 (1993): 30–47. *1 & 2 Corinthians:* Barth Campbell, "Flesh and Spirit in 1 Cor 5:5: An Exercise in Rhetorical Criticism of the NT," *Journal of the Evangelical Theological Society* 36 (September 1993): 331–42; Margaret M. Mitchell, *Paul and the Rhetoric of Reconciliation: An Exegetical Investigation of the Language and Composition of 1 Corinthians,* Hermeneutische Untersuchungen zur Theologie 28 (Tübingen: J. C. B. Mohr [Paul Siebeck], 1991); J. Smit, "The Genre of 1 Corinthians 13 in the Light of Classical Rhetoric," *Novum Testamentum* 33 (1991): 193–216; Franz Zeilinger, "Die Echtheit von 2 Cor. 6:14–7:1," *Journal of Biblical Literature* 12 (Spring 1993): 71–80. *Galatians:* Richard N. Longenecker, *Galatians,* Word Biblical Commentary 41 (Dallas: Word Books, 1990); Frank J. Matera, "The Culmination of Paul's Argument to the Galatians: Gal. 5.1–6.17," *Journal for the Study of the New Testament* 32 (February 1988): 79–91 [not in either of Watson's bibliographies]. *Philippians:* L. Gregory Bloomquist, *The Function of Suffering in Philippians,* JSNT Supplement Series 78 (Sheffield: JSOT Press, 1993). *Colossians:* Petr Pokorny,, *Colossians: A Commentary,* trans. Siegfried S. Schatzmann (Peabody, MA: Hendrickson, 1991). *1 & 2 Thessalonians:* Charles A. Wanamaker, *The Epistles to the Thessalonians: A Commentary on the Greek Text,* The New International Greek Testament Commentary, ed. I. Howard Marshall and W. Ward Gasque (Grand Rapids: William B. Eerdmans, 1990; Exeter: Paternoster Press, 1990). **General Epistles:** *James:* Duane F. Watson, "James 2 in Light of Greco-Roman Schemes of Argumentation," *New Testament Studies* 39 (1993): 94–121; idem, "The Rhetoric of James 3:1–12 and a Classical Pattern of Argumentation," *Novum Testamentum* 35 (1993): 48–64.

[16] See Black, "Rhetorical Criticism," 254–55; Kennedy, *NT Interpretation,* 33–38; Watson, *Invention,* 8–28.

can be completely or partially removed if discourse, introduced into the situation, can so constrain human decision or action as to bring about the significant modification of the exigence. Prior to the creation and presentation of discourse, there are three constituents of any rhetorical situation: the first is the *exigence;* the second and third are elements of the complex, namely the *audience* to be constrained in decision and action, and the *constraints* which influence the rhetor and can be brought to bear upon the audience.[17]

According to Bitzer, a rhetorical exigence is "an imperfection marked by urgency; it is a defect, an obstacle, something waiting to be done, a thing which is other than it should be." This imperfection is amenable to modification through discourse.[18] The rhetorical audience is those persons who, upon the reception of discourse, can be influenced and become agents of change. The constraints of which Bitzer speaks refer to those objects, events, persons, and relations that have the power to constrain the decision and action that are necessary for the modification of the exigence. The orator furnishes her/his own personal character (ethos), logical proofs, and style as constraints in the rhetorical situation and thus adds to those already present. These latter originate from standards sources like beliefs, attitudes, traditions, documents, and facts.[19] So important is the rhetorical situation for Bitzer that he asserts, "not the rhetor and not persuasive intent, but the situation is the source and ground of rhetorical activity—and, I should add, of rhetorical criticism."[20]

3. Determine the overriding rhetorical problem. In the third step of classical-rhetorical analysis, the rhetorical *species, stasis,* and *question* are determined. The determination of (A) the *species* of rhetoric in a text is of foremost concern to the classical-rhetorical critic, for the rhetorical species clarifies the rhetor's overall purpose in addressing his audience. There are three species of

---

[17] Lloyd F. Bitzer, "The Rhetorical Situation," *Philosophy & Rhetoric* 1 (Winter 1968): 6.

[18] Ibid., 6–7.

[19] Ibid., 7–8.

[20] Ibid., 6. See also Kennedy, *NT Interpretation,* 34–36; Wilhelm Wuellner, "Where Is Rhetorical Criticism Taking Us?" *Catholic Biblical Quarterly* 49 (1987): 455–56.

rhetoric:[21] judicial, deliberative, and epideictic. Judicial rhetoric concerns accusation and defence and is the language of the courtroom. The past comes under the scrutiny of judicial rhetoric. In deliberative rhetoric, the orator seeks to persuade the audience to take a course of action or to dissuade the hearers from it. The future is of primary importance. The proper subjects of epideictic, or demonstrative, rhetoric are praise and blame, approbation and censure. Although this species is basically oriented to the present, the past and future can be its time referents as well. A discourse may incorporate all three species within it, but one normally predominates.

The rhetorical problem involves (B) *stasis*[22] as well as species of rhetoric. Stasis is the basic issue of a case. Three main forms of stases are fact (whether something is), definition (what something is), quality (what kind something is). For example, a trial of one accused of murder may hinge on either fact (did the accused do it?), definition (the accused did it, but it was not murder), or quality (under the circumstances, the best course for the accused was to kill, but it was a noble act or one beneficial to many). Judicial rhetoric effectively employs any of the stases; the stasis of quality usually corresponds best with epideictic and deliberative discourse.

(C) The questions[23] of rhetorical discourse are legal; they concern word and intention of the law, contradictory laws, analogous cases (placing a case under a law by syllogism when that law does not specifically deal with it), and ambiguity in laws. Each of these questions can take one of the three stases as its starting point.

4. Investigate the invention, arrangement, and style. The fourth stage of CRCNT is the analysis of the invention, arrangement, and style of a discourse. In Greco-Roman oratory, memory and

---

[21] See, e.g., Arist. *Rh.* 1.3.1358b.3–1359a.9; Cic. *Top.* 24.91; *Her.* 1.2.2; Kennedy, *NT Interpretation*, 19–20, 36–37; Watson, *Invention*, 9–10.

[22] Arist. *Rh.* 3.17.1417b.1; Cic. *De Or.* 2.24.26; *Inv.* 1.8.10; *Or.* 15; *Top.* 21.79–23.90; Hermogenes, *On Stases*; Quint. *Inst. Or.* 3.6.66–67, 80, 86; Clark, *Rhetoric*, 72–73; Kennedy, *NT Interpretation*, 18–19; Watson, *Invention*, 11–13.

[23] Quint. *Inst. Or.* 3.66, 68; Watson, *Invention*, 13.

delivery were of importance in oral presentations, but are omitted in CRCNT since its concern is written discourse.[24] (A) *Invention*[25] refers to the devising of material, known as proofs, that contributes to the convincing nature of a case. Proofs are of two kinds, artificial and inartificial. Those whose existence is due to the artifice or creativity of the rhetor are artificial, whereas inartificial proofs are such things as witnesses, documents, and legal precedents. They present themselves to the orator ready-made and do not owe their susbsistence to the skill or ingenuity of the orator.

Artificial proofs include *ethos* (the integrity and authority of the rhetor in their power to persuade), *pathos* (positive and negative emotions of the audience concerning the case and those involved in it), and *logos* (the logical argument of a discourse). Rhetorical logos is either inductive (using examples) or deductive (using premises and a conclusion derived from them).

Both induction and deduction utilize topics or "places" (τόποι/ *loci*) where one looks for material for a discourse. Topics can be stock themes and subjects of a particular body of knowledge (material topics) or argumentative strategies (possible and impossible, greater and lesser), or desirable qualities and their opposites such as the just-unjust, honor-dishonor, and advantage-disadvantage.

Once the materials for a discourse are assembled, the rhetor seeks to provide them with a coherent and persuasive (B) *arrangement.*[26] The classical-rhetorical critic attempts to ascertain the orator's arrangement, the structure for the whole. Variations between the rhetorical species and between classical theorists of rhetoric occur, but the general speech pattern for judicial

---

[24] Kennedy, *NT Interpretation*, 13–14.

[25] See Arist. *Rh.* 1.2.1356a.1; Cic. *Inv.* 1.31.51 37.67; *Top.*; *Her.* 3.2.3–5.9; Black, "Recent Studies," 255; Kennedy, *NT Interpretation*, 14–18; Watson, *Invention*, 14–20

[26] See Arist. *Rh.* 3.13.1414a.2–1414b.4; *Her.* 2.18.28–29.46; 3.9.16; Quint. *Inst. Or.* 3.9.1–6; Black, "Recent Studies," 254–55; Clark, *Rhetoric*, 12–30; Kennedy, *NT Interpretation*, 23–24; Mack, *Rhetoric and the NT*, 41–48; Watson, *Invention*, 20–21; idem, "James 2," 94–97.

rhetoric serves as a standard outline on which alterations are made. A proem or exordium that seeks to obtain the auditors' attention and goodwill precedes a narration (*narratio*) of the facts of the case and the proposition (*propositio*) that sometimes features a partition (*partitio*) into separate headings. The proof (*probatio*) contains the speaker's arguments and refutation (*refutatio*) of the opponent's views. Finally an epilogue or peroration (*peroratio*) sums up the rhetor's arguments and seeks to sway the emotions of the hearers toward the orator's view. Deliberative and epideictic rhetoric simplify this arrangement.

(C) Style,[27] that choice of literary devices and language chosen by the rhetor to package his argument, is next examined in CRCNT. Much of what has been termed "rhetoric" in literary and biblical studies has really been a study of style, diction, figures of speech, and figures of thought. Stylistics is name often given to this kind of inquiry which is but one aspect of CRCNT.

Tropes, such as metaphor and simile, are concerns of an examination of style. Attention, too, to the degree of force and ornament in the language of a discourse is of importance to a classical-rhetorical critic. Hence the critic seeks to distinguish between the grand, middle, and plain styles. In a discourse, all three styles may be represented, but one predominates, whether it be the majestic grand, the simplified plain, or relaxed but uncolloquial middle style.

5. *Evaluate the rhetorical effectiveness.*[28] CRCNT seeks to determine the degree of success that the rhetor has achieved in addressing the rhetorical situation. This fifth step draws together the findings of a study of the New Testament in light of classical-rhetorical concerns.

---

[27] Arist. *Rh.* 3.1–12; Demet. *Eloc.*; *Her.* 4; Long. *Subl.*; Ernest W. Bullinger, *Figures of Speech Used in the Bible Explained and Illustrated* (London: Eyre & Spottiswoode, 1898).

[28] Black, "Rhetorical Criticism," 255; Watson, *Invention*, 28.

An Alliance of Classical-Rhetorical Criticism with Social-Scientific Criticism in New Testament Study

In his monumental investigation of 1 Peter and the communities to which it is addressed, John H. Elliott calls for a "methodological consolidation" of rhetorical criticism and social-scientific criticism since "both criticisms are necessary for the full exposure of both the social situation and the rhetorical strategy of any New Testament document."[29] Elliott devotes considerable attention to the situation and strategy of the letter since he believes the concerns of each method to be interrelated.[30] Duane F. Watson, in 1992, predicted that the next phase of rhetorical-critical studies would involve the combination of rhetorical criticism with social-scientific analysis for which Elliott calls.[31] Some works that employ such a combination have already begun to appear. What is social-scientific criticism of the New Testament (SSCNT)? What has been done to date that draws from both CRCNT and SSCNT?

SSCNT: Definition[32]

Social-scientific criticism of the New Testament analyzes the cultural dimensions of the biblical texts through the perspectives

---

[29] John H. Elliott, *A Home for the Homeless: A Social-Scientific Criticism of 1 Peter, Its Situation and Strategy* (Minneapolis: Fortress Press, 1981, 1990), xxxi.

[30] Ibid., xxxi, 19 n. 22.

[31] Duane F. Watson, to Barth Campbell, 10 February 1992, Barth Campbell's personal files, Redding, CA [hereafter referred to as Watson, "Letter"].

[32] Orientations to SSCNT are O. C. Edwards, "Sociology as a Tool for Interpreting the New Testament," *Anglican Theological Review* 65 (October 1983): 431–48; John H. Elliott, ed., *Social-Scientific Criticism of the New Testament and Its Social World*, Semeia 35 (Decatur, GA: Scholars Press, 1986); idem, *What Is Social-Scientific Criticism?* Guides to Biblical Scholarship, New Testament Series, ed. Dan O. Via, Jr. (Minneapolis: Fortress Press, 1993); Susan R. Garrett, "Sociology of Early Christianity," *ABD*, 6:89–99; Bengt Holmberg, *Sociology and the New Testament: An Appraisal* (Minneapolis: Fortress Press, 1990); Howard Clark Kee, *Knowing the Truth: A Sociological Approach to New Testament Interpretation* (Minneapolis: Fortress Press, 1989); Bruce J. Malina, *Christian Origins and Cultural Anthropology: Practical Models for*

and models of the social sciences. The method provides "lenses" through which to examine the New Testament for cultural codes, modes of interaction, and values. Rather than replacing historical-critical approaches, social-scientific criticism of the New Testament promises to provide insight into the *Sitz im Leben* of the New Testament documents and traditions that they embody.[33]

The term "social-scientific criticism" is used variously in the field of New Testament study. As time progresses, the identification of species within the discipline may attain greater precision, but presently their distinctions are somewhat blurred. (For instance, where does an anthropological examination leave off and a sociological one begin?[34]) Nevertheless, the method is of great benefit to the interpreter who attempts "to enter analytically into the life-world(s) of the communities in and for which the documents and other evidence we possess were produced."[35] The degrees to which thinking, behavior, discourse, and literary texts are conditioned socially and culturally are recognized by SSCNT. The approach enables the interpreter to connect phenomena in the biblical text with analogous social aspects in the interpreter's own world.[36]

SSCNT provides heuristic models for the study of scriptural texts.[37] "Models," says Malina, "are abstract, simplified representa-

---

Biblical Interpretation (Atlanta: John Knox Press, 1986); idem, *The New Testament World: Insights from Cultural Anthropology* (Louisville: John Knox Press, 1981); Robin Scroggs, "The Sociological Interpretation of the New Testament: The Present State of Research," *New Testament Studies* 26 (1980): 164–79; Jonathan Z. Smith, "The Social Description of Early Christianity," *Religious Studies Review* 1 (September 1975): 19–25.

[33] John H. Elliott, "On Wooing Crocodiles for Fun and Profit: Exegesis and the Social Sciences; Confessions of an Intact Admirer," paper presented at the annual meeting of the Society of Biblical Literature, San Francisco, CA, 21–24 November, 1992.

[34] Elliott, *Home*, xix, distinguishes between anthropology (primarily the study of preindustrial social systems) and sociology (primarily the study of modern social systems). These disciplines join economics, socio-linguistics, semiotics, and other related subdisciplines in the field of the social sciences.

[35] Kee, *Knowing the Truth*, 22.

[36] Edwards, "Sociology as a Tool," 445.

[37] Holmberg, *Sociology and the NT*, 15.

tions of more complex real world objects and interactions."[38]
Elliott further states:

> Models are thus conceptual vehicles for articulating, applying, testing, and possibly reconstructing theories used in the analysis and interpretation of specific social data. The difference between a model and an analogy or metaphor lies in the fact that the model is *consciously structured* and *systematically arranged* in order to serve as a *speculative instrument* for the purpose of organizing, profiling, and interpreting a complex welter of detail.[39]

Honor and Shame

The pivotal value in first-century Mediterranean society is honor.[40] Almost all one's social interaction with people outside her/his family constitutes a challenge to honor. The honor contest, which marks Mediterranean society as agonistic, comprises a cultural model. According to Malina,[41] honor is a claim to worth and the social acknowledgement of that worth. To honor someone means to acknowledge publicly that her/his actions conform to social obligations.

Two kinds of honor obtain in the honor model: ascribed honor, which is passively attained (as by birth or inheritance), and acquired honor, which is gained by excellence in the social interaction of challenge and response. The agonistic contest for honor is initiated by a challenge that can either be postive (e.g., praise, a request, a gift) or negative (such as an insult or physical attack). Usual social norms inform the recipient of a challenge as to the degree of potential dishonor inherent in it. A response is called for from the challengee, a response that will be exposed to

---

[38] Malina, *NT World*, 17.

[39] John H. Elliott, "Social-Scientific Criticism of the New Testament: More on Methods and Models," in *Social-Scientific Criticism*, ed. John H. Elliott, 5.

[40] Malina, *NT World*, 26–46; Bruce J. Malina and Jerome H. Neyrey, "Honor and Shame in Luke-Acts: Pivotal Values of the Mediterranean World," in *The Social World of Luke-Acts: Models for Interpretation*, ed. Jerome H. Neyrey (Peabody, MA: Hendrickson, 1991), 25–65. Cf. David D. Gilmore, "Anthropology of the Mediterranean Area," *Annual Review of Anthropology* 11 (1982): 175–205.

[41] Malina, *NT World*, 28.

the scrutiny of the public that issues a judgment granting to the participants either honor or dishonor.[42]

The range of responses open to the challengee runs from positive rejection to the challenge (in the form of scorn, disdain, or contempt) to negative refusal (no response), which is dishonorable. Between these two extremes is the receiver's acceptance of the challenge: a counter-challenge ensues which continues the contest. A true honor contest can occur only between social equals, since a superior cannot be affronted with the challenge of an inferior, nor can an inferior respond to the slight of a superior since the former does not have sufficient dignity to enable her/him to play on the latter's level.[43]

I shall explore the value of honor in the ancient Mediterranean world further in this dissertation. Its primary position among the values of antiquity make it one of the crucial foci of SSCNT.

Examples of an Alliance of CRCNT and SSCNT

Vernon K. Robbins[44] has integrated CRCNT and SSCNT in a method that he calls "socio-rhetorical." David B. Gowler[45]

---

[42] All things in life, including honor, are susceptible to the principle of limited good, i.e., they are limited in quantity and to increase one's share in a commodity means someone else's is decreased. See Malina, *NT World*, 75–76.

[43] Hence, as Malina perceptibly remarks (*NT World*, 32), the challengers to Jesus in the Gospels imply by their actions that he is their equal. The high priest and Pilate, however, regard Jesus as an annoying inferior who is not worthy of their attention in an honor contest.

[44] Vernon K. Robbins, *Jesus the Teacher: A Socio-Rhetorical Interpretation of Mark* (Philadelphia: Fortress Press, 1984); idem, "Rhetorical Argument about Lamps and Light in Early Christian Gospels," in *Context: Festskrift til Peder Johan Borgen/Essays in Honour of Peder Johan Borgen*, ed. Peter Wilhelm Bøckman and Roald E. Kristiansen, Relieff 24 (Trondheim, Norway: Tapir, 1987); idem, "Using a Socio-Rhetorical Poetics to Develop a Unified Method: The Woman Who Anointed Jesus as a Test Case," paper presented at the annual meeting of the Society of Biblical Literature, San Francisco, CA, 21–24 November 1992.

[45] David B. Gowler, *Host, Guest, Enemy and Friend: Portraits of the Pharisees in Luke and Acts*, Emory Studies in Early Christianity 2 (New York: Peter Lang, 1991).

describes his analysis of Luke-Acts as one that uses a "socio-narratological approach."[46] In it, he supplements narrative criticism with analyses of cultural contexts implicit in the Lukan documents. Both Gowler and Robbins practice a rhetorical method that most resembles a literary criticism of style in combination with social scientific analysis.

Robert Jewett[47] and Charles A. Wanamaker[48] have written commentaries on the Thessalonian letters from the standpoint of SSCNT and CRCNT. Ben Witherington III[49] has produced a "socio-rhetorical" commentary on 1 and 2 Corinthians. A recent article by John H. Elliott[50] combines rhetorical and social-scientific methods in an investigation of James. My intention in this dissertation is to augment the growing body of literature employing both these methods. My study of 1 Peter is essentially an exercise in CRCNT that considers aspects of SSCNT, particularly the honor shame contest as reflected in the text of the letter.

---

[46] Ibid., 9.

[47] Robert Jewett, *The Thessalonian Correspondence: Pauline Rhetoric and Millenarian Piety*, Foundations and Facets (Philadelphia: Fortress Press, 1986).

[48] Wanamaker, *Thessalonians.*

[49] Ben Witherington III, *Conflict and Community in Corinth: A Socio-Rhetorical Commentary on 1 & 2 Corinthians* (Grand Rapids: William B. Eerdmans, 1993).

[50] John H. Elliott, "The Epistle of James in Rhetorical and Social-Scientific Perspective: Holiness-Wholeness and Patterns of Replication," *Biblical Theology Bulletin* 23 (Summer 1993): 71–81.

CHAPTER TWO

Toward a Classical-Rhetorical Investigation of 1 Peter

Recent Research on 1 Peter[1]

The student of 1 Peter will profit from Troy W. Martin's *Metaphor and Composition in 1 Peter*.[2] His book is an invaluable treatment of various structural theories and of crucial imagery within the letter. The work constitutes the most recent thorough review of research on 1 Peter. Since the presentation of *Metaphor* as the author's Ph.D. dissertation at the University of Chicago in 1990, several important works on 1 Peter have appeared.[3]

---

[1] Reviews of the study of 1 Pt. include Paul J. Achtemeier, "Newborn Babes and Living Stones: Literal and Figurative in 1 Peter," in *To Touch the Text: Biblical and Related Studies in Honor of Joseph A. Fitzmyer, S. J.*, ed. Maurya P. Horgan and Paul J. Kobelski (New York: Crossroad, 1989), 207–36; Édouard Cothenet, "Les orientations actuelles de l'exégèse de la première lettre de Pierre," in *Études sur la première lettre de Pierre*, C. Perrot et al., Lectio divina 102 (Paris: Cerf, 1980), 13–42; John H. Elliott, "The Rehabilitation of an Exegetical Step-Child: 1 Peter in Recent Research," *Journal of Biblical Literature* 95 (1976): 243–54 [repr. in Charles H. Talbert, ed., *Perspectives on First Peter*, NABPR Special Studies Series 9 (Macon, GA: Mercer University Press, 1986), 3–16]; Ralph P. Martin, "The Composition of 1 Peter in Recent Study," *Vox Evangelica* 1 (1962): 29–42; idem, "Peter, First," in *The International Standard Bible Encyclopedia*, ed. Geoffrey Bromiley et al. (Grand Rapids: William B. Eerdmans, 1986), 3:807–15; Troy W. Martin, *Metaphor and Composition in 1 Peter*, Society of Biblical Literature Dissertation Series 131 (Atlanta: Scholars Press, 1992); Birger A. Pearson, "James, 1–2 Peter, Jude," in *The New Testament and Its Modern Interpreters*, ed. Eldon Jay Epp and George W. MacRae (Atlanta: Scholars Press, 1989), 376–82; F. J. Schierse, "Ein Hirtenbrief und viele Bücher," *Bibel und Kirche* 31 (1976): 86–88; Dennis Sylva, "A 1 Peter Bibliography," *Journal of the Evangelical Theological Society* 25 (March 1982): 75–89 [repr. in Talbert, ed., *Perspectives*, 17–36, as "The Critical Exploration of 1 Peter"]; idem, "1 Peter Studies: The State of the Discipline," *Biblical Theology Bulletin* 10 (October 1980): 155–63.

[2] See full ref. under n. 1.

[3] **Commentaries:** Wayne A. Grudem, *The First Epistle of Peter: An Introduction and Commentary*, Tyndale New Testament Commentaries

Most important to note for my study are three works that treat the rhetoric of 1 Peter: Ellul's article "Cheminement rhétorique," Martin's *Metaphor*, and Thurén's monograph *Rhetorical Strategy* (full references for these works in ns. 1 and 3 above). These three works constitute the only studies of rhetoric in 1 Peter of which I am aware.[4] As a prelude to my own rhetorical investigation of 1 Peter, I shall briefly review these three studies.

(Leicester: InterVarsity Press, 1988; Grand Rapids: William B. Eerdmans, 1988) [despite its publication before Martin submitted his diss., Grudem's work is overlooked by Martin in *Metaphor*]; Norman Hillyer, *1 and 2 Peter, Jude*, New International Biblical Commentary (Peabody, MA: Hendrickson, 1992); I. Howard Marshall, *1 Peter*, IVP New Testament Commentary Series (Downers Grove, IL, and Leicester: InterVarsity Press, 1991); **Dissertations and Monographs:** Reinhard Feldmeier, *Die Christen als Fremde: Die Metapher der Fremde in der antiken Welt, im Urchristentum und im 1. Petrusbrief*, Wissenschaftliche Untersuchungen zum neuen Testament 64 (Tübingen: J. C. B. Mohr [Paul Siebeck], 1992; Marlis Gielen, *Tradition und Theologie neutestamentlicher Haustafelethik: Ein Beitrag zur Frage einer christlichen Auseinandersetzung mit gesellschaftlichen Normen*, Athenäums Monografien Theologie; Bonner biblische Beiträge 75 (Frankfurt on Main: Hain, 1990); Sharon Clark Pearson, "The Christological Hymnic Pattern of 1 Peter" (Ph.D. diss., Fuller Theological Seminary, 1993); Ferdinand Rupert Prostmeier, *Handlungsmodelle im ersten Petrusbrief*, FB 63 (Würzburg: Echter, 1990); Angelika Reichert, *Eine urchristliche praeparatio ad martyrium: Studien zur Komposition, Traditionsgeschichte und Theologie des 1. Petrusbriefes*, Beiträge zur biblischen Exegese und Theologie 22 (Frankfurt on Main: Peter Lang, 1989); Lauri Thurén, *The Rhetorical Strategy of 1 Peter: With Special Regard to Ambiguous Expressions* (Åbo, Finland: Åbo Academy Press, 1990). **Articles:** David L. Balch, "The First Letter of Peter" [introduction and annotations], in *The HarperCollins Study Bible*, ed. Wayne A. Meeks (New York: HarperCollins Publishers, 1993), 2277–85; Ernest Best, "1 Peter," in *The Oxford Companion to the Bible*, ed. Bruce M. Metzger and Michael D. Coogan (New York and Oxford: Oxford University Press, 1993), 583–86; John H. Elliott, "Peter, First Epistle of," *ABD*, 5:269–78; Danielle Ellul, "Un exemple de cheminement rhétorique: 1 Pierre," *Revue d'histoire et de philosophie religieuses* 70 (1990/1): 17–34; José Cervantes Gabarrón, "El pastor en la teologia de 1 Pe," *Estudios biblicos* 49 (1991): 331–51; Pierre Prigent, "1 Pierre 2,4–10," *Revue d'histoire et de philosophie religieuses* 72 (1992): 53–60.

[4] I am indebted to Watson, "Letter," for bringing these works to my attention as the only ones of which he is aware that address the rhetoric of 1 Pt.

Danielle Ellul, "Un exemple de cheminement rhétorique: 1 Pierre"

According to Ellul, the structure of 1 Peter is a series of alternating exhortative and proclamatory material blocks. These are not arranged in a simple back-and-forth manner,[5] but as an A-B-A-B-C-B-A-B pattern where A=proclamation, B=exhortation, and C=the corner-stone of the scheme[6] which Ellul identifies as a rhetorical one.[7] Her structure of 1 Peter is as follows:[8]

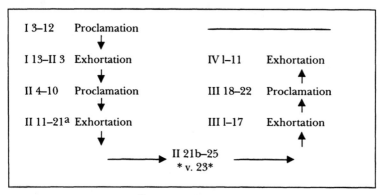

Like John H. Elliott,[9] Ellul perceives the centrality of 2:21–25 in 1 Peter, but for a different reason. Because of the association that Peter draws of the suffering and enduring Christ with the afflicted οἰκέται, says Elliott, the household servants in following Christ become paradigmatic for the entire community. To follow

---

[5] Cf. Edward Gordon Selwyn, *The First Epistle of St. Peter: The Greek Text with Introduction, Notes and Essays* (London: Macmillan & Co., 1949), 4–6, who (within an epistolary framework of 1:1–2 and 5:12–14) has three doctrinal sections (1:3–12; 2:4–10; 3:13–4:19) alternating with three hortatory ones (1:13–2:3; 2:11–3:12; 5:1–11).

[6] "La pierre angulaire de tout cet édifice nous semble être en effet II 21b–25, et plus particulièrement le v. 23 qui met au coeur de la lettre, le Christ modèle de non-violence active" (Ellul, "Cheminement rhétorique," 34).

[7] Ibid., 31, 33, 34. 24

[8] Ibid., 33–34.

[9] Elliott, *Home*, 206–7.

the slaves' example is to follow Christ's own example. Furthermore, since in the household code the οἰκέται are mentioned first, they hold the primary and exemplary position concerning household conduct. 1 Pt. 2:21–25, then, serves as the theological and social basis for that paradigmatic function of the οἰκέται. According to Ellul, the centrality of the passages is stressed not because the address to the οἰκέται with its Christological pattern precedes the instructions to others in a catalogue of household duties. The crucial nature of the passage 2:21–25 lies in its pivotal position in the rhetorical structure of the epistle. Ellul's analysis rightfully stresses the importance of 1 Pt. 2:21–25 in the strategy of the whole letter.

Three problems, in my opinion, encumber Ellul's study. (1) Although her compositional scheme helpfully points to many parallels between different blocks of material in the letter, I question whether these parallels are indicators of macrostructural poles rather than merely replications of Petrine language and themes. The readiness that Ellul exhibits to link exhorative and proclamatory sections before 2:21–25 with those after appears strained. Like other analyses[10] of 1 Peter that seek inclusions, repetitions, chiasmus, and parallelisms as landmarks to the discursive structure, Ellul's *cheminement rhétorique* finds corresponding structural poles where they do not really seem to exist.

(2) Overlooked is the clearly major divisional break at 3:12/13 where a subsantial scriptural citation, a clear indication of a conclusion to a large block of material,[11] occurs. Ellul, instead of breaking the section at 3:12/13, carries it over to vv. 17/18. The section 3:18–22 is not rely a major structural division of the letter, but is an argumentative proof for what precedes it in 3:13–17.

---

[10] Cf. H. J. B. Combrink, "The Structure of 1 Peter," *Neotestamentica* 9 (1975, 1980²): 34–63; A. B. du Toit, "The Significance of Discourse Analysis for New Testament Interpretation and Translation: Introductory Remarks with Special Reference to 1 Peter 1:3–13," *Neotestamentica* 8 (1974): 54–79.

[11] William J. Dalton, *Christ's Proclamation to the Spirits: A Study of 1 Peter 3:18–4:6*, 2nd ed., Analecta Biblica 23 (Rome: Editrice Pontificio Istituto Biblico, 1989), 95: "The more important and massive the scripture citation, the more emphatic is the break between this [an argument or devlopment of thought] section and the following."

Furthermore, according to Ellul, the particle οὖν demarcates a new section at 4:1, whereas the same particle in 2:1 only resumes the argument interrupted by a biblical citation (1:24–25a).[12] Why could not the particle at 2:1 signify a new section as well since the sentences of both particles are functionally similar (i.e., they resume exhortation)?

Perhaps in a future publication Ellul will produce a satisfactory explanation of the relationship of 1:3–12 (proclamation) and 4:12–5:11 to one another. However, in "Cheminement rhétorique," the connection between these passages is equivocal. Is 4:12–5:11 the counterpart of 1:3–12, or is it a recapitulation of the entire letter? Ellul considers answering the question in a later work.[13] Until the appearance of the future work, however, 1 Pt. 1:3–12 intrudes on the symmetry of Ellul's outline and leaves open the matter of 4:12–5:11 and its place in the rhetorical design of 1 Peter.

Troy W. Martin, *Metaphor and Composition in 1 Peter*

Martin's work resembles that of Elliott in its attention to the motif of the alienation experienced by God's chosen people. Martin emphasizes that the Diaspora is "the overarching and controlling metaphor" that issues in two types of images in 1 Peter: general and specific images. The former consist of indicators that Peter regards the Christian life as an "eschatological journey" that commences at the new birth and leads to the salvation revealed at the end time (cf. 1:3–5). The author is concerned for the hearers' conduct while on the way. That concern is one of the two main purposes that he has in writing.

A second general image of the Diaspora in 1 Peter is that of the danger of assimilation to a pagan environment and the subsequent defection of the chosen people of God. Hope, sobriety, and steadfastness (e.g., 1:13; 4:7; 5:8–9) become the focus of Peter, whose purpose for his audience is that they will not

---

[12] Ellul, "Cheminement rhétorique," 20, 32.

[13] Ibid, 33 n. 24.

succumb to hostile and ungodly influences in the society around them. The general images reveal the rhetorical situation and purpose of the letter.

These general images are supplemented by specific images that function as the means of accomplishing the authorial purposes and delineate the sections of the letter-body. These specific images, joined through the chief metaphor of the Diaspora, form the core of three metaphor clusters that determine the major sections of the body-middle of the letter. Their core images are announced in the identification of the addressees in 1:1: ἐκλεκτοῖς παρεπιδήμοις διασπορᾶς.[14] The metaphor clusters in Martin's treatment of 1 Peter are: (1) the οἶκος-cluster, the elect household of God (1:14–2:10); (2) the παρεπίδημος/πάροικος-cluster, aliens in this world (2:11–3:12); (3) the παθήματα-cluster, sufferers of the Dispersion (3:13–5:11).[15]

Martin correctly perceives the basic fault of letter-analysis: it can identify basic parts of the letter (prescript; body-opening, middle, and closing; and postscript), and their termini, but it cannot account for the composition of the letter-body. Other analytical methods must be employed to explain that part of the letter.[16] 1 Peter, whose major literary genre is epistolary, displays characteristics of parenetic as its specific literary genre.[17] According to Martin, the parenetic genre exhibits no fixed form and, "therefore, the identification of 1 Peter as a paraenesis does not provide an explanation of its compositional structure."[18] Has

---

[14] Martin, *Metaphor*, 144–61.

[15] From the outline, ibid., 271–73.

[16] Ibid., 75.

[17] Ibid., 41, 99, 105, 107, 269–70.

[18] Ibid., 270. Cf. also Martin's admission on 119–20: "Because the primary genre determiner of paraenesis is social context instead of literary form, the identification of 1 Peter as a paraenesis does not resolve its compositional structure. The literary features of paraenesis are helpful in analyzing the individual elements in a paraenetic document, but they do not explain how they are arranged and put together nor how the entire document is composed since the paraenetic genre adopts many compostional devices and assumes many different compositional structures. Therefore, each individual

some characteristic of parenesis functioned to provide a compositional framework for the letter-body? Martin believes so: Peter utilizes the ontological status of his readers as the basis of exhortations that he issues. The parenetic genre typically features such an interrelationship of ontological status and exhortation. This relationship of ontological status and exhortation is the compositional key of 1 Peter.[19]

How are we to evaluate Martin's work? He has clearly understood the importance that the Diaspora and its attendant imagery have for the argument of 1 Peter. In this he agrees with Elliott. However, Martin disputes Elliott's view that the alienation and estrangement conveyed by the Diaspora motif are social realities. Martin contends that the Diaspora image is metaphorical as are the images it controls ("metaphor clusters"). "Elliott," Martin asserts, "has already recognized the importance of the notion of the Diaspora in the description of the readers' ontological status. Unfortunately he refuses to see the metaphorical dimension of this notion in 1 Peter and its consequent role in the composition of the letter."[20]

In my opinion, Martin dismisses Elliott's social-scientific approach too quickly, neglecting the evidence that weighs heavily in favor of a social and cultural significance for the motif of the readers' παροικία that is not metaphorical. The viewpoint that πάροικοι and παρεπίδημοι in 1 Pt. 2:11 indicate that the letter contrasts a heavenly future life with a present earthly existence[21] is refuted by Elliott with a fivefold argument:[22] (1) The words

---

paraenetic document must be analyzed in order to ascertain the compositional devices used by the author."

[19] Ibid., 270.

[20] Ibid., 148 n. 52. Martin here responds to Elliott, *Home*, 48, where the latter affirms that the Diaspora imagery (including the words διασπορά, πάροικοι, παροικία, παρεπίδημοι, and βαβυλών) in 1 Pt. recognizes social and religious estrangement and alienation.

[21] As in Francis Wright Beare, *The First Epistle of Peter: The Greek Text with Introduction and Notes*, 3rd ed. (Oxford: Basil Blackwell, 1970), 135, cited by Elliott, *Home*, 42.

[22] Elliott, *Home*, 42–44.

maintain political and social currency in literature contemporary with 1 Peter. (2) The postulation of mutually exclusive literal or figurative meanings of the terms is unnecessary since the terms describe both religious and social circumstances in 1 Peter. (3) The picture of social alienation and conflict in the letter is consistent with the treatment that literal resident aliens and visiting strangers in Asia Minor could expect. (4) A sociological, not cosmological conflict, is the situation of 1 Peter. Finally, (5) the selfish desires from which the Christians are to abstain are not simply those of this world; they are the vices of the unbelieving society around them. Hence good conduct according to the will of God is summoned, with the anticipated result being the glorification of God (cf. 2:12; 4:1–6).

The term Diaspora for Peter's audience would have reference to religious, geographical, and social realities.[23] Surprisingly, Martin does not consider the socio-cultural dimensions of the Diaspora complex in 1 Peter, despite his thorough grammatical-historical investigation of the terms πάροικος and παρεπίδημος. He notes their social and cultural reference in ancient times, but makes a semantic leap to a metaphorical reference for them in 1 Peter.[24]

Still, Martin's view of the organization of 1 Peter (with three metaphor clusters at its core) is accurately attentive to the major and minor breaks of the document. One might think of his "metaphor clusters" as "image clusters" instead.

Lauri Thurén, *The Rhetorical Strategy of 1 Peter*

Thurén's work is welcome, for it constitutes what is probably the first rhetorical-critical study of the entire letter of 1 Peter. I find his summary of a premliminary rhetorical analysis of a text, discussion of the epistolary genre, and bibliography to be quite

---

[23] Ibid., 46.

[24] Martin, *Metaphor*, 188–92. Elliott has drawn fire from others over his judgment that the readers of 1 Pt. ought to be understood as politically, socially, and culturally estranged. Among his critics (besides Martin) on this point are Feldmeier, *Die Christen als Fremde*, 5 n. 3, 203–10; Holmberg, *Sociology and the NT*, 94–95; and Garrett, "Sociology," 94–95.

valuable.[25] Nevertheless, the treatment of his chosen concern, the ambiguities of the letter, is inadequate, in my opinion.

Thurén correctly identifies problematic ambiguities in 1 Peter's language. For example, ought the participles ἀναζωσά-μενοι and νήφοντες in 1:13 to be construed as imperatival ('gird up' and 'discipline yourselves') or as modal or circumstantial ('having [your minds] girded up,' 'being disciplined')? Thurén suggests that this ambiguity and others in the section 1:13–2:10 indicate that two kinds of recipients are being addressed: active recipients, Christians who are too abrasive in their relationship toward society, and passive ones, believers who assimilate too much to society in order to avoid suffering.

The actives hear 1:13–2:10 as an extension of the exordium that praises (1:1–12). The passives sense a shift to an imperatival mood at 1:13. 1 Pt. 2:11–3:12 is pivotal for the actives, for, after its clear commands, they perceive all that was uttered in 1:13–2:10 was really command to them, not affirmation of their values. At subsequent readings of 1 Peter, the passage 1:13–2:10 would be seen in new ways. After 3:12, the letter becomes more homogeneous—the passive-active dichotomy is dismantled.[26]

My credulity is somewhat strained by Thurén's theory. First of all, would a writer be that subtle in a circular letter for diverse readership? How could he know that his subtleties would be percieved? Not only so, but, as Duane F. Watson notes,[27] Thurén's notion of ambiguity derives mainly from modern rhetoric. Ambiguity of meaning and multiple possibilities of interpretations are potentially present in discourse according to the New Rhetoric to which Thurén is indebted. The emphasis in it is not any longer on securing an authorized interpretation, but of

---

[25] Thurén, *Rhetorical Strategy*, 58–67, 68–78, 187–204.

[26] Ibid., 12–53.

[27] Duane Frederick Watson, review of *The Rhetorical Strategy of 1 Peter: With Special Regard to Ambiguous Expressions*, by Lauri Thurén, in *Journal of Biblical Literature* 10 (Winter 1991): 748.

limiting interpretive possibilities.[28] C. Perelman recognized the "fringe of indefiniteness" around the most precisely stated terms[29] and the fact that the hearer listens and understands arguments in her/his own way, creating new arguments that modify the final results of argumentation. In the course of argumentation, however, the speaker can guide this creative response of the hearer.[30]

Ancient rhetorical notions of ambiguity, however, are different from modern ones. In Greco-Roman rhetoric, ambiguity is useful for jests and puns, but its obscurity is generally disparaged. In *Rhetorica ad Herennium*, something "is faulty which can be taken in another sense than the speaker intended."[31] The author of 1 Peter has no guarantee that the so-called actives will shift in comprehending that 1:13–2:10 is really command, not the praise that Thurén believes they originally heard. Peter's rhetorical art strongly suggests that he would not have been so careless as not to make his case clearer. Would Peter, who evinces an acquaintance with rhetorical principles, have based his argument on a device that his contemporaries would have likely judged to be unsound in serious discourse?

Two other points at which I take issue with Thurén concern his hypothetical multiplicities of readings of the letter and groups to

---

[28] C. Perelman and L. Olbrechts-Tyteca, *The New Rhetoric: A Treatise on Argumentation*, trans. John Wilkinson and Purcell Weaver (Notre Dame: University of Notre Dame Press, 1969), 123–26, 130–37, 508. See Thurén, *Rhetorical Strategy*, 166–67, for a positive evaluation of ambiguity in Perelman and Olbrechts-Tyteca, *The New Rhetoric*.

[29] Perelman and Olbrechts-Tyteca, *The New Rhetoric*, 130–33.

[30] Ibid., 189.

[31] *Her.* 2.26.40 (item vitiosum est quod in aliam partem ac dictum sit potest accipi). Cf. Arist. *Top.* 1.15.106a.1–18.108a.37; Cic. *Inv.* 1.13.17, 15.20–21; *Her.* 2.11.16; Quint. *Inst. Or.* 6.3.48; 8.3.56–57; Harry Caplan, in *Rhetorica ad Herennium*, trans. Harry Caplan, Loeb Classical Library (Cambridge, MA: Harvard University Press, 1954; London: William Heinemann, 1954), 86–87 note b; Lausberg, *Handbuch*, 222–23, 1068, 1070, 1073; Watson, review of *Rhetorical Strategy*, by Thurén, 748. Thurén himself admits that, because *perspicuitas* is one of the main virtues of classical rhetoric, the ancients did not favor ambiguity. Nevertheless, Thurén maintains that is employed by the author of 1 Pt. as a way to minimize negative expectations and meet diverse needs of the audience (*Rhetorical Strategy*, 165, 175, 178).

which it is addressed. He seems to be certain, without warrant in my judgment, that 1 Peter would be read ("performed")[32] several times. Perhaps, but no evidence exists that multiple readings are anticipated. A theory whose condition is a multiplicity of verbal performances is tenuous. In the rhetorical analysis that follows, I submit the 'ambiguous' participles to examination in light of the total rhetorical context in order to determine their function (imperatival or descriptive). The Petrine ambiguity may be resolved by closer examination. Furthermore, no evidence arises from the text of 1 Peter for Thurén's active and passive groups. His theory of these groups cannot be sustained in light of the document itself.

The species of rhetoric is predominantly, according to Thurén, epideictic. The audience is aware of Christian values, but its willingness to live by them is the focus of 1 Peter. Thurén claims that the action which Peter expects of the readers is not specified as in the deliberative species of rhetoric. One must remember, however, that 1 Peter is a circular letter. Any injunctions are, therefore, bound to be somewhat general. Nevertheless, they are present, and introduce each major section of the letter (cf. 1:13; 2:11; 3:14b–16b; 4:12–13). Moreover, the injunctions are not for continuation of present and acceptable behavior. Peter gives no indication whether the conduct that he enjoins is present to any degree among his readers. He writes as if it is not.[33]

New Directions

None of the three rhetorical studies of 1 Peter that I have reviewed is a comprehensive classical rhetorical study of the letter that observes its invention, arrangement, and style as discourse.

---

[32] Thurén, *Rhetorical Strategy*, 152.

[33] Ibid. 73, 96–98. Watson agrees with Thurén's assessment (review of *Rhetorical Strategy*, by Lauri Thurén, 747). Wanamaker, *Thessalonians*, 48, identifies 1 Thess. as epideictic since it seeks to confirm the readers in their present behavior whereas 2 Thess., in its intention to encourage different behavior, is deliberative. 1 Pt. is like 2 Thess. in its persuasive intention and ought to be classified as deliberative rhetoric.

Ellul's article is a literary-critical study that examines the surface structure of 1 Peter, especially parallelisms. Martin's focus is also literary-critical in that he explores the composition of the work which he believes revolves around three metaphor-clusters. Thurén employs principles of modern rhetoric and skirts a detailed analysis based on the ancient rhetorical handbooks. He concentrates basically on one problem: the ambiguous Petrine expressions. A need therefore exists for a classical-rhetorical investigation of 1 Peter, since rhetorical studies of the document to date have not employed that approach.

The thesis argued in this dissertation is that 1 Peter conforms to certain principles of Greco-Roman rhetoric (especially a pattern of argumentation located in *Rhetorica ad Herennium*). The epistolary author maintains that the audience, though presently slandered and held as outcasts, will receive vindication and honor. My analysis follows the contours of the rhetorical arguments in the letter, and is therefore an exercise in CRCNT. In that it is cognizant of the cultural value of honor in 1 Peter, it is secondarily a work of SSCNT.

Presuppositions

The scope of this dissertation does not allow me to address, even briefly, the many important critical issues that surround 1 Peter. I must, therefore, simply state some of my working presuppositions.

The letter originates in Rome, sometime between 62 and 92 CE. If the document has not been authored by the apostle Peter (perhaps through Silvanus as amanuensis), then a Petrine circle in the imperial capital has composed it, attaching his name, as a representation of the apostle's mind and heart. In this dissertation, "Peter" refers to the author(s), whoever he/they may have been.

The recipients are scattered throughout Asia Minor (1:1). The integrity of 1 Peter has been challenged without success. The document is a genuine letter, not a baptismal homily or liturgy in an epistolary frame.

The Rhetorical Unit and the Rhetorical Situation

In the present study, the entire letter of 1 Peter constitutes the rhetorical unit. The epistle is obviously a complete unit with a beginning, middle, and end.

One must ask questions of the New Testament documents that will lead to the identification of the social matrix of their intended and original audiences. The queries ought to ask whether honor, the pivotal value in Mediterranean society of the first century,[34] is reflected within the text. Readily apparent in 1 Peter is the issue of conflict: that of the Christian community with pagan outsiders (2:12; 2:18–20; 3:9, 14–17; 4:4, 12–16; 5:8–9). Can that conflict in 1 Peter be examined in light of the honor contest with its challenges to honor and responses to those challenges?

My theory is that conflict in 1 Peter is best seen in light of the honor contest. The suffering experienced by the Christians whom Peter addresses is not an official persecution on any scale, but primarily defamation of the community.[35] Defamation in the Mediterranean world is a challenge to honor. If not properly answered, its recipient is dishonored. Could Peter's audience be experiencing dishonor because of an unsatisfactory response to public ridicule and its challenge to honor? I believe so, and in order to test the feasibility of the theory that the suffering of the Christians in 1 Peter is the experience of dishonor, I have developed a semantic field of honor and shame that includes

---

[34] "Mediterranean" refers to those lands of Europe, Asia, and Africa that share common geographical, climatic, and social features that are characteristic of regions contiguous with the Mediterranean Sea. Areas that have such features in common do not necessarily adjoin the Mediterranean Sea.

[35] See J. N. D. Kelly, *A Commentary on the Epistles of Peter and of Jude*, Harper's New Testament Commentaries (New York: Harper & Row, 1969), 5–11; John A. T. Robinson, *Redating the New Testament* (Philadelphia: Westminster Press, 1976), 152–53. Both leave open the possibility of hearings before civil authorities, but they are not the persecutor (as in Rev.).

those words plus all cognates, synonyms, antonyms, and related terms.[36]

The honor-shame terminology is abundant in the letter. Remarkable is the fact that, whenever an explicit reference to insider-outsider conflict in 1 Peter occurs, there is a corresponding reference to the honor to be granted the believers. Peter's intention is to encourage in his audience an honorable response in the honor-shame contest. He simultaneously assures them of the bestowal of honor that they have received from God and that they can expect from God and outsiders in the future. They must, however, respond honorably and live as God's holy people (which they are).

The honor code in 1 Peter has been overlooked in scholarship as a factor in the cultural situation that the author of the letter faces. It is a significant element in the interpersonal relations that contribute to the rhetorical situation.[37] A favorable verdict in the honor contest for the Christians is related to the motif of reversal in the letter (cf. 2:12, 3:16).[38]

Elliott's opinion that πάροικοι ("resident aliens," 1 Pt. 2:11; cf. 1:17) and παρεπίδημοι ("visiting strangers," 1:1; 2:11) denote cultural displacement and disadvantage appears valid, as does his view that Peter encourages his readers to remain aliens and

---

[36] See Appendix 1, "The Semantic Field of Honor and Shame in 1 Peter," below. Others who use a semantic field of honor/shame to demonstrate convincingly that honor categories are present in a text are Halvor Moxnes, "Honour and Righteousness in Romans," *Journal for the Study of the New Testament* 32 (1988): 63–64, 77 n. 15; Malina and Neyrey, "Honor and Shame," 46.

[37] Both Elliott (*Home*, 122, 143, 228, 233) and Martin (*Metaphor*, 107–20) recognize the presence of honor in 1 Peter, but do not develop an analysis of its function in the Petrine argument from a social-scientific perspective.

[38] The motif of reversal in 1 Pt. is, for Pearson, "Hymnic Pattern," the pattern of righteous suffering followed by vindication and "glories" (10–14). In fact, "in 1 Peter, the S/G [suffering/glories] pattern, derived from and couched in traditional deposits, has become the message and method of the document" (13). See also 263, 265. The suffering/glories schema of 1 Pt. is identified also by William L. Schutter, *Hermeneutic and Composition in I Peter,* Wissenschaftliche Untersuchungen zum neuen Testament, 2nd series, 30 (Tübingen: J. C. B. Mohr [Paul Siebeck], 1989), 122–23.

strangers in a religious and moral sense.[39] Thus Peter uses terms of dishonor in an unpejorative way.

Why were these strangers subject to even further disadvantage and dishonor upon becoming Christians (1 Pt. 2:12; 3:9, 16; 4:4, 14)? To many, Christianity represented various dangers to the social order and was, therefore, at times savagely slandered. Among the imagined threats of the sect were:[40] (1) the independence of Christian slaves and wives in choosing their own religion apart from the *pater potestas* and (2) the reputed character of Christianity as *superstitio*.[41] Some regarded the sect as promoting (3) sexual immorality, (4) cannibalism, (5) magic, (6) sedition, (7) atheism, (8) and contempt for death coupled with a show in martyrdom. The church's (9) withdrawal of economic support for pagan interests (cf. Acts 19:18–41) was resisted as was its alleged (10) hatred of the human race. The believers were often regarded as an invasive foreign body[42] whose adverse influences required countermeasures. In 1 Peter, those countermeasures are slanders against the community.

The Christians' suffering, already actual and present (1 Pt. 1:6–7; 4:12–13), prompts a response from Peter. The exigence, the defect requiring eradication that things may be restored to what they should be, is the believers' experience of dishonor for doing right rather than the reception of honor for good behavior (2:12, 19–20; 3:16; 4:4, 13–14, 16).[43] Peter recognizes the status of

---

[39] Elliott, *Home*, 25–26, 42–44, 48–49.

[40] The ten dangers listed above, perceived in Christianity by paganism, may have been issues at the time 1 Peter was written even if they are attested to later. See David L. Balch, *Let Wives Be Submissive: The Domestic Code in 1 Peter*, Society of Biblical Literature Monograph Series 26 (Atlanta: Scholars Press, 1981); Stephen Benko, *Pagan Rome and the Early Christians* (Bloomington and Indianapolis: Indiana University Press, 1984); Feldmeier, *Die Christen als Fremde* (esp. 106–32); W. M. Ramsay, *The Church in the Roman Empire before A. D. 170* (New York and London: G. P. Putnam's Sons, Knickerbocker Press, 1919).

[41] Cf. Suet. *Nero* 16.2; Tacitus, *Ann.* 15.44.

[42] Feldmeier, *Die Christen als Fremde*, 174.

[43] Martin, *Metaphor*, 11.

his readers as πάροικοι, but informs them that their distinctive status as aliens and strangers coexists with their exalted status as the οἶκος τοῦ θεοῦ. As such they have an honored position before God (2:4–10; 4:17) and shall receive greater honor still because of it, both in the present age and the eschaton (cf. 1:7; 2:12, 19–20; 3:14; 4:13–14; 5:4, 10). In the honor contest, a correct response to challenges from the pagans shall issue in a verdict of honor and vindication by God, the one who grants the greatest honor.

The Rhetorical Problem: Species, Stasis and Question

Of what rhetorical species is 1 Peter? For clues, we may look to the commencements of the major divisions of 1 Peter, for there we would expect the propositions to be stated. The nature of 1:3–12 is that of an introduction.[44] The major argumentative divisions of the letter which follow are identifiable by means of certain indicators of literary structure:[45] 1:13—change from statement to exhortation, διό; 2:11—change from statement to exhortation, vocative ἀγαπητοί; 3:13—preceding scriptural citation at 3:10–12, link words κακά and κακώσων in vv. 12–13, inclusion of 3:13–17; 4:12—vocative ἀγαπητοί, preceding doxology at v. 11. Each verse features an imperative verb (1:13; 2:11 with παρακαλῶ; 4:12) or introduces a section whose mood is decisively imperatival (3:13). The sections 1:1–2 and 5:13–14 are epistolary forms of address and conclusion, respectively.

Since the major sections of the letter reflect exhortation to take future action, the species of the rhetoric of 1 Peter is deliberative.[46] Petrine argumentation is typically deliberative in that it utilizes example and comparison of example[47] (2:24; 3:18–22) as well as the *topoi* (sources of argument) of "what is

---

[44] Specifically, a blessing section. Elliott, *Home*, 43, 139, 234; Martin, *Metaphor*, 28–29, 39, 47–68, 269–75. Less so in Dalton, *Proclamation*, 97–98.

[45] Cf. those in Dalton, *Proclamation*, 94–95.

[46] *Pace* Thurén, *Rhetorical Strategy*, 73, 95–98, 177; and Watson, review of *Rhetorical Strategy*, by Lauri Thurén, 747, who agree that the rhetorical genus is, in the main, epideictic.

[47] Quint. *Inst. Or.* 5.11.1–21; 3.8.36–40; *Her.* 4.49.62; Watson, "James 2," 101.

advantageous, expedient, honourable, profitable, necessary and their opposites."[48]

The basic definite question at issue, the stasis, is primarily one of quality. Deliberative rhetoric generally utilizes the stasis of quality as the most effective basis of issue.[49] In the first conflict of causes in 1 Peter 1:6–7,[50] the stasis of quality becomes apparent: the πειρασμοί of 1:6 serve to purify as by fire the genuineness of the faith of Peter's readers. The quality of faith will "be found to result in praise and glory and honor when Jesus Christ is revealed." In answer to their question, 'What sort of trial is that of our sufferings?' Peter answers the addressees that they have the quality of purification and subsequent honor.[51] Hence the audience's situation involves an indefinite question involving knowledge of a thing (sc. suffering) and its quality.[52]

Now an examination of the invention, arrangement, and style of 1 Peter is in order. In the following pages, the Greek text cited

---

[48] Watson, "James 2," 101. See the discussions of these *topoi* in Cic. *Inv.* 1.15.20; 2.48.141, 51.156, 57.170–58.175; *Top.* 24.90–26.100; Quint. *Inst. Or.* 3.8.1–70; *Her.* 3.2.3–5.9. In 1 Pt. the advantageous and honorable are coterminous since honor is a claim to worth and its concomitant public acknowledgement that bring social prestige and benefit to the one who claims that worth. In Cic. *Inv.* 2.55.166, the combination of the honorable and advantage result in glory, "a person's having a widespread reputation accompanied by praise." In *Her.*, honor is one of two subdivisions of advantage, the other being security. The acquisition of advantage is the aim of deliberative speech (3.2.3).

[49] Watson, *Invention*, 11–13; idem, "James 2," 101–2.

[50] Quint. *Inst. Or.* 3.6.5, 17, 10.1–5. A cause is basically a reason (or denial) of an action that one seeks to prove in court. A conflict of causes occurs when an accusation is denied or the facts contradict themselves.

[51] The πειρασμοί (1:6; 4:12; cf. 4:17) of 1 Peter constitute a variety of the Messianic woes that befall the earth and God's people in the last time. See Selwyn, *St. Peter*, 128–29; 300–3. Other NT refs. to this time of woe and testing are Mk. 13:1–36; Rom. 8:18–25; 2 Thess. 2:3–12; Rev. 8:1–9:21. The notion of purification, apparent in Rom. 5:1–5; Jas. 1:2–4; and 1 Pt. 1:6–7, 4:12–13, is evident in the OT at Ps. 12:6; Prov. 17:3; Isa. 48:10; Zech. 13:9; Mal. 3:2–3. See Selwyn, *St. Peter*, 129–30.

[52] On the matter of questions in rhetorical species, see Watson, *Invention*, 10–11.

(unless otherwise noted) is the United Bible Societies' third edition. English scriptural quotations are from the NRSV unless stated otherwise.

CHAPTER THREE

The Exordium: 1 Peter 1:3–12

The Three Concerns of the Exordium

Rhetorical argumentation has as its preface an exordium,[1] a prologue whose major concerns are three: (1) the introduction of matters to be discussed in the *probatio* and *peroratio*, (2) the establishment of positive ethos for the speaker, and (3) the acquisition of the attentiveness and goodwill of the audience. In 1 Pt. 1:3–12 each of these concerns is addressed.[2]

(1) Matters to Be Discussed

The predominant subject in all of 1 Peter is suffering.[3] The word πάσχω or its cognates appear sixteen times[4] in the letter.

---

[1] Arist. *Rh.* 3.13.1414b.3, 14.1415a.7; *Her.* 1.4.6; Watson, *Invention*, 20–21.

[2] Cic. *De Or.* 2.80.325; Quint. *Inst. Or.* 4.1.23–27; cf. Cic. *De Or.* 2.79.320; Thurén, *Rhetorical Strategy*, 128–29, who identifies 1:1–12 as the exordium and *captatio benevolentiae*.

[3] Dalton, *Proclamation*, recognizes the inclusion of 1:6–7 and 4:12–13/5:10 (the latter verse constellation falls within the final section of the letter before the personal note and greetings). Several echoes of the former constellation appear in the latter (96). Cf. the following diagram:

1:6–7	*4:12–13*	*5:10*
ὀλίγον		ὀλίγον
πειρασμοῖς	πειρασμόν	
πυρός	πυρώσει	
λυπηθέντες	παθήμασιν	παθόντας
ἐν ἀποκαλύψει	ἐν τῇ ἀποκαλύψει	
Ἰησοῦ Χριστοῦ		
δόξαν	τῆς δόξης	δόξαν
		ἐν Χριστῷ

The importance of an inclusion is that it "not merely binds the section between the common words or phrases into a unity, but indicates that the unifying idea of the section is that expressed by the inclusion" (95). Dalton omits mention of the parallel of ἀγαλλιᾶσθε (1:6) with ἀγαλλιώμενοι (4:13) although it stresses the dimension of joyous vindication in spite of/because of suffering.

Nominal and verbal equivalents and explicative terms expand the πάσχω word field remarkably.[5] The topic of suffering is introduced in 1:6 (ὀλίγον ἄρτι εἰ δέον [ἐστὶν] λυπηθέντες ἐν ποικίλοις πειρασμοῖς) and 1:11 (τὰ εἰς Χριστὸν παθήματα).

The distresses of the believers are from the outset linked to those of Christ: he suffered just as they do. The fact that the believers' sufferings are called πειρασμοί (1:6) in which they have had to "suffer grief" (NIV for λυπέω), and not παθήματα, does not mean that their suffering is necessarily essentially different from the παθήματα of Christ. ἡ πύρωσις πρὸς πειρασμόν of 4:12 is defined in v. 13 as a partnership in Christ's sufferings (παθήματα). Hence λυπέω/λύπη and πειρασμός (linked in 1:6) in 1 Peter are both closely allied (if not equivalent to) the πάσχω/πάθημα word group.

The author's occupation with suffering is evident in every section of 1 Peter, especially in the latter two *argumentationes* (2:11–3:12 and 3:13–4:11) and in the *peroratio* (4:12–5:11). In the first *argumentatio* 1:13–2:10 the notion of affliction is explicit only at 1 Pt. 2:4 and 7,[6] in relation to Christ, who is rejected (ἀποδοκιμάζω) by humans, "the builders." Christ's experience of rejection by mortals/vindication by God is established as a paradigm by Peter in the letter for the Christian's own experience in suffering.

The subject of suffering overlaps with another Petrine concern that finds its introduction in the exordium: the honor/shame motif. Some terms in 1 Peter are common to the semantic field of

---

One ought also to notice the related parallel ἀγαλλιᾶσθε χαρᾷ ἀνεκλαλήτῳ καὶ δεδοξασμένῃ (1:8) with χαίρετε . . . χαρῆτε ἀγαλλιώμενοι (4:13). Both parallels indicate that Peter not only discusses suffering in the letter, but its honorable, glorious, and joyful outcome for the faithful endurers of it.

[4] πάσχω: 2:19, 20, 21, 23; 3:14, 17, 18; 4:1 (2x), 15, 19; 5:10. πάθημα: 1:11; 4:13; 5:1, 9.

[5] Cf. Appendix 1, "The Semantic Field of Honor and Shame in 1 Peter," below.

[6] The reference to the τίμιον αἷμα Χριστοῦ in 1:19 obliquely points to his suffering that is more directly mentioned elsewhere (1:2, 11; 2:21–24; 3:18; 4:1, 13; 5:1).

honor/shame and that of suffering.[7] Suffering in 1 Peter is related to the social distinction of dishonor. The Christians of Asia Minor suffer because acknowledgement of their claims to worth is withheld and replaced by slander and vituperation.

(2) Positive Ethos

Another purpose of the rhetorical exordium is the establishment of positive ethos, a high esteem and regard for the author that are held by the audience who believe her/him to be trustworthy and authoritative.[8] Nothing is said by Peter of himself in the exordium of 1 Peter. However, his identification of himself as Πέτρος ἀπόστολος Ἰησοῦ Χριστοῦ in the prescript at 1:1 has already established him as authoritative, reliable as a witness, and a good man.[9]

Peter identifies with his audience in his use of the first person in v. 3 (emphases mine):

> Blessed be the God and Father of *our* Lord Jesus Christ! By his great mercy he has given *us* a new birth into a living hope through the resurrection of Jesus Christ from the dead.

The commonality of Lord and new birth serves to unify Peter and his readers.[10] At v. 4, Peter switches to the second person in which he speaks through the remainder of the exordium.[11] By so

---

[7] Cf. 1:11, πάθημα; 2:1, κακία, καταλαλιά; 2:4, 7, ἀποδοκιμάζω; 2:12, καταλαλέω; 2:19, πάσχω ἀδίκως; 2:23, λοιδορέω; 2:24, ξύλον; 3:9, κακός, λοιδορία; 3:10–12, κακός; 3:13, κακόω; 4:14, ὀνειδίζω; 4:16, αἰσχύνω.

[8] The three categories of artistic proof are ethos, pathos (the emotional response elicited by the orator's craft), and logos (reasoned argument). See Kennedy, *NT Interpretation*, 15; on ethos, see Arist. *Rh.* 1.2.1356a.3–4; 3.14.1415a.7; Quint. *Inst. Or.* 4.1.7.

[9] Cf. Watson, *Invention*, 90, on ethos in 2 Peter and 38 on ethos in Jude.

[10] Cf. Watson, *Invention*, 38, regarding ἡ κοινὴ σωτηρία ἡμῶν (Jd. 3) of Jude and his readers: "His [Jude's] assumption that he and the audience share a common salvation emphasizes his relation to the audience—the corporate nature of his own and their salvation."

[11] εἰς ὑμᾶς, v. 4; ἀγγαλιᾶσθε (2 pers. pl.), v. 6; τὸ δοκίμιον ὑμῶν τῆς πίστεως, v. 7; ἀγαπᾶτε (2 pers. pl.), ἀγαλλιᾶσθε (2 pers. pl.), v. 8; τῆς πίστεως [ὑμῶν], v. 9; τῆς εἰς ὑμᾶς χάριτος, v. 10; ὑμῖν δέ, ἃ νῦν ἀνηγγέλη ὑμῖν διὰ τῶν εὐαγγελισαμένων ὑμᾶς, v. 12.

doing, he has set himself apart from his readers, although he still remains identified with them as having a common Lord and new birth (v. 3). Through second-person speech, Peter aligns himself with the esteemed prophets "who prophesied of the grace that was to be yours" (v. 10) and testified in advance about Christ's sufferings and glories that followed them (v. 11). The prophets were inspired by the same Spirit who empowered those who preached the gospel to the Christians of Asia Minor (v. 12). Peter, as an apostle, would be considered as one of these respected heralds and, therefore, as one guided by the Spirit like the other heralds and prophets. Peter's ethos is greatly enhanced by this pneumatic association,[12] not only because of his inclusion in select company, but also by reason that his discourse would be regarded as divinely inspired.[13]

(3) The Acquisition of Attentiveness and Goodwill

In 1 Pt. 1:3–12, the readers are commended for a variety of traits by the author in terms that are designed to win their goodwill. The rhetorical proem states the honorable nature of a cause when that quality is the issue. Peter deems his readers and

---

[12] The association is augmented by the link of (ὁ?) μάρτυς τῶν τοῦ Χριστοῦ παθημάτων in 5:1 with προμαρτυρόμενον in 1:11. Although Peter is (the) μάρτυς in 5:1 and the Spirit is the one who testifies beforehand in 1:11, the association that Peter has drawn of himself with the prophets and Christian heralds implies that he, as they, possesses the Spirit who animates the prophetic and kerygmatic work of them all. His function as μάρτυς is thus pneumatically exercised. The connection of μάρτυς with προμαρτυρό-μενον suggests that the former term carries an active sense (witness who testifies) rather than a passive one (witness who observes) since the participle is active in meaning. See further discussion below in the section on *peroratio*.

[13] Quintilian (*Inst. Or.* 10.1.48) praises Homer, who virtually establishes the regulations for the exordium: "For, by his invocation of the goddesses believed to preside over poetry he wins the goodwill of his audience, by the statement of the greatness of his themes he excites their attention and renders them receptive by the briefness of the summary."

Cf. Hom. *Od.* 1.1–10, where the muse is invoked and Odysseus is praised. Homer extols him as a man of many devices and the sacker of the Trojan temple, who not only saw and learned much on his return travels from Troy, but suffered (πάθεν) many woes as he sought to conduct himself and his comrades safely home.

their cause of faith to be honorable (contrary to what their experience with the outsiders would suggest). The Christians, despite their trials, can anticipate praise, glory, and honor when the proven character of their faith becomes evident, at the revelation of Jesus Christ (v. 7). The themes of suffering and honor have now coalesced: present suffering moves to future glory, as David W. Kendall notes.[14] Yet the present suffering also involves present honor for Peter's readers, a fact that Kendall largely overlooks.[15] How Christian sufferers who are publicly disgraced can nevertheless bear honor is a development of Peter's epistolary discourse. The two Petrine themes of coexistent suffering and honor are introduced in the rhetorical exordium.[16]

When a rhetor identifies matters of importance to be discussed, s/he is on the way toward gaining the attentiveness of the audience.[17] Peter wins the attention of his audience in mentioning the living hope to which he and his readers were born (v. 3), the permanent inheritance (v. 4), and salvation ready to be revealed (vv. 5, 9; cf. v. 7). The appearance of important characters in the drama óf salvation history (prophets, v. 10; the Spirit, vv. 11–12; preachers, v. 12; angels, v. 12) adds weight to the importance of Peter's discourse.

Receptivity follows closely upon the winning of the hearers' attention[18] and when the speaker provides a brief summary of the

---

[14] David W. Kendall, "1 Peter 1:3–12," in *Perspectives on First Peter*, ed. Charles H. Talbert, 112–17.

[15] Kendall does note in relation to 2:4–8 that "believers may face their own rejection with the confidence that they also [with Christ] are honored and chosen by God." That honor brings the experience of vindication and glory in the future, however. Hence for Kendall that honor is essentially something anticipated, not presently enjoyed ("1 Peter 1:3–12," 112).

[16] The function of 1 Pt. 1:3–12 as introduction to the entire letter and its contents is affirmed by Kendall, "1 Peter 1:3–12," 106, 115; and Martin, *Metaphor*, 51–68. Both authors perceive an eschatological context for the instructions of Peter.

[17] *Her.* 1.4.7; Quint. *Inst. Or.* 10.1.48.

[18] *Her.* 1.4.7; Quint. *Inst. Or.* 4.1.34.

case.[19] In 1 Peter, the exordium serves as a summary only insofar as it identifies the exigence of the document (the trials that have brought the readers grief, 1:6).

The goodwill of the audience is crucial for the success of rhetorical argument. A rhetor, in order to obtain the favor of the audience, may choose to focus on the facts of the case and/or upon the persons connected with it. Those persons are the rhetor her/himself, the audience, and the opposition.[20] In 1 Pt. 1:3–12, the writer concentrates upon the audience. He says nothing of the outsiders whose reproaches plague the readers in the *argumentationes* and *peroratio* of the letter. Peter gives only inferences of his own association with the prophets and heralds in vv. 10–12. Of the audience's interests and qualities he has much to say. Indeed, the exordium of 1 Pt. 1:3–12 evinces characteristics of an encomium, a detailed epideictic discourse that praises the attributes and deeds of its subject. In 1 Peter, the encomium shows the honorable esteem in which Peter holds his readers and thus fosters their goodwill. In what follows I shall analyze 1 Pt. 1:3–12 as an encomium on the Christians of Asia Minor.

· 1 Peter 1:3–12 as Encomium

Encomium, a kind of epideictic speech,[21] furnishes examples of a person's or institution's honorable qualities and the rationale

---

[19] Arist. *Rh.* 3.14.1415a.6; Cic. *Inv.* 1.16.23; Quint. *Inst. Or.* 4.1.34; 10.1.48.

[20] Arist. *Rh.* 3.14.1415a–1415b.7; Cic. *Inv.* 1.16.22; *De Or.* 2.79.321–22; *Part. Or.* 8.28; *Her.* 1.4.8–5.8; Quint. *Inst. Or.* 4.1.6–22. Aristotle says that "to make his hearers inattentive, the speaker must persuade them that the matter is unimportant, that it does not concern them that it is painful" (ὅτι λυπηρόν) (*Rh.* 3.14.1415b.7). Although Peter mentions trials by which his readers have been grieved (λυπηθέντες, 1:6), the use of λυπέω does not foster inattentiveness, but rather attention since the readers' grief eventuates in the honored approbation of tested faith (v. 7).

[21] *Rh. Al.* 1.1421b.8–17 identifies three kinds of public speeches: the parliamentary (τὸ δημηγορικόν), the ceremonial (τὸ ἐπιδεικτικόν) and the forensic (τὸ δικανικόν). Each kind has its species; ceremonial, or epideictic, has eulogy (ἐγκωμιαστικόν), and vituperation (ψεκτικόν; also κακολογικόν, 35.1440b.5–6). Quint. *Inst. Or.* 3.4.12–14 defines *demonstrativus* as speech concerning praise and blame, the equivalent of ἐπιδεικτικόν and ἐγκωμιαστικόν. In his opinion, however, a great difference exists between

for an honor or memorial bestowed upon that person or institution. Although the encomium is not a patterned discourse (as are deliberative and judicial speeches), it provides the orator opportunities for using persuasive skills within a generally topical, not logical, outline. That outline is given by Burton L. Mack in his introductory treatment on rhetoric in the New Testament:[22]

The Encomium
1. Introduction
2. Narration Origin/Genealogy/Birth
3. Achievements
   a. Education/Pursuits
   b. Virtues
   c. Deeds
   d. Blessings/Endowments
4. Conclusion Honor/Memorial

Encomium is closely associated with praise in Aristotle's terminology. The former has to do with achievements, whereas the latter concerns greatness of virtue.[23] Not only is encomium linked with praise as sub-species of epideictic rhetoric,[24] but it bears resemblance to deliberative discourse. Suggestions in counsel become encomia by alterations in language. As Aristotle has it:

---

the latter two, since epideictic seems to imply display rather than demonstration. Nevertheless, Quintilian points out the virtual synonymity of the terms in rhetorical parlance, although he disagrees with it.

[22] Mack, *Rhetoric and the NT*, 47–48. Cf. Baldwin, *Medieval Rhetoric*, 31 n. 60; Hermogenes, *Elementary Exercises* [προγυμνάσματα], trans. Baldwin in his *Medieval Rhetoric*, 23–38. The pattern for epideictic is fluid in the handbooks; a great variety of arrangements is permissible (Cic. *Part. Or.* 4.12).

[23] Arist. *Rh.* 1.9.1367b.33–34, where Aristotle nevertheless asserts that "achievements, in fact, are signs of moral habit" (τὰ δ᾽ ἔργα σημεῖα τῆς ἕξεώς ἐστιν), or, in other words, virtuous. Praise (ἔπαινος) and encomium (ἐγκώμιον) are indeed virtually synonymous in 1.9.1367b.35–36: ἔχει δὲ κοινὸν εἶδος ὁ ἔπαινος καὶ αἱ συμβουλαί· ἃ γὰρ ἐν τῷ συμβουλεύειν ὑπόθειο ἄν, ταῦτα μετατεθέντα τῇ λέξει ἐγκώμια γίγεται.

[24] See 38–39 n. 21 above.

> For instance, the statement that "one ought not to pride oneself on goods which are due to fortune, but on those which are due to oneself alone," when expressed in this way, has the force of a suggestion; but expressed thus, "he was proud, not of goods which were due to fortune, but of those which were due to himself alone," it becomes praise. Accordingly, if you desire to praise, look what you would suggest; if you desire to suggest, look what you would praise.[25]

Encomium, from the very earliest times, had served a deliberative purpose. That is, the great were praised in order to provide others with a noble example in their pursuit of virtue and honor.[26] Hence encomium is like epideictic generally in its possession of deliberative value.[27]

Few examples of encomiastic discourse are present in the New Testament. Mack identifies three: Paul's defense in 1 Cor. 9, an encomium on ἀγάπη in 1 Cor. 13, and a speech in praise of πίστις in Heb. 11.[28] There are, however, several passages that are epideictic in nature without being encomiastic. Kennedy identifies Mt. 23, the Magnificat (Lk. 1:46–55), the Johannine Farewell Discourse of Jesus (Jn. 13–17), Philippians and 2 Peter as

---

[25] Arist. *Rh.* 1.9.1368a.36–37; Kennedy, *Art of Rhetoric*, 172.

[26] Clark, *Rhetoric*, 136, who cites the poetical encomium of Pindaric hymns and the prose encomia of Isocrates (e.g., the *Euagoras*).

[27] Quint. *Inst. Or.* 3.7.28; cf. 2.4.20.

[28] Mack, *Rhetoric and the NT*, 60–64, 64–66, 73–76, who understands 1 Cor. 9 to be a judicial speech with an epideictic issue (Paul's authority and honor as an apostle) at stake.

Within Heb. 11, two passages themselves resemble encomia and may be classified as encomia within the encomium (Heb. 11) that Mack identifies. Abraham (11:8–12), after a brief narration of his call (v. 8), is praised for his noble achievements: his sojourn by faith (a pursuit, v. 9), his vision of faith (virtue, v. 10), his miraculous procreative ability (a deed, v. 11), his innumerable progeny (an endowment, v. 12). Along with Abel, Enoch, and Noah, Abraham receives the honor of a city prepared for them (v. 16). The mention of Abraham again in v. 17 is perhaps an introduction to the testimony about Isaac, or further acclaim of Abraham's virtuous faith and deeds. Moses (11:23–28) is the offspring of noble (=faithful) parentage (v. 23). The virtue of Moses lay in his identification with God's people (vv. 24–25). The faith of Moses inspired noble deeds, suffering of abuse for Christ (v. 26), perseverance (v. 27), and obedience (v. 28).

epideictic speech.[29] To the examples of Kennedy and Mack, one ought to add Mt. 11:7–19; Lk. 1:67–79; Lk. 7:24–35; Jude.

Although, in the main, the exordium in 1 Peter introduces deliberative speech, it is epideictic in nature and especially encomiastic. In ancient rhetoric, one species of rhetoric often contained other species within it.[30] The praise or censure of epideictic often appears in judicial or deliberative discourse.[31] The concern of epideictic speech is 'honor' (*honestum*),[32] which is, as we have seen, the primary concern for Peter's suffering readers.[33]

Peter opens his exordium with a blessing of God that resembles other opening epistolary benedictions in the New Testament.[34] The blessing of v. 3 extends, according to Martin, through v. 12. The section demarcated by the two verses comprises a blessing section that is a substitute for the more common health wish or thanksgiving clause of Greek epistolography. The blessing section supplies the context for an understanding of the letter which, Martin says, is eschatological.[35]

---

[29] Kennedy, *NT Interpretation*, 77–85. The Beatitudes, celebrating qualities, are epideictic although they function in the Sermon on the Mount/Plain (Mt. 5:3–14; Lk. 6:20–23) as a proem. "A proem," affirms Kennedy, "regularly shows epideictic traits" (45).

[30] *Rh. Al.* 5.1427b.32–38.

[31] *Her.* 3.8.15.

[32] Cic. *Top.* 23.89, 91, where the end of the encomiastic speech (*laudatio*) is honor (*honestas*); of the judicial speech, justice; of the deliberative speech, advantage. Yet in Cic. *Inv.* 2.51.156, the end of all three species of oratory is honor. More specifically: of forensic, equity (a subdivision of honor); of deliberative, honor and advantage; of epideictic, honor alone (*in demonstrativo, honestatem*).

[33] See 27–30 above.

[34] 2 Cor. 1:3; Eph. 1:3, each of which begins with the blessing colon that is identical to that of 1 Pt. 1:3: εὐλογητὸς ὁ θεὸς καὶ πατὴρ τοῦ κυρίου ἡμῶν Ἰησοῦ Χριστοῦ. The Corinthian passage is followed by the appositional ὁ πατὴρ τῶν οἰκτιρμῶν καὶ θεὸς πάσης παρακλήσεως. Like 1 Pt., Eph. has a relative clause after the blessing colon: ὁ εὐλογήσας ἡμᾶς ἐν πάσῃ εὐλογίᾳ πνευματικῇ ἐν τοῖς ἐπουρανίοις ἐν Χριστῷ.

[35] Martin, *Metaphor*, 47–52, 68.

While the section does open, as Martin points out, with a benediction that is akin to those of the *Hodayot Psalms* of Qumran and the *Odes of Solomon*,[36] the passage 1:3–12 as a whole ought to be taken, not as a praise of God (although it opens with it), but as an encomium on the Christians of Asia Minor. It concerns itself with their endowments, virtues, and deeds, not primarily with God's activity (although he is the confessed source of the Christians' bounty).[37] A detailed analysis of the encomium 1 Pt. 1:3–12 follows:

1. Introduction (1 Pt. 1:1–2)

Although the encomium proper is 1:3–12, one must take into account the rhetorical function of the prescript to the letter. Verses 1 and 2 not only function as a preface to identify the author and the recipients of the letter, but, in these verses, rhetorical tactics already surface as Peter establishes his ethos and endeavors to evoke pathos in his audience. Peter succinctly asserts his authority to address his hearers in his self-identification: "Peter, an apostle of Jesus Christ." Essential to the promotion of a rhetor's positive ethos is the audience's recognition of the rhetor as a good person. Such a recognition is the strongest influence in a case. Peter, as an apostle, would be recognized as good.[38] Furthermore, the orator must be regarded as a reliable witness in order to obtain positive pathos; an apostle, like Peter, would be so regarded.[39]

---

[36] Ibid., 48–49, where Martin observes εὐλογητός to be a translation of the Heb. בָּרוּךְ; the blessing section substitutes for the expected thanksgiving section because of the liturgical nature of the letter. That nature is exhibited by εὐλογητός which acquires its liturgical character as the equivalent of בָּרוּךְ in the Psalms (cf. Ps. 28:6; 31:21; 41:13; 72:18–19; 89:52; 106:48; 119:12; 124:6; 135:21; 144:1). Note the resemblance of 1 Pt. 1:3 esp. to 31:21 LXX which reads, εὐλογητὸς κύριος, ὅτι ἐθαυμάστωσε τὸ ἔλεος αὐτοῦ ἐν πόλει περιοχῆς.

[37] Hence, neither is 1 Pet. 1:3–12 foremost a rehearsal of the life of grace as Kendall ("1 Peter 1:3–12," *passim*) maintains.

[38] Arist. *Rh.* 1.2.1356a.3–4; 3.14.1415a.7; Quint. *Inst. Or.* 4.1.7; Watson, *Invention*, 37–38, 41 (on Jd.), 95 (on 2 Pt.).

[39] Quint. *Inst. Or.* 4.1.7; Watson, *Invention*, 95 (on 2 Pt.).

The addressees are not only residents of Asia Minor whose regions are listed. Although they are παρεπίδημοι διασπορᾶς (visiting strangers who are culturally alienated), they are ἐκλεκτοί, those "who have been chosen and destined by God the Father and sanctified by the Spirit to be obedient to Jesus Christ and to be sprinkled with his blood." These people are special indeed! Peter's intention is to help them experience a marvelous status. The election by God, the sanctification by the Holy Spirit, and the high calling and purpose (obedience to Christ and sprinkling with his blood) indicate the honored esteem that the hearers enjoy before God and before Peter.[40] Thus Peter arouses a positive pathos in them.

Does 1 Pt. 1:1–2 have any contribution to make to the letter other than to supply merely conventional greetings as preamble to the real heart of the letter? The answer must be yes. 1 Pt. 1:1–2 has a distinctly epistolary form and value, yet performs a rhetorical function in the letter (and especially in the encomium) as well. In the verses, Peter begins to establish his own ethos[41] and the hearers' pathos, both positive. Furthermore, as Dalton observes, motifs that are developed throughout 1 Peter (especially in chapter one) are announced in the address 1:1–2.[42] What, then, is the appropriate rhetorical designation of 1 Pt. 1:1–2? It is certainly an epistolary address and the introduction to the encomium of 1:3–12, but what is its role in the entire document?

---

[40] *Her.* 1.5.8.

[41] I disagree with Leonhard Goppelt, *Der erste Petrusbrief*, Kritisch-exegetischer Kommentar über das neue Testament 12/1, 8th ed. (Göttingen: Vandenhoeck & Ruprecht, 1978), 77, who maintains that 1 Pt. (unlike 2 Pt.) never urges the formal authority of its author. The argument is made from the subject matter alone. The Eng. trans., Leonhard Goppelt, *A Commentary on 1 Peter*, trans. and ed. John E. Alsup (Grand Rapids: William B. Eerdmans, 1993), appeared well after I had entered my research for the diss. Thus I refer to the Ger. ed. throughout.

[42] Dalton, *Proclamation*, 95–97, 99. He notes the inclusion of 1:1 and 5:13 by means of the ἐκλεκτ- words (cognates appear also at 1:15; 2:4, 6, 9, 21; 3:9; 5:10) and the announcement in the address of the main themes of the first chapter.

Duane F. Watson,[43] in his rhetorical-critical study of 2 Peter and Jude, assigns to the epistolary openings of those letters the role of "quasi-exordium." That is, they display rhetorical functions for the letters that they introduce, but are not formally part of rhetorical discourse. Regarding the epistolary prescript of Jude (vv. 1–2), Watson states:

> The epistolary prescript, although necessitated by the epistolary form of the discourse and not technically a recognized element in rhetorical arrangement, does function like the *exordium*. This is particularly true of making the audience attentive, receptive, and well-disposed; establishing desired ethos; and introducing topics to be developed in the *probatio*.[44]

Since 1 Pt. 1:1–2 functions in the same way as do the prescripts of 2 Peter and Jude, it, too, is a quasi-exordium. Rather than being an insignificant addition to the letter, 1 Pt. 1:1–2 demonstrates a clear connection to the rest of the letter. The Petrine address is not something joined to the body of the epistle later, but has always been synchronous with it, so as to serve its rhetorical purpose.

2. Narration (v. 3)

In a narration, an encomium recognizes the origin, genealogy, and birth of the person(s) extolled. Verse 3 provides that information about Peter's readers. Their origin is God the Father. The relative clause ὁ κατὰ τὸ πολὺ αὐτοῦ ἔλεος ἀναγεννήσας κτλ. is in reference to God since he is the Father who generates the new birth through the resurrection of Jesus Christ. Although not a parent, Jesus Christ is a member of the readers' ancestry in that his resurrection from the dead furnishes the precedent for their own rebirth. The phrase ἐκ νεκρῶν constitutes a *circumlocutio*[45] and serves to formulate a bond between the "rebirth" of Christ with their own (cf. 3:21 in the link of baptism-resurrection). Although not in degree, the new life of Christ and that of Peter's audience is similar. Thus, he is like a first-born sibling who undergoes the experiences of the brothers and sisters who follow

---

[43] Watson, *Invention*, 40–43, 95–96.

[44] Ibid., 41. Cf. his similar statement on the prescript 2 Pt. 1:1–2 (95).

[45] Quint. *Inst. Or.* 8.6.59–61. Gk. περίφρασις.

him.[46] The account of the ancestry of the Christians is brief, yet significant. God the Father and Jesus Christ in his resurrection are their ancestors responsible for their existence. The birth is "a new birth into a living hope." The origin, genealogy, and birth of the letter's recipients are thus noble. Their positive description corresponds to the congratulation of the well-born (εὐγενεῖς) that encomium contains[47] and serves to create positive pathos and elicit the readers' goodwill.

3. "Achievements" (vv. 4–8)

Peter's catalogue of his readers' "achievements" includes both blessings/endowments and virtues. "An inheritance that is imperishable, undefiled, and unfading, kept in heaven" is the first endowment in the Petrine inventory. The first three adjectives that modify κληρονομία compose, in Greek, a pleasing *homoeoptoton*[48] that coexists with alliteration[49] of the same words (ἄφθαρτον, ἀμίαντον, ἀμάραντον). Thus Peter has fashioned an ornate double figure. With it Peter stresses the eternal quality of the inheritance; by describing it three different ways, the certainty of the inheritance for the believers is emphasized and thus assured.

---

[46] Cf. Col. 1:15, [Χρίστος] ὅς ἐστιν . . . πρωτότοκος πάσης κτίσεως; v. 18, πρωτότοκος ἐκ τῶν νεκρῶν. Cf. 1 Cor. 15:20, where Christ is the ἀπαρχὴ τῶν κεκοιμημένων.

[47] *Rh. Al.* 35.1440b.13–1441a.20. Although it is proper for the well-born and others possessing goods external to virtue to receive congratulation, μακαρίζειν, not praise, οὐκ ἐπαινεῖν, for their good fortune (35.1440b.20), congratulation is still a conferment of honor.

[48] Lat. *exornatio/similiter cadens*, a figure of speech that occurs "when in the same period two or more words appear in the same case, and with like terminations" (*Her.* 4.20.28; cf. 4.17.18). According to Quint. *Inst. Or.* 9.3.78, the case endings need not be identical in appearance.

[49] When alliteration occurs at the beginning of clauses, it is *paromoiosis*. There the entire words show similarity as in the example cited by Arist. *Rh.* 3.1410a.9 from Ar. *Frag.* 649: ἀγρὸν γὰρ ἔλαβεν ἀργὸν παρ' αὐτοῦ="for he received from him land untilled."

The inheritance, furthermore, is reserved in heaven for the Christians to whom Peter writes.[50] The metonymy[51] ἐν οὐρανοῖς avoids an excessive transplacement in the next verse. That is to say, an unpleasant duplication of the same word.[52] The instrumental phrase ἐν δυνάμει θεοῦ could easily have replaced ἐν οὐρανοῖς. Similarly, φρουρουμένους avoids a further transplacement of τηρέω from v. 4 and indicates that the sovereignty of God protects both inheritance and its heirs:

κληρονομία   εἰς ὑμᾶς
τετηρημένην   τοὺς φρουρουμένους
ἐν οὐρανοῖς   ἐν δυνάμει θεοῦ

To insure their eventual receipt of the blessing of the inheritance, Peter's audience is "being protected by the power of God [a further contribution to the pathos in the letter] through faith." The notion of the addressees' faith, a highly prized Christian virtue, is expounded in verses 7 and 8. The "salvation" of v. 5 appears to be a synonym[53] for "a living hope" of v. 3 and the "inheritance" of v. 4. By examining it from three perspectives, the

---

[50] The echoes of the Gospel tradition ought not to be missed here. Cf. Mt. 6:19–20; Lk. 12:33.

[51] Lat. *denominatio*, a trope "which draws from an object closely akin or associated an expression suggesting the object meant, but not called by its own name." *Her.* 4.32.43. The passive τετηρημένην ἐν οὐρανοῖς is a circumlocution for God as active keeper of the inheritance; the passive encomiastically stresses the readers' fortune, not God's power.

[52] *Her.* 4.12.18. The figure (*traductio*) can be effectively utilized in order to enhance style (4.14.20).

[53] συνωνυμία/*interpretatio*, a figure of speech in which one word is replaced by another of the same meaning and, by which replacement, the force of the first expression is renewed by its synonym. *Her.* 4.28.38 (where the following illustrative example appears: "You have overturned the republic from its roots; you have demolished the state from its foundations"); Quint. *Inst. Or.* 8.4.26; 9.3.45; 9.3.98 (synonymity is not a figure); Lausberg, *Handbuch*, 649–56. The synonymity of the terms in 1 Pt. 1:3–5 is recognized by Norbert Brox, *Der erste Petrusbrief*, 2nd ed., Evangelisch-katholischer Kommentar über das neue Testament 21 (Zürich: Benziger Verlag, 1986; Neukirchen-Vluyn: Neukirchener Verlag, 1986), 62–63; Goppelt, *Der erste Petrusbrief*, 96–97; and J. Ramsey Michaels, *1 Peter*, Word Biblical Commentary 49 (Waco, TX: Word Books, 1988), 19.

author hopes that the readers will more greatly value and understand their destiny.

A series of virtues ensues in vv. 6–8. The hearers rejoice in the last time because of all the endowments that they have received (vv. 3–5), despite the fact that they "have had to suffer various trials" (6). In panegyric, one's bearing adversity without loss of dignity or being crushed was admirable.[54]

The genuineness of the readers' faith is tested in the refining fire of trials (vv. 6–7). Peter uses the figure of comparison.[55] The adjective πολύτιμος in the comparative degree signifies that the *similitudo* leads from the lesser to the greater (*ex minore ad maius ductum*), both elements of the comparison being similar but unequal.[56] Purification by fire is a Christian topic, borrowed from

---

[54] Cic. *De Or.* 2.85.346–47.

[55] παραβολή/*similitudo*, a figure of thought which, though invented by the rhetor, is drawn from real life. In *similitudo*, an element of likeness from one thing is carried over to a different thing. The figure serves to embellish, prove, clarify, and vivify a rhetorical argument. The four forms of comparison are contrast, negation, the detailed parallel, and the abridged comparison (*Her.* 4.45.59–48.61; cf. Cic. *Inv.* 1.30.49; Lausberg, *Handbuch*, 422–25). Among the rhetorical theorists, the usage of *similitudo* and its subdivisions is fluid. See Cic. *Inv.* 1.30.47–49 for one set of subdivisions and definitions.

The παραβολαί of Jesus are examples of the *similitudo*, specifically of its subdivision *collatio* (wherein a comparison is made between things that bear some degree of similarity). Jesus' parables are short discourses that make a comparison. Often expressing but one thought, the evangelists frequently accompany them with interpretation, since they can be obscure (Walter Bauer, *A Greek-English Lexicon of the New Testament and Other Early Christian Literature*, 2nd ed., trans and ed. William F. Arndt, F. Wilbur Gingrich, and Frederick W. Danker [Chicago: University of Chicago Press, 1979] [hereafter cited as BAGD], 612–13 [s.v. "παραβολή"]). See Arist. *Rh.* 2.20.1393b.4 for discussion of the παραβολή.

Peter here employs the abridged comparison since he does not elaborate on the ways that the refining process acts on faith. The transference of likeness from metallurgy to πίστις is stressed by the δοκ- words in v. 7a-c: ἵνα τὸ δοκίμιον ὑμῶν τῆς πίστεως πολυτιμότερον χρυσίου τοῦ ἀπολλυμένου, διὰ πυρὸς δὲ δοκιμαζομένου.

[56] Quint. *Inst. Or.* 5.11.30–31.

the Old Testament.[57] 'If perishable gold must be refined by fire in order to demonstrate its genuine worth, how much more must your faith be tested, since it is far more valuable than gold,' Peter maintains. After all, πίστις eventuates in the imperishable benefits of salvation (1:6, 9) and deliverance from suffering (5:10).

How are Peter's readers being purified? The nature of their refinement became evident in our examination of the rhetorical situation of 1 Peter. The readers, Christians in Asia Minor, under hostile verbal assault, were grieved and suffering. The pathos of Peter's readers may be even more clearly understood by reference to what Aristotle affirms as the source of λύπη. The discussion occurs within the context of rhetorical procedure for obtaining audience goodwill through the creation of pathos that is agreeable with the argument. Peter is not, of course, instructing his auditors in oratorical practice, but he evinces an acquaintance with the psychology of λύπη in his encomium on the addressees (a crucial place where pathos would be developed).

---

[57] On the beneficial nature of difficulties/refinement for God's people in the OT see Job 23:10; Ps. 17:3, 26:1-2, 66:10-12, 119:67; 139:1, 23, Prov. 17:3, 27:21; Isa. 48:10; Jer. 6:27-30; Zech. 13:9; Mal. 3:2-3; cf. Ps. 12:6; Prov. 25:4-5. The passage from Ps. 66 probably recounts the Exodus deliverance when the Lord brought Israel out of Egypt, the "iron-smelting furnace" (Dt. 4:20; Jer. 11:4, NIV).

Cf. Ezek. 22:18-22 for the notion that Israel is but the dross of the refining process, i.e., that she has failed the test and will fail it again. G. R. Beasley-Murray, on that passage, affirms that "the real point of the figure is the judgment involved in the idea of smelting. Unlike other prophets who use this figure, Ezekiel excludes the possibility of refinement; his generation is but slag!" ("Ezekiel," in *The New Bible Commentary: Revised*, ed. D[onald] Guthrie and J.A. Motyer (Grand Rapids: Eerdmans, 1970), 675.

For the image of fire as that which tests the righteous in the Apocrypha, see Wis. Sol. 3:5-6; Ecclus. 2:1-5; 2 Esd. 16:73.

For the Christian topic of trials as salutary see Rom. 5:3-5; 2 Cor. 1:3-7, 9; Phil. 1:12-18; Jas. 1:2-4, 12; 1 Pt. 1:6-7; 4:12-13. Cf. 2 Cor. 13:5; 1 Thess. 2:4.

Northrop Frye identifies the furnace as a variation of the authentic myth of creative descent and ascent. The archetype of the furnace is present in the Bible (e.g., the Exodus, Job) and Western literature, where the smelter continues as a biblical 'topic.' See Frye's *The Great Code: The Bible and Literature* (New York and London: Harcourt, Brace, Jovanovich, 1982), 193-98; idem, *Words with Power: Being a Second Study of "The Bible and Literature"* (San Diego: Harcourt, Brace, Jovanovich, 1990), 272-313.

According to Aristotle, one who insults (ὁ ὑβρίζων) another person slights (ὀλιγωρεῖ) her/him. To insult a person means to cause injury or annoyance that disgraces the sufferer (ἔστι γὰρ ὕβρις τὸ βλάπτειν καὶ λυπεῖν ἐφ᾽ οἷς αἰσχύνη ἐστὶ τῷ πάσχοντι).[58] In Attic law, ὕβρις (insulting, dishonoring treatment) was even more serious than αἰκία (bodily injury) and could invoke a capital sentence if it were proved in a state criminal trial that the defendant first caused injury with a verbal insult.[59] The recognition that the readers are grieved (λυπηθέντες) by reason of outsiders' insults (=ὕβρις, cf. 1 Pt. 4:14), augments the ethos that Peter enjoys since he would be recognized as one who understands his audience's dificulties. The discussion of λύπη also fashions the readers' positive pathos: The acknowledgement of their griefs by a respected authority assures the recipients of the letter that their feelings are not illegitimate.

Remarkable is the compression into a short section of The "Art" of Rhetoric[60] so many terms that are germane to the issue of rhetorical situation in 1 Peter. The terms λυπέω, αἰσχύνη, πάσχω, τιμωρέω, κακῶς, ἀτιμία, ἀτιμάζω, τιμή, ἀγαθός, and κακός all find counterparts in the vocabulary of 1 Peter.[61] I do not

---

[58] Arist. Rh. 2.2.1378b.5.

[59] John Henry Freese, Aristotle: The "Art" of Rhetoric, Loeb Classical Library (Cambridge, MA: Harvard University Press, 1947; London: William Heinemann, 1947), 174–75 note d.

[60] The section from Arist. Rh. 2.2.1378b.5–6 is in part: καὶ ὁ ὑβρίζων δ᾽ ὀλιγωρεῖ· ἔστι γὰρ ὕβρις τὸ βλάπτειν καὶ λυπεῖν ἐφ᾽ οἷς αἰσχύνη ἐστὶ τῷ πάσχοντι, μὴ ἵνα τι γένηται αὐτῷ ἄλλο ἢ ὅτι ἐγένετο, ἀλλ᾽ ὅπως ἡσθῇ· οἱ γὰρ ἀντιποιοῦντες οὐχ ὑβρίζουσιν ἀλλὰ τιμωροῦνται. αἴτιον δὲ τῆς ἡδονῆς τοῖς ὑβρίζουσιν, ὅτι οἴονται κακῶς δρῶντες αὐτοὺς ὑπερέχειν μᾶλλον. διὸ οἱ νέοι καὶ οἱ πλούσιοι ὑβρισταί· ὑπερέχειν γὰρ οἴονται ὑβρίζοντες. ὕβρεως δὲ ἀτιμία, ὁ δ᾽ ἀτιμάζων ὀλιγωρεῖ· τὸ γὰρ μηδενὸς ἄξιον οὐδεμίαν ἔχει τιμήν, οὔτ᾽ ἀγαθοῦ οὔτε κακοῦ.

[61] The counterparts in 1 Pt.: λυπέω: 1:6, 2:19; αἰσχύνη: 2:6, 4:16, cf. 5:2 αἰσχροκερδῶς; πάσχω: 2:19, 20, 21, 23, 3:14, 17, 18, 4:1 (bis), 13, 15, (16), 19, 5:1, 9, 10; τιμή word group: 1:7, 19, 2:4, 6, 7, 17 (bis), 3:7; κακῶς/κακός: 2:2, 12, 14, 16, 3:9 (bis), 10, 11, 12, 13, 17, 4:15; ἀγαθός: 2:14, 15, 18, 20, 3:6, 10, 11, 13, 16 (bis), 17, 21, 4:19. I have not included clearly synonymous terms that do not have a corresponding cognate in Arist. Rh. 2.2.1378b.5–6.

contend that Peter consciously borrows from Aristotle. That cannot be proven. What is possible, however, is a Petrine employment of the notions ὕβρις and λύπη that figure prominently in the ancient honor contest as explained in one critical passage of Aristotle. The reason for the readers' experience of λύπη is not elaborated in the discussion of 1 Pt. 1:6. The πειρασμοί are not identified since they are evident to the particular audience-communities within their respective geographical regions. Moreover, rehearsal of them would be out of place in an encomium. In the passage that is reciprocal[62] to 1:6, however, the difficulties of the readers are more clearly defined. The πύρωσις πρὸς πειρασμόν of 4:12 and the παθήματα τοῦ Χριστοῦ of 4:13 explain the nature of the trials in 1:6. Furthermore, reviling endured for the name of Christ in v. 14 (εἰ ὀνειδίζεσθε ἐν ὀνόματι Χριστοῦ) points to slander and public disgrace as the nature of the believers' tribulations. Their suffering as Christians (v. 16) is social dishonor.

As the audience is praised for their joy in suffering, it increases in goodwill toward Peter's message; a positive pathos is engendered. The same is true in the case of the other virtues pointed out here by Peter: their love for Jesus Christ (lack of sight notwithstanding) and belief in him. The repetition in 1:8 of "faith" and "joy" (cf. ἀγαλλιάω and the πιστ- root at vv. 6 and 7, respectively) represent the stylistic figure of transplacement: the (frequent) reintroduction of the same word in a tasteful, elegant way.[63] By understanding that they indeed have faith and joy the hearers will be encouraged to practice these virtues yet more.

The concept in 1:8 of faith without sight is another topic from the primitive Christian didactic repertoire (Jn. 20:29; 2 Cor. 5:7; Heb. 11:1, 7).[64] The shift between tenses of the verb ὁράω

---

[62] The inclusion formed by 1:6 and 4:12–13 is observed by Dalton, *Proclamation*, 96. 1 Pt. 4:14 and 16 further define the nature of the παθήματα τοῦ Χριστοῦ of v. 13.

[63] Lat. *traductio. Her.* 4.14.20–21.

[64] Noticeable verbal similarity between the Petrine and Johannine passages exists. Jn. 20:29 reads: λέγει αὐτῷ ὁ Ἰησοῦς, ὅτι ἑώρακάς με πεπίστευκας; μακάριοι οἱ μὴ ἰδόντες καὶ πιστεύσαντες. Peter's vocabulary

constitutes another transplacement. Peter elegantly praises both the love for Christ and faith in him that flourish in his audience despite their lack of sight of Christ. The believers in Asia Minor are the μακάριοι of the Fourth Gospel who do not see the risen Jesus, yet trust in him. Peter's readers, who have such a love and belief in Jesus, presently "rejoice with an indescribable and glorious joy" (1 Pt. 1:8). The verb ἀγαλλιᾶσθε is most likely a present indicative just as it is in v. 6. The linkage of ἀγαλλιᾶσθε to the present indicative ἀγαπᾶτε in v. 8 dictates against an imperatival sense for the former.[65] There is no reason to assume a present indicative with a future meaning for ἀγαλλιᾶσθε in v. 8, just as there was none in v. 6.[66] Rhetorical epideictic praises that which it desires to be existent in its subject. Peter commends his listeners for whatever rejoicing they may practice and thus intends to motivate even more.

Concerning the verb ἀγαλλιᾶσθε, Peter probably would not, in such close succession, repeat an identical verbal form with different moods at each occurrence. Inconsistency in moods for ἀγαλλιᾶσθε between verses 6 and 8 would introduce an element of ambiguity in Peter's exordium. Since his composition exhibits

---

is similar to John's. The former duplicates a double usage of ὁράω; he keeps ἰδόντες (aor. ptc.), but then utilizes a pres. ptc. (ὁρῶντες), whereas the latter employs a perf. (ἑώρακας). Like John, Peter makes use of the verb πιστεύω. However, Peter alters John's aorist πιστεύσαντες to a pres., πιστεύοντες (both ptcs.): ὃν οὐκ ἰδόντες ἀγαπᾶτε, εἰς ὃν ἄρτι μὴ ὁρῶντες πιστεύοντες δὲ ἀγαλλιᾶσθε χαρᾷ ἀνεκλαλήτῳ καὶ δεδοξασμένῃ (1 Pt. 1:8).

[65] Michaels, *1 Peter*, 28.

[66] *Pace* Goppelt, *Der erste Petrusbrief*, 98–99; and Michaels, *1 Peter*, 34. The latter views the ptc. κομιζόμενοι as establishing the time reference for ἀγαλλιᾶσθε. Thus the tense value is eschatological. The two ptcs. κομιζόμενοι and πιστεύοντες may receive their temporal sense from the finite verb, however. In that case, the believing is current as is the receiving of "the outcome of your faith, the salvation of your souls." The reception of that outcome is an eschatological phenomenon that has already begun (cf. Rom. 6:22). That is particularly true if the eschatological benefit is a complete exoneration of the Christians and an elevation of them to full honor by God. Thus salvation would equal deliverance from the ignominy and shame that they now endure before the pagans.

characteristics of classical rhetorical practice, one may assume that he attempts to avoid ambiguity, something that ancient rhetoric generally devalues.[67]

The introduction of the adverbial phrase χαρᾷ ἀνεκλαλήτῳ καὶ δεδοξασμένῃ creates a pleonasm in Peter's description of the joy for which he commends the audience. When more language than is absolutely required is used, the wording is pleonastic. When the figure serves to strengthen and emphasize the author's meaning, it is desirable; when it is merely superfluous, the pleonasm is faulty.[68] The pleonasm of v. 8 is effective and pleasing in that it intensifies the description of rejoicing without superfluity, as would be the case if Peter had written χαίρετε χαρᾷ κτλ. The joining of cognates would have been grating.[69] The words ἀνεκλάλητος and δεδοξασμένη give greater adornment to the noun χαρά; δεδοξασμένη returns us to the δόξα of v. 7: already the believers experience the eschatological joy that inheres in the glory that God will bestow on them when their honor and vindication are fully manifest. In their joy, that honor is already theirs. Peter's laudatory recognition of love, faith, and joy among his listeners promotes their goodwill toward him,

---

[67] See the discussion on ambiguity at 23–25 above.

[68] Quint. *Inst. Or.* 8.3.53; 9.3.46–47. In recent English idiom, pleonasm can sometimes be used effectively, but is often an instance of trite expression or indefensible repetition of ideas. See H. W. Fowler, *A Dictionary of Modern English Usage*, 2nd ed. revised by Sir Ernest Gowers (New York and Oxford: Oxford University Press, 1965), 455–56.

[69] The pleonasm χαρᾷ χαίρει in Jn. 3:29 ought not to be judged as unattractive. It becomes a transplacement with the presence of χαρά (nom. case), reinforcing the transplacement of the νυμφ- words. See *Her.* 4.14.20. The construction χαρᾷ χαίρει may reflect the Heb. infinitive absolute or be a variation on the cognate accusative construction evident in Mt. 2:10, ἐχάρησαν χαρὰν μεγάλην σφόδρα. See C. F. D. Moule, *An Idiom Book of New Testament Greek*, 2nd ed. (Cambridge: Cambridge University Press, 1959), 32–33, 177–78.

Peter's ἀγαλλιᾶσθε χαρᾷ is not found elsewhere in the NT, but the verbs χαίρω and ἀγαλλιάω appear in tandem in Mt. 5:12; 1 Pet. 4:13; and Rev. 19:7. Equivalent NT expressions are χαίρω λίαν (Lk. 23:8; 2 Jn. 4; 3 Jn. 3; cf. *BGU* 2.632; *PGiess.* 21:3; *PYale* 42, cited in BAGD, 473); χαίρω χαρὰν μεγάλην σφόδρα (Mt. 2:10); and χαίρω ἐν κυρίῳ μεγάλως (Phil 4:10).

makes them more receptive to the epistolary message, and instructs them in the virtuous Christian life.

4. Conclusion (vv. 9–12)

Peter concludes his encomium with an appeal to a fourfold authority that confirms the readers' participation in salvation (vv. 5, 9). The mention of σωτηρία yet again in v. 10 indicates another transplacement. The prophets who spoke of the grace/salvation to come to the Christians of Asia Minor, the Spirit of Christ who prompted them to prophesy, the preachers who brought the Good News and were inspired by that same Spirit, and the angels who maintain a keen interest in these things all serve as oracular authorities. Quintilian[70] identifies oracles as either supernatural evidence (argument inherent in the case itself) and supernatural argument (advanced from without).[71] Inhering in the case of Christian salvation are the prophets and the preachers; external agents to the case are the Holy Spirit and the inquisitive angels.

The functions of the prophets (vv. 10–12) in relation to the audience are prophecy of the grace that was destined to come to the hearers and service to the hearers in the matter of things foretold. Their activity, evident as fact to all because of the scriptural record,[72] and that of the Christian heralds (οἱ εὐαγγελισάμενοι,

---

[70] Quint. *Inst. Or.* 5.11.42–44.

[71] Quint. *Inst. Or.* 5.11.42: Quae cum propria causae sunt, divina testimonia vocantur; cum aliunde arcessuntur, argumentio.

[72] The προφῆται are almost certainly the OT prophets rather than prophets of the Christian communities. Presumed is a significant passage of time between the prophets and the Christian hearers of 1 Pt. The statement "the prophets who prophesied of the grace that was to be yours" (προφῆται οἱ περὶ τῆς εἰς ὑμᾶς χάριτος προφητεύσαντες) casts their activity back before the time of those who receive the grace. Furthermore, the presence of νῦν in v. 12 separates the period of the prophets (when it was revealed that they served not themselves, but those to come with the things forecast) from that of Peter's Christian audience (who have heard the words of prediction and grace announced to them through those who have preached the gospel by the Holy Spirit). Selwyn (*St. Peter*, 134, 260–67) believes that the

v. 12) stand as supernatural evidence supporting Peter's contention that his readers are honorable by reason of their Christian
virtues. The work of the prophets and preachers is incontestable
as fact; its concern with divinely sent salvation and grace make it
supernatural testimony. Since that evidence is inherent in the
matter of the readers' life of Christian virtue, it is an example of
inartificial proof; the orator does not invent or discover it, but it
comes as a ready characteristic of his case.[73]

Peter buttresses that evidence with artificial proof: the effects
of the Holy Spirit in salvation history and the interest of the
angels. Such matters constitute artificial proof because their role
in the argument is imported to the argument; the functions of the
Holy Spirit and the angels are not evident to the readers as are
the workings of the prophets and preachers, whose deeds are
readily substantiated by the Scripture and the memory of the
hearers. Peter "discovers" the part that the supernatural beings
have in the Christian experience of his audience. That part is not
evident to them. Hence, Peter defines that part for his auditors.
The Holy Spirit pointed to a person or time that was unclear to
the prophets he inspired. The Spirit's activity in this sense is to
'testify beforehand' (προμαρτυρέω) to the sufferings of Christ
and the glories to follow them.

The fact that Peter has the ability to comment on the
pneumatic activity behind prophecy and Christian preaching
serves two purposes. First, Peter's ethos is greatly enhanced as one
who himself speaks with oracular authority. One who discerns the
activity of the Spirit and the meaning of messages that were
obscure even to prophets is certainly one to whom the
communities of faith ought to give heed. Peter dissociates himself

---

προφῆται include those within the entire prophetic tradition. The Christian
prophets are especially prominent in his view.

[73] For discussion of artificial and inartificial proofs, see Arist. *Rh*.
1.2.1355b.2, in light of whom Peter's prophets and preachers are witnesses,
μάρτυρες; they already exist apart from the rhetor's artifice. When Peter
discusses the characteristics of the Spirit of Christ/Holy Spirit, he constructs
a theology of the Spirit by, as Aristotle says, fashioning proofs by system and
his effort (διὰ τῆς μεθόδου καὶ δι' ἡμῶν κατασκευασθῆναι δυνατόν).

from the prophets, preachers, and his audience (he avoids using the first person in vv. 10–12). His role as an omniscient observer who stands above the unfolding of salvation history fortifies his ethos. Yet he is restrained in his description of his role and is thus neither arrogant nor obtrusive.

The second purpose to be served by Peter's interpretive insight is pathetic: the readers' conviction of their own good, noble, and honorable standing is strengthened by the knowledge that the Spirit, prophets, and preachers all have exercised themselves for the sake of Peter's readers. The believers have a more privileged position than any of the others. The prophets served, not themselves, but the believers in the things they announced (οὐχ ἑαυτοῖς ὑμῖν δὲ διηκόνουν αὐτά); likewise the Christian messengers (ἃ νῦν ἀνηγγέλη ὑμῖν διὰ τῶν εὐαγγελισαμένων ὑμᾶς). The prophets "made careful search and inquiry" (ἐξεζήτησαν καὶ ἐξηραύνησαν) about salvation and could only inquire (ἐραυνάω) about the person or time indicated by the Spirit, whereas the believers know (according to what Peter says here and will say in the course of the letter!) the referent of prophecy: Christ. The Holy Spirit empowering the messengers was sent from heaven[74] for the express purpose of enabling those heralds in their task. Thus, ultimately, he was sent for the sakes of the preachers' hearers.

---

[74] In the phrase [ἐν] πνεύματι ἁγίῳ ἀποσταλέντι ἀπ᾽ οὐρανοῦ, the word οὐρανός constitutes a metonymy, a trope in which an attribute or adjunct of something stands for it. In the case of οὐρανός, the relationship is one of symbol (οὐρανός) to referent (God). For discussion of metonymy, see *Her.* 4.32.43; Cic. *De Or.* 3.42.167–68, 50.196; Cic. *Or.* 27.92–93; Quint. *Inst. Or.* 8.6.23–27, 41; Lausberg, *Handbuch*, 565–71.

Other uses of οὐρανός in a metonymical sense for God in the NT are Mt. 5:3, 10; Mk. 11:30; Lk. 15:18, 21; Jn. 3:27. For a thorough discussion of οὐρανός see Hans Bietenhard in Hans Bietenhard, Colin Brown, and Burghard Siede, "Heaven, Ascend, Above," in *The New International Dictionary of New Testament Theology* [hereafter cited as *NIDNTT*] (Grand Rapids: Zondervan, 1976), 2:184–96.

The angels are in a sense inferior in rank to Peter's readers in that the former long "to look"[75] into the things that the latter have heard by way of kerygmatic announcement. Whereas the believers understand the gospel, the angels desire yet to comprehend it.

The first occurrence in 1 Peter of a word from the πάσχω word group comes at 1:11, τὰ εἰς Χριστὸν παθήματα. The readers, who themselves face suffering (1:6; 2:12, 19–21; 3:14, 16–17; 4:1, 12–19; 5:9–10), have the experience of Christ himself from which to derive comfort: his sufferings gave way to subsequent glories (δόξαι).

The plural is not commonly used. An example of it is at 2 Macc. 4:15 where its meaning of "honors" (NRSV) suggests its connection to the honor-shame nexus of terms. That linkage appears in 1 Pt. 1:11 also, where the term δόξαι may point to the glorious sequence of events in 3:18 22: Christ's resurrection, victorious proclamation, and heavenly enthronement.

Since the Christians' fate is bound to that of Christ, their present sufferings are to give way to glory and honor from God just as Christ's did.[76] The motif of future glory continues in 1 Pt. 1:10–12 and reflects a topic of panegyric: prophecy of future greatness (cf. 1:3–5, 7, 9).[77]

---

[75] Gk. παρακύψαι, which here can also be translated either "gain a clear glance" or "steal a glance" at the gospel that proclaims the suffering and glorified Christ (BAGD, 619).

[76] A Petrine emphasis well observed by Kendall, "1 Peter 1:3–12," 12, 14–17, 120, who stresses that "the movement from present suffering to future glory not only depicts the vocation of Christ but also becomes paradigmatic for the believers' life in grace" (15).

[77] Quint. *Inst. Or.* 3.7.11 says that praise of a person may consider the time preceding her/his birth. Topics of praise from that time are those which refer to oracles and prophecies or omens forecasting the future renown of the one praised (quae responsis vel auguriis futuram claritatem promiserint). 1 Pt. 1:10–12 does not expressly state that Peter's readers are the subject of an OT prophecy, but since Christ's glories to which they are also destined were foretold by the Spirit, the hearers are bound up with that glorious prediction—that is the intention of the χάρις (v. 10) prophesied for them. On divine evidence (oracles, prophecies, etc.) cf. Cic. *Part. Or.* 2.6.

The honor of being the object and focus of such charismatic and supernatural activity would promote a healthy pathos among Peter's scattered communities. The testimony of prophetic Scripture stands as an honor to the addressees' life of hope and grace. It is the honor or memorial that an ancient encomium would identify in order to demonstrate the dignity of its honoree.[78] Rhetorically, the function of 1 Pt. 1:10–12 is to express the present and future honor of the epistle's addressees.[79]

Having introduced critical matters of the argument, having acquired the attentiveness and goodwill of the audience, and having established positive ethos for himself, Peter embarks on the first of three *argumentationes* in 1 Peter. Each demonstrates a pattern of argumentation that appears in *Rhetorica ad Herennium*:

> The most complete and perfect argument, then, is that which is comprised of five parts: the Proposition [*propositio*], the Reason [*ratio*], the Proof of the Reason [*confirmatio*], the Embellishment [*exornatio*], and the Résumé [*conplexio*]. Through the Proposition we set forth summarily what we intend to prove. The Reason, by means of a brief explanation subjoined, sets forth the causal basis for the Proposition, establishing the truth of what we are urging. The Proof of the Reason corroborates, by means of additional arguments, the briefly presented Reason. Embellishment we use in order to adorn and enrich the argument, after the Proof has been established. The Résumé is a brief conclusion, drawing together the parts of the argument.[80]

The first *argumentatio*, 1 Pt. 1:13–2:10, is the subject of my fourth chapter that now follows below.

---

[78] Mack, *Rhetoric and the NT*, 47–48.

[79] Schutter, *Hermeneutic*, 109, states that 1 Pt. 1:10–12, the letter's hermeneutical key, is where the author discloses his pesher hermeneutic that is at work throughout the correspondence (122–66).

[80] *Her.* 2.18.28 (cf. 2.18.28–29.46 for elaboration and 3.9.16 for summary); Watson, "James 2," 94–121; idem, "James 3:1–12," 48–64.

CHAPTER FOUR

First *Argumentatio*: 1 Peter 1:13–2:10

Propositio (1:13–16)

"Set All Your Hope . . ." (v. 13)

In the *argumentatio* that is described in *Rhetorica ad Herennium*, the *propositio* stands first and through it "we set forth summarily what we intend to prove."[1] At the head of the first Petrine *argumentatio* stands v. 13: διὸ ἀναζωσάμενοι τὰς ὀσφύας τῆς διανοίας ὑμῶν, νήφοντες, τελείως ἐλπίσατε ἐπὶ τὴν φερομένην ὑμῖν χάριν ἐν ἀποκαλύψει Ἰησοῦ Χριστοῦ. This is the first of two exhortations that comprise the proposition. The conjunction "therefore" (διό) indicates that a new section commences with what follows it. The notable change in mood, from indicative to imperative, also signifies the structural division.[2] The *argumentatio* is decidedly imperatival in tone; a number of verbs in the argument bear that mood: ἐλπίσατε (1:13), γενήθητε (v. 15), ἀναστράφητε (v. 17), ἀγαπήσατε (v. 22), ἐπιποθήσατε (2:2). One ought to include ἔσεσθε (1:16),[3] the imperatival participle μὴ συσχηματιζόμενοι (1:14),[4] and perhaps the verb οἰκοδομεῖσθε in

---

[1] *Her.* 2.18.28: Propositio est per quam ostendimus summatim quid sit quod probari volumus. Thereafter, the *propositio* is called *expositio*.

[2] Karl Hermann Schelkle, *Die Petrusbriefe, der Judasbrief*, Herders theologischer Kommentar zum neuen Testament (Freiburg: Herder, 1961), 43–44; Dalton, *Proclamation*, 94 n. 7, 98; Helmut Millauer, *Leiden als Gnade: Eine traditionsgeschichtliche Untersuchung zur Leidenstheologie des ersten Petrusbriefes*, Europäische Hochschulschriften 23, Theologie 56 (Bern: Herbert Lang, 1976; Frankfurt on Main: Peter Lang, 1976), 37.

[3] ἔσεσθε is a substitute for the 2nd pers. pl. impv. ἔστε/ἴστε which does not appear in the NT (cf. Mt. 6:5). The same form appears at Lev. 11:44–45, 19:2; 20:7 in the LXX, which 1 Pt. 1:16 cites. See discussion of this use of the fut. ind. in F. Blass and A. Debrunner, *A Greek Grammar of the New Testament and Other Early Christian Literature*, trans. and revised Robert W. Funk (Chicago and London: University of Chicago Press, 1961) [hereafter cited as BDF], 49, 183.

[4] Millauer, *Leiden als Gnade*, 37 n. 16.

2:5.[5] The exhortation of 1 Pt. 1:13 is complex: the finite verb is accompanied by two participles that are either adjectival or imperatival. Their connection to ἐλπίσατε lends them a hortatory sense even if they are merely adjectival. The states they depict indicate the means by which hope is completely set upon the grace that is to be brought to believers at the revelation of Jesus Christ. Hence there is not just one point advanced in the *propositio*, but three: (main) set all your hope on grace, (subordinate) prepare your minds for action, (subordinate) discipline yourselves.

Petrine invention for the content of the proposition reveals a predilection for topics in the Gospel tradition. The metaphor of girding up the loins echoes the tradition preserved in Lk. 12:35. There, the notion of one's loins being girded up conveys readiness, the kind of preparation expressed also in the twin Lukan image of lit and burning lamps.[6] The long gowns of men

---

[5] The verb is an impv. according to Charles Bigg, *A Critical and Exegetical Commentary on the Epistles of St. Peter and St. Jude*, International Critical Commentary (Edinburgh: T. & T. Clark, n.d.), 128; Goppelt, *Der erste Petrusbrief*, 144; NEB; NRSV. Taking οἰκοδομεῖσθε as an ind. are Peter H. Davids, *The First Epistle of Peter*, New International Commentary on the New Testament (Grand Rapids: William B. Eerdmans, 1990), 86–87; Michaels, *1 Peter*, 100; Selwyn, *St. Peter*, 159; and NIV.

[6] ἔστωσαν ὑμῶν αἱ ὀσφύες περιεζωσμέναι καὶ οἱ λύχνοι καιόμενοι. Luke may have interpolated an element of Matthew's parable of the virgins (25:1–13) here, yet the two evangelists use different words for lamp (Mt.- λαμπάς; Lk.- λύχνος). The message in both is to watch, γρηγορέω (Lk. 12:37; Mt. 25:13). That verb does not appear at 1 Pt. 1:13, but νήφω, similar in meaning, does. The two verbs appear in tandem at 1 Pt. 5:8 (νήψατε, γρηγορήσατε) and at 1 Thess. 5:6 (γρηγορῶμεν καὶ νήφωμεν). Cf. Eph. 6:14, στῆτε οὖν περιζωσάμενοι τὴν ὀσφὺν ὑμῶν ἐν ἀληθείᾳ.

Selwyn argues for the Matthaean, Pauline, and Petrine passages here to derive from material with a *Filii Lucis* theme. This material constitutes part of a body of early baptismal-catechetical material (B[1]). Strangely, Lk. 12:37 is not considered among the *verba Christi* in this strand of tradition. See Selwyn, *St. Peter*, 369–82. He also regards the metaphor of girding of one's loins and the idea of (spiritual) sobriety as components of a persecution-form (P) that is reflected in 1 Pt., 1 Thess. 2 Thess., Jas. and other epistles, Acts, and the *verba Christi* (439–58). On the relationship of 1 Pt. 1:13 to the Gospel tradition/*verba Christi*, see Robert H. Gundry, "'Verba Christi' in 1 Peter:

of the ancient Mediterranean were girded up when strenuous effort was required. Peter calls in the *propositio* for an earnest and urgent mental awakening and outlook.[7] Such a perspective requires disciplined behavior (νήφοντες),[8] Peter tells his listeners, so that they can set their hope fully on the grace Jesus Christ brings at his revelation. With the injunction ἐλπίσατε, Peter furthers what he has said about ἐλπίς in the exordium (1 Pt. 1:3). That living hope has as its object the χάρις to be granted to the faithful at the parousia.

χάρις *in 1 Peter*

In 1 Peter, χάρις belongs to the semantic field of honor and shame. Generally, χάρις in the New Testament means 'favor,' 'goodwill,' 'grace,' 'kindness,' or 'thanks,' and is supremely in reference to the gracious lovingkindness of God.[9] The word appears ten times in 1 Peter. It occurs in the opening (1:2) and then receives a definition in the following nine usages of it. The prophets foretold of the χάρις that the hearers of the letter have received (1:10). Upon that grace, which will come at the revelation of Jesus Christ, they are to set their hope completely (1:13). At the revelation of Jesus Christ, the genuineness of the

---

Their Implications concerning the Authorship of 1 Peter and the Authenticity of the Gospel Tradition," *New Testament Studies* 13 (1966–67): 339, and his later article "Further *Verba* on *Verba Christi* in First Peter," *Biblica* 55 (1974): 216.

[7] Alan M. Stibbs and Andrew F. Walls, *The First Epistle General of Peter*, Tyndale New Testament Commentaries (Grand Rapids: William B. Eerdmans, 1959), 85, where the colorful idiomatic expression "roll up one's sleeves" is a suggested modern equivalent to Peter's phrase ἀναζωσάμενοι τὰς ὀσφύας τῆς διανοίας ὑμῶν. Selwyn has "pull yourselves together" (*St. Peter*, 139).

[8] The verb νήφω can refer to sobriety in regard to alcohol, but seems to carry its figurative sense in 1 Pt. 1:13; 4:7; 5:8. Cf. NRSV "discipline yourselves" at all three occurrences. Yet cf. 1 Pt. 4:3–4. BAGD, 538–39, attribute only figurative usage to the word in the NT.

[9] My generalization does not do justice to the many dimensions of this word, but suffices as a working definition in this dissertation. Some representative verses in the NT are Acts 15:11; Rom. 3:24; 5:2, 17; Eph. 2:5, 7, 8. See the discussions of χάρις in BAGD, 877–78; and H. H. Esser, "Grace, Spiritual Gifts," *NIDNTT*, 2:15–24.

recipients' faith shall be found to result in praise, glory, and honor according to 1:7. Grace is thus linked to the ἔπαινος, δόξα, and τιμή granted to the faithful at the parousia. All these terms are indicative of the bestowal of divine favor: the coming grace means the granting of honor to those faithful.

In 2:19 and 20, χάρις should be rendered as "approval," "credit," "favor," "honor," or "that which brings God's favor" (cf. NRSV; Lk. 2:52, 6:32–34). The expression κλέος is a synonym for χάρις; κλέος, too, has the sense of "credit," "fame," "glory."[10]

Because their wives jointly share with them in the grace of life (χάρις ζωῆς, 3:7), husbands are enjoined to pay honor (τιμή) to them. Since the women have been honored with "the gracious gift of life," they are to receive honor from their mates. Since χάρις is indicative of divine favor, the person who receives χάρις receives divine honor and is worthy of honor from a fellow human. That is why reciprocal service is obligatory within the community. As each has received a gift (χάρισμα), s/he is to use it in service to others

---

[10] BAGD, 434, 877; Grudem, *1 Peter,* 126–28; Marshall, *1 Peter,* 89; Michaels, *1 Peter,* 135, 139–42. Other options for the meaning of χάρις in vv. 19–20 may be discounted for various reasons. Selwyn, *St. Peter,* 176, understands it to signify "a gracious act pleasing to God." The relationship of 1 Pt. 2:19–20 and Lk. 6:32–34 (note the threefold use of ποία ὑμῖν χάρις ἐστίν;) to a common tradition is evident. Yet Mt. 5:43–48 also reflects the tradition, and employs μισθός ἔχειν (to have a reward) and ποιεῖν περισσόν (to do what is remarkable). All the terms seem to be interchangeable in the tradition (cf. μισθός in Lk. 6:35) and the context is that of reward and credit to one's account, not the performance of a gracious act.

The parallelism of χάρις with κλέος in 1 Pt. 2:19–20 indicates that Peter signifies "credit" or "approval" with the former term. The two words are synonyms. Hence the views of Brox, *Der erste Petrusbrief,* 132–34, and Goppelt, *Der erste Petrusbrief,* 194, 197, are suspect. Brox suggests that undeserved suffering serves as the way to salvation and is hence "grace." Goppelt believes that to endure pain is χάρις, i.e., proof of God's love; it is an expression of the call to salvation. Endurance of unjust suffering is to have a part in Christ's experience, the way of salvation (cf. 3:17–22; 4:13). Cf. REB for χάρις: "a sign of grace" (v. 19) and "a sign of grace in the sight of God" (v. 20) plus "credit" for κλέος in v. 20. The synonymity of χάρις with κλέος, however, indicates to me that the former signifies reward or credit in 1 Pt. 2:19–20.

as a good steward of God's χάρις (4:10). The χάρισμα is a token of honor by God.

Furthermore, since God opposes the proud, but gives grace to the humble, all are to be clothed in humility to one another (5:5). Such humility is involved in what it means to be humble before God who, according to the next verse, exalts the meek. Exaltation and grace are synonymous: χάρις refers to vindication, honor, and deliverance from a humble state (the state of Peter's suffering audience). The exaltation of the sufferers is connected with χάρις once again in 5:10. Additionally, the term is linked with δόξα and thus acquires an eschatological dimension in its denotation of honored elevation for suffering ones. Indeed the entire letter attests to the true grace of God in which the addressees are to stand (5:12).

Hence the significance of χάρις for Peter seems to be that of honor divinely bestowed on those who presently suffer shameful treatment by those outside the community (cf. 2:12; 3:16; 4:4). The term has a socio-cultural denotation as much as a theological one—in fact, the former determines the import of the latter.[11] The honor that Peter holds out for his audience is something that they already enjoy (cf. the exordium) and is to be realized at the parousia (1:13; cf. 4:13). At some places, Peter could mean that God's vindication is either in the present age or in the eschaton (2:12; 3:16).[12] At any rate in 1:13, the focus is on the future revelation of Jesus Christ.

---

[11] In view of the Petrine usages of χάρις, one must wonder to what degree, if any, other NT occurrences of the term (theologically typical are Rom. 3:24, 6:14–15, 11:6; Gal. 5:4; Eph. 2:8; Tit. 2:11, 3:7) have reference to the honor contest of the first-century Mediterranean world.

[12] The prevalence of honor language in 1 Pt. argues for a temporal manifestation of honor for the believers vis-à-vis their slanderous opponents. ἐν ἡμέρᾳ ἐπισκοπῆς in 2:12 could be simply "when he comes to judge" (NRSV), whether on the day of the final eschatological judgment or on some occasion prior to it when he visits the ungodly with retribution for their oppression. That retribution may be no more dramatic than a reversal of roles in the honor contest (cf. 3:16).

"Be Holy" (vv. 14–16)

The Petrine proposition extends into a second exhortation that is a call for holy conduct. Peter utilizes two rhetorical figures of speech in order to set up the premises for an enthymeme[13] that concludes his statement of the *propositio*. Peter posits the simile[14] of the obedient children (ὡς τέκνα ὑπακοῆς) that will constitute one of his most vital topics in the letter: the household of God.[15] The topic serves the strategy of Peter to convey to his audience that their status before God (despite the hostility they experience from the godless) is one of honor and distinction. As Elliott observes:

> The strategy of 1 Peter, therefore, was to motivate the communal self-consciousness and to mobilize the solidarity and steadfastness of the audience by appealing to them as uniquely graced and honored members of the household of God. In this message the household of God functioned as a potent symbol socially, psychologically and religiously, for articulating and integrating the expressions of faith and the experiences of life.[16]

To be children in the household of God was a supreme honor for the letter's recipients. The simile in v. 14 stresses one aspect of that privilege: the responsibility of obedience that it confers.

Peter's simile of obedient children is expanded (after its introduction in v. 14) throughout vv. 15–18. A correlative to the

---

[13] An enthymeme is a syllogism with one of its components suppressed, assumed, or implied. Logical argument can be either inductive (which uses examples) or deductive (enthymematic). Both are species of logos which, with ethos and pathos, constitutes a mode of artistic proof. For discussion see Arist. *Rh.* 1.2.1357a.13–14; 2.22–26; 3.17.1418a–6.1418b.17; Quint. *Inst. Or.* 5.10.1–3; 5.14.1–4, 24–26; *Rh. Al.* 7.1428a.20; 10; Kennedy, *NT Interpretation*, 16–17; Watson, *Invention*, 17–18.

[14] παραβολή, which is invented, unlike historical facts (Arist. *Rh.* 2.20.1394a.7). Simile (*similitudo*) for Quintilian is a stylistic device (*Inst. Or.* 8.3.72–81) as well as an argumentative proof (5.11.1, 22–35). Cf. 8.6.8–9 (=*comparatio*), 49; 9.1.31; 2:2. With the presence of ὡς in v. 14, the figure seems to be more precisely an *imago* (=εἰκών/"simile" in Caplan's transl.) than a *similitudo* (*Her.* 4.45.59–48.61; 49.62).

[15] See Elliott, *Home*, 165–266.

[16] Ibid., 233.

simile is obedience (=holiness) as is the notion of God as Father
to whom children are responsible. Hence the obedient children
are to live, not in conformity to the desires to which they
previously succumbed, but in conformity to the holiness of the
Father who judges each one impartially. Of the four kinds of
similes that *Rhetorica ad Herennium* recognizes, the simile of the
obedient children is a detailed parallel in which a similitude is
established, then all like elements are related.[17] The point of the
simile is that the Christians/children embrace behavior that is
"according to, in accordance with, in conformity with,
corresponding to"[18] that of the one who has called them/their
Father.[19]

An antithesis[20] defines the requisite behavior of children. First
is described what it is not to be: μὴ συσχηματιζόμενοι ταῖς
πρότερον ἐν τῇ ἀγνοίᾳ ὑμῶν ἐπιθυμίαις[21] and what it is to be:
ἀλλὰ κατὰ τὸν καλέσαντα ὑμᾶς ἅγιον καὶ αὐτοὶ ἅγιοι ἐν
πάσῃ ἀναστροφῇ γενήθητε. Both clauses are not only, in
combination, an antithesis, but embody the figure of adjunction.
That is, the verb (γενήθητε) holding the two clauses is at the

---

[17] The other types are the contrast, negation, and abridgement. See *Her.*
4.45.59–48.61 (on the detailed parallel, *collatio*, see 47.60), where *similitudo* is
treated as an element of style, as a figure of thought. Simile also can be
utilized in the *exornatio* as an argumentative proof (2.29.46).

[18] BAGD, 407 (s.v. "κατά" in 1 Pt. 1:15).

[19] Τὸν καλέσαντα is an example of *pronominatio*. See the discussion on 65
n. 25 below.

[20] ἀντίθετον, a figure in which "either terminology or meaning, or both at
once, are opposite in the opposed clauses" (*Rh. Al.* 26. 1435b.25–38). Peter's
antithesis is in meaning, with no opposition of terms.

[21] The emphasis of the antithesis is upon the adversative clause
introduced by ἀλλά. Unlike the preceding clause, the adversative clause has
a finite verb (γενήθητε, 1st aor. pass. impv.) and the intensive pronoun
αὐτοί. The mid./pass. part. συσχηματιζόμενοι is probably here adjectival
rather than imperatival: "as obedient children who are not (being)
conformed to the desires of their former ignorance" (my transl.). To
attribute an adjectival sense to μὴ συσχηματιζόμενοι is to respect the
preponderant emphasis given to the following clause whose more emphatic
tone is set by the finite verb and intensive pronoun. For further discussion
on συσχηματιζόμενοι, see 65 n. 23 below.

end.[22] Adjunction lends embellishment to Peter's style and magnifies its persuasive power. So does the compound word συσχηματιζόμενοι[23] for in such words a writer's style achieves a measure of decoration and majesty.[24]

In the adversative clause, Peter employs *pronominatio* of God so that his characteristic elective activity is highlighted. The readers are to be holy κατὰ τὸν καλέσαντα.[25] The theme of election[26] in 1 Peter is closely related to the motif of the household of God. Those who are members of that household are a chosen race (γένος ἐκλεκτόν, 2:9) and, as chosen, enjoy honor from God just as Christ does (2:4, 6, 7). In vv. 15–16, the repetition of ἅγιος in various declensions (ἅγιον, ἅγιοι *bis*, ἅγιος) is an effective transplacement[27] that stresses the importance of holiness. A crucial text from the Holiness Code of Leviticus furnishes Peter with a τόπος that leads to the deduction that obedient children ought to be holy. The text is itself an enthymeme, which fact is

---

[22] *Adiunctio* could exhibit a verb at the beginning as well. See *Her.* 4.27.38. The ptc. συσχηματιζόμενοι, in the *adiunctio*, assumes an adjectival function in parallelism with ἅγιοι in the following clause. The construction γενήθητε συσχηματιζόμενοι gives way to the adjunctive one without an earlier γενήθητε.

[23] σύν + σχηματίζω. Cf. Rom. 12:2, μὴ συσχηματίζεσθε τῷ αἰῶνι τούτῳ.

[24] Demetr. *Eloc.* 2.91–92.

[25] *Her.* 4.31.42. Also called *antonomasia, pronominatio* "substitutes something else for a proper name" (Quint. *Inst. Or.* 8.6.29). Antonomasia/*pronominatio* can also be an epithet like that in v. 17: πατήρ for God. The same substitution occurs in 2 Pt. 1:3, τοῦ καλέσαντος ἡμᾶς. See Watson, *Invention*, 98.

[26] 1 Pt. 1:15; 2:4, 6, 9, 21; 3:9; 5:10, 13.

[27] *Traductio*/πλοκή is the frequent reintroduction of the same word in a tasteful, elegant way (*Her.* 4.14.20–21; cf. Quint. *Inst. Or.* 9.3.41–42). Transplacement is practically identical to reduplication (*conduplicatio*/ἀναδίπλωσις), "the repetition of one or more words for the purpose of amplification or appeal to pity" (*Her.* 4.28.38). Watson, *Invention,* 202, differentiates between the two figures of speech: "It [reduplication] is akin to transplacement, but according to the handbook examples, the repetition is always immediate and the word used in the same part of speech (*Her.* 4.28.38; Quint. *Inst. Or.* 9.3.28)."

evinced by the presence of ὅτι.[28] In the case of 1 Pt. 1:16, the syllogistic minor premise is excluded from the presence of the major premise and the conclusion:

Major premise: I (God) am holy
Minor premise: You (God's people) should be like God
Conclusion: You (God's people) shall be holy

In Peter's context, God's people become his obedient children who exhibit holy behavior that Peter deduces from God's own holiness. Thus the *propositio* is complete. The hearers ought to set their hope upon the grace that is to come at the revelation of Jesus Christ and live holy lives.

Ratio (1:17)

Why should the Christian set his hope fully on the grace to come? Why should she be holy in all her conduct? The reason for the twin exhortations of the proposition is the rhetorical *ratio* of v. 17. The verse is a reason and a basis for the proposition.[29]

In v. 17, ἀναστρέφειν ἐν φόβῳ is parallel to γίνεσθαι ἅγιος ἐν πάσῃ ἀναστροφῇ of v. 15. The duplication of ἀναστροφ- in v. 17, a transplacement, indicates that the latter instance is either a replication, elucidation, or commentary upon the first.[30] The resumptive καί that begins v. 17 indicates a continuation of the same thought.[31] ἀναστρέφειν ἐν φόβῳ becomes an alternative mode of expression for γίνεσθαι ἅγιος ἐν πάσῃ ἀναστροφῇ (v. 15). The entire verse (17) is a *ratio* for the proposition.

---

[28] Kennedy, *NT Interpretation*, 16. The particle γάρ may also indicate an enthymeme.

[29] *Her.* 2.18.28.

[30] See 65 n. 27 above.

[31] καί εἰ is better read as "and if" than "even if" or "although." The phrase is a first-class conditional clause with the pres. mid. ind. of ἐπικαλέω (Archibald Thomas Robertson, *Word Pictures in the New Testament*, vol. 6, *The General Epistles and the Revelation of John* [Nashville: Broadman Press, 1933], 89. It may (less likely) be a concessive clause. Between conditional and concessive clauses, however, there is little difference. On the matter of conditional and concessive clauses, as well as the construction καὶ εἰ in them, see BDF, 374, 457; and H. E. Dana and Julius R. Mantey, *A Manual Grammar of the Greek New Testament* (n.p.: Macmillan, 1955), secs. 271–79.

As in v. 15, the character of God demands an appropriate response here in v. 17. In v. 15, the holiness of God requires holiness in return. In v. 17, the impartiality of the divine adjudication obligates the one who invokes the judge as Father to live in reverent honor toward him.[32]

The English versions tend to overlook the rhetorical situation and its concern for honor in their translations of ἐπικαλέομαι in v. 17.[33] The verb appears elsewhere in the New Testament in the legal sense of 'to lodge an appeal for honor/vindication.'[34] I suggest this to be the meaning at 1 Pt. 1:17.

---

[32] Although not specifically stated in v. 17, ἐν φόβῳ almost certainly is in reference to one's attitude toward God. Despite the fact that Peter elsewhere enjoins honor toward other people (2:13–14, 17, 18; 3:1–2, 5, 7; 5:14), φόβος appears to be reserved for God alone (2:17). Peter alters Prov. 24:21a LXX, φοβοῦ τὸν θεὸν υἱέ, καί βασιλέα in order to express his intention that God alone should receive φόβος: τὸν θεὸν φοβεῖσθε, τὸν βασιλέα τιμᾶτε (cf. Michaels, *1 Peter*, 131–32). The arrangement τὸν βασιλέα τιμᾶτε not only creates an *inclusio* (with πάντας τιμήσατε), but (more significantly) signifies that φόβος is only for God. The other appearances of φόβος/φοβέω in 1 Pt. one ought to consider with the Petrine alteration at 2:17 in mind.

[33] Cf. "address" (NAS); "call on" (NIV) "invoke" (NRSV); "say" (REB). The commentators also neglect the agonistic restrict the significance of πατέρα ἐπικαλέομαι to its relationship to the dominical remarks on prayer as address to God as Father (cf. Ernest Best, *1 Peter*, New Century Bible Commentary [Grand Rapids: William B. Eerdmans, 1971; London: Marshall, Morgan & Scott, 1971], 87; Davids, *1 Peter*, 70; Hillyer, 1 *and 2 Peter, Jude*, 48; Selwyn, *St. Peter*, 142–43). Some interpreters, although allowing for the verb to be taken as 'to appeal for aid/help' (Grudem, *1 Peter*, 80; Stibbs and Walls, *1 Peter*, 89), do not observe the significance of the construction as indicative of the honor contest.

[34] The sense of lodging an appeal before a judicature is present in Acts 7:59 where Stephen cries out for divine vindication (τὸν Στέφανον ἐπικαλούμενον καὶ λέγοντα) before his executioners, κύριε Ἰησοῦ, δέξαι τὸ πνεῦμά μου). Luke also employs ἐπικαλέομαι in the account describing Paul's demand to appear before the emperor's tribunal in Rome. The construction is ἐπικαλέομαι (mid.) with the acc. (Καίσαρα, Acts 25:11, 12; 26:32; 28:19; τὸν Σεβαστόν, 25:25). In 25:21, the aor. pass. inf. τηρηθῆναι stands in the acc. with ἐπικαλέομαι (τοῦ δὲ Παύλου ἐπικαλεσαμένου τηρηθῆναι αὐτὸν εἰς τὴν τοῦ Σεβαστοῦ διάγνωσιν, "but when Paul had appealed to be kept in custody for the decision of his Imperial Majesty"). This legal sense of ἐπικαλέομαι presents itself also in secular Gk. lit. and the LXX (cf. Plut. *Marcel.* 2.4; *Tib. Grac.* 16.1.832b; 1 Ki. 18:24; Ps. 88:26 LXX).

In apposition to πατέρα is τόν ἀπροσωπολήμπτως κρίνοντα κατὰ τὸ ἑκάστου ἔργον.[35] The clause specifies that divine judicial decisions are dispensed with absolute impartiality. The appellation τὸν κρίνοντα is an instance of *pronominatio*, in which, for stylistic adornment, an epithet is used in place of a proper name.[36] The adverb ἀπροσωπολήμπτως is a neologism, a stylistic device in which something lacking an appropriate name (or a name entirely) is furnished with a suitable expression. It can be imitative of its referent (sound=onomatopoeia) or simply expressive of the character possessed by that to which the neologism refers.[37] The word, literally meaning 'not receiving the face,' indicates that God judges with complete fairness. He shows honor ('receiving the face') only to those whose works warrant it.

In light of divine infallibility regarding judgments, Peter exhorts his readers to "live your lives as strangers here in reverent

---

See discussions in Lothar Coenen, "Call: καλέω," *NIDNTT*, 1:271–76; Karl Ludwig Schmidt, "καλέω, κτλ.," in *Theological Dictionary of the New Testament* [hereafter cited as *TDNT*], ed. Gerhard Kittel, and Gerhard Friedrich, trans. and ed. Geoffrey Bromiley (Grand Rapids: William B. Eerdmans, 1965), 3:487–536.

[35] Bigg, *St. Peter*, 16; Robertson, *The General Epistles*, 89.

[36] *Her.* 4.31.42, where the Gracchi are called 'the grandsons of Africanus.' See also Martin, *Antike Rhetorik*, 263. For discussion of epithet itself as a quasi-trope, see Arist. *Rh.* 3.3.1406a.11–12; Quint. *Inst. Or.* 8.6.40; Martin, *Antike Rhetorik*, 264.

[37] *Her.* 4.31.42. ἀπροσωπολήμπτως is a *hapax legomenon* in the NT, but cf. Barn. 4:12; 1 Clem. 1:3, both of which apparently rely on the thought and language of 1 Pt. The neologism is an antonym for the more common προσωπολημπ- word group: προσωπολημψία (Rom. 2:11; Eph. 6:9; Col. 3:25; Jas. 2:1); λαμβάνειν πρόσωπον (ἀνθρώπου) (Lk. 20:21; Gal. 2:6; Did. 4:3; Barn. 19:4); προσωπολημπτέω (Jas. 2:9); προσωπολήμπτης (Acts 10:34). The idiom is found in the LXX (Mal. 1:8; Sir. 4:22; 35:13; 1 Esdr. 4:39) as the translation נָשָׂא פָנִים (with the parallel הָדַר פָּנִים). The idea is "to lift up the face" of one who has humbly bowed or prostrated oneself. Besides its negative connotation of partiality in judgment in the OT (Lev. 19:15; Dt. 10:17; Job 13:8 (not LXX), 10; 34:19; Ps. 82:2 (81:2 LXX); Prov. 18:5), פָּנִים נָשָׂא also has the sense of showing favor (cf. Num. 6:26). See BAGD, 720–21 (s.v. "πρόσωπον"); BDF, 4; Francis Brown, S. R. Driver, and Charles A. Briggs, *A Hebrew and English Lexicon of the Old Testament* (Oxford: Clarendon Press, n.d.), 213–14 (s.v. "הָדַר"), 670 (s.v. "נָשָׂא"); Erich Tiedtke, "Face: πρόσωπον," *NIDNTT*, 1:585–87.

fear" (NIV). The hearers can only expect honor in God's judgment of them if their behavior justifies it. The literal nature of παροικία ought not to be missed. The intended readers of Peter's letter, at least a preponderant number of them, are culturally and ethnically estranged from the societies of Asia Minor. Peter's instructions to live 'the time of your alien residence' (τὸν τῆς παροικίας ὑμῶν χρόνον) does not necessarily refer to a Christian's earthly life that is conducted in anticipation of a future migration to a true heavenly home. The phrase does not require such a metaphorical meaning in order to make sense. The duration of the readers' παροικία may not be that of their lives. Since παροικία is a term that connotes social dysfunction and maladjustment, it is a term of dishonor. A πάροικος cannot fully participate in social challenges and exchanges as an equal with natives or with those aliens who have become fully integrated into the new culture. For the πάροικοι to live the time of their alien residency[38] in fear is for them to conduct themselves properly as Christians until such time that the dishonorable status of resident aliens no longer adheres to them. The Father, as judge, vindicates those who live in fear of him with good works. His vindication spells the termination of dishonor. The Father's favorable verdict for the πάροικοι means that they no longer need to regret their disadvantage in social intercourse, for divine vindication (which elsewhere in 1 Peter is public)[39] elevates them. That verdict of honor by God takes place certainly at the glorious revelation of Jesus Christ (1 Pt. 1:7, 13; 5:10a; cf. 4:5–6), but seems to occur also somewhat proleptically or partially in the present, before the final judgment (2:12, 19–20; 3:14–17; 4:14; 5:10b). That possibility is suggested by the present participle

---

[38] παροικία seems to encompass both πάροικοι and παρεπίδημοι as those in an alien residency.

[39] 1 Pt. 3:16c, ἵνα ἐν ᾧ καταλαλεῖσθε καταισχυνθῶσιν οἱ ἐπηρεάζοντες ὑμῶν τὴν ἀγαθὴν ἐν Χριστῷ ἀναστροφήν. The verb καταισχύνω ('be put to shame', 'be ashamed') intimates shame that is a public verdict in the honor contest. Cf. Mt. 20:28D; Lk. 13:17; 2 Cor. 7:14, 9:4; Herm. man. 12.5.2; Malina and Neyrey, "Honor and Shame," 49–50 (on Lk. 13:17).

τὸν κρίνοντα.[40] One's παροικία does not vanish if s/he continues to live in a cultural and/or political entity to which s/he is not native. However, the opprobrium that person suffers as a πάροικος would appreciably diminish (if not pass) if that person receives a public verdict of honor in a significant social challenge. In terms of the honor contest, the term παροικία as a pejorative social designation would no longer apply. It is as terminology of shame that Peter uses the παροικ- word group (and its partner παρεπίδημος). That terminology would be inconsequential for him outside considerations of honor and shame.[41]

Confirmatio (1:18–21)

In the kind of argumentation that Peter employs, *confirmatio*, the proof of the reason, corroborates the *ratio* with additional arguments.[42] In 1 Pt. 1:18–21, Peter supplements his call for reverent conduct by mentioning the precious blood of Christ, the one chosen by God. In vv. 18–19, both negative and positive pathos are created. The precious blood of Christ, the ransom,[43] serves to arouse positive feelings of loyalty. φθαρτός (v. 18) acts as a foil for the κληρονομία ἄφθαρτος of 1:4 and creates negative pathos. The readers loathe the materials base and mean which were insufficient to ransom them from their pagan past. The Petrine construction φθαρτοῖς, ἀργυρίῳ ἢ χρυσίῳ represents the figure *interpretatio* (synonymy), whereby a word is replaced by

---

[40] A primary or even exclusive reference to present judgment and discipline by τὸν κρίνοντα is suggested by Grudem, *1 Peter*, 81.

[41] The instances of παροικ- (1:17; 2:11–12) or παρεπίδημος ([1:1 merely descriptive in address]; 2:11) in 1 Pt. clearly occur in discussions that involve the honor or shame of the readers.

[42] *Her.* 2.18.28.

[43] Cf. Isa. 52:3 LXX, καὶ οὐ μετὰ ἀργυρίου (gen.) λυτρωθήσεσθε (with instr. in 1 Pt. 1:18). On 'ransom,' see William Barclay, "*Lutron, Lutroun* and *Apolutrōsis*: The Debt and Its Payment," chapter in *New Testament Words* (Philadelphia: Westminster Press, 1964), 189–96; Leon Morris, *The Apostolic Preaching of the Cross* (Grand Rapids: William B. Eerdmans, 1955), 35–36, 41, 45 n. 1; idem, "Redeemer, Redemption," *New Bible Dictionary*, 2nd ed. [hereafter cited as *NBD*], ed. J. D. Douglas and N. Hillyer (Leicester: InterVarsity Press, 1982; Wheaton: Tyndale House, 1982), 1013–14.

another with the same meaning.[44] "Silver or gold" is an epexegesis on "perishable things."

In 1:18–21, Peter's style is grand and ornate. It features refined figures of diction and thought as well as amplification.[45] In addition to the synonymy in v. 18 of φθαρτοῖς[=]ἀργυρίῳ ἢ χρυσίῳ, that phrase carries with it a pleasing *homoeoptoton* (*similiter cadens*), a figure of speech "when in the same period two or more words appear in the same case, and with like terminations."[46] This figure aids the building effect of a portion of discourse.[47] Six instances of this figure are present in 1 Pt. 1:18–21.

ἀργυρίῳ ἢ χρυσίῳ 18a
ἀμνοῦ ἀμώμου . . . ἀσπίλου Χριστοῦ 19bc
προεγνωσμένου . . . κόσμου . . . ἐσχάτου . . . αὐτοῦ 20–21a
τοὺς πιστούς, 21a
θεὸν τὸν . . . αὐτόν 21ab[48]
ἐγείραντα . . . δόντα 21bc

---

[44] *Her.* 4.28.38; Lausberg, *Handbuch*, 649–56. In 1 Pt. 1:18, the Nestle-Aland[26] text indicates the synonymy with a minor stop after χρυσίῳ; the UBS[3] text omits a minor stop there so that the three instrumental-case nouns represent a series, the latter two nouns of which are not necessarily synonymous with the first. I agree with the Nestle-Aland[26] reading here and JB: "[18] the ransom that was paid . . . was not paid in anything corruptible, neither in silver nor gold, [19] but in the precious blood . . ."

[45] Arist. *Poet.* 22.1458a.18–1459a.14 discusses poetic style. It ought to be neither too lofty nor too frigid. The mean is best since excess in any matter of style vitiates one's oratory and its clarity. The handbooks do not restrict rhetorical style only to the middle style—all three styles (grand, middle, and plain) are generally to be found in a single work, as circumstances require (*Her.* 4.8.11, 10.15, 11.16, 12.17; Watson, *Invention*, 24–26). One ought to discourse with attention to *virtus* (excellence) even when the middle and plain styles are employed. Only then can *vitium* (defect) be avoided. Lausberg, *Handbuch*, 1063–77, catalogues the stylistic *vitia* in rhetoric. They especially concern ἔλλειψις/*detractio* (=das Zurückbleiben) and ὑπερβολή/*adiectio* (=das Hinausschiessen), the deficiency and the excess of that which *virtus* demands, respectively (1064).

[46] *Her.* 4.20.28.

[47] Watson, *Invention*, 98 (regarding 2 Pt. 1:5–7).

[48] If one accepts the broader definition of *homoeoptoton* in Quint. *Inst. Or.* 9.3.78 which does not require that case endings be identical in appearance, one may add several more instances of the figure.

A notable Petrine stylistic adornment is the compound
πατροπαράδοτος, "inherited, handed down from one's father
or forefathers,"[49] or, more inclusively, "inherited from your
ancestors" (NRSV).

The adversative particle ἀλλά at v. 19 signals an antithesis
(*contentio*), a figure that, built on contraries, lends distinction to
discursive style:[50]

(οὐ) φθαρτοῖς,	instrumental
ἀργυρίῳ ἢ χρυσίῳ	explanatory
	(synonymy)
ἐλυτρώθητε ἐκ	
τῆς ματαίας ὑμῶν	
ἀναστροφῆς	
πατροπαραδότου	
ἀλλά	
τιμίῳ αἵματι	instrumental
ὡς ἀμνοῦ = Χριστοῦ	explanatory
ἀμώμου καὶ	(simile)
ἀσπίλου	

The presence of *homoeoptoton* is accompanied by homoeoteleuton,
that figure which exists "when clauses conclude alike, the same

---

[49] BAGD, 637, where instances of this word in ancient texts are cited.
Some of these are from the first century BCE and may have been known to
Peter. Nevertheless, πατροπαράδοτος is a rare word, a NT *hapax legomenon*
and, if not constructed by the writer as a neologism, it is at least a compound
word that embellishes the writer's style.

In the elevated style (μεγαλοπρέπεια) of writing (prose and poetry)
identified by Demetrius, diction ought to be "superior, distinguished, and
inclined to the unfamiliar. It will thus possess the needed gravity, whereas
usual and current words, though clear, are unimpressive and liable to be
held cheap" (Demetr. *Eloc.* 2.77. His other types of style (2.36) are the plain
(ἰσχνός), elegant (γλαφυρός), and forcible (δεινός). Demetrius holds that
compound words (σύνθετα ὀνόματα) should find a place in elevated discourse. Such words ought to be formed to denote as yet unnamed things;
they may be fashioned from existing words or be completely new coinages
(onomatopoeia, *Eloc.* 2.91–98).

[50] (Gk. ἀντίθεσις/-τον) *Her.* 4.15.21; 45.58. In 1 Pt. 1:18–19, the *contentio* is
more of thought than of diction. See Lausberg, *Handbuch,* 787–807 (esp.
793, 795).

syllables being placed at the end of each."[51] Here the two clauses of the antithesis conclude with a genitival -ου (πατροπαρα-δότου, Χριστοῦ). These two figures increase the symmetry between the opposing clauses.[52] ἀμνοῦ ἀμώμου καὶ ἀσπίλου is a fine alliteration[53] that adds elegance to Peter's language.

The stylistic adornments to the *contentio* are all in service to the simile (εἰκών/*imago*) introduced by ὡς. Christ's blood is like that of the blameless and spotless Passover lamb (ἀλλὰ τιμίῳ αἵματι ὡς ἀμνοῦ ἀμώμου καὶ ἀσπίλου Χριστοῦ).[54] A simile is a figure of thought in which, because a certain resemblance exists between them, one object is compared with another.[55] Simile, used in praise and censure (*x* is like *y*) here increases positive audience pathos: Christ's death as Passover lamb/the Suffering Servant is portrayed in terms that would win their approval since they are hearers who appreciate the Old Testament.[56] His

---

[51] Quint. *Inst. Or.* 9.3.77.

[52] Cf. Quint. *Inst. Or.* 9.3.82, 86; Lausberg, *Handbuch*, 787.

[53] Alliteration (*homoeopropheron*) is a figure of speech that is "the repetition of the same letter or syllable at the beginning of two or more words in close succession" (Bullinger, *Figures of Speech*, 171; cf. Watson, *Invention*, 16, 200; Lausberg, *Handbuch*, 975–76).

[54] πρόβατον, not ἀμνός, appears in Ex. 12, as the designation for the Passover lamb sacrificed by the family. The instructions for the institutionalized annual paschal rites in Num. 28:16–25 LXX feature ἀμνοί (ἄμωμοι) (vv. 19, 21[*bis*]). Peter's ἀμνὸς ἄμωμος recalls the OT language of Passover (cf. λυτρόω, 1 Pt. 1:18; Ex. 15:13; Dt. 7:8 LXX). Peter's use of ἀμνός has associations also with the Isaianic ὡς ἀμνὸς ἐναντίον τοῦ κείροντος ἄφωνος (53:7 LXX; cf. 1 Pt. 2:23; Acts 8:32). The Passover and the Suffering Servant as lamb in Isa. 53 may both be present as influences in the Christian tradition utilized by Peter (see also Jn. 1:29, 36; 1 Cor. 5:7; Rev. 5:6, 9, 12; 12:11). The comparison of Jesus with the Paschal lamb may go back to Jesus himself (Mk. 14:22–24 and par.). The language of sacrifice is certainly present in the Synoptic accounts (σῶμα, αἷμα, ἐκχύννω) and in 1 Pt. 1:19 (αἷμα, ἀμνός). See the discussions in Joachim Jeremias, "ἀμνός, ἀρήν, ἀρνίον," *TDNT*, 1:338–41; idem, "πάσχα," *TDNT*, 5:900–901. A helpful general survey of the topic is R. A. Stewart, "Passover," *NBD*, 881–83.

[55] *Her.* 4.49.62; cf. Arist. *Rh.* 3.4.1406b.20; *similitudo, Her.* 4.45.59–48.61; Lausberg, *Handbuch*, 558, 843–47.

[56] For a detailed survey of authorial dependence on OT materials in 1 Pt., see Schutter, *Hermeneutic*, 35–49.

sacrifice should prompt their response ('live in reverent honor,' v. 17). The simile of the Passover lamb, in tandem with λυτρόω at v. 18, forms a metaphor[57] complex: Christ, the paschal lamb, shed his blood as the ransom[58] for those trapped in the vanity of living according to the ancestors' ways. The word τίμιος ("precious") belongs to the Petrine honor word-field. Here, the word contributes to the positive pathos the writer wishes to elicit regarding Christ's sacrifice. His shed blood is precious because it is shed according to God's plan (cf. v. 20) and thus honorably. If the suffering of Jesus is honorable, so is that of those it ransoms.[59]

Two adjectival clauses with participles that modify the genitive Χριστοῦ follow in v. 20. The two clauses are contraries: a visual opposition (destined/προεγνωσμένου and revealed/φανερω-θέντος) exists along with a temporal opposition (before the foundation of the world/πρὸ καταβολῆς κόσμου and at the end of the ages/ἐπ' ἐσχάτου τῶν χρόνων). Hence a double *contentio*[60] presents itself. Peter's antithesis is elegantly formed: in asyndeton[61] with an isocolon.[62]

Rudolf Bultmann's form-critical analysis of 1 Peter identifies v. 20 as a segment of an early Christian confession or hymn. The fragment evinces the metrical style of liturgical-poetical language. In the reconstruction by Bultmann of the confessional text, v. 20 is placed before a statement that is expanded in 3:18. The

---

[57] A metaphor (*translatio*) is a trope that "occurs a word applying to one thing is transferred to another, because the similarity seems to justify this transference" (*Her.* 4.34.45).

[58] λυτρόω recalls Mk. 10:45 and has the definite idea of 'to free by payment' (as at Tit. 2:14). F. Büchsel in F. Büchsel and O. Proksch, "λύω, κτλ," *TDNT*, 4:349–51.

[59] Cf. 1 Clem. 7:4.

[60] *Her.* 4.15.21, 45.58.

[61] ἀσύνδετον/*dissolutio*: a figure of speech in which an absence of connecting particles exists (Quint. *Inst. Or.* 9.3.50). Cf. Lausberg, *Handbuch*, 709–11, who remarks that "die Wirkung [of asyndeton] ist die der pathetisch-vereindringlichenden Steigerung" (709).

[62] In this figure of speech, a virtually equal number of syllables appears in plural *cola* (Lat. *conpar*). *Her.* 4.20.27; cf. Lausberg, *Handbuch*, 719–54, esp. 754 (antithesis).

participles are subordinate to a substantive in an alleged introductory credo. The presence of participles (προεγνωσμένου and φανερωθέντος) in v. 20, the rhythmical pattern of the verse, and its asyndetic nature suggest its hymnic or confessional origins.[63] The poetic[64] nature of the participial and asyndetic phraseology lends elegance to the Petrine *confirmatio.* Confessional material, hymnic or creedal, is enlisted in order to support rhetoric.

Verse 21 brings a phrase ὥστε τὴν πίστιν ὑμῶν καὶ ἐλπίδα εἶναι εἰς θεόν into hypotaxis with a phrase that comprises the two relative clauses τοὺς δι' αὐτοῦ πιστοὺς εἰς θεόν and τὸν ἐγείραντα αὐτὸν ἐκ νεκρῶν καὶ δόξαν αὐτῷ δόντα. The first of these relative clauses is in apposition to ὑμᾶς in v. 20. Peter wastes no opportunity to augment the positive pathos he began in the encomiastic proem and develops in the first *argumentatio.* The hearers are believers only δι' αὐτοῦ, through Christ, who was revealed in the last times for their sake (v. 20). Their faith is directed toward God who raised Jesus from the dead and gave him glory. Whether the hearers have become believers in God in order that their faith and hope might be in God,[65] or God has raised and glorified Jesus in order for their faith and hope to be directed thus[66] is difficult to determine. Rhetorically, the second alternative is preferable. In the epistle the destiny of believers is

---

[63] Rudolf Bultmann, "Bekenntnis- und Liedfragmente im ersten Petrusbrief," *Coniectanea Neotestamentica* 11 (1947): 10–12, 14. The three characteristics of v. 20 that I mention here (participles, rhythm, asyndeton) are among several features of creedal formulae in the NT that are identified in Ethelbert Stauffer, *New Testament Theology,* trans. John Marsh (New York: Macmillan, 1955), 338–39.

[64] If one accepts Bultmann's suggestion that δι' ὑμᾶς may be an insertion ("Liedfragmente," 11), one may regard the two as antithetical phrases that constitute a pair of lines in dactylic pentameter:

προ ε γνω σμε νου μεν προ κα τα βο λῆς κοσ μου

φα νε ρω θεν τος δε επ' εσ χα του των χρο νων

Each line contains a partial foot in addition to four dactyls.

[65] So NIV, NRSV, REB.

[66] So JB; Michaels, *1 Peter,* 70; UBS³.

bound indissolubly to that of Jesus. Since he has suffered and yet been vindicated/honored by God, so too will his people be exonerated from pagan slanders. His glory is to become their glory (1:7; 2:16–18, 22; 4:13; cf. 1:11; 2:4, 6–7, 12). The glorious destiny of Christ was foreknown (προεγνωσμένος), planned before creation. So it is with the believers: their election to a glorious future is "in the foreknowledge [πρόγνωσις] of God the Father" (1:2, REB). In v. 20, the destinies of Christ and hearers are linked by the προγνως- cognates. Peter's readers, dishonored aliens and strangers, are summoned to faith in God that he will vindicate them just as Jesus was vindicated. Jesus was raised from an ignominious death to a position of the highest δόξα and now, Peter says, his experience can be that of his followers. They must believe that his δόξα will be theirs and hope for χάρις, for his favorable judgment (cf. 1:13). Here, two τόποι[67] in early Christian preaching, the resurrection and glorification of Jesus, are employed for hortatory purposes in the Mediterranean social concerns of honor and shame.

Exornatio (1:22–25)

After a *confirmatio* has been put forth by the speaker in the complete argument that Peter emulates, the orator adorns and enriches the argument by the embellishment (*exornatio*).[68] Peter commences by introducing a familiar and standard material topic[69] of Christian deliberative discourse: love. Out of this topic he constructs a proposition (ἀλλήλους ἀγαπήσατε[70] ἐκτενῶς)

---

[67] The resurrection and glorification of Jesus are 'commonplaces' of past fact. Arist. *Rh.* 2.19.1393a.26–27.

[68] *Her.* 2.18.28; Watson, "James 2," 105–7, 113–16.

[69] Arist. *Rh.* 1.4.1359a.1–8.1366.7; Cic. *Top.* 21.79–23.90 on general theses both theoretical and practical. The topic of love is practical (i.e., it involves duty and emotion).

[70] In the Petrine tradition, a distinction between φιλαδελφία and ἀγάπη is present. In 2 Pt. 1:5–7 (where "mutual affection"=φιλαδελφία and "love"=ἀγάπη in NRSV), a climax (*gradatio, Her.* 4.25.34) is crowned with ἀγάπη. It is the highest virtue in the catechetical list, mentioned after φιλαδελφία (Watson, *Invention*, 98). Cf. also Jn. 21:15–17.

that is important in light of his discussion of the household of God that is to come (2:4–10). Those born into that house ought to have love for one another.

Immediately the *exornatio* advances the euphony of vv. 18–21. As there, so in vv. 22–23 it is achieved by means of *homoeoptoton*[71] (φιλαδελφίαν/ἀνυπόκριτον;[72] καθαρᾶς/καρδίας;[73] ζῶντος/ μένοντος) and *homoeopropheron*[74] (ὑμῶν/ὑπακοή; ἀληθείας/ἀνυπόκριτον; καθαρᾶς/καρδίας; ἀλλήλους/ἀγαπήσατε). Furthermore, φθαρτῆς ἀλλὰ ἀφθάρτου combines two figures: one of thought, *contentio*,[75] and one of diction, *antanaklasis*.[76] In the latter figure, two different meanings of the same word arise or differences in meaning are exhibited through the rhetor's use of words that are alike. The alpha-prefix negates the perishability of the seed in the first part of the *contentio*. The words ἀναγεννάω and ἄφθαρτος recall the encomium of the Christians in 1:3–12 where the words are used by Peter to describe the believers' new birth (ὁ θεὸς . . . ἀναγεννήσας ἡμᾶς, v. 3) and imperishable inheritance (κληρονομία ἄφθαρτος). Thus the words should evoke positive pathos in Peter's audience and prompt assent to

In 1 Pt. 1:22 the words φιλαδελφία and ἀγαπάω could form a synonymy (*Her.* 4.28.38), but more likely represent a lesser and higher grade of love, respectively. If they were synonymous, their qualifiers would likely also be; ἀνυπόκριτον and ἐκτενῶς are not synonymous.

[71] *Her.* 4.20.28.

[72] φιλαδελφίαν ἀνυπόκριτον contains two words in the acc. case whose terminations are different in spelling, but alike in sound.

[73] καθαρᾶς within square brackets of UBS³ indicates doubt on the part of its editors whether the word represents the superior reading. It is in p⁷², ℵ*, C, et al., but is lacking in A, B, Vg. In Nestle-Aland²⁶, the word καθαρᾶς is likewise enclosed in square brackets. For discussion of the textual options, see Bruce M. Metzger, *A Textual Commentary on the Greek New Testament* (n.p.: United Bible Societies, 1971), 688–89. In light of Peter's propensity for homoeoptoton in 1:18–22 and the textual witness in its favor, I believe καθαρᾶς is the superior reading (cf. also the homoeopropheron of καθαρᾶς with καρδίας in v. 22).

[74] Bullinger, *Figures of Speech*, 171.

[75] *Her.* 4.15.21.

[76] Quint. *Inst. Or.* 9.3.68.

his proposition ("love one another deeply from the heart"). The new birth ought to lead to a new life of love, love that grows increasingly deep.[77]

The new birth has had as its agent "the living and enduring word of God."[78] Since the σπορά is ἄφθαρτος, its life is divine and hence powerful in its regenerative effect. So powerful is the seed that it can vitalize love in even greater intensity, from φιλαδελφία to ἀγάπη. The imperishability of the regenerative word of God is the focus of the quotation from Isa. 40:6, 8. Unlike the perpetuity of God's word, flesh, like grass, withers and dies. As for the glory of flesh (its pride, honor, and esteem derived from vain and godless pursuits), it will disappear after a brief blaze of brilliance, just as the wild flower vanishes after its short season. The phrase τὸ δὲ ῥῆμα κυρίου μένει εἰς τὸν αἰῶνα substantiates the Petrine assertion concerning the incorruptibility and perpetuity of the λόγος. The simile of the wild grass maintains that the ῥῆμα κυρίου and its perpetual properties are antithetical to the flesh and its grasslike glory (δόξα).

Once again we have entered the semantic domain of honor and shame. The simile of the grass is important, for it illustrates the transient nature of that glory that is in opposition to the honor that God grants, the honor on which the hearers are to set their hope (1:13) and for which they are to lodge their appeal with God (1:17). The esteem of pagan society has been denied to the readers of 1 Peter. They have been slandered, abused, and reckoned as evil-doers (2:12; 3:16; 4:4). However, the pagan notion of glory is false; the glory and honor of the heathen will fade and fall[79] like the flowering wild grass. Yet the honor that

---

[77] See 76–77 n. 70 above.

[78] So NIV, NRSV, REB; cf. BAGD, 337. NRSVmg takes ζῶντος καὶ μένοντος as modifying θεοῦ, not λόγου. Michaels (*1 Peter*, 72, 77) favors this translation adopted also by JB. Since the OT quotation vv. 24–25 and the appended comment by the epistolary author has as its focus the ῥῆμα κυρίου, the participial emphasis ought to be placed on λόγος instead of θεός in v. 23.

[79] Not only does the word δόξα enable Peter to attack the false glory of the pagans, but the words ξηραίνω and ἐκπίπτω (both gnomic aorists in v. 24—these express proverbial and universal truths. See Michaels, *1 Peter*, 78)

God bestows, the honor that has already been bestowed upon Peter's audience through the preaching of the good news, remains forever. The word εὐαγγελίζω already has been associated with God's favor to the hearers in the encomium (1:10–12). They were honored in the preaching of the gospel, for in it they heard those things concerning which they were served by the prophets, the grace to come to believers, and the sufferings and glories of Christ. The very matters to which the Christians of Asia Minor have access are denied the angels. Peter's audience can take comfort in the midst of their distress, since the shame they experience is actually the false opinion of a false glory embraced by their opponents. The true glory of the gospel has been conferred on them already. They need only await its complete public recognition by their foes (cf. 2:12), the last stage in the honor contest.

Rhetorically, the quotation from Isaiah serves as a *iudicatio*, a judgment rendered by peoples, reputable citizens, judges, or one's opponents. Judgments made by the gods and supernatural oracles may be included in a *iudicatio*. A quotation from the Old Testament serves as such a divine pronouncement.[80] The *iudicatio* closes the Petrine *exornatio*. The argument advanced in the

---

are aligned with shame in the honor-shame word-field. The terms are in Peter's source, true, but the reason they are included with τὸ δὲ ῥῆμα κυρίου κτλ at all may very well be the function they serve in the matter of honor and shame. Jas. 1:11 redacts the Isaianic passage more creatively than Peter in that the former adds and changes words, whereas the latter essentially cites verbatim (whether absolutely one cannot say since we cannot with certainty reconstruct Peter's LXX text). Still, James employs ξηραίνω and ἐκπίπτω (again as gnomic aorists) and makes use of the Isaianic passage in a context of honor (to the lowly) and shame (to the rich). Both Peter and James may utilize Isa. 40:6–8 in a manner common to early Christian instruction about honor, shame, and vindication. Cf. the *indignatio* of the Petrine *peroratio* in 2 Pt. 3:17. There the negative topics of life (ἄθεσμος) and habit (πλάνη) of the false teachers are identified in order to elicit negative pathos from the audience that they might avoid their shameful behavior (2:1–3, 10–22; 3:3–6) and fate (2:1, 3–9; 3:7, 16). The concern of the author in 2 Pt. is the honor of his readers (1:11).

[80] *Her.* 2.29.46; Quint. *Inst. Or.* 5.11.36–37, 42–44; *Rh. Al.* 1.1422a.25ff. Cf. Cic. *Inv.* 1.30.48; *Part. Or.* 2.6; Watson, "James 2," 105.

propositio ('set your hope completely on the grace to come to you at the parousia') and the ensuing reason and confirmation is enhanced by the *exornatio*. The command to love one another not only is the first indication that the readers, social pariahs in a hostile environment, belong to a common οἶκος τοῦ θεοῦ;[81] it is a commentary on what it means to live in anticipation of the coming bestowal of favor and honor (χάρις, v. 13), on what holy living (vv. 14–16), and reverent honor of God (v. 17) signify.

Conplexio (2:1–10)

Verses 1–3

The particle οὖν signifies a new section, but the new section so designated is not a major section[82] of the letter, but another division in the rhetorical argument: the *conplexio*, or résumé,[83] that part of a rhetor's discourse that concludes and draws together the parts of the argument. In the *conplexio* 1 Pt. 2:1–10, the author develops the notion that his audience constitutes children and members of the household of God, an idea already introduced by him (1:3, 14, 23). In the *conplexio*, the repetition of the words ἐκλεκτός (2:4, 6, 9) and ἔντιμος (2:4, 6) suggests a

---

[81] The injunction ἀλλήλους ἀγαπήσατε ἐκτενῶς is given to those who have already known φιλαδελφία ἀνυπόκριτος ("sincere love for your brothers," NIV). Elliott states, "Those who have been reborn through the living and abiding word of God are to preserve their new familial solidarity by a 'sincere love of the brothers'" (*Home*, 202). On the contribution of 1:22 to the Petrine motif of the οἶκος τοῦ θεοῦ, cf. further Elliott, *Home*, 75, 83, 139, 145, 256 n. 151.

[82] Among interpreters of 1 Pt., Selwyn is rare in regarding 2:1 as the commencement of a new major section of the letter (*St. Peter*, 153), at the same time admitting 2:1–2 summarizes 1:13–25 and is thus closely linked with it. His view that 2:1–10 constitutes a (second) doctrinal section of the letter is not entirely tenable since the impv. ἐπιποθήσατε at v. 2 lends a distinctly hortative tone to the passage even if οἰκοδομεῖσθε at v. 5 is ind.: the hearers are to "long for the pure, spiritual milk" that by it they may grow since they are being built into a spiritual house. The ind. provides the basis for the impv.

[83] *Her.* 2.18.28, 29.46; 4.43.56; Watson, "James 2," 107–8, 16.

special authorial emphasis on election and honor.[84] These Greek words link to ἐκλεκτός in 1:1 and to τιμή in 1:7, respectively. In the *conplexio*, Peter wishes to remind his audience again of their honor and esteem before God. By so doing, he is augmenting the positive pathos of the readers toward themselves that he has already fostered. The résumé concludes with a beautifully crafted crescendo and climax in praise of the Christians.

The *conplexio* commences with a participial injunction[85] with a number of vices to be put off, metaphorically, as a garment:[86] "Rid yourselves, therefore, of all malice, and all guile, insincerity, envy, and all slander." The vice list incorporates *polysyndeton*,[87] which adds vigor and underlines its importance. The members of the catalogue are sins against the Christian community as brotherhood (cf. 1:22). Their elimination by the community would contribute to the further establishment and strengthening of the οἶκος τοῦ θεοῦ (cf. 2:5). After all, new-born babes, who Peter's

---

[84] ἔντιμος is a cognate of τιμή (1:7, 2:7), "precious" (from Lat. *pretiosus*) in NRSV. Its association with ἐκλεκτός suggests that its meaning is more than simply valuable or costly in a monetary or commercial sense (the word has this meaning figuratively in 2:4 and 6), but 'esteemed' and 'highly honored' also reflect the meaning of ἐντιμός. Because the stone is chosen, it is 'precious,' i.e., honored. It derives its value from the honor of its divine choice to serve as the cornerstone. Among the English translations that preserve the association of ἐντιμός with the cultural value of honor are Goodspeed ("prized," 2:4 [but "costly" at 2:6]); RVmg ("honourable," 2:4, 6); and Weymouth, "held in honour," 2:4, 6).

[85] ἀποθέμενοι takes its imperatival nature from the governing verb ἐπιποθήσατε in v. 2 Their relation is like that of ἀναζωσάμενοι and νήφοντες to ἐλπίσατε in 1:13. See Michaels, *1 Peter*, 84; cf. Goppelt, *Der erste Petrusbrief*, 133.

[86] The list is recognized as component of early Christian catechetical material by Philip Carrington, *The Primitive Christian Catechism: A Study in the Epistles* (Cambridge: Cambridge University Press, 1940), 32–37; Dalton, *Proclamation*, 99; Selwyn, *St. Peter*, 393–400. for similar instructions on 'putting off' sins, see Rom. 13:12; Eph. 4:22, 25; Col. 3:8–9; Heb. 12:1; Jas. 1:21.

[87] *Polysyndeton* is a figure of speech in which an excessive number of conjunctions exists (Quint. *Inst. Or.* 9.3.50–54; Watson, *Invention*, 54–55, 98, 201).

readers are by way of simile, ought to desire "the pure, spiritual milk," not the contention in the Christian family that Peter's forbidden practices engender. The metaphor, putting off the garment of sin, and the simile, new-borns desiring milk, are Christian commonplaces[88] and would be familiar and effective for those who had been baptized, as Peter's readers surely had been. From a modern standpoint, the metaphor-similes are incongruous: can a newborn babe be expected to take off clothing and put it aside? Yet the imagery was common in early Christian catechetical instruction and evidently posed no discordance for those forming the traditions of the church.[89]

The passage 2:1–3 contains an enthymeme:

[Major premise:] Newborn infants long for milk.

Minor premise: You are like newborn infants.

Conclusion: Long for the pure, spiritual milk (ridding yourselves of all malice, etc.) so that by it you may grow into salvation.

---

[88] For infants to be fed on milk is a Christian topic (1 Cor. 3:1–4; Heb. 5:11–14; cf. Od. Sol. 8:17, 19:1–4; Clement of Alexandria *The Instructor*, Ante-Nicene Fathers, 2:220–21. One need not look to the mystery religions for the origin of this topic as does Richard Perdelwitz, *Die Mysterienreligion und das Problem des I. Petrusbriefes: Ein literarischer und religionsgeschichtlicher Versuch* (Giessen: Alfred Töpelmann, 1911), 66–70, who believes that milk, the φάρμακον ἀθανασίας of the mysteries, is taken up by the Christians. See Selwyn, *St. Peter*, 154–55, 308–10 for discussion.

[89] The image of putting off sins and that of desiring a mother's milk are nowhere else combined in the NT, but the dual metaphors of putting off "the old self" and putting on "the new self" carry with them the idea of rebirth: Eph. 4:22–24, ἀποθέσθαι ὑμᾶς κατὰ τὴν προτέραν ἀναστροφὴν τὸν παλαιὸν ἄνθρωπον τὸν φθειρόμενον κατὰ τὰς ἐπιθυμίας τῆς ἀπάτης, ἀνανεοῦσθαι δὲ τῷ πνεύματι τοῦ νοὸς ὑμῶν, καὶ ἐνδύσασθαι τὸν καινὸν ἄνθρωπον τὸν κατὰ θεὸν κτισθέντα ἐν δικαιοσύνῃ καὶ ὁσιότητι τῆς ἀληθείας; Col. 3:8–10, νυνὶ δὲ ἀπόθεσθε καὶ ὑμεῖς τὰ πάντα, ὀργήν, θυμόν, κακίαν, βλασφημίαν, αἰσχρολογίαν ἐκ τοῦ στόματος ὑμῶν· μὴ ψεύδεσθε εἰς ἀλλήλους, ἀπεκδυσάμενοι τὸν παλαιὸν ἄνθρωπον σὺν ταῖς πράξεσιν αὐτοῦ, καὶ ἐνδυσάμενοι τὸν νέον τὸν ἀνακαινούμενον εἰς ἐπίγνωσιν κατ᾽ εἰκόνα τοῦ κτίσαντος αὐτόν. Cf. 1 Cor. 3:14; Heb. 5:11–14.

Appended to the enthymeme is a supporting maxim, a γνώμη/ *sententia*.[90] A *sententia* is a saying drawn from life that concisely shows either what may or ought to happen in life. The maxim has a universal application and is stylistically pleasing. The phrase εἰ ἐγεύσασθε ὅτι χρηστὸς ὁ κύριος is a kind of *sententia* that is more precisely called an epiphoneme, i.e., a concluding maxim that, as a reflective and confirming statement, accompanies an enthymeme. Epiphonemes could be intensely exclamatory or simply restrainedly proverbial.[91] The statement is from the LXX: γεύσασθε καὶ ἴδετε ὅτι χρηστὸς ὁ κύριος, μακάριος ἀνὴρ ὃς ἐλπίζει ἐπ' αὐτόν (Ps. 33:8). The association of γεύομαι with ἐλπίζω in the Psalm may have been in Peter's mind in his use of ἐλπίζω at 1:13 and of γεύομαι in 2:2.

Verses 4–10: Honor and Shame

Verses 4–10 constitute a *iudicatio* as in 1:24–25, the source of the *iudicatio* is the Old Testament and thus is a divine pronouncement, a supernatural oracle. The verses are an obvious example of the Petrine proclivity to utilize traditional materials within rhetorical argumentation.[92] A social-scientific approach attuned

---

[90] Arist. *Rh.* 2.21.1394a.20–1395b.19; *Her.* 4.17.24–25; Quint. *Inst. Or.* 8.5.3, 4, 6–8, 11, 15–34; Berger, "Gattungen," 1049–74; Kennedy, *NT Interpretation*, 17; Lausberg, *Handbuch*, 872–79; P. W. van der Horst, *The Sentences of Pseudo-Phocylides: With Introduction and Commentary*, Studia in Veteris Testamenti Pseudepigrapha 4 (Leiden: E. J. Brill, 1979), 79.

[91] Exclamatory: Verg. *Aen.* 1.33, "tantae molis erat Romanam condere gentem!" (cited by Quint. *Inst. Or.* 8.5.11, who says, "est enim epiphonema rei narratae vel probatae summa acclamatio"); proverbial: Quint. *Inst. Or.* 1.12.7, "adeo facilius est multa facere quam diu." See the full discussion in Lausberg, *Handbuch*, 879.

[92] Other examples are what Schutter (*Hermeneutic*, 35–37) calls Peter's explicit or implicit quotations of the OT: 1:16, 24–25; 2:6–8; 3:10–12; 4:8, 18; 5:5. In all, Schutter asserts that Peter makes reference to the OT approximately 46 times (nearly 1 for every 2 verses) by way of quotations and by way of allusions that are unequivocal in their appeal to OT materials. "Iterative allusions," those allusions that resume or anticipate an OT text cited elsewhere by Peter but that may have been undetected without a favorable literary context, would boost that total greatly. Neither these nor "biblicisms" (language influenced by expressions and idiom from Jewish

to the cultural values of honor and shame in 1 Pt. 2:4–10 ought first to consider the word-field of the passage, particularly in vv. 6–10 since those verses provide the scriptural foundation for the observations of vv. 4–5.[93] In vv. 6–10 appear the following words in respect to honor and shame:[94]

Honor		Shame
ἐκλεκτόν ἔντιμον ἀκρογωνιαῖον	v. 6	(οὐ μὴ) καταισχυνθῇ
τιμή (:πιστεύουσιν) (ἀπιστοῦσιν) κεφαλήν ἀπεδοκίμασαν	v. 7	
	v. 8	προσκόμματος σκανδάλου προσκόπτουσιν ἀπειθοῦντες
γένος ἐκλεκτόν βασίλειον ἱεράτευμα ἔθνος ἅγιον λαὸς εἰς περιποίησιν ἀρετὰς ἐξαγγείλητε καλέσαντος θαυμαστὸν φῶς	v. 9	
 (νῦν δὲ) λαὸς θεοῦ (νῦν δὲ) ἐλεηθέντες	v. 10	(ποτὲ) οὐ λαὸς οὐκ ἠλεημένοι

　　Four of the honor words are in reference to Christ. He is the "chosen" and "honourable" (RVmg) stone, the one "held in

piety and the LXX) are computed in Schutter's count. See Schutter's detailed discussion of the biblical sources of 1 Pt. in *Hermeneutic*, 35–43.

[93] As John Hall Elliott observes in *The Elect and the Holy: An Exegetical Examination of I Peter 2:4–10 and the Phrase* βασίλειον ἱεράτευμα, Supplements to Novum Testamentum 12 (Leiden: E. J. Brill, 1966), 48: "The relationship of vv. 4–5 to vv. 6–8 and 9–10 is that of secondary reformulation and interpretation of a primary source. That is, the OT passages of vv. 6–10 were not occasioned by the similar phraseology of vv. 4–5 and then added for substantiation; rather these OT verses provided the terminology and the thought for vv. 4–5."

[94] For the word-field of honor/shame for the entire letter of 1 Pt. see Appendix 1, "The Semantic Field of Honor and Shame in 1 Peter," below.

honor" (Weymouth), who becomes the "cornerstone," or, "the very head of the corner." Joachim Jeremias affirms the character of ἀκρογωνιαῖος (NRSV, "cornerstone." Cf. Luther, *"Eckstein"*; BCF, *"pierre d' angle"*) as an adjective that refers to the final stone in a building, the last to be laid in the construction of an edifice. The term is synonymous with κεφαλὴ γωνίας ('head of the corner,' Mk. 12:10 and par.; Acts 4:11; 1 Pt. 2:7/Ps. 17:22 LXX) and refers to the keystone that is probably set over the gate or porch. The builders reject the stone that becomes the capstone: Jesus, rejected by humans, is exalted by God to the highest place as the consummation of the heavenly sanctuary (cf. Eph. 2:20).[95] In other words, to the "head of the corner" (κεφαλὴ γωνίας). That stone is held in honor (ἔντιμος, vv. 4, 6) as the stone of the divine choice (ἐκλεκτός, vv. 4, 6) although rejected by humans (ἀποδοκιμάζω, vv. 4, 7). In Peter's mind, those who believe in Christ, the living stone (v. 4), share in the honor that their Lord enjoys. They indeed are living stones (v. 5). Many honorable epithets are bestowed upon the believing community in 2:4–10. They may easily be subsumed under the assertion in v. 7a: ὑμῖν οὖν ἡ τιμὴ τοῖς πιστεύουσιν (lit., 'Therefore, to you who are believing is the honor'). The antithesis of this sentence with v. 6d, καὶ ὁ πιστεύων ἐπ' αὐτῷ οὐ μὴ καταισχυνθῇ, serves to emphasize honor/shame as the central concern of 2:4–10. Everything else is subordinate to that dualism.

---

[95] Joachim Jeremias, "γωνία, ἀκρογωνιαῖος, κεφαλὴ γωνίας," *TDNT*, 1:791–93; idem, "λίθος, λίθινος," *TDNT*, 4:274–75. Even if λίθος ἀκρογωνιαῖος/κεφαλὴ γωνίας refers to cornerstone and not the keystone (Wilhelm Mundle, "Rock, Stone, Corner-Stone, Pearl, Precious Stones: γωνία," *NIDNTT*, 3:389–90), it still is a term that designates honor. A cornerstone is the most important stone in the foundation, being laid first (Mundle, "Rock" 389).

The word θεμέλιον, found 2x in the pl. in Isa. 28:16 LXX, is absent from the Petrine redaction. Peter may have intentionally omitted θεμέλιον in order to eliminate an association of ἀκρογωνιαῖος with the foundation, thus the word becomes more fluid and could stand for a stone placed, not at the foundation of the building, but at a higher level. Cf. Test. Sol. 22:7, 8; 23:2, cited by Jeremias, "γωνία," 792, who maintains that Isa. 28:16 LXX and quotations of it are the only instances of ἀκρογωνιαῖος=θεμέλιον.

The crucial sentence ὑμῖν οὖν ἡ τιμὴ τοῖς πιστεύουσιν is often mishandled by the translations. Typical is NRSV, "to you then who believe, he is precious," where the antecedent for "he" is the cornerstone (=Christ).[96] Thus NRSV understands something like 'to you then who believe is the preciousness (of Christ)'='he is precious.' This reading is very awkward in its attempt to refer τιμή to the ἀκρογωνιαῖος ἔντιμος of v. 6.

If, however, τιμή is understood within the cultural value system of honor and shame, the translation becomes a simpler matter, for τιμή is then easily regarded as a term than can apply to believers as well as Christ.[97] As living stones that comprise the οἶκος πνευματικός (v. 5), believers have a privileged status. They are living stones in the οἶκος because of their union to Christ, the living stone (v. 4). Not only do the believers derive their 'stoniness' from Christ, but their honored position derives from his dignity as the "cornerstone chosen and precious."[98]

Thus NJB has a very appropriate translation: "To you believers it [i.e., the cornerstone] brings honor." Weymouth also in his rendering of vv. 6–7 is accurate:

> For it is contained in Scripture, "See, I am placing on Mount Zion a Cornerstone, chosen, and held in honour, and he whose faith rests on Him shall never have reason to feel ashamed" (Isa. xxviii. 16). To you believers, therefore, that honour belongs; but for unbelievers—"A stone which the builders rejected has been made the Cornerstone" (Ps. cxviii. 22).

Beare and Hillyer are right to oppose the mistranslation of τιμή. The former understands τιμή to be the believers' honor that they receive in the present by virtue of their incorporation into the οἶκος πνευματικός. The honor that is Christ's (vv. 4, 6) is theirs also.[99] Hillyer asks, "Why should translators shy away from

---

[96] Similarly AV, NIV, REB.

[97] Cf. 1:7 in ref. to τὸ δοκίμιον ὑμῶν τῆς πίστεως; τιμάω with πάντας and ὁ βασιλεύς as objects in 2:17 and with ἀσθενέστερον σκεῦος τὸ γυναικεῖος in 3:7.

[98] Elliott, *Home*, 127.

[99] Beare, *1 Peter*, 124, who observes also that the article with "honor" (ἡ τιμή) makes clear the connection of τιμή with ἔντιμος.

suggesting that the people of God are to be honored?" He continues,

> Believers have been bought with the price (*timē*, 1 Cor. 6:20) of the precious (*timios*) blood of Christ (1 Pet. 1:19). They are his and are due to share both in the family inheritance (1:4) and in the divine family likeness.[100]

Hence the several appellations in 1 Pt. 2:4–10 all constitute an explication of the Christians' honored position as members of the spiritual house of God. A rhetorical-critical analysis for 2:4–10 remains to be done. To this we now turn.[101]

Verses 4–10: Rhetorical Analysis

A rhetorical analysis of 1 Pt. 2:4–10 as *iudicatio* is now in order. Peter describes[102] his readers as living stones who are being built (into) a spiritual house (v. 5). They are coming to the Lord[103]

---

[100] Hillyer, *1 and 2 Peter, Jude*, 63.

[101] Thorough source-critical, redaction-critical, and theological studies of the very important passage 1 Pt. 2:4–10 are outside the scope of this dissertation. In addition to the commentaries, I advise the reader interested in these subjects to consult Elliott, *The Elect and the Holy*.

[102] I work with the assumption that οἰκοδομεῖσθε in v. 5 is an ind. (NIV), not an impv. (NRSV). Hence, the ptc. προσερχόμενοι in v. 4 is an adjectival rather than an imperatival participle. Better sense is made of the ptc. if οἰκοδομεῖσθε is taken as its governing verb ('coming to him . . . you yourselves also as living stones are being built [into] a spiritual house,' etc.) rather than ἐπιποθήσατε in v. 2 ('desire the pure, spiritual milk . . . coming to him a living stone,' etc.) It makes more sense for the believers to, as stones, be fashioned into a spiritual house than for those same stones to be desiring spiritual milk. Furthermore, without a major break at vv. 3/4 (as in UBS³), the clauses are hopelessly run together.

Interpreters are not in agreement about the mood of οἰκοδομεῖσθε. Favoring it as an ind. are Best, *1 Peter*, 101; Kelly, *Peter and Jude*, 89; Marshall, *1 Peter*, 66; Michaels, *1 Peter*, 100; Robertson, *The General Epistles*, 96; Selwyn, *St. Peter*, 159. Opting for the impv. are Bigg, *St. Peter*, 128; Goppelt, *Der erste Petrusbrief*, 144, who thus predictably takes προσερχόμενοι as an impv. ptc. (141); BAGD, "οἰκοδομέω," 558 (pass. or mid.).

[103] ὁ κύριος is, for Peter, Jesus Christ: 1:3. Cf. 3:15a, κύριον δὲ τὸν Χριστὸν ἁγιάσατε ἐν ταῖς καρδίαις ὑμῶν, where that which applies to YHWH in Isa. 8:13 LXX is transferred by Peter to Christ. This is true also in 1 Pt. 2:8 (Isa. 8:14).

(antecedent in v. 3 of ὄν in v. 4), "a living stone, though rejected by mortals yet chosen and precious in God's sight." Confronting the audience is a powerful metaphor, the stone,[104] that is so prominent in the passage 2:4–10 that rhetorically it becomes an extended metaphor, or, more precisely, an instance of typology. Peter's stone motif exhibits the propensity of the early church to attribute to past events in salvation history a power to influence or press meaning onto future ones. The initial event, or type (τύπος), reproduces its 'image' on the antitype (ἀντίτυπος) as when a die transfers its image onto the coin that it strikes. The New Testament has many instances of typology.[105]

---

[104] Perdelwitz, *Die Mysterienreligion*, 66–70, suggests that the milk and stone metaphors ought to be considered as two aspects of a double metaphor that is drawn from the mystery religions. The milk refers to the drink of the initiation ceremonies as the φάρμακον ἀθανασίας. Meteor stones, the stone relief of Mithras, and the cone-shaped stone of Paphos that represents Aphrodite-Astarte are candidates for sources of Peter's lithic terminology which is linked with 'milk' in a cultic sense. This view, however, overlooks the obvious OT backgrounds for "stone" in the Petrine passage and the nature of milk as a Christian topic (see 82 n. 88 above). The two metaphors, milk and stone, are distinct.

[105] Lausberg, *Handbuch*, 901, who lists as NT examples of typology Adam-Christ, Eve-church, Eve-Mary, Melchizedek-Christ, David-Christ.

In his clarification-section of 1 Pt. 2:4–10, Brox refers to the *Allegorie* of the stone and the building (*Der erste Petrusbrief*, 96–107). Is the passage allegory and not typology? Is there a difference between the two? Lausberg distinguishes between them: "Verschieden von der Allegorie, deren Zweck die Textdeutung ist, ist die Typologie, die die Deutung der Wirklichkeit zum Ziele hat" (*Handbuch*, 901). Further, he states, "Die Typologie ist eine Semantik der Realitäten, die Allegorie (ἄλλο ἀγορεύειν) eine Semantik der Worte" (ibid.).

Since Peter does not so much extract hidden meanings from OT texts as make contemporary applications for passages which formerly had an historical context and meaning, his method is more typological than allegorical. His method is thus similar to the *pesherim* of the DSS.

In Gal. 4:21–31, Paul cites allegory to explain the significance for the Galatians of the incident of Hagar in Gen. For Paul, the terminology (ἅτινά ἐστιν ἀλληγορούμενα) may essentially mean an elaborate typology; one ought not to impose on him the associations that 'allegory' has for the later Christian allegorists, Clement and Origen of Alexandria (cf. the literal, moral, and spiritual meanings in the interpretations of the latter). In the story of Hagar and Sarah, the original historical context is only peripherally analogous to the situation in Galatia; the Isaianic passages that Peter

Not only is the stone metaphor powerfully prominent, but it is stylistically elegant. It is the kind of metaphor that, as Quintilian says, engenders a wonderful sublimity (*mira sublimitas*) since with it there are ascribed a certain activity and psychical capacity to an inanimate object.[106] Although the stone imagery is that imagery which is most pervasive in the section 1 Pt. 2:4–10, the typology of the stone serves the broader concept of the οἶκος (v. 5).[107] Peter's emphasis is on the stones which, as spiritual house or "Spirit-filled house(hold)"[108] are being built up (as) a spiritual household.[109]

---

produces find genuine circumstantial counterparts in the experience of Peter's audience. See discussion of allegory, typology, and the two compared in Carl Heinz Peisker and Colin Brown, "Parable, Allegory, Proverb: παραβολή, παροιμία," *NIDNTT*, 2:743–60.

[106] Quint. *Inst. Or.* 8.6.11–12; Martin, *Antike Rhetorik*, 267–68. In 1 Pt. 2:4–8, Christ is living (v. 4); the one who grants honor, not dishonor (vv. 6–7); he who becomes (apparently of his own activity) the head of the corner (v. 7). His role as a stumbling-stone and a rock that makes some fall seems to be more passive than active: "they stumble because they disobey the Word" (v. 8c). The believers, as λίθοι ζῶντες, are a functioning priesthood that offers spiritual sacrifices to God (v. 5).

[107] Martin, *Metaphor*, 161–88, maintains that the theme of election is developed in 1 Pt. 1:14–2:10 through metaphors pertaining to the οἶκος τοῦ θεοῦ: obedient children (1:14–16), children under a new *pater potestas* (1:17–21), children in a new brotherhood (1:22–25), newborn babies (2:1–3), and living stones forming a new temple (2:4–10). The first three metaphors concern the new birth and consequent familial relations, whereas the final two concern growth. The image of the household of God, argues Elliott, is the coordinating medium that gives unity to the literary, theological and social elements of 1 Pt. (*Home*, 220, 228–29, 231, 233, 270). In 2:3–10, οἶκος πνευματικός combines independent traditions regarding the Messiah (vv. 6–8) and his community (vv. 9–10) (229).

[108] Elliott, *Home*, 133 (cf. 168), who elsewhere translates οἶκος πνευματικός as "house(hold) of the Spirit" (167, 201, 204). I agree with Elliott in his opinion that the prominence of οἶκος as a social and family designation in 1 Pt. determines its translation as "household" rather than "temple." See *Home*, 167–69, 186, 241–43 for discussion.

[109] Since λίθοι ζῶντες is preceded by ὡς, it is, in precise terms, a simile. In apposition to λίθοι ζῶντες is οἶκος πνευματικός (nom. case), not οἶκον πνευματικόν (acc. case) as one would expect if καὶ αὐτοὶ ὡς λίθοι ζῶντες οἰκοδομεῖσθε οἶκος πνευματικός is translated "you also, like living stones, are being built into a spiritual house" (NIV). An English trans. that preserves the apposition would be 'and you yourselves, as living stones, a spiritual house,

These living stones derive their animation from Christ who is a living stone *par excellence* (v. 4). The appearance of οἶκος immediately after οἰκοδομεῖσθε constitutes a *derivatio*, a figure in which a word is derived from one that precedes it.[110]

The metaphor/simile of the stone and of the house gives way to that of the holy priesthood (ἱεράτευμα ἅγιον). Both the holiness and priesthood of the believing community are picked up in v. 9, but in conjunction with other images and not each other (βασίλειον ἱεράτευμα/ἔθνος ἅγιον). The believers as living stones and spiritual house are being built up for the purpose (εἰς) of becoming a holy priesthood. The preposition εἰς marks off the metaphor of the priesthood from the double metaphor of stones and house. Thus, no mixing of metaphors[111] occurs here, but a sudden transition to a completely new one.[112] The Christian priesthood exists in order "to offer spiritual sacrifices acceptable to God through Jesus Christ" (ἀνενέγκαι πνευματικὰς θυσίας

---

are being built up.' The syntax is altered to underscore that οἶκος πνευματικός is not an object but nom. and appositional to λίθοι ζῶντες.

[110] Cf. Verg. *Aen.*: ultro ipse gravis graviterque ad terram pondere vasto concidit (5.446); voce vocans Hecaten (6.247); oppetere ingentem atque ingenti vulnere victum (12.640). Cited by Lausberg, *Handbuch*, 648.

[111] To achieve the exquisite speech of metaphor, one must conclude with the same kind of metaphor with which s/he has begun. One cannot, for example, begin with a storm and finish with a conflagration and collapse. Quint. *Inst. Or.* 8.6.49–51; Martin, *Antike Rhetorik*, 263.

1 Pt. 2:5 contains two compatible metaphors (living stones, spiritual house) succeeded by another unrelated metaphor, but without mixing. For the view (to which I subscribe) that οἶκος in v. 5 is to be understood as "house(hold)" rather than "temple," see 89 n. 108 above.

A helpful discussion of mixed metaphor in modern English may be found in Fowler, *Modern English Usage*, 361–63, who differentiates between mixed and successive metaphors. A change in metaphors is legitimate and allowable in proper English.

[112] If "holy priesthood" were in grammatical apposition to λίθοι ζῶντες and οἶκος πνευματικός, one could justly charge the author with mixing metaphors. However, the introduction of εἰς makes clear that ἱεράτευμα ἅγιον is in the acc. case, not nom., and hence is not appositional with the previous two metaphors.

εὐπροσδέκτους [τῷ]¹¹³ θεῷ διὰ Ἰησοῦ Χριστοῦ). The idea of non-cultic (metaphorical) sacrifices is a topic in early Christian discussion.¹¹⁴ These sacrifices are 'spiritual' in the sense that they pertain to the life and service of those who live in grace and worship in spirit and truth.¹¹⁵ The imagery of stone and house in vv. 4–10 is vital for Peter's purposes of defining the Christians' social identity (a family, or, household of God) and achieving positive pathos. The image of a ἱεράτευμα augments that pathos. As the community understands itself as a priesthood whose functionaries approach God in worship, thanksgiving, and repentance on behalf of the people, they acquire a sense of a unique and privileged identity. They have an honored position above that of those outside the priestly community, the Gentiles. Yet that privileged status can be understood as one that is mediatory: the believers proclaim the mighty acts of him who called them out of darkness into his marvelous light (v. 9). Positive pathos is largely the goal of the writer in his presentation of a chain of epithets in vv. 9–10.

The Old Testament citations in vv. 6–8 are the heart of the *iudicatio* which is vv. 4–10. Specifically, the citations are rhetorically a typology concerning the stone. The style is pleasing: it features *homoeoptoton*¹¹⁶ in v. 6 (λίθον, ἀκρογωνιαῖον, ἐκλεκτόν, ἔντιμον), v. 7 (ὑμῖν, πιστεύουσιν, ἀπιστοῦσιν), and v. 8 (λίθος,

---

¹¹³ Here I follow Nestle-Aland²⁶ and UBS³ by placing τῷ within brackets. See the apparatus in the former for witnesses to the readings with and without the article.

¹¹⁴ For this sense of θυσία, see Rom. 12:1; Phil. 2:17, 4:18; Heb. 13:15–16; 1 Clem. 18:16–17, 35:12, 52:3–4; Barn. 2:10; Ign. Rom. 4:2; Mart. Pol. 14:2; Herm. Sim. 5.3.8. See BAGD, "θυσία," 366.

¹¹⁵ Selwyn, *St. Peter*, 285, who goes beyond the NT evidence when he suggests that the πνευματικαὶ θυσίαι (consisting of righteousness, prayer, praise, penitence, kind and loving deeds, etc.) have a sacramental (Eucharistic and baptismal) association, i.e., that they are components of the celebration of the Lord's Supper in the church (294–98). The association does indeed occur, however, in the 2nd cent. (Did. 14:1–2; Justin, *Apol.* 1.65, 67; cf. *Dial.* 41, where the sacrifices that Christians offer are the Eucharistic bread and cup).

¹¹⁶ *Her.* 4.20.28.

προσκόμματος). The frequent reintroduction of λίθος in vv. 6–8 (and in vv. 4–5) constitutes a transplacement (*traductio*).[117] "Stone," although it appears thrice in close succession within vv. 6–8, is repeated tastefully and elegantly. Its dominance in the passage is unobtrusive. The quotation from Ps. 17:22 LXX is an antithesis, a figure of thought in which contraries meet. The builders rejected the stone, but it is chosen by God to occupy the place of honor in the building which is, one must assume by the context, the οἶκος πνευματικός, the household of the Spirit. That household is the church, the Christian community that is a family of brothers and sisters in faith. The family members, although themselves rejected by the natives and majority ethnic groups in the society of Asia Minor, have found a place of belonging, as God's elect children. Hence, to them is the honor (v. 7a).

All the benefits that the believers enjoy derive from the λίθος that God has placed in Zion. The stone's function is revealed through epithets that are in three pairs of synonymy:[118]

v. 6 λίθον—ἀκρογωνιαῖον ἐκλεκτὸν ἔντιμον
v. 7 λίθος ὃν ἀπεδοκίμασαν—κεφαλὴν γωνίας
v. 8 λίθος προσκόμματος—καὶ πέτρα σκανδάλου

The figure of synonymy stresses the greatness of the stone and its importance in Peter's thought. Not only does Peter give synonyms for λίθος but for a key attribute of it in v. 8. The stone that is Christ is for those who disbelieve "a stone of stumbling and a rock of offence" (AV).

---

[117] *Her.* 4.14.20–21. Cf. the figure reduplication (*conduplicatio*): the repetition of one or more words for amplification or appeal to pity (*Her.* 4.28.38; Quint. *Inst. Or.* 9.3.28). The difference between reduplication and transplacement seems to be one of intensity—reduplication is effective in impassioned pleas and instances where the arousal of audience pathos is of major concern.

[118] συνωνυμία/*interpretatio*/*communio nominis* is a figure in which the replacement of a word by another of the same meaning is present, or (more specifically) the sense of a given word is repeated through one or more different words of the same meaning. This stylistic device occurs when one word will not suffice to demonstrate the dignity or greatness of something. *Her.* 4.28.38; Lausberg, *Handbuch*, 649–56.

Two human destinies in relation to Christ are presented in 1
Pt. 2:4–10.[119] The first is the destiny to honor (τιμή) for those
who believe in the stone whom God has chosen (v. 6). The
second is to stumbling and falling for those who disbelieve.
Peter's discussion of the unbelievers (vv. 7b–8) is a digression.[120]
The digression serves to emphasize the present dignity of the
cornerstone (οὗτος ἐγενήθη εἰς κεφαλὴν γωνίας) despite its
rejection by the builders. The audience thus is encouraged that it,
too, has present dignity despite the present slander. The vivid
image of builders tripping over the stone that they have rejected
during their work and cast aside serves as *indignatio,* a device in
rhetorical *peroratio* where the orator stirs up hatred for someone
or severe aversion for something.[121] Here, Peter seeks to arouse
repugnance for dishonorable disobedience.

For Peter, the fate of stumbling and falling is an inviolable
consequence of disobedience to the Word. Since God's decree is
that those who choose to disobey shall stumble, those who do
disobey the Word are destined to fall.[122] One must keep in mind
Peter's rhetorical situation which is one of honor and shame. His
purpose is to encourage his audience that the honor denied them

---

[119] See esp. Beare, *1 Peter,* 124–25.

[120] παρέκβασις/*digressio* is a divergence from an argument into an
unrelated matter for the purpose of solidifying the argument (Quint. *Inst.
Or.* 4.3.12–17; 9.1.28, 2.56; 10.1.49; Cic. *De Or.* 3.53.203; *Inv.* 1.51.97;
Lausberg, *Handbuch,* 340–42. The figure is also known in Lat. as *egressio,
egressus, digressus,* and *ex cursis.*

[121] Cic. *Inv.* 1.53.100; Lausberg, *Handbuch,* 438.

[122] εἰς ὃ καὶ ἐτέθησαν signifies that whoever disbelieves/disobeys the Word
will stumble, such is God's decree. The result of disobedience is
foreordained, not the decision to disobey (and thus fall) (so Bigg, *St. Peter,*
133; Marshall, *1 Peter,* 71, 73). Hence the idea that the opponents in Asia
Minor were predestined to unbelief (and thus to damnation) is not present
in 1 Pt. 2:8. The honored position of the cornerstone is the concern of 2:4–8
first of all. The passage, then, treats the standing of those who believe and
disbelieve in the stone: either honor or shame. As Michaels (*1 Peter,* 106) says
regarding stumbling in 2:8, "it is the opposite of divine vindication, the
negative equivalent of the 'honor' reserved for Christian believers of not
being 'put to shame' (vv 6b–7)."

by the surrounding pagan culture is already theirs and will be even more fully disclosed as such in the future, both before and at the revelation of Jesus Christ (cf. 1:7, 13; 2:12, 19, 20; 3:16; 4:13; 5:10). The readers' vindication and honor necessarily require their opponents' dishonor and shame, an agonistic reversal (3:16; cf. 2:12). The shame of the opponents is what Peter has in view in his extended antithesis of believers and unbelievers.

God has ordained that honor comes to the one who believes in the cornerstone chosen and honorable: that person will not come to shame (vv. 6d–7a). Correspondingly, God has decreed that the one who disbelieves will stumble (vv. 7–8). Synonymous with disbelief in the cornerstone/stone/rock is disobedience to the Word (v. 8c). τῷ λόγῳ is the object of ἀπειθοῦντες, not προσκόπτουσιν, since in 8a the stumbling is against the λίθος, not the λόγος.[123] Hence τῷ λόγῳ ἀπειθοῦντες elucidates the nature of disbelief; προσκόπτω/πρόσκομμα-σκάνδαλον define the dishonor that comes to those who reject the stone that God has chosen.[124]

In the comparison of the two groups, the τιμή of the first has its counterpart in the πρόσκομμα/σκάνδαλον of the second. The disbelieving Gentiles who are the antagonists in 1 Peter now meet (and shall meet) shame and disgrace.[125] These antagonists are like builders who, having refused to incorporate a certain stone in

---

[123] See Beare, *1 Peter*, 125.

[124] Both προσκόπτουσιν and ἀπειθοῦντες are in the pres. tense: to stumble is to fall into shame, into a dishonorable verdict that is now assigned by Peter to the antagonists of the letter since they currently oppose the audience by rejecting their message (λόγος. Cf. 3:1 for ἀπειθέω τῷ λόγῳ as=disobey the message of the gospel. That usage of λόγος is a pun on its other appearance in the verse where it=a word, verbal utterance). By contrast, the readers enjoy an exalted status (pres. copula understood, v. 7a).

[125] Although in the stone typology of 1 Pt. 2:4–8, the one who exercises the prerogative of judgment is unspecified, just as it is throughout 1 Pt., God (YHWH in Isa. 28:16 LXX) is evidently the one who lays the stone in Zion and establishes faith in him as the criterion for an honorable verdict (v. 6). Hence one may presume that God is the judge; judgment is not explicitly assigned to Jesus Christ as his agent. See 1:7, 13; 2:12; 3:16; 4:5–6, 17; 5:10. Jesus apparently is the judge in 5:4 (as the ἀρχιποίμην). God/the Father is clearly the judge in 1:17 and 2:23.

their building and cast it aside, turn only to trip against it. Peter's *iudicatio* is not just about eternal destinies (heaven or hell), but about honor and shame, his primary rhetorical concerns.[126]

In vv. 9–10, Peter returns to the believers, those who are aligned with the corner-stone in a spiritual house. A series of epithets serves as a peroration[127] for the *iudicatio* (vv. 4–10), the *conplexio* itself (of which the *iudicatio* is a part [2:1–10]), and, indeed, the entire *argumentatio* (1:13–2:10).

The *peroratio* effectively accomplishes the twofold aim of that rhetorical component. First, it intensifies the positive pathos of the audience for themselves as the privileged and honored people of God. Peter affirms his Christian readers with titles drawn from the Old Testament. What were once significations of Israel are now those of the church, the new Israel. The identification of the believers in Asia Minor with Israel is a motif of 1 Peter from the beginning of the letter (1:1—ἐκλεκτοῖς παρεπιδήμοις διασπορᾶς), most notably in the first *argumentatio* where the Levitical holiness code is invoked for substantiation of the element of the *propositio* which states: "You shall be holy, for I am

---

[126] Beare, *1 Peter*, 124, perceptibly remarks: "The thought is not at all eschatological; the honour is not that which is to be bestowed upon the faithful in the Judgment Day, but that which is given them here and now, in their incorporation into the divine temple which rests upon the 'honourable' cornerstone, Jesus Christ." Of course, elsewhere in the letter, the eschatological dimension of the believers' honor is present (1:7, 13; 4:13; cf. 2:12).

[127] *Peroratio* in classical rhetoric serves a dual purpose: to intensify the pathos of the audience and to bring to its remembrance the points of argument. The first element consists of *conquestio/commiseratio* (=eliciting sympathy) and *indignatio* (=eliciting anger). *Enumeratio/recapitulatio*=ἀνακεφαλαίωσις repeats and collects the rhetor's evidence in order to refresh the memory of the hearers. In this concluding portion of one's speech, one may give full rein to eloquent expression, since it is the final opportunity to influence the judges/hearers. *Peroratio* is utilized, not only at the conclusion of the entire speech, but also whenever the subject matter is complex or the memory of the audience must be refreshed. See Arist. *Rh.* 3.19.1419b.10–1420b.4; Cic. *Inv.* 1.52.98, 53.100–54.105, 55.107–56.109; *Her.* 2.30.47–49, 31.50; Quint. *Inst. Or.* 6.1.1–2, 11, 21–35, 51; Lausberg, *Handbuch*, 431–42.

holy" (1:16).[128] Thus the terms γένος ἐκλεκτόν (Isa. 43:20), βασίλειον ἱεράτευμα (Ex. 19:6), ἔθνος ἅγιον (Ex. 19:6), and λαὸς εἰς περιποίησιν (cf. Ex. 19:5, 23:22; Dt. 4:20, 7:6, 14:2; Isa. 43:21; Mal. 3:17) recall that identification made earlier in the letter. The fact that these believers are "chosen," "royal," and "holy" intensifies the honorable nature of the attributes that these adjectives modify. Thus they are a good example of amplification.[129] The Petrine amplification in vv. 9–10 is through accumulation.[130] The ordering of attributes in ascending grades of value[131] is not present here; the epithets are somewhat synonymous.

In verse 9, the epithets are attended by five notable stylistic devices: (1) asyndeton[132] in the *cola*[133] before the dependent clause

---

[128] The identification of the church as the new Israel may be implicit at 1:2, 10–12, 15, 17, 19; 2:5.

[129] Although the adjectives are in Peter's source, the LXX, they still function rhetorically as *amplificatio*. On *amplificatio/*αὔξησις, see the detailed treatments in Arist. *Rh.* 1.9.1368a.38–40; Cic. *De Or.* 3.26.104–27.107; *Part. Or.* 15.52–17.58; Long. *Subl.* 11.1–12.2; Quint. *Inst. Or.* 8.4; Lausberg,. *Handbuch*, 401–9; Martin, *Antike Rhetorik*, 208–10; Watson, *Invention*, 26–28.

[130] *Frequentatio*, one of 9 types of amplification identified in Watson's brief and helpful survey of the subject (*Invention*, 26–28, esp. 27 on accumulation). See Quint. *Inst. Or.* 8.4.26–27; Long. *Subl.* 12.2; *Her.* 4.40.52–41.53.

[131] Augmentation is the name for this method of amplification which includes *gradatio/climax*, the figure in which a word appears only after the speaker has advanced by steps to the preceding one. See Cic. *Part. Or.* 15.54; *Her.* 4.25.34; Quint. *Inst. Or.* 8.4.3–9; Watson, *Invention*, 26, 97 (on 2 Pt. 1:5–11, a good example of *gradatio*-augmentation of Christian virtue capped with supersession of the *gradatio* by something even greater than its subject: rich provision of entrance into Christ's kingdom). Another prominent NT example of *gradatio* is Rom. 5:3–5.

[132] Quint. *Inst. Or.* 9.3.50; *Her.* 4.30.41.

[133] A colon (κῶλον/*membrum*) is a brief phrase that is complete yet does not express an entire thought until it is supplemented with one or more *cola*. The figure is stylistically better with three *cola* than with two (*Her.* 4.19.26).

The four *cola* in 9 are two pairs of *isocola* (*conpar, Her.* 4.20.27), i.e., two pairs whose respective phrases have virtually equal numbers of syllables. However, the quantity of syllables in each pair differs:

A) γέ/νος ἐ/κλεκ/τόν = 5
A') ἔ/θνος ἅ/γι/ον = 5
B) βα/σί/λει/ον ἱ/ερ/ά/τευ/μα = 9
B') λα/ὸς εἰς πε/ρι/ποί/η/σιν = 8

ὅπως τὰς ἀρετὰς κτλ; (2) *homoeoptoton*[134] with ος- (3x) and -ον endings (3x); (3) the utilization of the common Christian *topoi* of darkness and light.[135] The pre-Christian life of ignorance (1 Pt. 1:14) and futility (1:18) is that out of which the believers have been called. Furthermore (4), the adjective θαυμαστός is emotive, recalling the language of praise and worship in the Psalms,[136] and is an example of grand diction, a word that imparts grandeur, beauty, and force.[137] (5) The *pronominatio* τοῦ καλέσαντος recalls 1:15 where the same figure is used for God as it is here.

Verse 10 is an outstanding example of antithesis. The figure, again two pairs of *isocola*,[138] is a Petrine conflation of material in Hosea.[139] It has been reworked to produce a symmetrical figure of contrast between the believers' past and present modes of existence. Whereas the resident aliens and visiting strangers of Asia Minor knew no honor and no sense of belonging before receiving the gospel, now they have a distinguished identity (λαὸς θεοῦ). Their incorporation into the people of God, despite a previous way of life marked by futility (1:18), is an inexpressibly

---

The *isocolon* is broken up by an A-B-A'-B' pattern. Read aloud, the Petrine epithets would be rhythmically pleasant and symmetrical, a somewhat euphonic flourish to the *peroratio*.

[134] *Her*.4.20.28.

[135] See Selwyn, *St. Peter*, 375–82, for a treatment of the light-darkness motif in the NT (especially in the catechetical material).

[136] Cf. LXX Ps. 8:1, 9; 9:1; 25:7; 70:17; 85:10. The entire clause ὅπως τὰς ἀρετὰς ἐξαγγείλητε τοῦ ἐκ σκότους ὑμᾶς καλέσαντος εἰς τὸ θαυμαστὸν αὐτοῦ φῶς appears to be a Petrine creation that conflates (with redaction) Isa. 42:16 ([ποιήσω αὐτοῖς]τὸ σκότος εἰς φῶς), 43:21 (τὰς ἀρετάς μου διηγεῖσθαι), and the θαυμασ- words of the Pss.

[137] Long. *Subl.* 30.

[138] See 96–97 n. 133 above. Here, v. 10a-b=6 syllables each and v. 10c-d=7 syllables each.

[139] Cf. Hos. 1:9, οὐ λαός μου (*bis*); 2:1, λαός μου; 2:23, καὶ ἐρῶ τῷ οὐ λαῷ μου, λαός μου εἶ σύ; 1:6, οὐκ ἠλεημένη. Peter may have understood ἀγαπάω and ἐλεέω to be virtually synonymous for Hosea and substituted the latter for the former in 1 Pt. 2:10c-d. Hence καὶ ἀγαπήσω τὴν οὐκ ἠγαπημένην in Hos. 2:23 may also lie behind 1 Pt. 2:10 c-d as Hos. 1:6 certainly does.

generous act of divine mercy. To be showered with such compassion is the supreme honor, and it has been granted to Peter's audience.

The exordium and the first *argumentatio* of 1 Peter have established that the Christian alien residents and visiting strangers of Asia Minor have an honored and dignified position as members of the οἶκος τοῦ θεοῦ. The specific instructions to follow in 2:11–3:12 thus will have an attentive and kindly hearing of the audience. To those instructions we now turn.

CHAPTER FIVE
Second *Argumentatio*: 1 Peter 2:11–3:12

Propositio (2:11–12a)
πάροικοι καὶ παρεπίδημοι

A definite shift in verbal mood at 1 Pt. 2:11 signifies the transition to another major section of the epistle: an imperatival παρακαλῶ presents itself in v. 11 after an extended description (2:4–10) of the letter's recipients where the indicative mood prevails.[1] The vocative ἀγαπητοί is further evidence that a transition exists at v. 11.[2] The author arouses positive pathos with the term of endearment. Again, the species of rhetoric is deliberative since Peter urges his audience to take some course of action in the future.[3] That course is for the resident aliens and visiting strangers (πάροικοι καὶ παρεπίδημοι) to whom Peter writes "to abstain from the desires of the flesh that wage war against the soul."

Elliott[4] argues for the socio-political dimensions of the words πάροικοι and παρεπίδημοι as opposed to metaphorical denotations. My assumption in this dissertation is that Elliott is correct. The presence of ὡς in no way requires an understanding of ὡς παροίκους καὶ παρεπιδήμους as metaphorical.[5] The particle

---

[1] 1 Pt. 2:4–10 is the *iudicatio* of the *conplexio* that is 1 Pt. 2:1–10. The final impv. of the section is ἐπιποθήσατε at 2:2 (I take οἰκοδομεῖσθε at 2:5 as ind.). See discussion at 80–98 above.

[2] For Peter, ἀγαπητοί is a favorite transitional term. It is used as such at 1 Pt. 2:11; 4:12, transition from *argumentatio* to *peroratio*; 2 Pt. 3:14, transition from *probatio* to *peroratio* (esp. *repetitio*); and 3:17, transition within *peroratio* from *repetitio* to *adfectus* (emotional appeal). At 2 Pt. 3:8, ἀγαπητοί appears to be merely emphatic. See Watson, *Invention*, 130, 135–41, for the significance of ἀγαπητοί in 2 Pt. at the passages cited in this note.

[3] See the discussion on the species of rhetoric in 1 Pt. at 30 above.

[4] Elliott, *Home*, 21–58. See discussion at 28–30 above.

[5] A metaphorical sense for the phrase is argued by Martin, *Metaphor*, 188–92. NIV ("as aliens and strangers in the world") is particularly

here introduces an actual quality rather than a metaphorical one.[6] The prominence of language that pertains to honor and shame in 1 Peter should advise the reader to consider agonistic dimensions in any epithets given the audience in this letter. Metaphor is important to Peter, but so are honor and shame. Since the encouragement of the recipients in their apparent dishonor is of central concern to Peter, πάροικος and παρεπίδημος in 1 Pt. 2:11 may well have reference to the contest for honor. I suggest this to be the case. The two words are identifications that will assist the readers in plotting their position in the challenge and response of the honor contest. Peter will demonstrate how the contest will eventuate favorably for his readers. Thus I work with the assumption that 'resident alien' and 'visiting stranger' carry socio-political meaning and are Petrine terms suitable for reference to roles in the honor contest. They are not, in my opinion, metaphorical.

---

misleading since nothing in the Gk. warrants the prepositional phrase "in the world."

[6] ὡς followed by the acc., the usual case for παρακαλέω. ὑμᾶς is understood from the immediate context as in Jd. 3 (cf. BDF, 407). Within the NT, the particle is used non-metaphorically with the acc. at Rom. 1:21; 1 Cor. 4:14; Phlm. 16; and Heb. 11:9. The Corinthian passage recalls 1 Pt. 2:11 in its hortatory focus: οὐκ ἐντρέπων ὑμᾶς γράφω ταῦτα, ἀλλ᾽ ὡς τέκνα μου ἀγαπητὰ νουθετῶ[ν] cf. v. 16). Of interest is the text from Heb. where ὡς ἀλλοτρίαν appears with the verb παροικέω (['Αβραὰμ] πίστει παρῴκησεν εἰς γῆν τῆς ἐπαγγελίας ὡς ἀλλοτρίαν). Not only does this passage indicate that παροικ- words could refer to one's actual socio-political status (resident alien), but it illuminates ὡς as a designation of an actual (not metaphorical) condition. ὡς ἀλλοτρίαν is not a simile, but a relative adverbial clause that is subordinate to πίστει . . . ἐπαγγελίας.   ὡς ἀλλοτρίαν expresses the reason that Abraham assumed an *alien* residence in the promised land: it was indeed at that time a land foreign to him. Thus, '(Abraham) took up alien residence in the promised land as/since it was a foreign land.' BAGD, 898 (s.v. "ὡς"; cf. 40 [s.v. "ἀλλότριος"], "as if it were foreign"—not a metaphorical, but a subjunctive phrase). Although Heb., unlike 1 Pt., opts for a heavenly home as response to the social alienation experienced by the Christian community in relation to the world (Elliott, *Home*, 251 n. 106), the metaphorical sense of 'stranger' is not in view in Heb. 11 until at least v. 10, certainly v. 13.

"The Desires of the Flesh"

A literal frame of reference for πάροικος and παρεπίδημος does not preclude, however, metaphorical elements in the passage 1 Pt. 2:11. To describe fleshly lusts as waging war (στρατεύονται) against the soul is an instance of the type of metaphor known as personification, the most impressive form of sensate metaphor.[7] The metaphor invokes toward those lusts a negative pathos: the hearers are alerted to the grave danger to their spiritual welfare that the desires represent and the audience is led to a revulsion of them.[8] The *adfectus* that the martial image creates makes Peter's proposition all the more forceful. The *propositio* is amplified by means of several instances of *homoeoptoton* as well.[9]

Although the typical enthymematic particles (γάρ, ὅτι) are not present in v. 11, the *propositio* is based on a syllogism. The Petrine *propositio* and its syllogistic categories would be universal and acceptable in definition for the audience. (A dualism like that of flesh-soul is common in ancient thought.) The major premise, one must abstain from those things that combat the soul,

---

[7] *Conformatio/translatio/*προσωποποιία. *Her.* 4.53.66; Quint. *Inst. Or.* 8.6.11; Lausberg, *Handbuch*, 559. Brox (*Der erste Petrusbrief*, 12–13) cautions against attributing metaphysical and theological significations to Peter's description of an inner conflict in a human person. An anthropological dichotomy between body/flesh and soul ought not to be inferred here. σαρκικός refers to that which is sinful and ψυχή to the human person in her/his concern for the good and right. The description of the inner conflict, typical and conventional for the NT, is an element of persuasive oratorical style.

[8] Revulsion (or hatred) is one aspect of negative pathos that the rhetorical theorists discuss. Arist. *Rh.* 2.4.1380b.1–32; Cic. *De Or.* 2.42.178; Quint. *Inst. Or.* 6.2.20–22. Negative pathos for human opponents is only infrequently aroused in 1 Pt., and interestingly so since the slanderers have made life difficult for the audience. They are not so much castigated (cf. the false teachers of 2 Pt. 2:1–22, 3:3–5, 16) as placed in an inferior position in Peter's honor contest.

[9] *Her.* 4.20.28. This figure of speech lends attractiveness to the period in which it is contained through the repetitive sounds -ους (2x), -ων (4x), -ες (2x), -ης (2x), and -ην (3x).

is supplemented with the minor premise, fleshly lusts battle the soul. The conclusion then becomes Peter's exhortation: abstain from fleshly lusts which wage war with the soul. The antithesis of flesh and soul here is an opposition to which Peter returns again.[10] Specifically what the ἐπιθυμίαι[11] are is not stated. They probably are the inclinations to respond wrongly to persons in authority.

Negative and Positive Aspects of the Proposition

The verse divisions hinder one from seeing the rhetorical progression between *propositio* and *ratio*. The *colon* of v. 12a is actually part of the *propositio*. ἔχοντες, rather than being a genuine imperatival participle, is more likely attached to ἀγαπητοί, παρακαλῶ . . . ἀπέχεσθαι. The participle and all that accompanies it (τὴν ἀναστροφὴν ὑμῶν ἐν τοῖς ἔθνεσιν ἔχοντες καλήν) form a restatement of the imperatival ἀπέχεσθαι κτλ.[12] Together, ἀπέχεσθαι κτλ and ἔχοντες κτλ form a synonym.[13] The former phrase states negatively what the latter states positively.[14] The *ratio* begins properly at v. 12b with ἵνα. The function of ἔχοντες κτλ is, however, more than mere restatement and definition of ἀπέχεσθαι τῶν σαρκικῶν ἐπιθυμιῶν. The presence of καλήν is of critical importance, for it is a word that

---

[10] The antithesis is repeated in 1 Pt. 3:18 and 4:6.

[11] At 1 Pt. 2:11, σαρκικός is probably in reference to "all that partakes of the self-centeredness of human beings" (the general Pauline sense) and not to sins of the body, esp. sexual sins. Davids, *1 Peter*, 95.

[12] David Daube, "Appended Note: Participle and Imperative in I Peter," in *St. Peter*, by Selwyn, 482; Michaels, *1 Peter*, 17; Selwyn, *St. Peter*, 141. ἀπέχεσθαι (pres. mid. inf.) is an indirect command after παρακαλῶ (Robertson, *The General Epistles*, 99). ἔχοντες is a "circumstantial" ptc., describing the circumstances (positive) that attend the command ἀπέχεσθαι (negative).

A v.l. (attested in 614, 630, *pc*) suggests that v. 12a is to be read as a restatement of v. 11: παρακαλῶ δὲ καὶ τοῦτο τὴν ἐν τοῖς ἔθνεσιν ὑμῶν ἀναστροφὴν ἔχειν καλήν ('and I also urge [you to do] this: maintain your honorable conduct among the pagans'). Nestle-Aland[26], 601 (critical apparatus at 1 Pt. 2:12).

[13] *Her.* 4.28.38.

[14] Brox, *Der erste Petrusbrief*, 13; Davids, *1 Peter*, 95–96. Cf. Cic. *Top.* 11.47–49 for the topic of argument from contraries.

pertains to the honor contest and indicates that the behavior called for is honorable.[15] "Honour is the token of a man's being famous for doing good."[16] The doing of good is the avenue for the ancients to honor.

For Cicero,[17] honor and advantage are the twin ends of deliberative oratory. By pursuing virtue, one does good and attains those qualities that make for honor and advantage. The virtuous qualities that Peter encourages in the *propositio* are *continentia*, "the control of desire by the guidance of wisdom"[18] (ἀπέχεσθαι κτλ) and *patientia*, "a willing and sustained endurance of difficult and arduous tasks for a noble and useful end"[19] (ἔχοντες κτλ). The result will be honor, particularly glory which "consists in a person's having a widespread reputation accompanied by praise."[20] Glory comes to the audience as glory is given to God. The present slanderers will give glory to God as they see the honorable deeds of those whom they presently defame. A reversal of status will take place. In the classic honor contest, revenge would have been required[21] of the disdained challengee(s) (in 2:12, the Christians). Peter instructs his readers, the challengees, to instead abstain from fleshly lusts and maintain good and

---

[15] NRSV perceptively translates both occurrences of καλός at 2:12 as "honorable" and "honorably." Cf. JB "honorably" and "good." Peter reflects the language of the Jesus tradition at v. 12c-d: Mt. 5:16, ὅπως ἴδωσιν ὑμῶν τὰ καλὰ ἔργα καὶ δοξάσωσιν τὸν πατέρα ὑμῶν τὸν ἐν τοῖς οὐρανοῖς. For Peter, καλός is essentially synonymous with ἀγαθός: cf. 1 Pt. 2:12a with 3:16d, ὑμῶν τὴν ἀγαθὴν ἐν Χριστῷ ἀναστροφήν (cf. v. 16b, συνείδησιν ἔχοντες ἀγαθήν). The virtual equivalence of the terms is throughout the NT (see discussion in Erich Beyreuther, "Good, Beautiful, Kind: ἀγαθός, καλός, χρηστός," *NIDNTT*, 2:98–107), although "noble" or "praiseworthy" could be the nuance of καλός when applied to behavior (Beyreuther, "Good," *NIDNTT*, 2:98; BAGD, 3 (s.v. "ἀγαθός"), 400 (s.v. "καλός").

[16] Arist. *Rh.* 1.5.1361a.27 (Roberts's trans.).

[17] Cic. *Inv.* 2.51.156–58.175 for full discussion of the honorable and advantageous in deliberative oratory.

[18] Cic. *Inv.* 2.54.164.

[19] Cic. *Inv.* 2.54.163–64.

[20] Cic. *Inv.* 2.55.166.

[21] Malina, *NT World*, 31–32.

honorable behavior in their social exchanges with the outsiders.[22] In a sense, he is rewriting the social code of honor, taking his cue from Jesus himself (2:23).

"The desires of the flesh" from which the hearers are to abstain may well include the desire for revenge and the attempt to exact it by answering malign words with the same. Peter has already instructed his readers in 2:1 to put off all slander (καταλαλία).[23] The temptation for the believers to repay slander in kind would have been great, but would not have contributed toward their ultimately favorable outcome in the honor contest (i.e., the future glorification of God by the present slanderers). The *confirmatio* of the present argument emphasizes the necessity for the community to refrain from returning abuse for abuse or threats for suffering (2:23). The submission that Peter enjoins may largely be of a verbal nature: grumbling and defamation would be common responses to political authorites, masters of slaves, and unbelieving husbands among others with whom members of the community were dissatisfied for some reason (2:13, 18; 3:1). Although silence is sometimes required in the face of unbelief (3:1), the entire *argumentatio* is concluded with a summons to repay abusive speech with blessing (3:9–12).[24]

---

[22] Since virtually all social exchanges outside the family or one's circle of friends constitute an honor contest in the world of the readers (Malina, *NT World*, 32–33), ἡ ἀναστροφὴ ἐν τοῖς ἔθνεσιν may well refer to the entire network of societal intercourse.

[23] As a subst., κατάλαλος appears in a vice list at Rom. 1:30. Such a list includes sins that may be considered as σαρκικαὶ ἐπιθυμίαι as in Gal. 5:16–21, where the items in the list are subsumed under the twin headings ἐπιθυμία σαρκός and τὰ ἔργα τῆς σαρκός. Paul does not use σάρξ in connection with the offenses of Rom. 1:18–32, but the term αἱ ἐπιθυμίαι τῶν καρδίων αὐτῶν may be a heading under which κατάλαλος falls.

[24] The similarity of 1 Pt. 3:9 with Rom. 12:17 (μηδενὶ κακὸν ἀντὶ κακοῦ τινι ἀποδῷ) and 1 Thess. 5:15 (ὁρᾶτε μὴ τις κακὸν ἀντὶ κακοῦ τινι ἀποδῷ) is likely due to common catechetical tradition (Selwyn, *St. Peter*, 189, 408, 412–13). The context of the prohibition against repaying evil for evil in Rom. 12:17 is personal revenge. One is not to take revenge, but leave room for God's vengeance (μὴ ἑαυτοὺς ἐκδικοῦντες . . . ἐμοὶ ἐκδίκησις, ἐγὼ ἀνταποδώσω, λέγει κύριος, Rom. 12:19). I suggest that Peter's context is similar to Paul's: he is thinking of the matter of revenge in the honor contest, but instructs his readers to avoid it and take another path, that of

The praise of God by the pagans constitutes not only their verdict on the God of the Christian community, but an honorable public verdict of the believers themselves and their honorable behavior (καλὰ ἔργα, v. 12c). Thus the believers will receive honor at the conclusion of the exchange of challenge and response.

Ratio 2:12b-d

Form and Style

Why does Peter summon his readers to abstinence from fleshly desires? Why ought they to conduct themselves "honorably among the Gentiles"? Only by so doing will there be a favorable verdict for them in the honor contest. Although now the Christian community is culturally despised, socially estranged, and politically displaced, it can anticipate a reversal of status in the arena of challenge and response, in the honor contest. God has granted them a marvelous new identity (1:3–2:10). Only it now remains for the pagans in their cultural environment to recognize the believers' true holy character.

The *ratio* is a purpose (pure final) clause with ἵνα (*colon* d) that is interrupted by two *cola* which serve as somewhat parenthetical qualifications. In other words, the conjunction ἵνα is separated from the clause that it properly introduces by two intervening *cola*. Peter has embellished his style in the *ratio* by augmenting the purpose clause with these two additional *cola*.[25]

12a τὴν ἀναστροφὴν ὑμῶν ἐν τοῖς ἔθνεσιν ἔχοντες καλήν
ratio
12b (ἵνα,) ἐν ᾧ καταλαλοῦσιν ὑμῶν ὡς κακοποιῶν
12c ἐκ τῶν καλῶν ἔργων ἐποπτεύοντες
12d ἵνα . . . δοξάσωσιν τὸν θεὸν ἐν ἡμέρᾳ ἐπισκοπῆς

honorable conduct. Such conduct does not retaliate in the face of rejection and slander.

[25] ἵνα δοξάσωσιν τὸν θεὸν ἐν ἡμέρᾳ ἐπισκοπῆς could have stood alone as a *colon* in connection with vv. 11–12a. With the additional *cola* v. 12b and c, the statement still does not constitute a complete thought or period (*continuatio*, *Her.* 4.19.27); for such a completion it must be syntactically joined to the *propositio*. However, v. 12b-d is still a complete *ratio*.

The initial κ- sounds in v. 12b-d, a *homoeopropheron*,[26] phonetically hammer the reason home—the sounds are hard and striking, but not harsh. Peter again constructs a *homoeoptoton*[27] in the *ratio* for stylistic adornment.

The Petrine Honor Contest

In 1 Pt. 2:12 the author of the letter clearly delineates the pattern of challenge, response, and verdict that is typical of the honor contest. In the competition for honor between the Christian community and the unbelievers of Asia Minor, a favorable public verdict for the former can ensue only when it responds appropriately to the challenge that is made to them. The challenge has been laid down by the outsiders (τὰ ἔθνη)[28] in Asia Minor: a positive rejection of the Christ-community, its message, and behavior. That rejection, according to 2:12, has taken the form of a continuous stream of slanderous speech, defamation, and maligning words.[29]

Calumny comes like a torrent and specifies its objects to be[30] "evildoers." What the particular instances of evil may be of which the hearers are accused is impossible to know with certainty. The

---

[26] Bullinger, *Figures of Speech*, 171.

[27] *Her.* 4.20.28. -σιν (2x), -ων (5x). Although v. 12b-d is not a grammatical period, it is a distinct rhetorical segment and thus I consider the *homoeoptota* of vv. 11–12a and v. 12b-d separately.

[28] τὰ ἔθνη can mean "Gentiles" (NRSV), "nonbelievers" (Elliott, *Home*, 43), "pagans" (NIV), or "unbelievers" (REB). "Peter calls unbelievers Gentiles, not because he thinks that his readers were all Jewish Christians, but because he once again assumes that Christians (both literal Jews and literal Gentiles within the body of Christ) are the 'true Israel.' Therefore all who are not Christians (both literal Jews and literal Gentiles) are truly 'Gentiles' (cf. 4:3)" (Grudem, *1 Peter*, 16).

[29] The Gk. is, lit., the equivalent of the colloquial English expressions 'talk (someone) down' or 'put (someone) down' (κατά=down, λαλέω=talk, speak). Some of the better English translations are NRSV and REB "malign," JB "denounce," NAS "slander." The verb, pres. act. ind., signifies that the defamation is current at the writing of the letter.

[30] In the phrase ἐν ᾧ καταλαλοῦσιν ὑμῶν ὡς κακοποιῶν, the word ὡς has the non-metaphorical significance that it has at 2:11. The charge is false, but represents an actual condition for the accuser who brings it: 'in that for which you are slanderously accused of being (ὡς) evildoers.'

transgressors listed at 4:15 may provide a clue: μὴ γάρ τις ὑμῶν πασχέτω ὡς φονεὺς ἢ κλέπτης ἢ κακοποιὸς ἢ ὡς ἀλλοτρι-επίσκοπος.[31] Nonetheless, the Christian community in Asia Minor was perceived by the indigenous ethnic and/or religious majorities somehow to be a threat to the established order. The reason, therefore, for Peter's *propositio* (abstaining from fleshly lusts and maintaining good behavior) is that the reversal of status (from shame to honor) for those who are now being slandered may take place. The antithesis[32] ἐν ᾧ καταλαλοῦσιν δοξάσωσιν τὸν θεόν, wherein the first condition gives way to the second, suggests that the act of glorifying God is the expression of a different public verdict by the ἔθνη regarding the Christians. The non-retaliatory nature of Christian response does not meet with positive rejection (i.e., slander), but with a positive verdict (δοξά-σαι τὸν θεόν). The verdict of glory to God is at least partially public (as verdicts are in the honor contest) and is understood somehow by the indigenous inhabitants of Asia Minor.

Some interpreters suggest that the turnaround by the pagans is not at the final judgment, but at an undefined moment in present history. ἡ ἡμέρα ἐπισκοπῆς may refer to any time at which God visits to bring blessing or judgment.[33] We may diagram the challenge-response according to 1 Pt. 2:11–12 as in Figure 1.

---

[31] See the suggestions at 29 above.

[32] Here, a *contentio* of diction. *Her.* 4.15.21, 45.58.

[33] Lk. 19:44, ὁ καιρὸς τῆς ἐπισκοπῆς σου refers to the time of Jesus' ministry that was intended to bring blessing but, because that ministry was unrecognized, it stands in contrast to the impending judgment. Grudem, *1 Peter*, 16–17, and Marshall, *1 Peter*, 81–82, believe that δοξάσαι τὸν θεὸν ἐν ἡμέρα ἐπισκοπῆς refers to a change of heart in present time that may/does lead to conversion to Christ. Schelkle, *Die Petrusbriefe*, 72, believes that the day of visitation could mean either that Last Day or a time when the pagans praise God, are converted to the Christian faith, and enter into the church. Best, *1 Peter*, 112, maintains that ἡ ἡμέρα ἐπισκοπῆς is best understood as a reference to the final day of judgment. My analysis, as an examination of the cultural values of honor and shame in 1 Pt., does not underline an emphasis on the evangelistic value of good works in the letter. That emphasis, however, is surely also present (see Grudem, *1 Peter*, 117).

Confirmatio (2:13–17)

In 1 Pt. 2:13–17, the hearers encounter additional and corroborating arguments in support of the *ratio* of v. 12b-d. Hence, one would expect this section, as *confirmatio*, to elucidate the reason and purpose for the Petrine summons to abstain from lusts of the flesh and to maintain an honorable conduct. One finds such elucidation in vv. 13–17. Such expressions as διὰ τὸν κύριον, εἰς ἐκδίκησιν κακοποιῶν ἔπαινον δὲ ἀγαθοποιῶν, and the enthymematic ὅτι οὕτως ἐστὶν τὸ θέλημα τοῦ θεοῦ indicate that the section stresses cause. As summary, v. 17 supports Peter's case for his hearers to maintain an honorable conduct. "Honor everyone. Love the family of believers. Fear God. Honor the emperor."[34]

Figure 1: Challenge and Response in 1 Pt. 2:11–12	
Action*	Threat πάροικοι & παρεπίδημοι → τὰ ἔθνη
Perception*	Attack on self-esteem/established order
Challenge (Reaction)	Positive Rejection ἐν ᾧ καταλαλοῦσιν ὑμῶν ὡς κακοποιῶν ↓ |
Response (Counter-reaction)	↓ | ἀπέχεσθαι τῶν [revenge] σαρκικῶν ἐπιθυμιῶν = τὴν ἀναστροφὴν ὑμῶν ἐν τοῖς ἔθνεσιν ἔχοντες καλήν
Verdict	ἵνα δοξάσωσιν τὸν θεὸν ἐν ἡμέρᾳ ἐπισκοπῆς (Honor for the πάροικοι & παρεπίδημοι)
(* refers to stages not explicitly discussed by Peter.)	

---

[34] 1 Pt. 2:13–17 is closest to the original version of a common source that may underlie, not only that passage, but Rom. 13:1–7; 1 Tim. 2:1–3; Tit. 3:1–3, 8. Selwyn, *St. Peter*, 426–29.

The particular arrangement that Peter's *confirmatio* takes is very close to that of a thesis (also known as "the complete argument" or an "elaboration"). In the compact outline of the thesis were contained the major types of proof and subdivisions of the standard deliberative speech. The complicated rhetorical discussions of the handbooks were reduced to this popular and teachable form at some time during the second century BCE. My analysis conforms to the pattern of the thesis:[35]

The Thesis	The Standard Speech
1. Introduction	I. *Exordium*
2. Proposition	II. *Narratio*
3. Reason (Rationale)	
	III. *Confirmatio*
4. Opposite (Contrary)	
5. Analogy (Comparison)	
6. Example	
7. Citation (Authority)	
8. Conclusion	IV. *Conclusio*

Thesis (vv. 13–17)

Proposition (vv. 13–14)

Deference to all

Since Peter's thesis does not stand alone, but is embedded in a larger *argumentatio*, it omits the introduction or exordium. The proposition, as in the other Petrine propositions thus far, is an exhortation. Although ὑποτάγητε (aor. pass. impv.) could have the sense of 'subject yourselves, be subjected or subordinated, obey,'[36] another translation is possible according to Michaels.[37] Peter distinguishes between the kind of primary and radical

---

[35] Mack, *Rhetoric and the NT*, 42. An example of the thesis form utilized in relation to a *chreia* (a memorable and beneficial action or saying by a famous authority) is by Hermogenes in his *progymnasmata*. See Mack, *Rhetoric and the NT*, 44, for text in English trans. The pattern of the thesis, although with some variation, appears in *Her.* 4.43.56–44.57; cf. 4.42.54.

[36] BAGD, 848 (s.v. "ὑποτάσσω").

[37] Michaels, *1 Peter*, 121, 123–24.

obedience that only God deserves (ὑπακοή, 1:2, 14, 22)[38] and a secondary, limited commitment to "human creatures" (i.e., every person: πάσῃ ἀνθρωπίνῃ κτίσει).[39] Hence "respect" or "defer to" is more appropriate than "submit to," or "be subject" as renderings for the verb ὑποτάσσω. I suggest "honor" as a synonym for Michaels's terms. Such deference is for the sake of the Lord (διὰ τὸν κύριον). The author's concern in the thesis is good and honorable conduct toward all, just as it was in vv. 11–12a.

In order to confirm the reason of v. 12b-d, he first restates, in a more specific fashion, the *propositio* of the entire argument. To this point in the letter, Peter's hortatory thrust has been general and unspecific: 'abstain from fleshly lusts' (v. 11) and 'maintain good conduct among the unbelievers' (v. 12a). Now it is specifically 'defer to every person' (v. 13a).

Emperor and governors

Peter identifies some of those to whom one is to give respect. The "emperor" and "governors" are mentioned asyndetically[40] with *pronominationes*: 'the emperor as the supreme one' and 'the governors as those sent by him' (i.e., 'by the Lord').[41] The

---

[38] 1 Pt. 3:6, Σάρρα ὑπήκουσεν τῷ Ἀβραάμ, as "one passing reference . . . within a biblical illustration," is an exception to the consistency within 1 Pt. that applies ὑποτάσσω to human relationships (2:13, 18; 3:1, 5; 5:5) and ὑπακοή to God/Christ and the Christian message (1:2, 14, 22). Michaels, *1 Peter*, 124.

[39] Best, *1 Peter*, 13–14, suggests that πάσῃ ἀνθρωπίνῃ κτίσει may function as a title for the entire social code (1 Pt. 2:13–3:7). He thus follows NRSVmg "accept the authority of every institution ordained for human beings" and reads κτίσις as "institution" whose itemization occurs in three areas (each of which is an institution created by God in the human sphere): the State, the master-slave relationship, and the family. One could assume such an interpretation of πάσῃ ἀνθρωπίνῃ κτίσει and yet not take v. 13 as a heading for 2:13–3:7. As a rhetorical *exornatio*, 2:18–3:7(12) may simply continue, as a new section, to embellish the proposition, reason, and proof of the reason already stated.

[40] Lat. *dissolutum*, a figure which is the omission of conjunction(s) so that each part of a period is presented separately. *Her.* 4.30.41.

[41] *Her.* 4.31.42. Commencing with Augustus, Roman provinces, including those that were the destinations of 1 Pt. (see 1:1; Pontus and Bithynia are a single, unified province), would each have either a governor appointed by

repetition of εἴτε before each (εἴτε βασιλεῖ ὡς ὑπερέχοντι, εἴτε ἡγεμόσιν ὡς δι' αὐτοῦ πεμπομένοις εἰς ἐκδίκησιν κακοποιῶν ἔπαινον δὲ ἀγαθοποιῶν, vv. 13b–14)[42] tends to establish both parties as deserving of respect.

The governors and their deputies would have been more likely than the emperor to exert direct or indirect influence in the lives of the provincials to whom Peter writes.[43] As an appointed emissary, the governor was supposed to work for the correct application of Roman justice.[44] The ἐκδίκησιν κακοποιῶν and the ἔπαινος ἀγαθοποιῶν are not only the opposite poles of Roman justice, but represent for Peter's audience the reversed roles in the pattern of challenge and response. In 2:12, Peter says that, though the community is now maligned as evildoers, that verdict will be reversed. That same assertion is made here again in a different way. His sense is that the governors will see to it that

---

the Senate or one appointed by the Emperor. Evidently, according to Best, Peter failed to distinguish the two kinds of governors and assumes all are sent by the Emperor (*1 Peter*, 14). Peter may, however, intend ὡς δι' αὐτοῦ πεμπομένοις to make reference to the Lord as the sender of the governors (τὸν κύριον is thus the antecedent of αὐτοῦ). To understand the Lord as the dispatcher of the governors accords with the purpose of Peter to establish the reason for his exhortation to good behavior. Such behavior will be rewarded, says Peter, becuause the governors are sent for the purpose of (εἰς) administering justice. Not only so, but they are sent by *God*. Thus the justice of their decisions is virtually assured by Peter. For a brief explanation of Roman emperorship and governorship see John E. Stambaugh and David L. Balch, *The New Testament in Its Social Environment*, Library of Early Christianity 2 (Philadelphia: Westminster Press, 1986), 15–20.

[42] An example of *epanaphora* (*repetitio*), a figure in which like or different ideas are expressed in phrases that are begun in close succession by the same word. *Her.* 4.13.19.

[43] Gubernatorial functions and responsibilities (incl. judicial and police duties) are described in Stambaugh and Balch, *Social Environment*, 19, 32–35.

[44] Governors did not always exercise justice in legal and criminal matters. The NT gives evidence for the self-serving crookedness of some: Pilate (Mk. 15:6–15; Lk. 23:13–25; Jn. 19:12–16), Felix (Acts 24:26–27), and Festus (Acts 25:9–10). Cf. D. H. Wheaton, "Pilate," *NBD*, 939–40, for a brief yet illuminating article on the insensitive wickedness of Pilate that is attested in ancient sources. Peter does not imagine anything but just verdicts from the governors in 2:14, however.

honor (ἔπαινος) is accorded where it is due and punishment (or vengeance, ἐκδίκησις) likewise. The readers may be confident that ultimately they will receive the honor that is justly theirs. After all, they are ἀγαθοποιοῦντες who deserve praise, and not κακοποιοῦντες who deserve punishment.

"To praise those who do right"

Perhaps some kind of public recognition or exoneration from governors or their agents is envisaged. Van Unnik believes that ἀγαθοποιοῦντες in vv. 14–15 must signify more than those who merely conform to the law, an act that is expected. He states:

> It is well known that εὐεργέται [=ἀγαθοποιοῦντες] of Greek communities were often honoured by tablets in the market-place extolling the great services they rendered to the State. Therefore something more than doing one's duty is implied here; it means, people who do something deserving a special distinction.[45]

Giving public distinction (ἔπαινος) to benefactors is a role of the Roman ruler.[46] If the Christians of Asia Minor work for the public good, the official commendations that they receive will silence the ignorant criticisms of their foolish accusers.

The New Testament provides an example of someone who may have been so honored with a monument. Erastus, the Corinthian city treasurer whom Paul mentions in Rom. 16:23, may be the same Erastus whose role as a civic benefactor was commended in a Latin inscription discovered at Corinth: "Erastus laid this pavement at his own expense, in appreciation of his appointment as aedile."[47] One cannot be certain if the Erastus of the inscription is Paul's companion of Rom. 16:23, but the identification of one with the other is argued by some.[48] Nevertheless, the

---

[45] W. C. Van Unnik, "The Teaching of Good Works in 1 Peter," chap. in *Sparsa Collecta: The Collected Essays of W. C. Van Unnik*, part 2, *1 Peter, Canon, Corpus Hellenisticum, Generalia*, Supplements to *Novum Testamentum*, vol. 30 (Leiden: E. J. Brill, 1980), 92.

[46] W. C. Van Unnik, "A Classical Parallel to 1 Peter II 14 and 20," chap. in *Sparsa Collecta*, 107, 109.

[47] A. F. Walls, "Erastus," *NBD*, 341.

[48] E.g., Gerd Theissen, "Social Stratification in the Corinthian Community: A Contribution to the Sociology of Early Hellenistic

kindness of Erastus the benefactor is an example of ἀγαθοποιεῖν among the Greeks and Romans: 'to do good' means the friendly and willing gift of material or spiritual assistance to anyone in need. This idea of doing good in general has its Christian motivation in the teaching of Jesus and is paralleled in Paul.[49]

In Acts 18:12–17, Annius Gallio, proconsul of Achaia, dismisses the case by the Jews against Paul. The governor's refusal to hear the case constitutes a negative refusal in an honor contest between himself and the Jewish accusers. No response implies dishonor. Furthermore, the proconsul, by not responding to the Jews, at v. 17 demonstrates that he did not regard his honor to be affronted by the challenge to his decision. He regards himself as 'superior' to the 'inferior' plaintiffs.

Paul, the defendant, maintains honor in this incident. Since the Jewish accusers cannot bring a valid charge against Paul, his honor is upheld. Not only so, but (1) it is dishonorable for one to take another to court in the first place. The action publicizes the grievance and (2) implies that one cannot deal with one's equals. The Jews are dishonored on both counts. They take Paul to court and show that they cannot deal with him as their equal.[50] Peter's

---

Christianity," chap. in *The Social Setting of Pauline Christianity: Essays on Corinth*, trans. and ed. John H. Schutz (Philadelphia: Fortress Press, 1982). An Erastus is also mentioned at Acts 19:22 and 2 Tim. 4:20.

[49] Van Unnik, "Good Works," 105.

[50] Cf. Malina, *NT World*, 30–36, 39, for discussion of the honor contest as it applies to the legal proceedings described above. Nothing in the text of 1 Pt. demands that one interpret the letter against a backdrop of official imperial or local persecution (see e.g., Marshall, *1 Peter*, 23; Robinson, *Redating the NT*, 151–56). Still, disputes between Christians and unbelieving, hostile neighbors may have led to situations like that in Acts 18:12–17.

The fact that Gallio refuses to hear the case against Paul does not sustain the view that Christianity is a *religio licita*. Although the Jews did have advantages with and enjoy concessions from the Romans, religions and religious controversies were dealt with ad hoc. No juridical category of *religio licita* existed according to Philip Francis Esler, *Community and Gospel in Luke-Acts: The Social and Political Motivations of Lucan Theology*, Society for New Testament Studies Monograph Series 57 (Cambridge: Cambridge University Press, 1987), 205–19. He believes that Lk.-Acts is a legitimation for Christians inside the community, esp. Roman believers who may have felt tension trying

notion of "praise" may involve legal vindications that will establish the honor of his readers—that is, if they persist in well-doing.

At any rate, in Peter's estimation, such a verdict cannot fail to come since the governors are God's very agents sent by him for the purpose of dispensing honorable verdicts where they are due. The praise that is to be awarded to the genuinely faithful at the revelation of Christ (cf. 1:7) is also to be publicly recognized before that event, affirmed by the political powers!

Reason (v. 15)

The reason of the thesis is quite similar to the *ratio* (v. 12b-d) for the entire argument.[51] One would expect this to be so since Peter's thesis serves as a *confirmatio* for that *ratio*. The reason in v. 15 is an enthymeme in support of the propositional exhortation. It is somewhat unusual, for the conclusion with ὅτι (ὅτι οὕτως ἐστὶν τὸ θέλημα τοῦ θεοῦ) is listed first.[52] The major premise is unstated (God's will is to silence the ignorance of the foolish), but the minor premise is stated (doing right silences the ignorance of the foolish). Therefore, doing right (including the deference to political authorities)[53] is God's will. The silencing of the foolish ignorance of which Peter speaks may envisage the kind

---

to be good Roman citizens and Christians too. The political implications of Christianity may have been a concern for such an audience. Luke assuages such fears, however, in his portrayal of the faith as an ancestral religion that promotes conservatism (cf. Acts 3:13; 5:30; 15:10; 22:14; 24:14; 26:6; 28:17, 25).

[51] "Verse 15 is essentially a restatement of verse 12 within a more specific context." Scot Snyder, "1 Peter 2:17: A Reconsideration," *Filologia Neotestamentaria* 4 (November 1991): 214 n. 15.

[52] The syntax is an example of the figure hyperbaton, "a putting together of words in a way contrary to or different from the usual order" (Bullinger, *Figures of Speech*, 692). See also *Her.* 4.32.44.

[53] On ἀγαθοποιέω, Marshall (*1 Peter*, 84) comments: "Here Peter speaks the language of the Greco-Roman world, which commended 'doing good.' The implication is that Christians are not only to avoid breaking the law but also to do what will win recognition as good deeds. At the extreme, rich citizens were expected to provide lavishly for the needs of the community. The benefactor was a recognized figure. Here is an implicit justification for a positive contribution to the life of the community according to a person's ability."

of silence described in Acts 18:12–17. The refusal of the magistrates to hear charges against the Christians is a shameful rebuff to the accusers, an action that brings dishonor on them.

The construction φιμοῦν τὴν τῶν ἀφρόνων ἀνθρώπων ἀγνωσίαν is stylistically rich. The deficiency of the people to be silenced is stressed by alliteration of three consecutive α-sounds,[54] two of which are alpha-privative: ἀνθρώπων is surrounded by two negative characteristics on either side of it. The object of φιμοῦν is ἀγνωσίαν. One would expect ἀνθρώπους here since the normal idiom is φιμοῦν τινά.[55] 'To silence ignorance' is an occurrence of metonymy, a figure of diction in which an expression closely asociated with the object is used in place of it.[56] Ignorance stands for the people who are its possessors.

The phrase 'to silence ignorance' also furnishes Peter another term of reproach for his motif of role reversal in the honor contest. The verb φιμοῦν is, in Peter's usage at v. 15, a term loaded with negative pathos and dishonor. It refers to the muzzling of oxen as they tread the grain on the threshing floor (1 Cor. 9:9 v.l.; 1 Tim. 5:18). In that the opponents are compared to oxen that require a muzzle(!), the construction φιμοῦν τὴν ἀγνωσίαν is metaphorical; specifically, a *katachresis.*[57]

Opposite (v. 16a-b) and Analogy (v. 16c)

Simile in v. 16

In the thesis or elaboration, an opposite is employed in order to support the reason. "The logic of the principle proposed is

---

[54] *Homeopropheron* with α-. Bullinger, *Figures of Speech,* 171.

[55] People: Mt. 22:12 (pass.), 34; animals: 1 Cor. 9:9 v.l.; 1 Tim 5:18.

[56] Lat. *denominatio. Her.* 4.32.43.

[57] κατάχρησις/*abusio,* a figure of diction in which an inexact use of a like and kindred word occurs for the precise and proper one (e.g., "the long wisdom in the man"). *Her.* 4.33.45. Cf. Cic. *De Or.* 3.43.169–70 (*verbo in transferendo*); Quint. *Inst. Or.* 8.2.4–6, 6.34; Lausberg, *Handbuch,* 562. The word φιμόω is used as a *katachresis* at Mt. 22:12, 34.

confirmed if the inverse also is true."⁵⁸ The phrase καὶ μὴ ὡς ἐπικάλυμμα ἔχοντες τῆς κακίας τὴν ἐλευθερίαν indicates that this verse concerns itself with some kind of opposite. In v. 16, Peter uses two paradoxical similes each introduced by ὡς: ἐλεύθεροι yet (θεοῦ) δοῦλοι. A third simile explicates the way the ἐλεύθεροι are not to use their liberty, καὶ μὴ ὡς ἐπικάλυμμα ἔχοντες τῆς κακίας τὴν ἐλευθερίαν.

The positive exercise of that freedom (one of the paradoxical similes) is set off from its negative use by ἀλλά (hence it is an instance of antithesis): ἀλλ᾽ ὡς θεοῦ δοῦλοι. The adverb ὡς requires the reader to join the adverbial clauses to the preceding verb, ὑποτάγητε.⁵⁹ ὡς resumes the instructions to respect others that were interrupted parenthetically by the reason of v. 15. The translations tend to obscure the connection of the ὡς phrases to

---

⁵⁸ Mack, *Rhetoric and the NT*, 45. Mack's citation (44–47) of a *chreia* (attributed to Isocrates) and his discussion of it provides the student an opportunity to see how a *chreia* is contrasted with its opposite: "Isocrates said that the root of education is bitter, but its fruit is sweet" (*chreia*); "for ordinary (or chance) affairs do not need toil, and they have an outcome that is entirely without pleasure; but serious affairs have the opposite outcome" (opposite).

⁵⁹ In the rhetorical subdivision that commences at v. 13, the verbs through v. 15 are ὑποτάγητε, ὑπερέχοντι (v. 13); πεμπομένοις, κακοποιῶν, ἀγαθοποιῶν (v. 14); ἐστίν, ἀγαθοποιοῦντας, and φιμοῦν (v. 15). It is unlikely that the ptcs. control the adv. phrases; each ptc. serves an obvious grammatical or rhetorical function prior to v. 16. The copula ἐστίν has τὸ θέλημα τοῦ θεοῦ as its subject and cannot logically govern the advs. One is left with either the impv. ὑποτάγητε (v. 13) or the infin. φιμοῦν (v. 15). The proximity of φιμοῦν weighs in its favor, but 'to silence someone as free people . . . as servants of God' (cf. RV, Vg) makes less sense than 'defer to . . . as free people . . . as servants of God.' The phrases ὡς ἐλεύθεροι and ὡς θεοῦ δοῦλοι ought to be connected to ὑποτάγητε. The WH text (see UBS³ punctuation apparatus at 1 Pt. 2:15, 795) expresses this understanding with parentheses surrounding v. 15.

In the translations, additions exist that do not appear in the Gk. text: "conduisez-vous en hommes libres . . . agissez en serviteurs de Dieu" (BFC); "you are slaves of no one except God, so behave like free men" (JB); "live as free men . . . live as servants of God" (NIV); "as servants of God live as free people" (NRSV); "durch Christus seid ihr frei . . . [Menschen] über deren Leben Gott verfügt" (NTHD); "live as those who are free . . . as slaves in God's service" (REB).

ὑποτάγητε in v. 13 and the rhetorical function of v. 16 as opposite.

The interpretation of Troy W. Martin

Martin[60] denies the metaphorical role of the word ἐλεύθερος in 1 Pt. 2:16. It is, says he, rather in reference to a socio-political reality, whereas he is inclined to understand the rest of the Diaspora matrix as figurative. Nevertheless, Martin applies the conditions of the Jewish Diaspora to the Christians of Asia Minor in their cultural state as ἐλεύθεροι. The concept of the free people in 1 Pt. 2:16, however, is clearly metaphorical. The antithetical ὡς θεοῦ δοῦλοι in v. 16c applies even to those who are not οἰκέται (v. 18).

The fact that the addressees are to show deference to all humans ὡς θεοῦ δοῦλοι signifies that Peter is using metaphor in v. 16. The similar paradoxical appearance of ἐλεύθερος and δοῦλος at 1 Cor. 7:22[61] indicates that both terms could be metaphorical in early Christian thinking: although one is a slave, one is (metaphorically) a free person and vice versa. The concept of 'free' versus its metaphorical opposite 'slave' is a Christian topic

---

[60] Of ἐλεύθερος, Martin states: "Because of the significant theological tradition behind this term many commentators deny it has any political connotation in this passage. However, I argue it does have political connotations in this context that contains political terms drawn from the Diaspora and discusses various groups of aliens" (*Metaphor*, 192). Here, Martin admits a social dimension to the terminology he elsewhere maintains is metaphorical! Perhaps he means that originally political terms have acquired a metaphorical significance for 1 Pt.

Michaels understands ἐλεύθεροι to be metaphorical. He perceptively comments on 2:16: "Peter has in mind not political or social freedom (which for household servants [2:18–25] and wives [3:1–6] was limited at best), but freedom in Christ from the 'ignorance' (1:14) or 'darkness' (2:9) of paganism. The freedom of the epistle's readers was the result of being 'redeemed' (ἐλυτρώθητε, 1:18) with the blood of Christ" (*1 Peter*, 128, brackets Michaels's).

[61] ὁ γὰρ ἐν κυρίῳ κληθεὶς δοῦλος ἀπελεύθερος κυρίου ἐστίν· ὁμοίως ὁ ἐλεύθερος κληθεὶς δοῦλός ἐστιν Χριστοῦ.

of contraries.[62] Since the believers are servants of God already and understand something of deference from that condition, so they are to respect all humans in the same way (particularly here, political authorities). Thus ὡς θεοῦ δοῦλοι has the functions of an analogy.

Although the metaphor of the free people is set within a context of Diaspora terms that bear a socio-cultural sense, Martin postulates a social significance where he ought to apply a metaphorical one, and applies a metaphorical sense where a socio-cultural reality is functioning. The presence of ὡς is a clue to the possible metaphorical value of ἐλεύθεροι and δοῦλοι. The ascription θεοῦ with the latter confirms it.

"A pretext for evil"

The heart of the opposite that is v. 16 is the expression καὶ μὴ ὡς ἐπικάλυμμα ἔχοντες τῆς κακίας τὴν ἐλευθερίαν. Present is a similarity in syntax and vocabulary with v. 12a in the main *propositio*. The word order is not identical, but similar in that the participle ἔχοντες in both phrases emerges within the phrase and not at the beginning or end. The two expressions are opposites that express the same idea positively (v. 12a) and negatively (v. 16b).[63] That is, the honorable is encouraged (v. 12a) and the wicked (v. 16b) is discouraged.[64]

The *colon* v. 16b thus constitutes, within the opposite (v. 16a-b), a negative contrast that serves as a bridge between the reason (v. 15) and the analogy (v. 16c). The opposite, in a judicial context, might seek to refute opposing views that either have actually been advanced or are anticipated.[65] The abuse of Christian freedom that led to antinomianism is a prevalent error often addressed in

---

[62] Cf. Gal. 4:31–5:1 for another instance of the topic. Sometimes the topic of slavery for God's/Christ's sake is in effect (see Rom. 1:1; Jas. 1:1; 2 Pt. 1:1). Cic. *Top.* 11.47–49 discusses "from contraries" as a topic.

[63] V. 16a ὡς ἐλεύθεροι is positively stated, but introduces the actual negative contrast of v. 16b. Hence I consider v. 16a as logically part of the opposite. Only with v. 16c does Peter progress to a purely positive example.

[64] Cf. the discussion of the evils for which people feel shame in Arist. *Rh.* 2.6.1383b.1–13, where morals and honor/shame intersect.

[65] Mack, *Rhetoric and the NT*, 42–43.

the New Testament.[66] Peter perhaps here addresses, either responsively or proleptically, those who use their "freedom as a pretext [ἐπικάλυμμα] for evil" (NRSV), "for a cloke of wickedness" (RV). ἐπικάλυμμα is another simile,[67] the third in this verse alone. The particular expression of libertinism that Peter perhaps has in mind is one which denies the need to recognize any authority or show deference to anyone. 'We are free,' the libertines may have said. 'Why should we be subject to anyone?'

Conclusion with Citation (v. 17)

Petrine redaction of Prov. 24:21a

Omitted from Peter's thesis is an example.[68] From the analogy at v. 16c, the writer proceeds to the conclusion within which a citation from Prov. 24:21 is embedded rather than distinctly standing apart from it. The citation occurring within a thesis is a statement or judgment by a recognized authority, philosophical or literary, that becomes a precedent in favor of the proposition.[69] In v. 17, a scriptural citation is furnished, one that would carry great authority with Peter's audience. The citation demonstrates

---

[66] E.g., 1 Cor. 5:1–13; 2 Pt. 2:1–22; 1 Jn. 1:5–2:11, 3:4–10; Jd. 4–19. Cf. 1 Pt. 2:16 with Gal. 5:13, ὑμεῖς γὰρ ἐπ᾽ ἐλευθερίᾳ ἐκλήθητε, ἀδελφοί· μόνον μὴ τὴν ἐλευθερίαν εἰς ἀφορμὴν τῇ σαρκί, ἀλλὰ διὰ τῆς ἀγάπης δουλεύετε ἀλλήλοις.

[67] ἐπικάλυμμα is a *hapax legomenon* in the NT, but κάλυμμα as "veil" appears at 2 Cor. 3:13 (lit.) and 14 (fig.) (cf. Ex. 34:33–35). Therefore, ἐπικάλυμμα may well have a figurative sense at 1 Pt. 2:16, where (if so) it means not merely "covering" (NAS) or "pretext" (NRSV), but "cloak/cloke" (AV, REB, RV) as a simile. See BAGD, 294 (s.v. "ἐπικάλυμμα"), 400–401 (s.v. "κάλυμμα") for discussion.

[68] The omission is not surprising since *Her.* 4.43.56–44.56 concedes that a great many variations are used in the pattern of a thesis. See the chart of variations compared in Watson, "James 2," 97.

[69] Mack, *Rhetoric and the NT*, 43. In a judicial speech, such an inartificial proof (along with evidence of a witness or document and a legal decision as precedent) would be utilized. Arist. *Rh.* 1.2.1355b.2; 15.1375b.13–1376a.19 (ancient witnesses, the poets and reputable persons whose judgments are famous, are more reliable than recent ones since the former cannot be corrupted); cf. Quint. *Inst. Or.* 5.1.1–6.37.

the Petrine proclivity for concluding major and minor sections with scriptural allusions or citations.[70]

However, Peter has redacted his source quite significantly. Rather than Prov. 24:21a LXX, φοβοῦ τὸν θεὸν υἱέ, καὶ βασιλέα, 1 Pt. 2:17c-d reads τὸν θεὸν φοβεῖσθε, τὸν βασιλέα τιμᾶτε. The king/emperor is no longer to be feared, but honored. Although he creates an *inclusio*[71] with v. 17a in the repetition of τιμάω, Peter's reasons for his alteration of the passage are more than stylistic. Now, φόβος is reserved for God alone and the emperor is one of the 'all,' πάντας) who are to receive honor. The sovereign is an example of the particular stations and people to be given deference by the Christians just as he was in v. 13. Honor for all takes varying expressions. One gives honor to political authorities by granting them respect: ὑποτάγητε . . . βασιλεῖ . . . ἡγεμόσιν.[72] To fellow believers (ἡ ἀδελφότης) one ought to give love (1:22) as the expression of honor. To God, of course, honor is given by fear, reverent and holy awe (1:17). Peter's alteration of Prov. 24:21 LXX makes clear this unique expression of honor to God. With v. 17, Peter has restated crisply, concisely, and captivatingly his proposition of vv. 13–14. Asyndeton[73] helps create such verbal effects.

---

[70] In 1 Pt., scriptural allusions/citations conclude the following sections: *major*—2:10; 3:10–12; *minor*—1:16; 1:24–25; 2:25; 3:6; 5:7. Dalton, *Proclamation*, 95, observes that OT citations conclude arguments/sections in 1 Pt.

[71] *Inclusio* is also called *redditio*, ἐπαναδίπλωσις, προσαπόδοσις (Quint. *Inst. Or.* 9.3.34, 43; Lausberg, *Handbuch*, 625–27). 1 Pt. 2:17a-d forms a chiasmus (i.e., an inversion pattern a-b-b-a) according to E. Bammel, "The Commands in I Peter II.17," *New Testament Studies* 11 (1964–65): 280; and Combrink, "Structure," 40–41, 56. Their view fails because it wrongly judges v. 17b (τὴν ἀδελφότητα ἀγαπᾶτε) & c (τὸν θεὸν φοβεῖσθε) to be parallel. The repetition of τιμάω in v. 17a & d is not so much due to synecdoche (aor. impv. stresses the effectiveness of the expected deference for the emperor [Bammel]) as to the function of πάντας τιμήσατε as a heading for v. 17b-d.

[72] One must note, however, that ὑποτάγητε πάσῃ ἀνθρωπίνῃ κτίσει (v. 13) is a command to defer to *all* persons (see above). Hence πάντας τιμήσατε is an equivalent exhortation (C. E. B. Cranfield, *The First Epistle of Peter* [London: SCM Press, 1950], 61, 72). One would expect the conclusion of a thesis to sum up the entire argument and the proposition.

[73] *Her.* 4.30.41.

The thesis is determined by the so-called final headings, just as Hermogenes dictated:[74] justice, expediency, possibility, and propriety. Submission to all, especially rulers at this point, is just since it is on account of the Lord (v. 13); it is expedient since it issues in praise (v. 14); deference is possible by analogy: "as servants of God" (v. 16); fitting in that it fulfills the will of God (v. 15).

The function of πάντας τιμήσατε

Despite his misappropriation of the term ἐλεύθερος in 1 Pt. 2:16, Martin[75] offers an attractive suggestion for the organization of the major section (2:11–3:12)[76] in which the image occurs. Within the second metaphor cluster (strangers-aliens) of 2:11–3:12, the first sub-unit consists of 2:11–15, a call to abstain from fleshly lusts and to submit to 'every human creature' (πάσῃ ἀνθρωπίνῃ κτίσει, v. 13). Martin understands κτίσις to refer to "creature" or "human being." Hence Peter calls for submission to every human being in the sense that aliens, as guests in a host country, had limited rights and were obligated to submit to their hosts, to everyone in their host environment. The immediate example of submission is that rendered to the emperor and to the governor (vv. 13–14). The alien's social obligation to submit to all means to 'honor everyone' (πάντας τιμήσατε, v. 17a).

The command to honor all in v. 17a (πάντας τιμήσατε, aorist imperative) then becomes the heading for v. 17b-d and the subsections to follow (2:18–25; 3:1–6; 3:7; 3:8–12). Regarding τιμήσατε, Martin states:

> Everything that follows in verse seventeen and in the remaining part of this passage [2:18–3:12] is an explication of the exhortation to honor all that is expressed by the aorist imperative τιμήσατε. The three present

---

[74] See Hermogenes, "The Elementary Exercises (προγυμνάσματα)" in Baldwin, *Medieval Rhetoric*, 37.

[75] Martin, *Metaphor*, 203–5.

[76] Martin calls this section "The Παρεπίδημος/πάροικος- Cluster, Aliens in this world" (ibid., 188–208, 272).

imperatives that follow in this verse indicate they are subsidiary ideas of the command to honor all.[77]

Martin demonstrates the predominant role that τιμήσατε assumes in his citation of Theophylact,[78] where the present imperatives in 1 Pt. 2:17 (τὴν ἀδελφότητα ἀγαπᾶτε, τὸν θεὸν φοβεῖσθε, τὸν βασιλέα τιμᾶτε) are rendered as present participles: ἀγαπῶντες . . . φοβούμενοι . . . τιμῶντες. Hence the verse, in Theophylact, is πάντας τιμήσατε, τὴν ἀδελφότητα μὲν ἀγαπῶντες, τὸν δὲ θεὸν φοβούμενοι, τὸν βασιλέα τιμῶντες ("honor all by loving the brotherhood, by fearing God, by honoring the king").[79] The subordination of the present imperatives to the aorist imperative is correct, says Martin.

The sense of NEB at 2:17 is to give πάντας τιμήσατε a summary role in relation to the following present imperatives that serve to specify the meaning of the aorist imperative: "Give due honour to everyone: love to the brotherhood, reverence to God, honour to the sovereign." The translation of REB is similar: "Give due honour to everyone: lŏve your fellow-Christians, reverence God, honour the emperor." The senses of NEB and REB[80] are also advanced by Stanley E. Porter[81] and Scot Snyder.[82] They agree that the aorist imperative πάντας τιμήσατε is a general or head statement whose meaning is specified by particular instances expressed in the present tense. A view of the tenses based on

---

[77] Ibid., 204.

[78] Theophylact, *Expositio in Epistolam Primam S. Petri, Patrologia Graeca* (ed. J. P. Migne), 125: 1216, cited by Martin, *Metaphor*, 204 n. 236.

[79] Trans. Martin, *Metaphor*, 204 n. 236, who then asserts that Theophylact "renders the present imperatives as present participles, clearly demonstrating that he considers them to be subordinate to the aorist imperative τιμήσατε."

[80] Cf. also NIV "show proper respect to everyone: love the brotherhood of believers, fear God, honor the king."

[81] Stanley E. Porter, *Idioms of the Greek New Testament*, Biblical Languages: Greek 2 (Sheffield: JSOT Press, 1992), 54, 227; D. A. Carson, ed., *Studies in Biblical Greek* (New York: Peter Lang, 1989), vol. 1, *Verbal Aspect in the Greek of the New Testament, with Reference to Tense and Mood*, by Stanley E. Porter, 351, 360.

[82] Snyder, "1 Peter 2:17," 211–15 (five objections against Porter's and Snyder's viewpoint [set forth by Grudem, *1 Peter*, 122–23, and Kelly, *Peter and Jude*, 12] are effectively nullified at 213–15).

verbal aspect suggests that the aorist imperative denotes a complete process whereas the present imperative specifies and treats a command as in progress.[83]

"Circumstantial" participles

The participles from 1 Pt. 2:18 through 3:12 are, in Martin's view, "circumstantial," not imperatival as is sometimes believed. They describe circumstances attendant to the imperative πάντας τιμήσατε.[84] In my opinion, the participles are circumstantial, but the phrase πάντας τιμήσατε κτλ does not signal a heading for 1 Pt. 2:18–3:12, as Martin believes. As an expansion of a scriptural allusion that concludes a subsection (thesis, 2:13–17), πάντας τιμήσατε κτλ has no direct verbal control over what follows it. Because the *exornatio* expands, enriches, and adorns the *propositio, ratio*, and *confirmatio*, viz. the *argumentatio* unaugmented by the *exornatio* and *conplexio*,[85] I contend that the *exornatio* 1 Pt. 2:18–3:7 and its participles are more appropriately subsumed under the *propositio* (a brief statement of the entire *argumentatio*) than under πάντας τιμήσατε (part of the *confirmatio*). Like Martin, I understand the participles in 1 Pt. 2:18–3:12 to be circumstantial.

---

[83] "On this basis the artificial distinction between a general and a specific command is circumvented. Both tenses may be used for each ... " (Porter, *Verbal Aspect*, 351). This statement appears to contradict the assertion immediately before it (351) on aorist imperatives (complete process) and present imperatives (specifying, progressional). Porter seems, however, to attempt a correction of an erroneous temporal distinction between aorist and present imperatives that identifies the former as imprecise and the latter as precise as to when the commanded action is to occur.

[84] Cf. Daube, "Participle," 482–84; Goppelt, *Der erste Petrusbrief*, 193, 214, 220–21; Eduard Lohse, "Parenesis and Kerygma in 1 Peter," in *Perspectives on First Peter*, ed. Charles H. Talbert, 45–47. See Martin, *Metaphor*, 205, who at 205 n. 238 states: "My analysis does not understand these participles [in 2:18–3:12] to be imperatival but circumstantial, describing circumstances that attend to the imperative statement *honor all*" [πάντας τιμήσατε, 17] (emphases Martin's). The distinction is fine, but important in that it shows Martin's attempt to find logical connections between 2:18–3:12 and what has come before it.

[85] *Her.* 2.18.28, exornatio est qua utimur rei honestandae et conlocupletandae causa, confirmata argumentatione.

Unlike Martin, however, I regard the participles as, not attending τιμήσατε (v. 17a) only, but the entire *argumentatio* through 2:17, whose propositional summary is ἀπέχεσθαι κτλ (2:11–12a). More specifically, I consider the participles to attend all of 1 Pt. 2:11–17 rhetorically and ἀπέχεσθαι (not τιμήσατε) grammatically.[86] Nevertheless, the verb τιμάω in v. 17 does indicate that the entire discussion of appropriate conduct for Peter's Christian audience is bound to the cultural value of honor.

Exornatio (2:18–3:7)

The "circumstantial" participle ὑποτασσόμενοι (in 2:18) expresses specifically what it means to show deference to all (2:13a) and thus honor (v. 17a). The participle ὑποτασσόμενοι and the following participles at 3:1, 7, 8–9 explicate the argument that has already been presented: 'by the observation of good works (ἐκ τῶν καλῶν ἔργων ἐποπτεύοντες, 2:12c; cf. ἀγαθοποιοῦντας, v. 15b) those presently slandering you as evildoers (ἐν ᾧ καταλαλοῦσιν ὑμῶν ὡς κακοποιῶν, v. 12b) will be led to glorify God (δοξάσωσιν τὸν θεόν, v. 12d; cf. opp. φιμοῦν τὴν τῶν ἀφρόνων ἀνθρώπων ἀγνωσίαν, v. 15b). The argument is adorned and enriched by specific examples of the kinds of good works that Peter has in mind: submission and honor to all (vv. 13, 17).

The Petrine Haustafel

With v. 18 begins the Petrine *Haustafel* (household rules). The version of the household code that Peter incorporates is similar to the other forms in the New Testament (Eph. 5:22–6:9; Col.

---

[86] Davids, *1 Peter*, 98, believes that ὑποτάγητε is the main verb that controls the ptcs. of 2:18, 3:1, and 7. Such an arrangement to me seems awkward at 2:18 and 3:1 ('submit, submitting'), although possible at 3:7 ('submit, living considerately, showing honor'). Nevertheless, Davids does not recognize the rhetorical composition of 2:11–3:12 that incorporates the ptcs. as part of the *exornatio*, expanding the proposition 'to abstain/maintaining good conduct.' Thus the ptcs. attend the construction ἀπέχεσθαι/ἔχοντες τὴν ἀναστροφὴν καλήν in 2:11–12a, and then strictly only ἀπέχεσθαι because the other propositional verb ἔχοντες is itself a circumstantial ptc., used to describe positively the kind of behavior that accompanies the abstinence expressed by the infinitive ἀπέχεσθαι.

3:18–4:1; cf. 1 Tim 6:1–2; Tit. 2:1–10),[87] yet is obviously dissimilar in that it addresses οἰκέται rather than δοῦλοι. Elliott comments on the dissimilarity:

> The specific appeal to *household* servants [οἰκέται] (rather than the more general 'slaves' [δοῦλοι]) in 1 Peter and the paradigmatic function that their instruction serves in the letter support the likelihood that the communities addressed were those of households for whom a reminder of household responsibilities would have been most appropriate.[88]

The deference that these household servants are to render is to be given ἐν παντὶ φόβῳ (a phrase that the hearers probably understood in relation to God[89]).

The Petrine *Haustafel* is not a summons to the Christian community to acculturate itself to Roman society, as Balch maintains.[90] Rather, the code is an element of Peter's ethics that agrees with the morality of the larger Greco-Roman culture. Not all of his ethical instruction does harmonize with values of society (cf. 1 Pt. 1:14–16, 18; 4:3–4). At the points of ethical disagreement, Peter's audience finds itself in conflict with the unbelieving outsiders. When Peter's values converge with those of secular

---

[87] For discussion of the common *Haustafel* tradition, see Selwyn, *St. Peter*, 426–39 (incl. civic obedience and mutual submission in the church). Research on the NT household codes (esp. that of 1 Pt.) is surveyed in Balch, *Wives*, 1–10, and Elliott, *Home*, 208–20, 231.

[88] Elliott, *Home*, 69 (emphasis Elliott's).

[89] At 1 Pt. 2:17c, the author has just said τὸν θεὸν φοβεῖσθε. See above. Since Peter probably draws from an early Christian tradition on slavery (Selwyn, *St. Peter*, 429–31, 434) that emerges in passages elsewhere, then those other passages that concern slavery may shed light on 1 Pt. 2:18. ἐν φόβῳ more than likely refers to honor that is due to God since φοβ- words are so used on other redactions of the tradition: Col. 3:22, οἱ δοῦλοι, ὑπακούετε ... φοβούμενοι τὸν κύριον (where ὁ κύριος is clearly distinguished from οἱ κατὰ σάρκα κύριοι); Eph. 6:5, οἱ δοῦλοι, ὑπακούετε τοῖς κατὰ σάρκα κυρίοις μετὰ φόβου ... ὡς τῷ Χριστῷ does not unequivocally designate the Lord as the object of φόβος. The slavery tradition appears also at 1 Tim. 6:1–2; Tit. 2:9–10.

[90] David L. Balch, "Hellenization/Acculturation in 1 Peter," in *Perspectives on First Peter*, ed. Charles H. Talbert, 81, 88–90, 97–101.; idem, *Wives*, 93, 119.

society, however, he gives them a unique Christian motivation and foundation, just as he does the dissimilar values.[91]

Thesis (2:18–25)

Once again Peter exhibits the pattern for the thesis in a short argumentative discourse that is itself set within an *argumentatio*. The thesis 1 Pt. 2:18–25 concerns the household servants within the Christian communities to which Peter writes. (The outline that he follows has already been utilized at 2:13–17.)

Proposition (v. 18)

The proposition, unlike that of v. 13, is not a statement with an imperative verb, but one with a circumstantial participle. Nevertheless, the tone is hortatory since the participle describes the

---

[91] John H. Elliott, "1 Peter, Its Situation and Strategy: A Discussion with David Balch," in *Perspectives on First Peter*, ed. Charles H. Talbert, 63, 66, 68, 71–73, who maintains, against Balch, that the strategy of 1 Pt. is to encourage an enduring, distinctive communal identity and cohesion, not assimilation.

"My contention," says Elliott, "is that nothing in 1 Peter, including its discussion of household duties, indicates an interest in promoting social assimilation. It was precisely a temptation to assimilate so as to avoid further suffering that the letter intended to counteract" (72–73).

Agreeing with Elliott is Achtemeier, "Newborn Babes," 218–22. Achtemeier says on the matter of acculturation: "if one gains any impression from the whole of 1 Peter, it would have to be that the farthest thing from the author's mind is accomodation to Hellenistic culture; 4:1–4 ought to make that clear enough. Indeed, it is not the danger of avoiding acculturation, but the temptation to lapse into acculturation that seems uppermost in our author's mind. The contrast between 'formerly' and 'now,' which recurs repeatedly throughout the letter, with the implication of lesser value of 'formerly,' combined with the equally clear indications that such 'former' conduct was precisely the sort of thing advocated by Greco-Roman culture (esp. 4:3–4), present a telling argument against Balch's interpretation" (219–20).

Balch does admit to the rejection of common pagan social patterns in 1 Pt. 1:18, 4:3–4 ("Hellinization/Acculturation," 87).

I, therefore, believe that one ought to speak of a cultural adaptation (for purposes of Christian witness) by the believing communities of 1 Pt. rather than a cultural assimilation or acculturation. The author's call for deference to those in culturally recognized positions of authority (political rulers, masters, and husbands) is a summons to submit in culturally expected ways in order to demonstrate uniquely Christian character (see further Achtemeier, "Newborn Babes," 220–22).

kind of behavior that accompanies the commanded abstinence from desires of the flesh (2:11). Indeed, it is the imperatival ἀπέχεσθαι in 2:11 that functions as the heading for the participles in 2:18; 3:1, 7, and 9.[92] An explanatory subordinate clause serves to extend the instruction to all situations: not only to masters who are good (ἀγαθοῖς) and gentle (ἐπιεικέσιν), but also to those who are harsh (σκολιοῖς)[93] is deference to be given. Peter desires that honor be given, in deference, to all.[94]

Reason (vv. 19–20)

The particle γάρ indicates that a reason for the required action is to follow. τοῦτο γὰρ χάρις identifies the advantage to

---

[92] The ptc. ὄντες is understood in association with the adjs. of 3:8, according to Selwyn, *St. Peter*, 188, who calls it a "participial imperative." Thus, ὄντες (understood) is also subsidiary to ἀπέχεσθαι (2:11a).

[93] Harsh and angry treatment of slaves from the masters' viewpoint is found in Plut. *Mor.* 458F–464D/Penguin 189–201, who counsels against an angry disposition that leads to the maltreatment of one's servants. Probably dating from the late 90's CE, (Ian Kidd, "On the Avoidance of Anger: Introduction," in *Essays,* by Plutarch, trans. Robin Waterfield [London: Penguin Books, 1992], 175), Plutarch's words are valuable for the insight that they furnish regarding slave-master relationships in the first-cent. CE. "As for ourselves," writes Plutarch, "don't we often bungle the punishment of a slave who is misbehaving, because they get frightened at our threats and at what we are saying, and run away?" (459A/Penguin 190).

With his own servants, Plutarch had learned an important lesson: it is better for the master to have them become worse by his tolerating their badness than focussing on the servants' correction in harshness and anger that would corrupt their master (459C-D/Penguin 190–91). One's adoption of a simple life-style in which one is easy to please will assure one's gentler treatment of one's slaves. Otherwise improperly prepared food, iceless drinks, shop-bought bread, plain dishes, and hard mattresses create displeasure that leads to harshness towards servants (perhaps these items caused problems for Peter's οἰκέται!). A master, therefore, must train for a contented life, not one of feeble complaining (461B-C/Penguin 194–95).

[94] Cf. 1 Tim. 6:1, ὅσοι εἰσὶν ὑπὸ ζυγὸν δοῦλοι, τοὺς ἰδίους δεσπότας πάσης τιμῆς ἀξίους ἡγείσθωσαν, ἵνα μὴ τὸ ὄνομα τοῦ θεοῦ καὶ ἡ διδασκαλία βλασφημῆται. To regard someone as worthy of honor (ἡγεῖσθαι τινὰ ἄξιον τιμῆς) seems to be the equivalent of 'to accept the authority of someone' (ὑποτάσσεσθαι τινί) in the tradition (cf. 1 Tim. 6:1 with Tit. 2:9).

be gained through giving deference to masters. "Approval," "credit," "favor," "honor," or "that which brings God's favor" are appropriate translations of χάρις at 1 Pt. 2:19–20. The endurance of griefs (ὑπόφερειν λύπας, v. 19) is virtuous and thus honorable or desirable for its own sake, according to Cicero. When one willingly endures arduous tasks for a noble and advantageous purpose, her/his *patientia* is a display of courage, one of the four parts of virtue (with wisdom, justice, and temperance). Honorable and virtuous endurance, results in gain (χάρις) for its Christian practitioners, says Peter. Thus in his rhetoric he aims at both honor and advantage. Both topics can determine the orator's strategy in deliberative rhetoric.[95]

The structure of vv. 19–20 reflects a high degree of craftsmanship by the author. The reason (v. 19) and the restatement of in (v. 20b-c) form a chiasmus[96] whose triads are interrupted by the

---

[95] For a discussion of χάρις in 1 Pt., see above. On honor and advantage in deliberative rhetoric see Cic. *Inv.* 2.51.155–56.169, where his definition of *patientia* is exactly that which Peter advocates: "Patience is a willing and sustained endurance of difficult and arduous tasks for a noble and useful end" (2.54.163).

[96] From Gk. χιασμός: an inversion, in the second set of parallel expressions, of the order followed in the first set. E.g., a-b-c-c'-b'-a' (see Bullinger, *Figures of Speech*, 374–79; Soulen, *Handbook*, 40–41). Chiasmus receives surprisingly little attention in the handbooks. At *Her.* 4.42.54, in a discussion of *expolitio* (refining), the author prescribes changes and repetitions for descanting upon an idea. One idea can be stated repetitively by equivalent terms. The example of such refining is expressed not only in synonymous phraseology, but chiastically also: "[a] No peril is so great [b] that a wise man would think it ought to be avoided [c] when the safety of the fatherland is at stake. [c'] When the lasting security of the state is in question, [b'] the man endowed with good principles will undoubtedly believe that in defence of the fortunes of the republic [a'] he ought to shun no crisis of life [then comes the epilogue] and he will ever persist in the determiniation eagerly to enter, for the fatherland, any combat, however great the peril to life."

Cicero uses chiasmus at one point in his correspondence as a 'Homeric' device (*Att.* 1.16.1): "I shall answer you Homerically [ὡμηρικῶς], cart before horse" (Cicero, *Selected Letters*, trans. D. R. Shackleton Bailey, Penguin Classics [New York: Penguin Books, n.d.], 42). That is, Cicero answers two introductory questions in the reverse order in which he poses them. Cf. Odysseus's seven questions and his mother's answers in Homer, *The Odyssey*, Penguin Classics, pp. 175–76.

contrary (a rhetorical question) that opposes them.[97] The chiastic structure is most apparent in the Greek:[98]

In his book, *Chiasmus in the New Testament: A Study in Formgeschichte* (Chapel Hill: University of North Carolina Press, 1942), Nils Wilhelm Lund suggests a Hebrew origin for the inversion of word order in Homer (28–29, 130–31). He puts forth (43–44) some OT examples of chiasmus that evince an arrangement similar to that of 1 Pt. 2:19–20, i.e., positive statements chiastically arranged around a negative central section (Isa. 60:1–3) or around a central section of dissimilar subject matter to and from which the chiastic material shifts (Gen. 12:16).

Although Lund cites no passages from 1 or 2 Pt., he adduces (202–3) one example of chiasmus from Eph. 6:5–7, a passage that incorporates traditional material also found in 1 Pt. 2:18–21. I reproduce here Lund's text, emphases, and structure, but add the alphabetical line identifications (Lund's sec. A, vv. 8–9, I omit):

a   *Servants*, be obedient to them that according to the flesh are your *lords*,
b   With fear and trembling,
c   In singleness of your heart,
d   As unto Christ;
e   Not in the way of eye service,
       As men-pleasers,
d'   But as servants of Christ,
c'   Doing the will of God from the soul,
b'   With good will
a'   *Doing service* as unto the *Lord* and not unto men.

The middle negative explanatory phrase "e" is comparable to 1 Pt. 2:20a in its function within the chiasmus. In 1 Pt. 2:19–20, the structure is a-b-c CONTRARY c'-b'-a'; in Eph. 6:5–7, the pattern is a-b-c-d CONTRARY (e) d'-c'-b'-a'.

[97] See Combrink, "Structure," 41, 56; Michaels, *1 Peter*, 142.

[98] The pattern is obscured in NRSV. John H. Elliott, "Backward and Forward 'In His Steps': Folowing Jesus from Rome to Raymond and Beyond. The Tradition, Redaction, and Reception of 1 Peter 2:18–25," in *Discipleship in the New Testament*, ed. Fernando F. Segovia (Philadelphia: Fortress Press, 1985), 189, 203 n. 7, notes a chiastic structure, featuring an *inclusio* with χάρις, at vv. 19–20:

   A. "For one is approved (τοῦτο γὰρ χάρις) if, mindful of God"
     B. "If when you do wrong" (εἰ ἁμαρτάνοντες)
     B'. "If when you do right" (εἰ ἀγαθοποιοῦντες)
   A'. "you have God's approval" (τοῦτο χάρις παρὰ θεῷ)

Elliott's scheme, however, is incomplete. It gives no recognition to the duplication of πάσχω and ignores the fact that ὑποφέρω and ὑπομένω are synonymous and parallel in the chiasmus. I contend also that πάσχων ἀδίκως and ἀγαθοποιοῦντες καὶ πάσχοντες are parallel.

v. 19   a   τοῦτο γὰρ χάρις
         b   εἰ διὰ συνείδησιν θεοῦ ὑποφέρει τις λύπας
         c   πάσχων ἀδίκως

v. 20   CONTRARY
      ποῖον γὰρ κλέος εἰ ἁμαρτάνοντες
      καὶ κολαφιζόμενοι ὑπομενεῖτε;

         c'   ἀλλ' εἰ ἀγαθοποιοῦντες καὶ πάσχοντες
         b'   ὑπομενεῖτε,
         a'   τοῦτο χάρις παρὰ θεῷ

A repetition of identical words occurs in "a" and "a'" (χάρις), and in "c" and "c'" (πάσχω). The two verbs ὑποφέρω and ὑπομένω ("b" and "b'" respectively) are synonymous. The appearance of synonymous verbs avoids an unaesthetically excessive use of transplacement, the frequent reintroduction of the same word.[99] In the same manner a similar excess is avoided by the use of κλέος[100] in the contrary instead of χάρις. The favor of God is certain to follow endurance in the face of unjust suffering inflicted by the harsh masters.

A chiastic arrangement a-b-c-b'-a' in vv. 18–20 is observed by Maurice Carrez, "L'esclavage dans la première epître de Pierre," in *Études sur la première lettre de Pierre*, Lectio Divina no. 102 (Paris: Cerf, 1980), 207–8, 216. According to Carrez, the chiasmus is formed as follows:

a   18. Vous, gens de (la) maison, soyez soumis
        avec un respect total à vos maîtres,
b   non seulement aux bons et aux amicaux
        mais aussi aux acariâtres.
  c 19. Car e'est une grâce,
        si, par délicatesse pour Dieu,
        on supporte des peines
        en souffrant injustement.
b' 20. Quelle réputation, si c'est en commettant une
        faute que vous supportez des coups?
a'   Mais si, ayant bien agi,
        vous supportez la souffrance,
        c'est une grâce aux yeux de Dieu!

The rationale for the central place of c is that it is in the third person, whereas a, b, b', a' are in the second. The third person, however, merely personalizes an otherwise parallel affirmation, ὑπομενεῖτε. I contend further that my scheme joins the truer parallels in vv. 19–20 than does that of Carrez.

[99] *Her.* 4.12.18, 14.20.

[100] See above on κλέος and χάρις as synonyms.

Hence in vv. 19–20 the reason for the thesis proposition occurs as reason—contrary—restatement in a chiasmus. Peter endeavors in this thesis to show the way to honor for the mistreated slaves in their exchanges with harsh masters. Despite abusive and dishonorable treatment, the slaves can emerge honorably by endurance. The manner in which that endurance is practiced is made clear by means of a very powerful and persuasive example.

Example (vv. 21–24b)

The historical exemplum

Peter omits an analogy from his thesis on οἰκέται, but in support of his proposition furnishes a lengthy example[101] on the suffering Christ.[102] In the thesis, the example typically is drawn from history, although not all rhetorical examples are. Fable, myth, nature, and history serve as sources for the rhetorical example which is used inductively to point to a general conclusion. The example of the suffering Christ is an instance of the *res gesta*, an *exemplum* that is an artificial proof in that its relation to the fact of the reason is one of independence—it does not stand in immediate connection with the reason that it is enlisted to prove. The art of the rhetor draws the relationship between the *exemplum* and the reason. Thus it is an artificial proof.

In the present Petrine thesis, the relationship of the suffering Christ to the mistreated slaves is not self-apparent. The appeal to Christ's example of endurance in suffering is based upon the hymn of Christ's atoning death. In 1 Pt. 2:21–25, the emphasis is no longer on his vicarious sacrifice, but on the exemplary value of

---

[101] For my brief discussion of the *exemplum*/παράδειγμα I borrow from Arist. *Rh.* 1.2.1357b.25–37; *Her.* 1.8.13, 4.49.62; Quint. *Inst. Or.* 5.11.1, 3–5, 9, 17, 19, 36–37; Kennedy, *NT Interpretation*, 16; Lausberg, *Handbuch*, 410–26; Mack, *Rhetoric in the NT*, 46.

[102] Peter's debt to hymnic material in 1 Pt. 2:21–25 is widely recognized. The source obviously incorporates elements of Isa. 53. For discussion, see Bultmann, "Liedfragmente," 13–14 (for his reconstruction of the original hymn); Elliott, "Backward and Forward," 190–91, 204–5. Cf. Michaels, *1 Peter*, 136–37, for a dissenting view (i.e., vv. 21–25 is a midrash on Isa. 53:4–12).

that suffering. "Thus," affirms Lohse, "the kerygmatic accent of the hymn has been thrust aside in favor of the parenesis."[103] The *exemplum* of Christ in his passion is independent of the matter of grace awarded to the slaves through their endurance. Thus Peter, by his literary art, must forge a connection between the experience of Christ and that of the οἰκέται.

The historical *exemplum* (the example of vv. 21–23 is such a type) is more credible than either the poetic *exemplum*[104] or the *exemplum verisimile*[105] since the historical *exemplum* rests on truth. It is also the most frequently employed kind of *exemplum* in oratory.

In using the *exemplum*, the rhetor must establish its relationship to the *causa* (reason). The means by which the rhetor accomplishes that establishment is the *inductio*. That is to say, from things that are not doubted the certainty of something doubted is proven by its similarity to them. In 1 Pt. 2:18–25, the similarity of Christ's endurance in suffering to that required of the οἰκέται is established by an *exemplum impar*, specifically, an *exemplum ex maiore ad minus ductum*[106] (example from the greater to the lesser). Christ, the greater, is an example for his followers who are of lesser standing. The example of Christ's endurance, whose factuality, manner, and benefit are established, serves to argue the certain advantage (honor) of the slaves if they also endure.

Christ as ὑπογραμμός. Of course, the example (ὑπογραμμός) of endurance[107] par excellence for the slaves is Christ. His

---

[103] Lohse, "Parenesis," 58. For this reason, ὑμῖν ὑπολιμπάνων ὑπογραμμὸν ἵνα ἐπακολουθήσητε τοῖς ἴχνεσιν αὐτοῦ (v. 21c) must not have belonged to the original hymn.

[104] The poetic *exemplum* has two grades: the superior is the *poetica fabula*, the stuff of the tragedies. Neither it nor the inferior *fabella* contains truth or verisimilitude. The inferior grade, the *fabella*, is directed to the masses; Aesop's fables fall under this category. See *Her.* 1.8.13; Quint. *Inst. Or.* 5.11.19–21; Lausberg, *Handbuch*, 413.

[105] The *exemplum verisimile* is the stuff of comedy, resembles life, and is probable (*argumentum, Her.* 1.8.13).

[106] Quint. *Inst. Or.* 5.11.9; Lausberg, *Handbuch*, 420.

[107] With ὑπολιμπάνω, ὑπογραμμός is a NT *hapax legomenon*. It refers to the 'example' or 'pattern' of letters in ancient copybooks that were to be traced or copied by the student. The word is also used in reference to an

authority and prestige in the Christian communities of Asia Minor is indisputable (cf. 1:18–21). Therefore, his example has overwhelming importance and weight in the church.[108] Christ's passion is analogous to the suffering of the οἰκέται in that he had to submit to unjust suffering in order to fulfill God's purpose (vv. 21, 24), just as they must endure suffering to fulfill God's will and so that which is honorable as Christians. The verb πάσχω refers to both Christ (vv. 21, 23) and to the slaves (vv. 19, 20). Thus their experience is linked;[109] what Christ did the hearers are called to do also.[110] Christ's suffering and endurance are the ὑπογραμμός

artist's design in outline that he leaves for his pupils to fill in. Peter's intention is advanced more vividly with ὑπογραμμός than if he had used παράδειγμα or the synonymous ὑπόδειγμα. The sense is that Christ has left an outline or pattern that Christians are to follow: that of endurance in suffering. F F. Bruce, "ὑπογραμμός," *NIDNTT* 2:291; Selwyn, *St. Peter*, 92.

In later Christian literature, ὑπογραμμός refers to Christ's example of humility (1 Clem. 16:17, in the context of Isa. 53, cited vv. 3–14) and of endurance (Pol. Phil. 8:1–2). Polycarp appears to have properly understood the thrust of Peter's argument and the purpose for the example at 1 Pt. 2:21–23. Within a context replete with language from 1 Pt., πάντα ὑπέμεινεν signifies for Polycarp the endurance of the cross, Christ's innocent and guileless behavior (8:1). The ὑπογραμμός of 8:2 is the imitation of his endurance in suffering (μιμηταὶ οὖν γενώμεθα τῆς ὑπομονῆς [αὐτοῦ], καὶ ἐὰν πάσχομεν διὰ τὸ ὄνομα αὐτοῦ, δοξάζωμεν αὐτόν. τοῦτον γὰρ ἡμῖν τὸν ὑπογραμμὸν ἔθηκε δι᾽ ἑαυτοῦ, καὶ ἡμεῖς τοῦτο ἐπιστεύσαμεν). So also in 1 Pt. 2:21, the ὑπογραμμός is endurance in suffering. For endurance Peter has already argued in vv. 19–20; endurance results in honor (χάρις) from God. See discussion in Elliott, "Backward and Forward."

[108] The authority of the one adduced in examples is important and ought to be considered by the rhetor in deliberative oratory (Quint. *Inst. Or.* 3.8.36).

[109] Elliott, "Backward and Forward," 190, who stresses the bond of innocent suffering that unites believers and Christ and that is apparent throughout 1 Pt. I, however, understand Peter's main emphasis to be *endurance* in suffering. The example that the οἰκέται are to follow is their Lord's endurance as it is expressed in non-retaliatory conduct. Likewise, the servants are to endure their suffering (harsh treatment despite their good behavior) by giving deference to their masters (v. 18).

[110] εἰς τοῦτο γὰρ ἐκλήθητε has as its antecedent that which has immediately preceded: endurance despite suffering for/while doing good. Such endurance is the expression of deference to harsh masters (v. 18) (so Elliott, "Backward and Forward," 206 n. 29).

that he leaves his followers; he intends that they follow in his footsteps (ἵνα ἐπακολουθήσητε τοῖς ἴχνεσιν αὐτοῦ).[111] The paradigm of endurance in suffering is elucidated by means of two sets of cola.[112] The first set, v. 22, is a quotation from Isa. 53:9. The second colon of the set defines the first in synonymy.[113] Christ was not culpable of sin (ἁμαρτία), that is, of deceit or treachery (δόλος). Peter's interest in the Isaianic material may be that it points out Christ's innocent suffering and his blamelessness regarding every kind of evil speech.[114] His followers are likewise to eschew deceptive, treacherous, and abusive (cf. v. 23) speech.

Verse 23a-b contains a set of two cola that are two contrasts: ὃς λοιδορούμενος οὐκ ἀντελοιδόρει, πάσχων οὐκ ἠπείλει. The first colon (v. 23a) is defined by the second (v. 23b) by way of synonymy. By introducing πάσχων οὐκ ἠπείλει Peter connects the suffering of Christ with that of the οἰκέτης in v. 19, where one is πάσχων ἀδίκως. The servants can take comfort in the fact that, as they suffer, so did Christ suffer. They are now to follow his example of non-retaliation in suffering: despite cruel treatment from their masters or from the hostile pagan populace generally, abuse must not be answered with abuse; suffering must not engender threats. The repetition of the pronoun ὃς (vv. 22, 23, 24a; οὗ in v. 24c) is the stylistic figure *epanaphora* in which closely successive phrases, expressing like or different ideas, are begun by the same word.[115] The relative clauses and the participles λοιδορούμενος, πάσχων, κρίνοντι, and ἀπογενόμενοι in vv. 23–24 are characteristic of creedal formulae.[116] Legal language of

---

[111] That a primitive pre-Petrine and pre-synoptic tradition on discipleship is present at 2:21 is noted by Elliott, "Backward and Forward," 195–96. Cf. Mk. 1:16–20, 2:14, 8:27–37 with the notion of following and the suffering of those who do follow, elements that emerge in 1 Pt.

[112] *Her.* 4.19.26.

[113] *Interpretatio, Her.* 4.28.38, where the examples demonstrate replacements not just of single words, but of entire phrases.

[114] Cf. Michaels, *1 Peter*, 145.

[115] *Repetitio,* Her. 4.13.19.

[116] Cf. Acts 4:10; Rom. 1:3; Stauffer, *NT Theology*, 339.

appeal and vindication characterizes the construction παρεδίδου δὲ τῷ κρίνοντι δικαίως. The verb παραδίδωμι in association with κρίνω here has the the sense of handing over to someone's custody for trial or judgment.[117] Jesus does not retaliate to defend or vindicate himself and his honor. Rather, he entrusts himself and his honor to the one who is certain to bring an impartial and fair verdict (1 Pt. 1:17). Since Christ is innocent he can expect a favorable verdict from the one who judges righteously. So, too, can the οἰκέται expect a decision that exonerates them. To follow Christ's example involves awaiting God's just and fair declaration of their honor, despite the fact now that they are suffering unjustly (ἀδίκως).

A pun on φέρω *at v. 24a.* A further bond between Christ's suffering and that of the household slaves is established by a pun on φέρω in v. 24. The word-play is like ἀντανάκλασις, a figure by which two different meanings of the same word arise, a change occurs within a word to create a pun, or a verb's meaning is reversed by a change in its prepositional prefix.[118] In vv. 19 and 24, the verb φέρω undergoes an alteration in meaning as the

---

[117] On this sense of παραδίδωμι τινὰ τινί as a t.t. of the police and courts cf. Mk. 10:33, 15:1; Lk. 20:20, 22:4; Jn. 18:30; BAGD, 614–15 (s.v. "παραδίδωμι"). Similar to 1 Pt. 2:23c is (Χριστός) παρέδωκεν ἑαυτὸν ὑπὲρ ἡμῶν προφορὰν καὶ θυσίαν τῷ θεῷ, Eph. 5:2. The reflexive pronoun is understood at 1 Pt. 2:23 where Jesus "handed himself and his cause over to the Father who judges righteously" (Robertson, *The General Epistles*, 105–6).

Cf. κρίνω as a legal t.t. (human court) in Jn. 18:31; Acts 13:27, 23:3, 25:10, 26:6; (divine court) 1 Pt. 1:17, 4:5–6.

[118] According to Quint. *Inst. Or.* 9.3.68–77. However, since Quintilian's examples all involve changes of words within the same sentence, the Petrine alteration of φέρω (ὑποφέρει, v. 19b; ἀνήνεγκεν, v. 24) is not strictly *antanaklasis*. Bullinger (*Figures of Speech*, 286) stipulates that for *antanaklasis* to occur, the word change must be within the same sentence. The repetition of φέρω in vv. 19 and 24 could be classified as *polyptoton* (repetition of the same verb in different tenses), but the punning element tends to be absent from NT examples of this figure whereas it is present in 1 Pt. 2:19, 24 (Bullinger, *Figures of Speech*, 267–85, on *polyptoton*). Peter may be taking liberty in the exercise of his word-play, perhaps bending the rules of style in order to achieve his effect.

author attaches two different prefixes to it: ὑπο- in v. 19 and ἀνα-in v. 24.[119] Thus a Christian οἰκέτης "bears up under the pain of unjust suffering" (NIV), whereas Christ "bore our sins in his body on the tree" (NIV), or "brought our sins in his body to the cross" (as a sacrifice).[120] The pun unites the experiences of both the believers and Christ. It emphasizes to the audience that Christ has endured, or carried, suffering as they now do. Christ's suffering is different in that it atones for sin (ἵνα ταῖς ἁμαρτίαις ἀπογενόμενοι τῇ δικαιοσύνῃ ζήσωμεν, v. 24b) and the suffering of the slaves does not. However, the experience of suffering verbal abuse is common to them and Christ: as he suffered verbal abuse (v. 23; cf. 3:8), so do the slaves with the entire congregations of believers (2:12; 3:9, 16; 4:4, 14; cf. 3:14, 17; 4:1, 12–13, 16, 19, 5:9, 10). The unjust treatment of verbal abuse is a major source of shame for the hearers of 1 Peter.

Granted, the two φέρω verbs in word-play are not visually parallel: ὑποφέρει is in the present tense and ἀνήνεγκεν is an aorist. However, visual or audile correspondence is not necessary for a connection of ideas to exist. For example, an anglophone understands the different forms 'goes' and 'went' to refer to the same word ('go') and mentally joins them when hearing them. I contend a similar phenomenon may be at work in 1 Peter. The irregularity in the aorist form of φέρω does not obscure the connection with its present-tense counterpart in v. 19.

Petrine redaction in v. 24a. Peter has evidently embellished his Isaianic/hymnic source at v. 24a. Whereas Isa. 53:12e LXX reads

---

[119] Isa. 53:11e LXX, καὶ τὰς ἁμαρτίας αὐτῶν αὐτὸς ἀνοίσει (fut. of ἀναφέρω); v. 12e, καὶ αὐτὸς ἁμαρτίας πολλῶν ἀνήνεγκε (aor. of ἀναφέρω). Cf. v. 4a, οὗτος τὰς ἁμαρτίας ἡμῶν φέρει (pres. of φέρω).

[120] BAGD, 63 (s.v. "ἀναφέρω"); cf. NEB, NRSVmg. In 1 Pt. 2:24 appears the phrase ὃς τὰς ἁμαρτίας ἡμῶν αὐτὸς ἀνήνεγκεν ἐν τῷ σώματι αὐτοῦ ἐπὶ τὸ ξύλον. Two options are available in the translation of these words into English. NIV has "he himself bore our sins in his body on the tree." "In his own person he carried our sins to the gallows" is the rendering of NEB. The preposition ἐπί could have a reference to location ("on") or to motion toward ("to"). How one chooses to translate makes little difference. For a full discussion see Murray J. Harris, "Appendix: Prepositions and Theology in the Greek New Testament," *NIDNTT* 3:195–96.

(καὶ) αὐτὸς ἁμαρτίας πολλῶν ἀνήνεγκε, Peter has ὃς τὰς ἁμαρτίας ἡμῶν αὐτὸς ἀνήνεγκεν ἐν τῷ σώματι αὐτοῦ ἐπὶ τὸ ξύλον. Isaiah's πολλῶν becomes the typically hymnic ἡμῶν. The addition[121] of ὅς intensifies the subject of the verb: "he himself bore our sins." Furthermore, Peter adds (or retains from his hymnic source) two contiguous prepositional phrases that do not appear in Isaiah: ἐν τῷ σώματι αὐτοῦ ἐπὶ τὸ ξύλον. With the supplementary ὅς and the prepositional phrases, Peter employs a *demonstratio* (ἐνάργεια), an ocular demonstration by which an event is described so vividly by the rhetor that the audience can almost see it. This figure of thought is useful for amplification and arousal of pity.[122] Peter brings the crucified Christ before the very eyes of his hearers and awakes in them pity for the Christ who suffered for them and a determination to follow his example.

The Petrine language echoes the early Christian saying that Jesus, in his execution, was hung on a tree, ξύλον (Acts 5:30, 10:39; Gal. 3:13 [from Dt. 21:23]; cf. Barn. 5:13, "suffer on the tree").[123] The word ξύλον recalls the utter contemptibility and

---

[121] The addition of the article τάς to ἁμαρτίας is inconsequential.

[122] *Her.* 4.55.68–69; Quint. *Inst. Or.* 8.3.61–71 (*repraesentatio*), 9.2.40–44 (*sub oculos subiectio*); Cic. *De Or.* 3.53.202 (*sub aspectum paene subiectio*).
Selwyn remarks on the vividness that Peter's language lends to the thought of Jesus' sacrifice: "The dominant implication in all these passages (including also Deut. xxi. 22, 23) is that of *criminality*; and the atmosphere of this Petrine text is dramatic and spectacular rather than doctrinal. The words are such as we might expect if they came from one who witnessed Christ's progress, with a malefactor on either hand, to Calvary; and this would be so whether they were part of a hymn or were dictated by St. Peter himself. They portray 'the Lamb of God which taketh away the sin of the world' of Jn. i.29, and they give the idea a precision of time (aorist ἀνήνεγκεν), place (ἐπὶ τὸ ξύλον), and personal reference (plural τὰς ἁμαρτίας, and ἡμῶν) which bespeaks a primitive date" (*St. Peter*, 181).
Cf. Betz, *Galatians*, 131, for his comment on Gal. 3:1c οἷς κατ' ὀφθαλμοὺς Ἰησοῦς Χριστὸς προεγράφη ἐσταυρωμένος. Betz suggests that the phrase describes Paul's oratorical effort to preach the gospel with the vividness that *demonstratio* lends to a presentation.

[123] Peter is (co-)speaker in these passages. For discussion on the relation of 1 Pt. to the Petrine speeches of Acts and the authenticity of the latter, see Selwyn, *St. Peter*, 33–36, 180–81.

shamefulness of Christ's death, that of a malefactor cursed by God (Dt. 21:23; Gal. 3:13).[124] The word ξύλον itself, a part of pre-Petrine Christian nomenclature, constitutes a trope in the author's thesis. Specifically, ξύλον is a synecdoche, a figure in which a whole stands for the part of vice versa. Here it is the whole (tree) that represents the cross, a part that is made from it.[125]

The entire vivid presentation of Christ in his sacrifice in v. 24a awakens pity for the one whose shameful death is for their sakes. The hearers determine to follow Christ's example and endure shameful treatment, for by their endurance they gain God's approving honor. The final clause ἵνα ταῖς ἁμαρτίαις ἀπογενόμενοι τῇ δικαιοσύνῃ ζήσωμεν identifies the purpose[126] of Christ's bearing of sins on the cross, for his endurance of suffering. To follow Christ's example of suffering means to get away from or die to sins and then live for righteousness. In the context of the thesis, the ἁμαρτίαι to which the readers are to die are sins retaliatory and verbal (2:22–23), particularly deceitful speech, "insults" (JB), and "threats" (REB).

Death as public identification with Jesus (bearing one's cross) and renunciation of one's past life of sin is a Christian *topos* that elsewhere comes to expression in texts on discipleship[127] and in baptismal contexts[128] where it is paired with the new life and resurrection. Dying to sins is attendant to following (ἀκολουθεῖν)

---

[124] Cf. Burghard Siede (on ξύλον, 390) in Burghard Siede, Egon Brandenburger, and Colin Brown, "Cross, Wood, Tree," *NIDNTT*, 1:389–405. Martin Hengel, *Crucifixion in the Ancient World and the Folly of the Message of the Cross*, trans. John Bowden (Philadelphia: Fortress Press, 1977), 7–10, 86–90, expresses well the shame of crucifixion.

[125] Lat. *intellectio. Her.* 4.33.44–45.

[126] The ἵνα clause with the 1st aor. act. subj. ζήσωμεν is identified as a purpose clause by Robertson, *The General Epistles*, 106. Thus the clause does not indicate mere consequence, but intention in Christ's act of bearing sins.

[127] Mk. 8:34–35 and parallels. Q: Mt. 10:38; Lk. 14:27. See discussion of the cross-bearing sayings by Brandenburger and Brown in Siede, *et illi* "Cross," 402–4.

[128] Rom. 6:1–7 (cf. vv. 8–23); Col. 2:12–13, 3:1–5. Cf. also Gal. 2:20; 6:14; Selwyn, *St. Peter*, 389–93.

Jesus in pre-synoptic and pre-Petrine tradition. The force of Christ's example of suffering is the motivation for his people to follow him (2:21) and to die for/with him and to sins.

Citation (v. 24c) and Conclusion (v. 25)

"By his wounds you have been healed." An Old Testament citation clinches the argument from Christ's example. οὗ τῷ μώλωπι ἰάθητε (v. 24c) is a phrase from Isa. 53:5. Other language from the Suffering Servant passage has appeared, but this statement comes at the place where an authoritative citation would be introduced by the rhetor to enhance the weight of the argument by example just given.[129] The citation has likely undergone some revision by Peter. The original form of the LXX used by Peter cannot with certainty be recovered, but apparently either he or a previous hymnic redactor has changed the pronominal features of Isa. 53:5d in order to make a relative clause that complements the relative clauses of 1 Pt. 2:22, 23, and 24a. Furthermore, the first person of the verb has given way to the second person. Thus τῷ μώλωπι <u>αὐτοῦ</u> ἡμεῖς ἰάθημεν[130] becomes <u>οὗ</u> τῷ μώλωπι ἰάθητε.

Although the hymnic tradition may have preserved the Isaianic first person, Peter switches to his customary second-person form of address in v. 24c. As he reflects on the pagan past of his readers (cf. 1:14, 18; 2:9–10; 4:3), the second person is appropriate: ἰάθητε, "you have been healed"; ἦτε γὰρ ὡς πρόβατα πλανώμενοι, "for you were going astray like sheep" (v. 25a), ἀλλὰ ἐπεστράφητε νῦν, "but now you have returned" (v. 25b). Peter, the Jew, distances himself from his readers in these discussions of their Gentile past by using the second person. The Isaianic first

---

[129] Mack, *Rhetoric and the NT*, 42–44, 46.

[130] 1 Clem. 16:3–14, an exact quotation from Isa. 53:1–12, indicates that Peter may have known the OT passage in a form close to the present LXX since 1 Clem. (originating from Rome as does 1 Pt.) knows it. Michaels, *1 Peter*, 136. Another explanation for the similarity of 1 Pt. to the LXX is that the hymnic material that Peter utilizes presumes a form of it close to our text. Michaels denies a hymnic source for 1 Pt. 2:21–25. See 140 n. 131 below.

person would have been inappropriate for him.[131] Additionally, the second person, by its more direct appeal to the hearers, fosters positive pathos for their experience as Christians and thus intensifies their resolve to follow the example of Christ.

Metonymy and metaphor. The citation, an inartificial proof, is not of Peter's invention, but its stylistic features as part of his discourse deserve attention. Two tropes give this citation its power. οὗ τῷ μώλωπι is a metonymy: μώλοψ (bruise, wounds) suggests the entire experience of Christ's suffering and death which constitute his redemptive sacrifice (v. 24a-c). His "wounds" are a metonymy of cause that stands for effect.[132] Christ's wounds brought about the effect of his death as its cause. The sacrificial death of Christ, as identified by his wounds, is the healing medium for the community. ἰάθητε is a metaphor[133] for deliverance from sin. By the metaphor sins are regarded as wounds or disease whose cure is effected by their transmission to another, Christ, whose bodily death annuls sins.[134]

"For you were going astray like sheep." The conclusion (v. 25) adds a further allusion to Isa. 53 in its appellation of the hearers as formerly wandering sheep (53:6) who have now returned to their souls' shepherd and guardian. The return of the slaves to Christ

---

[131] Michaels, *1 Peter*, 136–37, who, incidentally, denies the presence of hymnic tradition at 1 Pt. 2:21–25. Much of the passage is a midrash or paraphrase on Isa. 53:4–12 LXX according to Michaels who, I believe, wrongly overlooks the distinct hymnic style of vv. 21–25 over against its context. At any rate, since the rhetorical design in 1 Pt. 2:21–25 is my concern, of secondary importance is the identity of the redactor(s) who give(s) the passage its present form, whether Isaiah, Peter or (a) hymnic redactor(s).

[132] *Her.* 4.32.43; cf. Quint. *Inst. Or.* 8.6.23–27.

[133] Lat. *translatio*, that "occurs when a word applying to one thing is transferred to another, because the similarity seems to justify this transference." *Her.* 4.34.45.

[134] Heb. 12:13(?); Jas. 5:16; 2 Clem. 9:7; Herm. *Sim.* 9.28.5. Isa. 53:5, τῷ μώλωπι αὐτοῦ ἡμεῖς ἰάθησεν → 1 Clem. 16:5; Barn. 5:2; BAGD, 368 (s.v. "ἰάομαι"); Siede, "Cross," 390. Mt. 8:17 shows how the concepts of sin and disease could be interchangeable in early Christian thought.

(probable reference of ποιμήν and ἐπίσκοπος)[135] signifies that they are now in his care; he will provide them with protection and the power of endurance. The fact that the slaves have returned to the shepherd who died for them signifies that Christ's purpose in suffering ("for you") has been achieved—he has been honored, he and his cause which were committed to God have been vindicated (v. 23c). Hence the suffering believers can expect that, by following their shepherd, Christ, they shall be honored as well. After all, their call to follow (ἐπακολουθέω, v. 21) means to be led by a loving shepherd.

The honor that Christ has received is indicated by the epithets[136] ποιμήν and ἐπίσκοπος that apply to YHWH in the LXX, or, in the case of ποιμήν, to the Messiah. In v. 25 they stand in hendiadys[137] and thus denote 'guardian shepherd' or 'watchful shepherd.' These appellations, suggesting Christ's honorable (or even divine) status after he endured innocent suffering, signify for the readers that they too can anticipate their exoneration to an exalted status.

Simile and typology in v. 25. The simile[138] ὡς πρόβατα expands the Isaianic frame of reference for the passage to incorporate now, not only Christ as the bearer of sins, but also the aberrant 'sheep' for whose salvation he gave himself up. The particle γάρ

---

[135] God could be the reference of "shepherd" and "guardian." However, in light of the reference to the "chief shepherd" (ἀρχιποίμην) who brings the crown of glory in 1 Pt. 5:4 and because Peter regards Christ as the one who will come to honor his followers (1:7, 13; 4:13), Christ is probably intended in 2:25. BAGD, 13 (s.v. "ἀρχιποίμην"), 684 (s.v. "ποιμήν").

[136] Epithets constitute a form of antonomasia, a trope which substitutes a name or description of actions for a proper name. See Quint. *Inst. Or.* 8.6.29–30. For YHWH as ποιμήν in the LXX, cf. Ps. 22(23) (κύριος ποιμαίνει με); 77(78):52; 79(80):1; Isa. 40:11); for the Messiah as ποιμήν cf. Ezek. 34:23, 37:24; Erich Beyreuther, "Shepherd: ποιμήν," *NIDNTT*, 3:565–66. For God as ἐπίσκοπος in the LXX, cf. Job 20:29; Wisd. 1:6; BAGD, 299 (s.v. "ἐπίσκοπος").

[137] Hendiadys is a picturesque figure by which two words are used, but only one thing or idea is intended (Bullinger, *Figures of Speech*, 657).

[138] *Her.* 4.49.62.

in v. 25a signals an enthymeme that has been constructed from a syllogism formed from two originally distinct metaphors in Isa. 53:5–6.[139] Peter mixes them in his construction in order to smooth the transition from the citation (v. 24c) to the conclusion (v. 25). Behind vv. 24c–25 stands the syllogism:

Major Premise: Wandering sheep who return to their shepherd are healed by Christ's wounds.

Minor Premise: You were wandering sheep who have returned to your shepherd.

Conclusion: By Christ's wounds you are healed.

Thus the enthymeme reads: "By his wounds you have been healed. For you were going astray like sheep, but now you have returned to the shepherd and guardian of your souls" (vv. 24c–25).

The extended metaphor of Isaiah's Suffering Servant[140] is another instance of Petrine typology (cf. 1 Pt. 2:4–10; 3:20–21)[141] that, in v. 25, serves as a proof by way of the supernatural authority that is derived from oracles.[142] For the early Christians,

---

[139] Note the full stop (with no γάρ) at Isa. 53:5/6: τῷ μώλωπι αὐτοῦ ἡμεῖς ἰάθημεν. πάντες ὡς πρόβατα . . .

[140] Although παῖς is not found in 1 Pt., the influence of the entire Servant Song of Isa. 52:13–53:12 is evident in the NT tradition associated with Peter (Acts 3:13, 26; 4:27, 30; 1 Pt. 2:21–25, 3:18). Thus the concept of Jesus as the Suffering Servant likely influenced Peter's understanding of Jesus and his mission to a great degree. See R. T. France, "Servant of the Lord," *NBD*, 1093.

[141] See 88 above and 182–83 below.

[142] Auctoritas deorum, quae est ex responsis, Quint. *Inst. Or.* 5.11.42–44. Joan Liversidge, *Everyday Life in the Roman Empire* (London: B. T. Batsford, 1976; New York: G. P. Putnam's Sons, 1976), 203–4, explains briefly how oracles were sought at one site in the province of Asia: "Diana's twin brother Apollo had several important temples in Asia to which worshippers came to consult oracles. At Claros, near Notion, not far from Ephesus, there was a holy place in a wood by a sacred spring mentioned by Homer. A Hellenistic temple was approached by a processional way lined by statues. The oracle was always consulted at night when the priest entered a room beneath the temple and drank from the spring. The prophecies were delivered in verse. Inscriptions at Claros, many of them of the second century A.D., record delegates from eastern Europe and Thrace arriving with problems, and the oracle's replies are recorded from as far afield as southern Russia, Dalmatia,

the Old Testament functions as an oracle. The Servant concept of Isaiah is frequently cited in application to Jesus Christ to the extent that it becomes an early Christian *topos*.[143] The Servant *topos* strongly elicits pity for Christ from Peter's audience, but also the resolve to follow him as their example, shepherd, and souls' guardian.

The Honor-Shame Contest in 1 Pt. 2:18–25

Primacy of the οἰκέται *in 1 Peter*

The paradigmatic role of the οἰκέται for the entire community of believers has been noted by Elliott,[144] who affirms that whatever is said of the household servants in 1 Pt. 2:18–25 applies to all Christians. Their experience of innocent suffering and endurance despite doing good is exemplary for all believers as is the honor that they receive from God for their steadfastness. The primary place that these household slaves have among the specific groups within the Petrine parenesis suggests that the οἰκέται are paradigmatic for the entire οἶκος τοῦ θεοῦ. Furthermore, only the exhoration to the household servants is grounded to any degree Christologically. Whatever Peter suggests about the shame and honor of the slaves applies also to the church as a whole.

Provocation by the οἰκέται

That the cultural code of honor and shame is prevalent in this section is evident by Peter's abundant vocabulary of honor and dishonor.[145] The harsh treatment, presumably arbitrary and/or unjustified beatings (κολαφιζόμενοι, v. 20a; cf. v. 24) and verbal

---

Algeria and Rome itself." The activity of the Spirit in and through the OT prophets and Christian preachers as described in 1 Pt. 1:10–12 is véry much oracular.

[143] For the notion, with different NT traditions, of Jesus as the Isaianic Servant of the Lord, see France, "Servant of the Lord," 1093–94.

[144] Elliott, *Home*, 206–7; idem, "Backward and Forward," 187, 199. Cf. Carrez, "L'esclavage," 216–17.

[145] Cf. Appendix 1, "The Semantic Field of Honor and Shame in 1 Peter," below.

abuse (λοιδορούμενος, v. 23a) inflicted by brutal masters constitutes "pains" (λύπαι, v. 19b)[146] for the οἰκέται. The abuse could stem from a master's indulgent life-style: his unmet demands for comfort and pleasure lead to harshness in his dealings with his servants who, he believes, may be at least partially to blame for his frustration.[147] What the δεσπόται perceive as an attack by the slaves on their self-esteem or on the established order (as in the classic honor contest) could precipitate severity in the treatment of the latter by the former. Since slaves of a household generally conformed to the religious preferences of the *pater familias*,[148] adoption of their own beliefs was viewed as a disturbance of the social equilibrium. Balch declares:

> The Roman constitution insisted on proper worship of the state gods, so Romans reacted negatively when Jewish and Christian slaves—the first groups to do so—rejected the worship of their masters' gods, insisting on an exclusive worship of their own God.[149]

In any case, the οἰκέται incur a challenge to their honor. That challenge takes the form of cruelty, the infliction of pain, and unjustly severe treatment.

A New Honor to Defend

The οἰκέται, with the entire οἶκος τοῦ θεοῦ, have been honored by God (1:3–12; 2:4–10). Normally, slaves in the Roman world had no honor to defend since they were human chattels. Some did have considerable and important responsibility, being dear and loyal to their masters. However, the master still had the legal power of life and death over the slave. Despite the decided legal inferiority of the slaves, the honored status of the οἰκέται in the οἶκος τοῦ θεοῦ translates into a new self-perception which

---

[146] Generally in the NT, λύπη denotes both physical and emotional pain. Hermann Haarbeck and Hans-Georg Link, "λυπέω," *NIDNTT*, 2:420.

[147] Cf. Plutarch's description of the self-indulgent master whose demands are unsatisfied and so becomes harsh with his servants (*Mor.* 461B-C/Penguin, 194–95).

[148] Balch, *Wives*, 68–69, 74–75.

[149] Ibid., 74.

accepts their equality (cf. 1 Pt. 4:5–6) before God with the challengers.[150] Therefore, the dishonored slaves have honor within the household of God and that honor can be defended and upheld.

Normally, the challengee would seek revenge to defend her/his honor. However, in 1 Pt. 2:18–25, the prescribed action is not deceit, the return of abuse for abuse, or threats—any to which a mistreated slave could conceivably have resorted in order to get revenge on an acrimonious δεσπότης.[151] As in the case of Jesus, so in the case of the οἰκέται are the vengeful responses to give way to the endurance of pain in unjust suffering that comes to one despite doing right. The one treated in a humiliating way is to cede her/his rights according to Peter. Like Jesus, who "entrusted himself to the one who judges justly" (v. 23), so the οἰκέται along with all Christians are to commit themselves to God's care and righteous judgment (cf. v. 25; 4:19).[152] To allow God to come to their defense makes possible for the slaves a future reconciliation with their challengers instead of an inimical and possible ongoing

---

[150] E. A. Judge, "Slave, Slavery. II. In the New Testament," *NBD*, 124–25; Liversidge, *Everyday Life*, 29–31; Malina, *NT World*, 36; Malina and Neyrey, "Honor and Shame," 31; Wayne Gilbert Rollins, "Slavery in the NT," in *The Interpreter's Dictionary of the Bible*, ed. Keith Crim (Nashville: Abingdon, 1976), suppl. vol., 830–32; Paul Veyne, "The Roman Empire," chap. in *A History of Private Life: I. From Pagan Rome to Byzantium*, ed. Paul Veyne, trans. Arthur Goldhammer, A History of Private Life, ed. Philipe Aries and Georges Duby, no. 1 (Cambridge, MA: Harvard University Press, Belknap Press, 1987), 51–69, passim (sec. on slavery). An interesting story of οἰκέται who were entrusted with an important mission is found in Acts 10:1–24. The legal power of the master over the slave is illustrated in Phm., where Paul can do nothing more than appeal to Philemon to welcome back Onesimus leniently.

[151] Such vengeful tactics may have been particulary tempting for slaves who had Christian masters from whom they felt they could claim the right to brotherly treatment (cf. Phm.). I am indebted to Dr. John H. Elliott for this suggestion in a personal communication to me (1992).

[152] On the ceding of one's rights when the defense of honor would normally be required see Mt. 5:38–48; Lk. 6:27–36; Bruce Malina and Richard L. Rohrbaugh, *Social Science Commentary on the Synoptic Gospels* (Minneapolis: Fortress Press, 1992), 55 (on Mt. 5:38–42).

demand for satisfaction.[153] That future reconciliation is, for Peter, tantamount to the opponents' conversion to Christ (cf. 2:12; 3:1).

Ultimately, a favorable verdict in the social exchange will come for the Christian πάροικοι and παρεπίδημοι (exemplified in the οἰκέται) from God himself who is the audience in the slave-master exchange. He grants his credit or approval (χάρις) to the believers who endure unjust suffering as Jesus did. By way of Christlike endurance, the exigence of shameful treatment experienced by God's people will have been transformed and those who justly deserve honor, those who do good (cf. 2:14), will obtain it. Hence the contest for honor between slaves and masters may be diagrammed as in Figure 2.

Figure 2: The Honor Contest in 1 Pt. 2:18–25		
Action*	οἰκέται → δεσπόται	
Challenge (Reaction)	Positive Rejection Harsh treatment Pain Unjust suffering	
Response (Counter- reaction)	Endure pain, suffering unjustly Endure when you do right and suffer for it	[revenge] [no]sin=deceit [no]abuse [no]threats
Verdict	Credit/God's approval (χάρις)	
(* refers to stages not explicitly discussed by Peter.)		

---

[153] Cf. Malina and Rohrbaugh, *Commentary*, 55.

Thesis (3:1–6)

Proposition (v. 1a)

Again in 1 Pt. 3:1–6 the author displays his thesis pattern in the presentation of an argument whose proposition (v. 1a) is the submission of wives to their husbands, ὑποτασσόμεναι τοῖς ἀνδράσιν. The participle is, like its counterpart in 2:18, circumstantial in that it describes circumstances attendant to the proposition of the major rhetorical unit 1 Pt. 2:11–3:12: ἀπέχεσθαι τῶν σαρκικῶν ἐπιθυμιῶν (v. 11b).

The instructions to the γυναῖκες are extensive in contrast to a brief address to husbands (3:7), probably because of the potential explosiveness within a marriage where the wife has converted to Christ and the husband has not. The wife[154] of a Greco-Roman household typically adopted her husband's religious beliefs and observances. Her failure to do so was regarded as disruptive of the social order. The Romans suspected the worship of Dionysus-Bacchus as being revolutionary and accompanied by ritual murder and sexual immorality. The cult's alleged corruption of Roman women was of grave concern. As for the cult of Isis, the Romans accused it of promoting the woman's usurpation of the husband's authority.

The Jews were so castigated for their reversal of Roman marriage customs of male dominance that Philo and Josephus felt compelled to responsively argue for a woman's inferiority and necessary submission to the man. The mystery cult of Cybele and the Christian religion were also suspected of fomenting sedition. Hence the wife's worship of her husband's gods was of the utmost importance for public and domestic order:

> A wife ought not to make friends of her own, but to enjoy her husband's friends in common with him. The gods are the first and most important friends. Therefore it is becoming for a wife to worship and know only the gods that her husband believes in, and to shut the front door tight upon all queer rituals and outlandish superstitions. For with no god do stealthy

---

[154] For what follows, I rely on Balch, *Wives*, 65–80, 85, 96–97, 99; cf. also Davids, *1 Peter*, 115–17.

and secret rites performed by a woman find any favour. . . . Those who
have to go near elephants do not put on bright clothes, nor do those who
go near bulls put on red; for the animals are made especially furious by
these colours; and tigers, they say, when surrounded by the noise of
beaten drums go completely mad and tear themselves to pieces. Since,
then, this is also the case with men, that some cannot well endure the
sight of scarlet and purple clothes, while others are annoyed by cymbals
and drums, what terrible hardship is it for women to refrain from such
things, and not disquiet or irritate their husbands, but live with them in
constant gentleness?[155]

Peter's advice is, unlike Plutarch's quoted above, not for wives
to abandon the worship of Christ, but for them to continue in
Christian living[156] so as to win their unbelieving husbands over to
the Christian faith. The summons is not to acculturation to
Greco-Roman society, but to adaptation to its domestic realities
and norms. Thus will the Christian mission advance in a home
despite a mixture there of religious beliefs.

Reason (v. 1b–2)

Style

Easily discerned is Peter's reason for his thesis since it is
couched in a purpose clause with ἵνα which is separated from its
verb κερδηθήσονται by three *cola*: a conditional clause
(identifying those to be converted (καὶ εἴ τινες ἀπειθοῦσιν τῷ
λόγῳ) and two prepositional phrases, one expressing the agency
of conversion (διὰ τῆς τῶν γυναικῶν ἀναστροφῆς) and one
expresing the manner in which the domestic mission is to be
executed (ἄνευ λόγου). The three *cola* embody some stylistic

---

[155] Plut. *Mor.* 140D, 144D-E, cited by Balch, *Wives*, 85.

[156] 1 Pt. 3:2, ἐποπτεύσαντες τὴν ἐν φόβῳ ἁγνὴν ἀναστροφὴν ὑμῶν
echoes earlier language in the letter that refers to Christian living: ἐν φόβῳ
τὸν τῆς παροικίας ὑμῶν χρόνον ἀναστράφητε, 1:17b; τὰς ψυχὰς ὑμῶν
ἡγνικότες ἐν τῷ ὑπακοῇ τῆς ἀληθείας κτλ, 1:22a; τὴν ἀναστροφὴν ὑμῶν
ἐν τοῖς ἔθνεσιν ἔχοντες καλήν, 2:12a; ἐκ τῶν καλῶν ἔργων ἐποπτεύοντες,
2:12c. The submission in vv. 1, 5 is not restricted to the marital sexual
relationship (*pace* Hillyer, *1 and 2 Peter, Jude*, 92), but extends to the entire
life of a gentle and quiet spirit (v. 4). So, too, ἁγνὴ ἀναστροφή is not just
chaste sexual behavior (as Marshall, *1 Peter*, 101, maintains), but the wife's
entire life of purity.

adornments. Three instances of genitival *homoeoptoton*[157] occur: τῆς-ἀναστροφῆς, τῶν-γυναικῶν, and ἄνευ-λόγου. The double usage of λόγος ("word") is an instance of ἀντανάκλασις where the same word has two different meanings:[158] "even if some of them do not obey the word, they may be won over without a word." The first occurrence of λόγος is a synecdoche[159] in which a whole, the entire Christian kerygma, is known from a small part, a word (cf. 1 Pt. 2:8).[160]

κερδαίνω,[161] a commercial term, can have the meaning of 'to get commerical gain,' 'to win something,' 'to make a profit,' 'to gain,' or 'to gain advantage.' 'To win someone' is an early Christian missionary *topos* metaphorically signifying 'to make a person a Christian.' For Paul in 1 Cor. 9:19–22, his missionary task is one of becoming a slave to all that he might win (κερδαίνω) people. To gain converts means save (σώζω) them (v. 22d). Following the verb κερδηθήσονται is a participial clause (ἐποπτεύσαντες τὴν ἐν φόβῳ ἁγνὴν ἀναστροφὴν ὑμῶν) that further defines the behavior (ἀναστροφή) of the wives (mentioned in v. 1b) that influences the conversion of their pagan husbands.[162] The

---

[157] *Her.* 4.20.28.

[158] Quint. *Inst. Or.* 9.3.68.

[159] *Her.* 4.33.44–45.

[160] Peter is not unique in this absolute use of λόγος which from an early time meant simply "the gospel" (e.g., Acts 6:4; 16:6, 18:15; Gal. 6:6; Col. 4:3; 1 Thess. 1:6; Jas. 1:21; BAGD, 478 (s.v. "λόγος").

[161] For observations on metaphor, see *Her.* 4.34.45; Arist. *Poet.* 21; *Rh.* 3.2.1404b.6–1405b.13. On κερδαίνω see BAGD, 429 (s.v. "κερδαίνω"); David Daube, "κερδαίνω as a Missionary Term," *Harvard Theological Review* 40 (1947): 102–20; Davids, *1 Peter,* 16; Gordon D. Fee, *The First Epistle to the Corinthians,* The New International Commentary on the New Testament, (Grand Rapids: William B. Eerdmans, 1987), 426–27 n. 24 (under 1 Cor. 9:19); Burghard Siede, "κέρδος," *NIDNTT,* 3:136–37. Cf. the construction ἵνα κερδήσω/κερδαίνω in 1 Cor. 9:19–22 (5x) with ἵνα κερδηθήσονται in 1 Pt. 3:1.

[162] The sequential aspect of observing—being won is suggested by the aor. ptc. ἐποπτεύσαντες ('having observed') preceded by the fut. pass. ind. κερδηθήσονται ('they will be won'). Cf. Weymouth: "so that even if some of them disbelieve the Message, they may, apart from the Message, be won over

vocabulary recalls 2:12 and thus reminds the hearer that the rhetor embellishes here that which was pronounced in the *propositio* and *ratio* of the entire argument above.

Cicero's topics of honor and advantage[163]

Peter's use of κερδαίνω suggests that he pursues the aim of advantage in this particular thesis. Deliberative oratory, according to Cicero, aims at the topics of honor and advantage. That is, the orator seeks to persuade the audience to embrace honorable things that not only are attractive by their intrinsic worth, but are advantageous—desirable because of the profit or gain that they promise. Examples of the class of things that combine honor and advantage are friendship, a good reputation, rank, and influence. Throughout 1 Peter, the author chooses from the topics of honor and advantage (or their combination) in his deliberative discourse. In 2:18–25, the topic of advantage (God's approval) was the aim of the thesis, to be arrived at by honorable courage on the part of the οἰκέται.[164] With the wives, Peter reasons similarly, seeking not only to persuade them of the honorable course, but the one that is simultaneously to their advantage.

The *ratio* for the entire *argumentatio* 2:11–3:12 indicates that Peter aims at the honorable, for a reversal in attitude of the pagans (from slander to honorable recognition of the believers' true character) is the rationale for the πάροικοι and παρεπίδημοι to abstain from fleshly lusts/to maintain good conduct. The rhetor supplements the topic of honor with that of advantage in his appeal to Christian wives: their deference to their husbands (an honorable act, cf. 2:14b) will bring the women profit in that they will 'gain' (κερδαίνω) their disobedient or unbelieving husbands.

---

by the daily life of their wives, after watching your daily life—so full of reverence, and so blameless!"

[163] Cic. *Inv.* 2.51.155–58.176.

[164] God's approval (χάρις παρὰ θεῷ) in 2:20 is itself honor. However, Peter's reasoning is that the οἰκέται ought to endure suffering, not because endurance is honorable in itself (which it is), but because their steadfastness gains for them the advantage of the divine approval. Thus the topic in 2:18–25 is of advantage.

Peter's sub-topic of deference to husbands approximates that of friendship argued by Cicero as a class of things honorable and advantageous to be sought in deliberative oratory. "Friendship," affirms Cicero, "is a desire to do good to some one simply for the benefit of the person whom one loves, with a requital of feeling on his part" (amicitia voluntas erga aliquem rerum bonarum illius ipsius causa quem diligit cum eius pari voluntate).[165] Wives who recognize their pagan husbands' authority as the *pater familias*, a recognition that is culturally approved, do them a service since their display of blameless behavior might lead the husbands to Christ. The gain to be gotten in a conversion of a husband to Christ is not just the Lord's or the church's, but the wife's, and that especially since a converted husband is more likely to treat his wife understandably and honorably (cf. 3:7), without the friction that might well attend a religiously mixed marriage.

Undoubtedly, the Christian wives to whom Peter writes have virtually no chance for an egalitarian marital arrangement. Yet for them to remain faithful Christians, maintaining their own religious identity (independent of their husbands' religious practices) is quite revolutionary.[166] To this Peter calls the Christian wives. To defer to the husband is honorable for the Christian wife, to win him is advantageous.

---

[165] Cic. *Inv.* 2.55.166. This trans. by H. M. Hubbell in the LCL version appears altruistically to remove the legitimate pursuit of advantage for the one initiating love. "Simply" is not present in Latin and is not the best rendering of the intensive pronoun *ipsius*. The occurrence of the English word seems to make friendship a one-sided concern, the reciprocation of love being a mere accessory when it, however, is integral to friendship according to the Latin. I suggest the following trans. (*pace* Hubbell): 'Friendship is a desire of good things for the very sake of another whom one loves, accompanied with like desire on the part of the one who is loved.'

[166] An observation by Davids, *1 Peter*, 15–16. If Peter were truly advocating "acculturation" to Greco-Roman culture (as Balch maintains), he would discourage such religious independence and evangelistic determination since the wife was expected to follow the husband's religion.

Moral division of labor: the female

Until 1 Pt. 3:1, Peter's argument has concerned collective honor, that shared by males and females in what is regarded as a voluntary grouping, the church as the household of God. However, at 3:1, the author commences with instructions (extending through v. 7) that are gender-specific, addressed to either females (wives, vv. 1–6) or males (husbands, v. 7). The instructions involve daily concrete actions and conduct that are culturally assigned sexual roles. They reflect what is known in cultural anthropology as the moral division of labor.[167] The reputation of one's group as well as that of the individual is bound to performance in daily conduct. The public extends honor to the individual and her/his group if the everyday behavior conforms to the culturally expected norms.

Additionally, a female's honor is maintained in sexual purity (unmarried virginity and married exclusiveness), shyness, blushing, and modesty at her nakedness, all which contribute to

---

[167] For the following discussion on the moral division of labor for the female, I have consulted Abou A. M. Zeid, "Honour and Shame among the Bedouins of Egypt," in *Honour and Shame: The Values of Mediterranean Society*, ed. J. G. Peristiany, The Nature of Human Society Series (Chicago: University of Chicago Press, 1966; London: Weidenfeld & Nicolson, Midway Reprint, 1974), 253–54, 256–57; J. K. Campbell, "Honour and the Devil," in *Honour and Shame*, ed. J. G. Peristiany, 146–47; Carol Delaney, "Seeds of Honor, Fields of Shame," in *Honor and Shame and the Unity of the Mediterranean*, ed. David D. Gilmore, A Special Publication of the American Anthropological Association no. 22 (Washington: American Anthropological Association, 1987), 38–41; Gilmore, "Anthropology of the Mediterranean Area," 195; idem, "The Shame of Dishonor," in *Honor and Shame*, ed. David D. Gilmore, 4; Stuart L. Love, "A Macrosociological View: The Household: A Major Social Component for Gender Analysis in the Gospel of Matthew," *Biblical Theology Bulletin*, 23 (Spring 1993): 23, 27–29; Malina, *NT World*, 39–47; Malina and Neyrey, "Honor and Shame," 41–44, 61–64; Malina and Rohrbaugh, *Commentary*, 30–31, 77, 213–14, 241–42, 310–11; Michaels, *1 Peter*, 159–60; J. G. Peristiany, "Honour and Shame in a Cypriot Highland Village," in *Honour and Shame*, ed. J. G. Peristiany, 183–84; idem, "Introduction," in *Honour and Shame*, ed. J. G. Peristiany, 2, 7, 11–12; Julian Pitt-Rivers, "Honour and Social Status," in *Honour and Shame*, ed. J. G. Peristiany, 42–46, 68–70; Jane Schneider, "Of Vigilance and Virgins: Honor, Shame and Access to Resources in Mediterranean Societies," *Ethnology* 10 (1971): 17–18.

shame in a good sense. The female's purity or exclusiveness is embedded within the honor of a male, whether a father, husband, brother, or son, who protects her honor. From a husband, a wife receives honor through her bearing children—the more, the better, especially if they are males. Women who are not under the honor of a male become themselves dishonorable, viewed as sexually aggressive and outside the culturally encoded boundaries. A male anxiety that suspects female sexuality to be ungovernable and diabolical is exacerbated by women who are not legitimized by male honor.

The conjunction of female honor with that of a male clarifies Peter's summons to submission or deference to the husband in v. 1. The Petrine concern may well be that a Christian wife, who has found a new identity and honor within the οἶκος τοῦ θεοῦ (2:4–10) is tempted to find the context of her honor exclusively there, and not also in a home where her unbelieving husband has established pagan worship (as is his prerogative as the *pater familias*). After all, she, with all God's people, has been ransomed from the vanity of pagan ways by Christ's precious blood (1:18–19) to freedom (2:16).

The churches in Galatia, if not in all of Asia Minor, knew of the freedom in equality that union with Christ brings since Paul had written Galatia in the 50's, "There is no longer Jew or Greek, there is no longer slave or free, there is no longer male and female; for all of you are one in Christ Jesus" (Gal. 3:28). The women (and slaves) in the congregations of Asia Minor may have demanded greater liberty because of this baptismal formula, thereby creating tension with the surrounding culture that expected domestic female submission. The household codes of the New Testament may originate with the purpose of the writers to encourage slaves and women to respect the social roles and boundaries imposed on them.

David L. Balch[168] discusses the matter of Gal. 3:28 and its effect on early Christian communities. He believes that the problem

---

[168] Balch, *Wives*, 9–10, 106–7.

addressed by the household code in 1 Peter did not arise within the church, but from without as a protest against slaves and wives who refused to worship the traditional gods chosen by the *pater familias*. No evidence exists in the letter that wives endeavor to attain greater social equality with men.

I differ with Balch, however, and believe that women within the communities have pursued freedom from the cultural restraints that prohibited public displays of luxury and adornment.[169] Elegance in appearance is equated by ancient writers with immodesty and vice since a woman's honor is thought in the Greco-Roman world to be found in secluded and inconspicuous domesticity. Hence Peter denounces extravagance and ostentation in feminine dress and requires Christian women to preserve modesty and attend to habits of the heart (v. 4; cf. Isa. 3:16–4:1; 1 Tim. 2:9–10; Rev. 17:4). Modesty, gentleness, and quietness are the attributes of a wife who seeks to defer to her husband and honorably to preserve her positive shame, according to Peter.

Balch fails to note that public extravagance of a Christian woman could lead to slander from unbelieving society just as her independence in religion could. Both are likely the issue in 1 Peter and have led to unbelievers' denunciations of Christian women as shameless and without honor. The author argues for restraint in the wives' exercise of freedom: they are at liberty to believe in Christ, but must otherwise live within the dictates of the cultural honor code for wives. Their recognition of the husband's authority is to continue, thus preserving the identification of female honor with that of the male. Otherwise, the women are susceptible to the criticism from the surrounding society and from their unbelieving husbands that they are dishonorably shameless, having transgressed social boundaries.

The deferential attitude argued in vv. 1–6 compensates for any perceived outrage to the husband's honor by the wife's

---

[169] "The closely similar admonition in 1 Tim. ii. 9f. suggests that both passages draw on stock catechetical material, and also that the congregations addressed included a number of well-off women" (Kelly, *Peter and Jude*, 129).

independent choice of the Christian faith. Thus Peter affirms that unbelieving husbands whose wives have contravened their domestic religious authority (in becoming Christians) will be won over. The husbands will relent in the face of any perceived challenge to their status.

Deference is equivalent to obedience (ὑπακούω, v. 6) and upholds the honorable status of the husband since he is thus recognized as κύριος of the home (v. 6), a term that suggests he is the repository of family honor (including that of resident females). Peter's advice for women to concentrate on the inner beauty of a gentle and quiet spirit, if heeded, guarantees the properly centripetal focus of the female in the home, whereas the outward adornment (ὁ ἔξωθεν κόσμος) of v. 3 is centrifugal. Since only the male is to project himself and his honor outwardly from the home, a woman's ostentation projects her before the public gaze that judges her display not as modest, blushing, and restrained (marks of proper sexual exclusiveness), but as aggressive and wanton. The woman is suspected of being a seductress.

The foremost duty of women is to protect the honor of herself and her family from disparagements to her sexual modesty. Thus, as Peristiany says regarding Cypriot village women,

> In dress, looks, attitudes, speech, a woman, when men are present, should be virginal as a maiden and matronly as a wife. If it were possible to combine the concepts of virginity and motherhood the ideal married woman would be a married mother virginal in sensations and mind.[170]

---

[170] Peristiany, "Cypriot Highland Village," 182. In Andalusia, Pitt-Rivers ("Honour and Social Status," 71) observes that a woman of the aristocracy is not under the same rules as female plebeians. Since her power derives from economic rank, not sexuality, she incurs no dishonor if she is disobedient to her husband. Perhaps Lydia, a purple merchant mentioned in Acts 16:14–15, is a NT example of a woman who, because of a higher social standing, is not bound by typical female restrictions. Lydia apparently is religiously independent and leads her household in its religious preference. Although not an aristocrat, Lydia likely has economic power through her merchandising of a commodity in great demand (purple fabric was used for official Roman togas). For discussion of Lydia see Archibald Thomas Robertson, *Word Pictures in the New Testament*, vol. 3, *The Acts of the Apostles* (Nashville: Broadman Press, 1930), 251–54. The women whom Peter

What holds true in a modern Cypriot village has prevailed in Mediterranean society since ancient times.

Hence 1 Pt. 3:1–6 is not merely about female roles in a patriarchal society, but reflects the writer's concern for the honor of the married women in the churches, of their husbands who are shamed if their spouses become dishonorable, and for the testimony that the entire household of God manifests. The church should be socially irreproachable in order to win unbelievers, slanderers, and sceptics (2:12, 15; 3:1). Although Peter announces a new and radical dignity for Christian women (τιμή, συγκληρονόμοι, v. 7; cf. Gal. 3:28), he exhibits no inclination to alter the οἶκος pattern prevalent in Greco-Roman society. According to that pattern, the woman is subordinate and private.

Sometimes the repository of the household honor is not the male. A Mediterranean family's honor often rests with the females if the family or its lineage is unstable or if the family has no long-term economic interests. Christian πάροικοι could be of uncertain ancestry (especially in the eyes of outsiders) and without established financial interests in their area of residence. Female honor, therefore, as one of the few arenas where family honor could be demonstrated and defended, would be of the utmost importance in such cases. The positive shame of Christian women could be regarded by Peter as the best, and perhaps the only, arena of Christian testimony by a church of πάροικοι and παρεπίδημοι. As much as possible, he wishes that positive shame to be upheld in noble feminine behavior.

Opposite (vv. 3–4)

Verses 3–4 comprise a contrary to the thesis proposition. Peter counsels, therefore, against behavior that would contradict

---

addresses are not, despite the dress that they have assumed, necessarily aristocratic. Their husbands may be civic or diplomatic officials, successful craftsmen or merchants, or small or medium landowners. They certainly are not slaves since slaves, although allowed to cohabit, were not permitted to marry.

deferential conduct. The device called *congeries* (accumulation)[171] plays a role in this opposite. In v. 3, Peter accumulates details that pertain to and describe excess and preoccupation[172] with external adornment[173] which are somehow opposed to deference: braiding the hair (ἐμπλοκὴ τριχῶν), wearing gold[174] jewelry (περίθεσις χρυσίων), and wearing fine clothing. The conjunction ἀλλά introduces an antithesis[175] which returns the hearer to the topic of submission. "The lasting beauty of a gentle and quiet spirit" is a second restatement of the proposition in definition of it, ἡ ἐν φόβῳ ἁγνὴ ἀναστροφή being the first. These restatements constitute a *commoratio*,[176] a dwelling on and resumption of the crucial rhetorical point. *Commoratio* is present not only in vv. 1–4, but throughout 2:11–3:12. Whenever Peter touches on the subject of deference to others, he resorts to the strongest topic of his entire *argumentatio* that pleads for abstention from evil and maintenance of good behavior. πολυτελές ("very precious"), in reference to the gentle and quiet spirit,[177] is part of Peter's semantic field of honor and supports his argument that the wives' respectful attitude toward their husbands brings honor.

---

[171] Long. *Subl.* 12; Quint. *Inst. Or.* 8.4.26–27; Watson, *Invention*, 27; 15 (on 2 Pt. 2:12–14).

[172] Goppelt, *Der erste Petrusbrief*, 216, notes how the genitives of activity-words in v. 3 all describe the expenditure in work and time that the effort to create an attractive appearance demands!

[173] Cf. Balch, *Wives*, 101–2, who recounts Hellenistic ethical instruction against extravagance for the sake of proper morality. Balch also relates how the excesses criticized in 1 Pt. 3:3 accompany the cults of Artemis of Ephesus and Isis. Against these cults Balch finds no polemic in 1 Pt. 3:3–4, however.

[174] Gold has already been described as a perishable, and thus inferior, article in 1 Pt. 1:7.

[175] Lat. *contentio*, *Her.* 4.45.58, is one of diction since the various elements on either side of the *contentio* correspond to one another.

[176] *Her.* 4.45.58.

[177] Balch, *Wives*, 102; Kelly, *Peter and Jude*, 129–30. The neut. rel. pron. ὅ could refer to all of vv. 3–4 (Goppelt, *Der erste Petrusbrief*, 218). The immediacy of the neut. πνεῦμα does not require such a reference, however.

Analogy (v. 5), Example (v. 6a),
Citation (v. 6b), and Conclusion (v. 6c)

The holy women of long-ago

The choice of analogy, the holy women of long-ago, constitutes an exemplum,[178] an action of the past, that is adduced as proof for amplification in order to stir the hearers. The appeal to the holy women is the commonplace from authority that reveals of what concern the matter at hand has been to one's ancestors.[179] Peter hopes that the example of the female saints of the past motivates his female hearers to defer to their husbands since the women of old looked to God for his vindication of their honor (αἱ ἐλπίζουσαι, cf. 1:13) and deferred to their husbands in the very manner that Peter now urges (ὑποτασσόμεναι τοῖς ἰδίοις ἀνδράσιν, identical phraseology as in v. 1). The continual nature of their hope, expressed in the present participle ἐλπίζουσαι, is vocally emphasized with *homoeoptoton*[180] in nominative -αι endings (αἱ ἅγιαι . . . αἱ ἐλπίζουσαι . . . ὑποτασσόμεναι). The habitual nature of their submission in former times is stressed by the imperfect ἐκόσμουν.

The example of Sarah

The conjunction ὡς introduces the example of the argument and the conjoined authoritative citation.[181] Peter appeals to the story of Sarah who is presumably respected as a godly and deferential wife in the tradition that Peter shares with his readers.

---

[178] *Her.* 4.43.56–44.58; Quint. *Inst. Or.* 5.11.1–2; 5.6; Cic. *Part. Or.* 16.55; Watson, *Invention*, 27.

[179] *Her.* 2.30.48. The amplification under discussion pertains to forensic (*criminis causa*) rhetoric, but is equally valid in deliberative causes since the purpose of appealing to the past, to establish the importance of the theme and its sanction for ancestors, is identical in both species. Cf. Cic. *Inv.* 1.53.101.

[180] *Her.* 4.20.28. Quintilian's expanded def. of the figure, which includes words in the same case without like endings, would incorporate the ending of γυναῖκες in the *homoeoptoton* (*Inst. Or.* 9.3.78).

[181] See BAGD, 897 (s.v. "ὡς") for the introductory role of ὡς with examples and citations.

He, however, seems to misapply her story, since the LXX text (Gen. 18:12) where she calls Abraham 'lord' (κύριος) is not set within a context of deferential wifely behavior, but in one of incredulous amusement at the announcement of her future child bearing.

Peter, though, appears to have spun off the word κύριος: if Sarah called Abraham 'lord,' she must have respected his position as husband. The affirmation that she obeyed (ὑπήκουσεν) the patriarch features a verb that is equivalent to ὑποτάσσω, but is used as a stylistic variation to avoid excessive transplacement with that verb. Hence, in reasoning from the greater to the lesser (the γυναῖκες are Sarah's children, ἧς ἐγενήθητε τέκνα), Peter presents Sarah as a model of deference for Christian wives throughout Asia Minor.[182] The participial clause is subordinate to ὑπήκουσεν and serves as a brief and authoritative scriptural citation for the thesis.

Do good, have no fear

The conclusion in Peter's thesis addressed to the wives is not the thorough *conclusio* of a complete *argumentatio* in which stand an enumeration, amplification, and appeal to pity.[183] Rather, v. 6c is the figure *conclusio* in which the necessary consequences of what has already been advanced are deduced briefly.[184] By now calling the wives τέκνα Σάρρα, Peter utilizes the figure of *pronominatio* to evoke positive pathos of the women for themselves and their honored position. Thus he reinforces their resolve to continue in the virtuous behavior, ἀγαθοποιοῦσαι, that has advanced them to their esteemed status. To "do what is good" is on the plane of

---

[182] Cf. Michaels, *1 Peter*, 164–66, for a helpful discussion whose conclusions have shaped mine at this point. Warning against excessive transplacement (i.e., overrepetition of the same word) is in *Her.* 4.12.18. For further discussion of the argument from greater to lesser, see Quint. *Inst. Or.* 5.11.9.

[183] *Her.* 2.30.47–31.50.

[184] *Her.* 4.30.41.

the honorable and virtuous;[185] to be Sarah's children is in the realm of both the honorable and advantageous.[186] Thus Peter returns subtly to the twin topics of honor and advantage with which he began his thesis.

The specific context for ἀγαθοποιοῦσαι is defined by its placement in antithesis "do what is good and never let fears alarm you," μὴ φοβούμεναι μηδεμίαν πτόησιν, a phrase which may refer to the Christian wives' fear of their non-Christian husbands,[187] to the frightening circumstances that life of a Christian woman with a pagan husband might bring. The participles are subordinate to the aorist ἐγενήθητε and are conditional: the Christian wives have become Sarah's children if they do good and do not succumb to fear.[188] Women, however, who do not abide within cultural honor boundaries and who project their femininity publicly, even to excess (v. 3), do not seem to be ones who need any instruction regarding fear of husbands. Why does Peter encourage apparently fearless Christian wives not to allow fears to alarm them?

One must keep in mind the rhetorical function of v. 6c ἧς ἐγενήθητε τέκνα ἀγαθοποιοῦσαι καὶ μὴ φοβούμεναι μηδεμίαν

---

[185] "To do good" is virtuous in that it is an expression of justice, "a habit of mind which gives to every man his desert [*suam cuique tribuens dignitatem*] while preserving the common advantage." In the case of the husband in the Greco-Roman household, reverence (*observantia*) by the wife is the honorable course. Cic. *Inv.* 2.53.160–61.

[186] To be children of Sarah for the wives would be honorable and advantageous in that it confers a dignified and honorable position of respect (Cic. *Inv.* 2.55.166). "To be Sarah's daughter is to be a joint heir of the promises and the honour given to her and to Abraham" (Grudem, *1 Peter*, 142).

[187] Balch, "1 Peter," 2282.

[188] Kelly, *Peter and Jude*, 131. The view that understands the ptcs. as conditional is opposed by Michaels, *1 Peter*, 166–67, on the grounds that 1 Pt. is opposed to human initiative in redemption. True though this may be, Peter is not here, however, discussing Christian regeneration (becoming children of God, 1:3), but the ethical pattern of Sarah whose imitators become her children metaphorically. Michaels takes ἀγαθοποιοῦσαι as an impv. ptc. I differ with Martin, *Metaphor*, 205 n. 238, who says that the ptcs. from 2:18–3:12 attend τιμήσατε in 2:17. In my opinion, ἀγαθοποιοῦσαι and φοβούμεναι attend ἐγενήθητε in 3:6 and are circumstantial-conditional.

πτόησιν. The colon is a conclusion for the thesis 3:1–6. Peter sums up his argument, keeping in mind the two basic types of married women he believes are in the churches that will receive his letter. (1) For those women who have expressed their Christian liberty through a public display of elegance in adornment, Peter advises the doing of good (ἀγαθοποιοῦσαι). They are to keep a culturally expected reserve in dress and behavior, deferring to their husbands, thus proving themselves honorable. (2) For those women who have maintained culturally acceptable reserve in dress and demeanor, but fear the reactions of their unbelieving husbands to the wives' Christian commitment, Peter counsels an unfearing and unperturbed outlook (μὴ φοβούμεναι μηδεμίαν πτόησιν). The women need not fear any intimidation, but can expect the conversion of their husbands because of the wives' pure and reverent lives.

Expolitio (3:7)[189]

Syntax

The concise appeal to husbands is not a developed thesis like those of 2:13–17, 2:18–25, and 3:1–6, but an *expolitio*, a figure of refining in which the same idea is dwelt upon by the rhetor who expresses it in various ways. The shape of the *expolitio* is chiastic; added to it is the stylistic adornment of *homoeoptoton*.[190]

Address
   a οἱ ἄνδρες
   b ὁμοίως
Argument
   c συνοικοῦντες κατὰ γνῶσιν
   d ὡς ἀσθενεστέρῳ σκεύει
   d' τῷ γυναικείῳ
   c' ἀπονέμοντες τιμήν

---

[189] *Her.* 4.42.54, where the furnished example is chiastic like the *expolitio* in 1 Pt. 3:7 (although the a-b-c-c'-b'-a'-d pattern in the former differs from the Petrine pattern).

[190] *Her.* 4.20.28

Reasons

    e ὡς καὶ συνκληρονόμοις χάριτος ζωῆς

    f εἰς τὸ μὴ ἐγκόπτεσθαι τὰς προσευχὰς ὑμῶν

The participles are again circumstantial (cf. 2:18; 3:1, 6).[191]

In contrast to other syntactical hypotheses[192] for v. 7, my suggestion above respects the true parallelism that exists between the two dative clauses (d, d') and the participial clauses (c, c') that take them as objects. Moreover, the chiastic arrangement avoids the problem of supplying a noun to either συνοικοῦντες or ἀπονέμοντες—a traditional necessity recognized by Michaels, who understands ὡς ἀσθενεστέρῳ σκεύει τῷ γυναικείῳ as one syntactically difficult clause.[193] This dative construction is clear when resolved into a chiasmus. The adjective γυναικείος is a substantive[194]—the lone definite article of the dative construction is paired with it and suggests that τῷ γυναικείῳ has a referent distinct from ὡς ἀσθενεστέρῳ σκεύει.[195] 'To the feminine (person),' or 'to the woman' would serve as translations of τῷ γυναικείῳ.

---

[191] Martin, *Metaphor*, 205 n. 238.

[192] The possibilities are presented in Michaels, *1 Peter*, 168.

[193] Ibid. These alternatives are represented (my brackets designating supplied nouns in the translations) by NRSV "show consideration [for your wives] in your life together, paying honor to the woman as the weaker sex" and TEV "in living with your wives you must recognize that they are the weaker sex. So you must treat [them] with respect."

[194] NEB takes γυναικεῖος as a noun in the possessive case qualifying σκεῦος: "pay honour to the woman's body."

[195] My interpretation would require the minor stop after γνῶσιν in UBS[3] to be moved so that it immediately follows σκεύει. The Nestle-Aland[26] text places a minor stop after γυναικείῳ (thus making συγκληρονόμοις the obj. of ἀπονέμοντες τιμήν).

Moral division of labor: the male[196]

In Mediterranean culture, the male is the protector of female honor, the positive shame of her sexual exclusiveness and reserve. Pre-marital or extra-marital sexual activity brings shame not only to the woman, but to the male (brother, son, husband) whose responsibility was to safeguard feminine purity. Masculine honor is maintained by a man whose wife is not violated, whose unmarried daughter or sister remains chaste, who is himself not cuckolded, and who fulfills his wife's sexual needs. A man who fathers many children whose patrilineage to him is not questioned is ascribed honor that can be extended to his wife in her bearing many children. If one's daughter or wife becomes immoral, the man publicly denounces her conduct to preserve his honor.

In rabbinic thought, the woman is a vessel (כְּלִי) and 'to use as a vessel' means to have sexual intercourse. In a passage that throws light on 1 Pt. 3:7, Paul advocates that each Thessalonian man "know how to take a wife [σκεῦος κτᾶσθαι] for himself" (1 Thess. 4:4 NRSVmg). In other words, that each man 'possess his own wife sexually,' or 'live in sexual union with his wife' with sanctification and honor.[197]

The belief that the wife is a vessel is a sentiment that continues in Turkish village culture today. The woman is a vessel for the male's seed which grows within the nutritive environment of the womb. The woman is constitutionally inferior—not only does she have less physical strength, but she does not have the creative

---

[196] Abou, "Bedouins," 253–54, 256–57; Balch, *Wives*, 42, 56–57; Campbell, "Honour and the Devil," 146; Cranfield, *1 Peter*, 72–73; Delaney, "Seeds of Honor," 38–41, 47 n. 16; David D. Gilmore, "Honor, Honesty, Shame: Male Status in Contemporary Andalusia," in *Honor and Shame*, ed. David D. Gilmore, 96–97; Goppelt, *Der erste Petrusbrief*, 220–23; Malina, *NT World*, 43–44; Marshall, *1 Peter*, 102–3; Christian Maurer, "σκεῦος," *TDNT*, 7:358–67; Peristiany, "Cypriot Highland Village," 182–84; Veyne, "The Roman Empire," 33–49. See 152 n. 167 above.

[197] τὸ ἑαυτοῦ σκεῦος in 1 Thess. 4:4 is taken to signify 'his own wife' by Maurer, "σκεῦος," 365–67. Other possible meanings are 'his own body' or 'his own penis.' See BAGD, 754 (s.v. "σκεῦος") for a review of the options.

seed within her and hence is unable to project herself and assert an autonomous self as the male does in his procreative ability. In Anatolian culture, female deliberative and discretionary powers are regarded as inferior and render women incapable of domestic leadership. Sexually vulnerable because she lacks the power of resistance, the woman needs the protection of males.

Peter's words to husbands reflect a Mediterranean mind-set concerning male and female like that just described. The author's description of the woman as a weaker (intellectually, physically) vessel sounds like so much male chauvinism to twentieth-century Western ears, but is completely consonant with cultural attitudes of the Mediterranean, ancient and modern. Despite the fact that v. 7 reflects attitudes of a patriarchal culture, a powerful and somewhat equalizing Christian ethic surfaces in its instructions for husbands to live considerately (κατὰ γνῶσιν) with their wives and in paying the female honor (τιμή) as joint heirs of God's grace. The woman is herself sacred, according to Peter, and to be accorded due respect.

In the ancient Mediterranean world, 'to live considerately with a weaker vessel' and 'to pay honor to the woman' would include a husband's tenderness, affection, kindness, understanding of his wife's feelings, attention to her sexual needs, giving her children, protection of her sexual purity, insuring a mutual communion that respects the common advantage of husband and wife, his delegation to her the charge (*cura*) of the household (perhaps even the keys to the strong-box), speaking well to and of his wife publicly, and his certification in his will that his wife had been a good spouse. Husband and wife are spiritual equals, but, since they must live in a society where marked gender distinctions and roles are in effect, they must respect those distinctions and functions for the sake of their Christian testimony. In 3:8–12, Peter augments these cultural expectations with the Christian duties that all within the οἶκος τοῦ θεοῦ owe to one another.

Reasons for male sensitivity

Two reasons support Peter's argument for believing husbands to dwell considerately with their Christian wives, paying honor to them. (1) The first concerns the wives' status in the economy of grace within the οἶκος τοῦ θεοῦ. They, like the men, are heirs[198] of χάρις ζωῆς, a hendiadys for "the gracious gift of life."[199] Thus they deserve consideration and respect from their Christian husbands. A simple syllogism stands behind this reasoning. Co-heirs of grace deserve consideration and honor (major premise), wives are co-heirs of grace (minor premise). Therefore, show consideration and honor to your wives since they are co-heirs of grace (conclusion). The prefix συν-, already introduced with συνοικοῦντες, reappears now in συγκληρονόμοις and stresses the identity of the joint membership of husband and wife as heirs in the household of God and is intended (with other instances of συν- composites in 1 Peter) to encourage social cohesion.[200]

(2) The second reason that Peter advances to buttress his plea for a male's respect for his wife pertains to prayer. Live considerately, pay honor, "so that nothing may hinder your prayers." προσευχὰς ὑμῶν could refer to prayers jointly offered

---

[198] The *varia lectio* συγκληρονόμοι (appositional to οἱ ἄνδρες or in reference to wives in a new clause) has good support as original, but is probably a secondary reading that altered what some editor or copyist believed to be an incorrect reference of a pl. (συγκληρονόμοις) to a sing. antecedent (ἀσθενεστέρῳ σκεύει=τῷ γυναικείῳ). The dat. pl. in ref. to the wife is the preferred reading: the proximity of σκεύει-γυναικείῳ and the parallel between ὡς and ὡς καί demand it. The difference in number between σκεύει/τῷ γυναικείῳ and συγκληρονόμοις is not inimical to my suggested reading. For discussion and this view, see Goppelt, *Der erste Petrusbrief*, 222; Kelly, *Peter and Jude*, 134; Metzger, *Textual Commentary*, 690–91; and Michaels, *1 Peter*, 155.

[199] Bullinger, *Firgures of Speech*, 657–72 (on hendiadys). Kelly, *Peter and Jude*, 134, believes ζωῆς is epexegetical and renders the construction "the grace which consists in life." I suggest 'life-giving grace,' 'regenerative grace,' or 'vivifying grace' as possible translations also.

[200] Elliott, *Home*, 135–36. Cf. 1 Pt. 1:14, συσχηματιζόμενοι; 3:8, συμπαθεῖς; 4:4, συντρεχόντων; 5:1, συμπρεσβύτερος; 5:13, συνεκλεκτή.
    In the Roman Empire, women were the equals of men in inheritance laws and had the same right to make a will (Veyne, "The Roman Empire," 73, 75). Peter, therefore, does not emphasize some unusual hereditary right of women when he calls them "co-heirs," but stresses the closeness and bond that husbands and wives ought to have in their relationship together before God.

by husband and wife[201] or the husband's prayers only.[202] In my opinion ὑμῶν, is restricted to the prayers of those addressed in the verse: the husbands. Whether Peter means that answers to prayer will not be forthcoming[203] or that the very act of prayer is disrupted[204] makes little difference. Behind his assertion is the belief that respectful conduct is honored by God by means of an unhampered prayer life. He appeals to the husbands in terms of advantage, especially security. Their conduct assures them of a continued and secure link with God in prayer.[205]

Conplexio (3:8–12)
Style and Topic

. At 1 Pt. 3:8, Peter begins to summarize his arguments that he has presented in 2:11–3:7. The passage 3:8–12 is easily identifiable as a conclusion:[206] it is introduced by τὸ δὲ τέλος ("finally") and finishes with a sizable quotation from the Old Testament (Ps. 33:12–16 LXX), the longest in the letter.[207] ὁμόφρονες, συμπαθεῖς, φιλάδελφοι, εὔσπλαγχνοι, ταπεινόφρονες in v. 8 are all predicate adjectives that follow participial ὄντες that is understood.[208] The verse is what I call a circumstantial

---

[201] Goppelt, *Der erste Petrusbrief,* 222; Marshall, *1 Peter,* 103–4.

[202] Grudem, *1 Peter,* 145.

[203] Cf. ibid., 146.

[204] Cf. Phillips, "you will find it impossible to pray properly."

[205] Cic. *Inv.* 2.51.156–58; 56.168–69. "Security [*incolumitas*] is a reasoned and unbroken maintenance of safety" (2.56.169). Cf. Mt. 5:23; 6:12, 14–15; 18:19–35; 1 Cor. 11:17–34. See Kelly, *Peter and Jude,* 134, on the possible bearing of 1 Cor. 7:1–7 on 1 Pt. 3:7.

[206] The conclusion or *conplexio* of the argument whose pattern Peter follows has as its function the drawing together of the parts of the argument. Brevity and clarification of the preceding argument are its characteristics (*Her.* 2.18.28, 29.46–30.47).

[207] Dalton, *Proclamation,* 95, notes that OT citations conclude arguments in NT writings and affirms that "the more important and massive the scripture citation, the more emphatic is the break between this section [i.e., whatever section is at hand] and the following."

[208] Selwyn, *St. Peter,* 188, claims that ὄντες is understood, but is a ptc. impv. Consistently with Peter's ptc. usage to this point as I have described it, I

predicate—it is not truly a circumstantial participial clause since it lacks a given participle, in contrast to 2:18; 3:1, 7. The author's gathering of many positive characteristics that promote Christian solidarity is an example of the stylistic device known as accumulation.[209] Asyndeton[210] gives the impression of a great quantity and lends importance to the catalogue. Two instances of *homoeoptoton*[211] (with endings -ες [3x] and -οι [2x]) are present. The adjectives function appropriately in the conclusion since they summarize well the attitude of deference that Peter advocates as an expression of the proposition 'abstain from fleshly desires/ maintaining a good conduct.'

In interpersonal relationships of the readers, between fellow Christians and with unbelieving outsiders,[212] evil and abuse are not to be repaid in kind: μὴ ἀποδιδόντες κακὸν ἀντὶ κακοῦ ἢ λοιδορίαν ἀντὶ λοιδορίας, a recapitulation of 1 Pt. 2:23. Instead, blessing is the exchange for unjust and ill treatment (τοὐναντίον δὲ εὐλογοῦντες). The participles μὴ ἀποδιδόντες and εὐλογοῦντες are circumstantial in reference (grammatically and conceptually) to ἀπέχεσθαι in 2:11. The notion of non-retaliation and kindliness toward enemies is a Christian topic that finds its expression also in the Jesus tradition[213] and Paul.[214] Although in agonistic Mediterranean society an offense is typically met with a response in defense of one's honor, the conferment of kindness

---

maintain that ὄντες understood here is a circumstantial ptc. in attendance on ἀπέχεσθαι (2:11).

[209] Lat. *congeries*. Long. *Subl.* 12; Quint. *Inst. Or.* 8.4.26–27; Watson, *Invention*, 27; 15 (on 2 Pt. 2:12–14).

[210] Quint. *Inst. Or.* 9.3.50; Watson, *Invention*, 15.

[211] *Her.* 4.20.28.

[212] Since v. 9 follows so closely upon the instructions to husbands in a Christian marriage, it certainly applies to relations within a Christian family. The passage probably extends beyond the family in its application, though, since it echoes 2:23, a verse that is set within an address to slaves with masters who are in all likelihood unbelievers. Hence it has applicablility to all sorts of contacts with non-Christians.

[213] Mt. 5:44–48; Lk. 6:27–36.

[214] Rom. 12:14, 17, 19–21; 1 Thess. 5:15.

in place of vengeance is present. Paul, echoing Prov. 25:21–22, advocates benevolence toward enemies in Rom. 12:20 and Egyptian Bedouins count giving sanctuary to one's own enemy the highest grade of honorable conduct.[215] The prospect of inheriting a blessing (εὐλογία) after blessing one's enemies or opponents stirs the hearers and prompts their resolve to so act. εὐλογία, the conferring of a distinction of rank, wealth, and influence in the Old Testament, metaphorically expresses the honor bestowed by God for noble conduct as hereditary and here is a topic of honor and advantage.[216] Forbidden and prescribed responses to malicious actions by others are placed in antithesis with the construction τοὐναντίον δὲ ("on the contrary"), transplacement[217] being utilized with κακός, λοιδορία, and εὐλογ- words in order to emphasize both the prohibition and the prescription.

Syllogistic Reasoning

The proof in the *conplexio* is deductive, so indicated by the enthymematic ὅτι. 'Bless, for (ὅτι) to this you are called' is based

---

[215] Abou, "Bedouins," 254–55, 258, who describes the honorable custom of opening one's *beit* (tent) to one pursued by enemies. If one's own enemy by whom one has been victimized seeks sanctuary, honor demands that the victim open the *beit* to the fugitive—even if the fugitive has committed murder against the household where sanctuary is sought. One's giving of sanctuary to a person who has murdered an immediate family member is honor par excellence for the one who extends protection.

[216] Cic. *Inv.* 2.55.166. *Loci communes* ('commonplaces' or 'topics') serve as amplification in a *conplexio* or in another part of a discourse, developing and enhancing the rhetor's argument. They stir the hearers and win their assent to the points of the discourse. The many *loci* available to the rhetor in the peroration of judicial oratory are enumerated in Arist. *Rh.* 1.14.1374b.1–7; Cic. *Inv.* 1.53.100–54.105 (for *indignatio*/invective); and *Her.* 2.30.48–49. Amplification occurs anytime in rhetorical composition and in all species of rhetoric. On amplification generally see Cic. *Part. Or.* 8.27, 16.55–56; Kennedy, *NT Interpretation*, 21–22; and Watson, *Invention*, 26–28.

The particular topic of the inheritance of a blessing would be of great importance to Peter's audience and recalls the inheritance that they have already been promised in 1:4. εὐλογία, blessing, is a distinction of honor in the OT, highly prized (Gen. 27:1–41; Heb. 12:16–17; Hans-Georg Link, "Blessing, Blessed, Happy: εὐλογία," *NIDNTT* 1:206–15).

[217] *Her.* 4.14.20; Quint. *Inst. Or.* 9.3.41–43.

on the syllogism 'those called are to bless' (major premise), 'you were called' (minor premise), 'bless, for to this (i.e., the act of blessing) you were called' (hence τοῦτο has a backward reference). The ἵνα clause, the substantiating purpose for the action (conclusion) also reflects syllogistic reasoning: 'those who bless inherit a blessing' (major premise), 'you bless' (minor premise), 'you inherit a blessing, for you bless' (conclusion). The honor/advantage of εὐλογία becomes the inducement for blessing one's enemies.

The demonstrative pronoun τοῦτο could point forward, in which case the syllogism would be 'those called that they might inherit a blessing themselves bless (major premise), to this you were called: that you might inherit a blessing (minor premise), bless, for to this you were called: that you might inherit a blessing (conclusion). The fact that the phrase ὅτι εἰς τοῦτο ἐκλήθητε is so reminiscent of εἰς τοῦτο γὰρ ἐκλήθητε in 2:21 which also points backwards leads me to accept the same direction for τοῦτο at 3:9. After all, Peter is, at 3:9, summarizing what he has argued beforehand and his instruction for his readers 'to bless' is an explication of the endurance to which his audience has been called, the same endurance exemplified by Christ in his refusal to repay abuse for abuse (2:23).[218] I suggest as a translation of v. 9 "not repaying evil for evil or abuse for abuse, but blessing instead, for to this you were called. When you bless you inherit a blessing yourselves."

---

[218] Kelly, *Peter and Jude*, 137, assumes a forward reference for τοῦτο, inasmuch as it so has at 4:6 (cf. also 2:19), the backward orientation produces the awkward parenthesis "bless your insulters (for you were called to bless them) so that you may in turn secure a blessing," and the 'freely received—freely given' idea is more in harmony with a forward reference. A forward reference for τοῦτο is also advanced by Bigg, *St. Peter*, 156; Davids, *1 Peter*, 126–27; and Goppelt, *Der erste Petrusbrief*, 228 n. 15.

However, the syllogistic flow of the proof is not the muddle that Kelly believes it is and the reader ought not to impose the Jesus logion (Mt. 10:8) on Peter here since he is arguing for honor and advantage and not for the proper spirit for mission (as in Mt.). I contend that τοῦτο has a backward reference. Directing τοῦτο backward are Best, *1 Peter*, 130; Michaels, *1 Peter*, 178; and Robertson, *The General Epistles*, 112.

The Three Zones of
Human Personality and Honor

Furthermore, vv. 10–12 confirm[219] what is expressed in the proof—blessing others (one's using one's speech for good [ἀγαθός] and peaceful [εἰρήνη] purposes) leads to life and good days. The scriptural citation defines the inherited blessing of v. 9 and supports Peter's contention that blessing others leads to blessing. The text of Ps. 33 LXX does not appear to have undergone much revision at the hands of Peter. The third-person imperative does replace the second person in the verbs παυσάτω, ἐκκλινάτω, ποιησάτω, ζητησάτω, and διωξάτω.[220] The passage is marvelously suited to the author's intention of promoting irenic attitudes and speech. It comes immediately after the discussion of the necessary act of blessing one's opponents and is loaded with the imagery of the three zones of human experience described by Malina.[221] The three zones are Semitic biblical expressions that typically describe dyadic human personality in its (1) psychic processes (eyes-heart), (2) language and the reception thereof (mouth-ears) and (3) outward expression (hands-feet).

Each zone is represented in the quotation of Ps. 33:12–16 LXX: (1) desire life (lit., wish to love life), see good days, evil, deceit, seek peace; (2) tongues, lips, speak; (3) turn away from evil, do good, pursue peace, do evil. "Now when all three zones are explicitly mentioned," affirms Malina, "then the speaker or writer is alluding to a total human experience."[222]

God, in v. 12, is also described in terms of dyadic personality: his eyes (psychic zone) are on the righteous, his ears (language) are open to their prayer, and his face (psychic zone) is against the

---

[219] Cf. Quint. *Inst. Or.* 5.11.42–44 on oracular proof.

[220] Perhaps the 3rd pers. appeared in Peter's catechetical source. Selwyn, *St. Peter*, 190–91.

[221] Malina, *NT World*, 60–67; cf. Malina and Rohrbaugh, *Commentary*, 55–56, 226–27, 336.

[222] Malina, *NT World*, 62.

evil doers.[223] The head and face are associated with honor (crowning, bowing or being bowed to, etc.) and dishonor (slapped, uncovered, etc.).[224] 'To set one's face against' is to oppose another's honor with one's own, thus to dishonor another by means of a facial affront. The impossibility of answering a challenge from the Lord spells dishonor; it is extended to those who do evil in contradistinction to the favorable turning of the face (esp. the eyes and ears) to the the righteous.[225] They are the ones honored since the Lord's eyes are protectively upon them and ears are attentive to their prayer.

---

[223] πρόσωπον κυρίου here prob. is parallel to ὀφθαλμοὶ κυρίου in the same verse and thus is a second ref. to the psychic zone of eyes-heart, the faculty of seeing (BAGD, 721 [s.v. "πρόσωπον"]).

[224] Malina, *NT World*, 35; Malina and Neyrey, "Honor and Shame," 35.

[225] ἐπί with the acc. can take a neutral sense (as if to answer the question 'where?') or a hostile meaning ('against'). The first meaning attends ἐπὶ δικαίους, the second ἐπὶ ποιοῦντας κακά. The meaning of ἐπὶ δικαίους becomes positive in association with καὶ ὦτα αὐτοῦ εἰς δέησιν αὐτῶν. See BAGD, 288 (s.v. "ἐπί. III with the accusative").

CHAPTER SIX

Third *Argumentatio*: 1 Peter 3:13–4:11

Propositio (3:13–16b)

A Quasi-*Narratio* (vv. 13–14)

The third *argumentatio*[1] of 1 Peter looks back to the central portion of the letter, 2:11–3:12, and answers objections that the audience may produce as a result of its contents. καὶ τίς ὁ κακώσων ὑμᾶς ἐὰν τοῦ ἀγαθοῦ ζηλωταὶ γένησθε; (v. 13) resembles the question of a rhetor to an imaginary objector in diatribe[2] or the figure of *sibi ipsi responsio*.[3] By means of the rhetorical question, the orator hopes to raise the questions in the minds of his actual hearers and answer them. Peter, having called for endurance in good behavior generally (2:12) and specifically for deference to the civic authorities (2:15), to masters (2:20), and to husbands (3:6), evidently anticipates some in his audience to counter with some protestations. Their objections might have been something like, 'If we do good, we shall still continue to suffer,' 'our alien status still makes us the target of criticism and slander,' 'people will still think of us as evildoers,' or 'our calling is to suffer—we cannot escape hardship as Christians.'

---

[1] For Peter's argumentative design (demonstrated now for the third time), see *Her.* 2.18.28–31.50; 3.9.16.

[2] Cf. Rudolf Bultmann, *Der Stil der paulinischen Predigt und die kynisch-stoische Diatribe*, Forschungen zur Religion und Literatur des alten und neuen Testaments 13 (Göttingen: Vandenhoeck & Ruprecht, 1910), 10–19.

[3] Cic. *De Or.* 3.54.207. Cf. Quint. *Inst. Or.* 9.3.90, the *sermocinationes consequentes* in *Her.* 4.52.65, and *interrogatio* in *Her.* 4.15.22. See Watson, "James 2," 108–13, for a perceptive discussion of Jas. 2:14–26, where dialogue of question and answer between the rhetor and the rhetor's imaginary opponent(s) occurs. Bullinger, *Figures of Speech*, 943–56, discusses the figure *erōtēsis*/interrogating in which the speaker poses a question without expecting a reply as a vivid way of declaring something. The particular kind of *erōtēsis* in 1 Pt. 3:13 is "affirmative negation" (949–51).

Not so, retorts Peter, since he expects that even among the pagans there is a general consensus of right and wrong that recognizes the goodness of Christian behavior to some extent. That consensus may not be universally shared (cf. 4:3–4), but the author believes that his readers can expect it to provide the ground for at least a partial affirmation of their moral uprightness (2:12, 14–15). Besides, even if they should suffer for righteousness,[4] says Peter, his readers are blessed (μακάριοι) (v. 14a). The language here clearly echoes the dominical saying in the Beatitudes (Mt. 5:12). Verses 13–14a resemble a *narratio* in Peter's argument since the passage establishes the context and conditions for the *propositio*.

The Fourfold Proposition

The proposition, with four carefully blended segments, is designed to assuage the fears and to address the objections that the listeners may well have concerning the behavior described in 2:1–3:12.

(1) and (2) Antithesis (vv. 14b–15a)

The first two elements of the propositio are placed in antithesis: τὸν δὲ φόβον αὐτῶν μὴ φοβηθῆτε μηδὲ ταραχθῆτε, κύριον δὲ τὸν Χριστὸν ἁγιάσατε ἐν ταῖς καρδίαις ὑμῶν (with language again from Isaiah [8:12–13]). Peter emphatically prohibits his readers from being apprehensive of unbelievers and their slanderous intimidation. An antanaklasis,[5] in which the φοβ-root of the imperative is duplicated in the accusative of content[6] ("do not fear their fear" NRSVmg), furnishes the emphasis that is augmented by an additional verb in the imperatival mood: μηδὲ

---

[4] ἀλλ' εἰ καὶ πάσχοιτε διὰ δικαιοσύνην, a construction that features a rare optative vb., πάσχοιτε. See BDF, 385 on the potential optative (like the one here) in a hypothetical protasis as a mark of literary language.

[5] Quint. *Inst. Or.* 9.3.68–77.

[6] The simple accusative of content (cognate accusative) is reviewed in BDF, 153–54.

ταραχθῆτε.[7] In contrast to fearful response, Peter advocates the sanctification of Christ as Lord in the believers' hearts.[8]

(3) Predicate Adjectival Phrase with ἕτοιμοι (vv. 15b–16a)

The absence of ὄντες in v. 15b is in keeping with Peter's style—he has omitted the participle before in 3:8. With ὄντες understood, the construction is a predicate adjective phrase headed by the adjective ἕτοιμοι ("ready") and is subordinate to the imperative verb ἁγιάσατε. To be ready to give an answer (πρὸς ἀπολογίαν) does not necessarily mean that the readers are to be prepared to stand before a magistrate or tribunal in an official inquest or trial during a local or imperial persecution. The defense could very well be informal.[9]

Neither does the author suggest an outlining of a domestic behavioral constitution by which the Christians would prove their acculturation to Greco-Roman society and its acceptable norms of conduct. Such an explanation, Balch affirms,[10] would pacify pagans who feared that the Christian faith represented a threat to the social order. Such a fear arose since Christ's adherents in Asia Minor included slaves and wives who autonomously forsook the religion of the *pater familias* and followed their Lord. The

---

[7] Peter's dual prohibition is more than that: it reveals that he has accurately understood his audience and their natural emotions of fear and thus wins their goodwill (establishes his ethos). According to Aristotle (*Rh.* 2.1.1378a.5), an orator's knowledge of the emotions contributes to the inclination of the audience to trust her/him. One of those emotions is fear. "Let fear be defined," says Aristotle, "as a painful or troubled feeling caused by the impression of an imminent evil that causes destruction or pain [ἔστω δὴ φόβος λύπη τις ἢ ταραχὴ ἐκ φαντασίας μέλλοντος κακοῦ φθαρτικοῦ ἢ λυπηροῦ]" (*Rh.* 2.5.1382a.32). The correspondence to 1 Pt. 3:14b is unmistakable.

The construction τὸν δὲ φόβον αὐτῶν μὴ φοβηθῆτε μηδὲ ταραχθῆτε, although from Isa. 8:12, shows how a rhetor can make skillful use of traditional material.

[8] The hallowed place in the heart that was to be YHWH's in Isa. 8:12–13 is now to be that of Christ.

[9] The probability that the backdrop for πρὸς ἀπολογίαν παντὶ τῷ αἰτοῦντι ὑμᾶς λόγον is that of informal daily social exchange is affirmed by Michaels, *1 Peter*, 188, and Selwyn, *St. Peter*, 193–94.

[10] Balch, *Wives*, 90–93, 109.

domestic code of 1 Pt. 2:18–3:12 would serve as a defense (before masters, husbands, perhaps the governor) of Christian behavior, that it conformed to cultural expectations of submissiveness by slaves and wives.

While Balch is correct in understanding the autonomy of slaves and wives in choosing the Christian faith as a source of serious concern to Greco-Roman society, the ἀπολογία that Peter mentions is in response to inquiry about the reason for the believers' inner hope (ἐλπίς), not about their conduct.[11] The hope of the readers is to be set upon the grace to come at Christ's revelation (1:13), a likely reference to the hope in God's vindication to honor for his presently harassed people. When giving their reason for the hope that they cherish, Peter advises gentleness and reverence for God as accompanying characteristics (v. 16a). These qualities have been encouraged of the wives and now they are required of all.[12]

(4) "Keep Your Conscience Clear" (v. 16b)

The phrase συνείδησιν ἔχοντες ἀγαθήν is circumstantial-participial in attendance upon the imperative ἁγιάσατε in v. 15a. It is also parallel to τὴν ἀναστροφὴν ἔχοντες καλήν in 2:12a. In dyadic and agonistic cultures, such as that of Peter's auditors, the

---

[11] Balch, *Wives*, 90, points out that Paul's apology in Acts 26 (ἀπολογεῖσθαι, v. 2) involves a defense of his lifestyle after he was accused by the Jews concerning his hope (ἐλπίς, v. 7). The fundamental charge against Paul, however, is that he opposed Jewish custom and profaned the temple (21:27–29; 24:6). While in custody, Paul maintains his innocence by asserting that he has done nothing wrong and merely lives in accordance with the hope of Israel that his adversaries also share (24:15; 26:6–7). Defending himself against the charges that he has violated Jewish custom and defiled the temple, Paul describes his hope to show that, since he merely has acted in accord with the hope that he shares with his accusers, they really have no grounds for complaint. The defense in 1 Pt. 3:15 is not similar—the subject of inquiry there is specifically "the hope that is in you" and not criminal charges as clearly indicated in Acts.

[12] 1 Pt. 3:4, πραὺ πνεῦμα; 3:2, ἡ ἐν φόβῳ ἀγνὴ ἀναστροφή. ἐν φόβῳ in 1 Pt. (1:17; 2:18; 3:2) appears to be in reference to a reverent attitude toward God (cf. 2:17).

conscience is not the internal monitor and voice of right and wrong as in individualistic Western society with its emphasis on individual guilt.[13] The conscience, συνείδησις, is rather one's awareness of the sum of the expectations and demands of one's culture that, when met by an individual, signify honorable behavior. According to Malina and Rohrbaugh,

> A consequence of all this is that ancient people did not know each other very well in the way we think most important: psychologically or emotionally. They neither knew nor cared about psychological development and were not introspective. Our comments about the feelings and emotional states of characters in the biblical stories are simply anachronistic projections of our sensibilities onto them. Their concern was how others thought of them (honor), not how they thought of themselves (guilt). Conscience was the accusing voice of others, not an interior voice of guilt (note Paul's comments in 1 Cor. 4:1–4). Their question was not the modern one, Who am I? Rather, they asked the questions of Jesus in this classic text [Mt. 16:13–20]: "Who do people say that I (the Son of Man) am?" and "Who do you say that I am?" It is from significant others that such information came, not from the self.[14]

Good behavior in the Mediterranean milieu means to have a good conscience, since by the former one fulfills the collective requirements of the latter that continually present themselves to one's sense of what his society demands.

Ratio (3:16c)

The obvious indicator of the *ratio* is the particle ἵνα. That which follows constitutes the *ratio* for the *propositio*. Peter's instructions are to be carried out "so that, when you are maligned, those who abuse you for your good conduct in Christ may be put to shame" (v. 16c).

---

[13] In psychological terms, the super-ego.

[14] Malina and Rohrbaugh, *Commentary*, 13. Cf. similar statements on 231, 342–43. Whether Paul's usage of συνείδησις (17x in the undisputed letters; lx ea. in 2 Tim. and Tit.) is similar deserves investigation. In the quotation above, Malina and Rohrbaugh suggest that Paul's notion of guilt, at least in 1 Cor. 4:1–4, corresponds to that which they describe. For Peter, a dyadic dimension to "conscience" is likely, especially in light of his predominant themes of honor and shame.

The language is reminiscent of 2:12 and describes the same contest for honor between Christians and their slanderous opponents with the same reversal in status that eventuates from the process of challenge and riposte. Figure 3 gives the reader a visual diagram.

Figure 3: Challenge and Response in 1 Pt. 3:16	
Action*	Threat οἱ ζηλωταὶ τοῦ ἀγαθοῦ → τὰ ἔθνη/οἱ ἐπηρεάζοντες ὑμῶν τὴν ἀγαθὴν ἐν Χριστῷ ἀναστροφήν
Perception*	Attack on self-esteem/established order
Challenge (Reaction)	Positive Rejection ἐν ᾧ καταλαλεῖσθε[15]/οἱ ἐπηρεάζοντες ὑμῶν τὴν ἀγαθὴν ἐν Χριστῷ ἀναστροφήν
Response (Counter-reaction)	συνείδησιν ἔχοντες ἀγαθήν (v. 16b)=ὑμῶν τὴν ἀγαθὴν ἐν Χριστῷ ἀναστροφήν
Verdict	ἵνα καταισχυνθῶσιν οἱ ἐπηρεάζοντες ὑμῶν τὴν ἀγαθὴν ἐν Χριστῷ ἀναστροφήν
* refers to stages not explicitly discussed by Peter.	

Confirmatio (3:17)

A maxim (*sententia*)[16] corroborates the reason for Peter's commands in the proposition: "For it is better to suffer for doing good, if suffering should be God's will, than to suffer for doing evil." The particular kind of maxim that Peter utilizes here is what Berger[17] calls a *Besser-spruch*, a saying in which the speaker affirms 'better is x than y.'

---

[15] The shorter rdg. is to be preferred over the longer ones in the UBS³ apparatus. The longer rdgs. are apparently copyists' attempts to harmonize 3:16 with 2:12. See Metzger, *Textual Commentary*, 691–92.

[16] *Her.* 4.17.24–25.

[17] Berger, "Gattungen," 1064. Cf. Arist. *Rh.* 1.7.1364b.22, οἷον τὸ ἀδικεῖσθαι μᾶλλον ἢ ἀδικεῖν ("it is better to suffer wrong that to commit it").

For Peter, to suffer for doing good means that one is slandered for one's commitment to Christ, a commitment made in spite of the prevalent cultural expectations or of one's household. To so suffer signifies the loss of dignity and honor that comes when one does right, but is accused of doing evil. Such painful experiences may, for some reason perhaps unknown, be the will of God.

Exornatio (3:18–22)

As in 2:21–25, Peter adopts noble and lofty material from the church's confessional tradition for a parenetic purpose. The particle ὅτι introduces a section (vv. 18–22) that embellishes the argumentation of vv. 13–17. The theological meaning and significance of 3:18–22, as well as the reconstruction of its original underlying hymn, have been discussed elsewhere[18] and are

---

Some notable examples of *Besser-sprüche* are found in Henry Chadwick, *The Sentences of Sextus: A Contribution to the History of Early Christian Ethics* (Cambridge: University Press, 1959): *Sent.* 152, αἱρετώτερον λίθον εἰκῇ βάλλειν ἢ λόγον ('it is better chosen to cast a stone at random than a word'); *Sent.* 345, κρεῖττον ἀποθανεῖν λιμῷ ἢ διὰ γαστρὸς ἀκρασίαν ψυχὴν ἀμαυρῶσαι ('it is better to die of famine than to diminish the soul on account of incontinence of the belly'); cf. Clitarchus 114 (in Chadwick, *Sextus*, 82), κρεῖττον ἀποθανεῖν ἢ διὰ γαστρὸς ἀκρασίαν ψυχὴν ἀμαυρῶσαι ('it is better to die than to diminish the soul on account of incontinence of the belly'); Clitarchus 115 (in Chadwick, *Sextus*, 82), ἄμεινον εἰδέναι ἀγνοοῦντα ὅτι ἀγνοεῖ ἢ δοκεῖν μή γινώσκοντα γινώσκειν ('it is better for one to know that he does not know unknown things than to think that he understands things that are not understood').

[18] Besides the commentaries, the reader may consult Bultmann, "Liedfragmente," 1–14; William J. Dalton, "1 Peter 3:19 Reconsidered," in *The New Testament Age: Essays in Honor of Bo Reicke*, ed. William C. Weinrich, (Macon, GA: Mercer University Press, 1984), 1:95–105; idem, *Proclamation*, esp. 64–65, 117–19; R. T. France, "Exegesis in Practice: Two Samples," in *New Testament Interpretation: Essays on Principles and Methods*, ed. I. Howard Marshall (Grand Rapids: William B. Eerdmans, 1977), 264–81 (on 1 Pt. 3:18–22); Martin Hengel, "Hymns and Christology," chap. in *Between Jesus and Paul: Studies in the Earliest History of Christianity* (n.p.: Fortress Press, 1983), 85–87; George Eldon Ladd, *A Theology of the New Testament* (Grand Rapids: William B. Eerdmans, 1974), 600–601; Pearson, "Hymnic Pattern," 182–245; Bo Reicke, *The Disobedient Spirits and Christian Baptism: A Study of 1 Pet. III. 19 and Its Context*, Acta Seminarii Neotestamentici Upsaliensis Edenda Curavit A. Fridrichsen (Copenhagen: Ejnar Munksgaard, 1946); Schelkle, *Die Petrusbriefe*, 102–12.

outside the scope of this dissertation. A classical-rhetorical examination of the passage, sensitive to the possible presence of the cultural values of honor and shame, is now in order.

1 Pt. 3:18–22 as Proof for the Argument

Here is the historical *exemplum* of Christ par excellence, the recounting of his sacrificial death, resurrection and triumphant ascension to the supreme place of glory. The confessional/ hymnic material constitutes for Peter's rhetorical scheme an *exemplum*[19] as proof. As in 1 Pt. 2:21–25, traditional material that originally served as a kind of encomium of Christ's redemptive activity is enlisted for a parenetic purpose, i.e., the proposition of vv. 14–15. The *exemplum* is thus an artificial proof—it is not in a naturally observable relationship to the argument and thus its applicability must be established by the rhetor's art.

Peter's point is this: just as Christ who suffered[20] innocently ("the righteous for the unrighteous") was exalted to honor, so those who faithfully follow him can anticipate the divinely bestowed honor. The maligned Christians also suffer unjustly, being defamed as evildoers (2:12) despite their good and irreproachable behavior, their ἀγαθὴ/καλὴ ἀναστροφή (2:12; 3:16). The logic of Peter's proof is an argument from the greater to the lesser:[21] what is true of Christ must certainly be true for his

---

[19] Specifically, a *res gesta*. See discussion at 131–32 above. Following Dalton, *Proclamation*, 117–19, I take 3:19–21 to contain catechetical material that digresses from the confessional tradition of vv. 18 and 22. My sub-headings thus identify the contents of vv. 19–21 as rhetorical *digressiones*.

[20] The textual witnesses are divided between ἔπαθεν and ἀπέθανεν at 3:18. I follow UBS[3] and Nestle-Aland[26] in reading ἔπαθεν. See discussion in Metzger, *Textual Commentary*, 692–93, who, despite the variety of witnesses for ἀπέθανεν, argues strongly for ἔπαθεν. Metzger contends that ἔπαθεν is preferable to ἀπέθανεν since πάσχω is a favored term in 1 Pt. (12x), whereas ἀποθνήσκω is nowhere found in it (except in some inferior witnesses for the word at 2:21). πάσχω has already been introduced (v. 14) as the subject of the present major section. For ἀποθνήσκω to suddenly appear at 3:18 would be strange.

[21] Quint. *Inst. Or.* 5.11.9.

followers.[22] Each element of the hymn has a function in the proof.

The Rhetorical Functions of the Confessional Articles

"For Christ also suffered . . ." (v. 18)

Christ's suffering for sins was not only once for all (ἄπαξ), but it was an instance of the just suffering in place of (ὑπέρ)[23] the unjust. *Antanaklasis*[24] with δίκαιος-ἀδίκων and the antithesis[25] θανατωθεὶς μὲν σαρκὶ ζῳοποιηθεὶς δὲ πνεύματι (with its *homoeoptoton*[26] in -εις and -ι) preserves the cadence of the hymn. The antithesis is both of diction (put to death—made alive; flesh—spirit), and of thought since the status of Christ in the flesh was reversed in his resurrection and ascension to glory.

Digressio 1. ". . . A proclamation to the spirits in prison" (vv. 19–20a)

Some recent scholarship has seen the journey of Christ[27] to the imprisoned spirits in v. 19 not as the pre-Easter *descensus ad inferna*

---

[22] Cf. Jn. 15:20b-c, "If they persecuted me, they will persecute you; if they kept my word, they will keep yours also." The shared experiences of suffering (shame) and honor are present in this passage as they are in 1 Pt. 3:18–22.

[23] Donald Guthrie, *New Testament Theology* (Leicester and Downers Grove, IL: Inter-Varsity Press, 1981), 474, states: "Although the preposition [ὑπέρ] used does not in itself demand a substitutionary meaning, the context shows this to be Peter's intention. It would weaken the force of the argument if a representative and not a substitutionary interpretation is in mind. The meaning is unmistakable—the righteous took the place of the unrighteous." For general discussion of ὑπέρ in this context, see Harris, "Prepositions," 196–97.

[24] Quint. *Inst. Or.* 9.3.68–77.

[25] *Her.* 4.15.21, 45.58.

[26] *Her.* 4.20.28.

[27] ἐν ᾧ could refer to the event of Christ's death and thus have the temporal sense 'on which occasion' (sc. when he died) according to Reicke, *Disobedient Spirits*, 13. However, the immediacy of πνεύματι to the rel. pron. ᾧ argues more strongly for the kind of option represented by JB "and, in the spirit, he went to preach to the spirits in prison." Grudem, *1 Peter*, 157, also connects ᾧ to πνεύματι in his suggested renderings: "'in which realm, namely, the spiritual realm,'" or "'in the realm of the Spirit's activity' (the realm in which Christ was raised from the dead, v. 18)."

as in the Apostles' Creed, but rather an ascent by the risen Christ to the ethereal realm of the disobedient spirits.[28] To these fallen angels, probably in the primitive Christian tradition the supernatural Watchers who sinned with mortal women (Gen. 6:1–4)[29] and were imprisoned for final judgment, Christ proclaims his victory (cf. v. 22). Such an interpretation is consistent with Peter's concern to emphasize Christ's exaltation to honor as paradigmatic for his audience.[30] Peter probably includes the cryptic material because of its correspondence to the need of his readers to understand their future honor. If v. 19

Untenable is the theory that ἐν ᾧ καί was originally followed by "Enoch" which, because of its similarity in sound to the prepositional phrase, was dropped by an early copyist. Enoch is said to have preached to the Watchers (cf. 1 En. 12:4–6), but Moffatt ("It was in the Spirit that Enoch also went and preached to the imprisoned spirits;" cf. Goodspeed) adopts the theory without any textual warrant. See discussion in Best, *1 Peter*, 139–40, and Marshall, *1 Peter*, 123–25.

[28] Dalton, "1 Peter 3:19," 99–105, comprehensively surveys the interpretation of v. 19 between 1965 (the date of the 1st ed. of his *Proclamation*) and c. 1977.

[29] Dalton, "1 Peter 3:19," 98–99; idem, *Proclamation*, 64–65, 117–19; Marshall, *1 Peter*, 123–26; Reicke, *Disobedient Spirits*, 66–67, 69, 90–91, 116–17, 132.

[30] If one believes that Peter is concerned with the witness of his audience to the non-Christians around them, then one might understand the verb to be 'to preach the gospel' (Reicke, *Disobedient Spirits*, 18–25; idem, *The Epistles of James, Peter, and Jude*, The Anchor Bible [Garden City, NY: Doubleday & Co., 1964], 111). If one presupposes that endurance in suffering is the Petrine focus, one might take κηρύσσειν in a neutral sense: 'to proclaim,' so that v. 19 has to do with an announcement of victory over the evil powers that subjects those powers and frees humanity (Dalton, "1 Peter 3:19," 97–99).

I work with an assumption that Peter's concentration is upon the motif of honor and shame and the reversal of status to be experienced by his readers (shame → honor) and their adversaries (honor → shame). Hence, the interpretation of Dalton seems preferable. However, whereas he ("1 Peter 3:19," 97) believes that 3:19, in asserting Christ's victory over evil, encourages Christians to overcome the evil active in their unbelieving opponents, I maintain that the verse asserts the honor that Christ has acquired through his unjust suffering and thus encourages believers that God will also honor them.

establishes an evangelistic *descensus ad inferna*, for the benefit of recalcitrant spirits (human and/or otherwise), its analogous value would be minimal since the proclamation does not then concern Christ's honor as much as the eternal doom or deliverance of the spirits to whom he preaches. The understanding of ἐκήρυξεν as Christ's triumphant proclamation of his honor in victory, however, respects the honor-motif of the letter.

Digressio 2. The ark-baptism typology[31] (vv. 20b–21b)

Baptism is the antitype (ἀντίτυπον) to the ark-Flood event[32] for Peter's theology. The saving significance of the latter corresponds to the ritual significance of the former in Christian practice.[33] As a symbolically significant ritual act, baptism marks the transition from the old life, which for Peter is the dis-honorable past,[34] to the new life of honor in the οἶκος τοῦ θεοῦ. Those baptized are linked to faithful Noah in contradistinction to the imprisoned spirits whose disobedience has won for them an irrevocable verdict of dishonor, the same verdict pronounced on the disobedient builders in 1 Pt. 2:7–8. The verb ἀπειθέω is used of the rebel spirits (3:20) and of the unbelieving builders (2:8).

---

[31] For definition and a brief discussion of typology, see 88–89 above. For the word ἀντίτυπος, see BAGD, 76 (s.v. "ἀντίτυπος").

[32] The neut. rel. pron. ὅ in v. 21a strictly refers to ὕδωρ immediately before. However, following A. T. Robertson, *A Grammar of the Greek New Testament in the Light of Historical Research* (Nashville: Broadman Press, 1934), 714, I apply it to the entire complex of events related to the Flood of which v. 20 speaks—without them the Flood would have no salvific or typological significance. The syntax is difficult: ὃ καὶ ὑμᾶς ἀντίτυπον νῦν σῴζει βάπτισμα ('which an antitype baptism also now saves you') is, however, satisfactorily smoothed by NRSV "and baptism, which this prefigured, now saves you."

[33] The meaning of baptism as a ritual marking the crossing of a boundary in Paul is explored (along with other rites) by Jerome H. Neyrey, *Paul, in Other Words: A Cultural Reading of His Letters* (Louisville: Westminster/John Knox Press, 1990), 79–92. A general analysis of the importance of rite to group identity is in Malina, *Christian Origins*, 21–22, 139–43.

[34] Cf. 1 Pt. 1:18 where the readers are said to be ransomed from their vanity of life inherited from their ancestors by the precious (τίμιος) blood of Christ. The new ransomed life is thus associated with that which is honorably valued (τίμιος). In 2:1–10, the believers are praised and have τιμή (2:7).

The rite of baptism signifies, for Peter's audience, a passage to honor and, as typological, connects the baptized readers to Noah. In the primitive Christian community, Noah is a historical personage of eminence. The respectable Noah would arouse positive pathos among the audience as its members are identified with him.[35]

The specific value of baptism as a ritual of crossing boundaries is its nature as an "appeal made to God from a good conscience" (REB). This rendering is by no means unanimously accepted—the word ἐπερώτημα has been variously understood as 'appeal,' 'request,' 'pledge,' 'question,' or the like, and options in translation of the word with the genitive συνειδήσεως ἀγαθῆς vary, depending on whether the construction is regarded as a subjective or an objective genitive.[36] If one accepts the translation of REB, however, the desire for vindication and honor by those presently denied them may very well be present as it may be with ἐπικαλέομαι in 1:17.

In such a case, ἐπερώτημα denotes a plea to God, in baptism, by resident aliens and visiting strangers for the vindication and honor society has refused them. Since these pariahs have submitted to baptism in faith (1:21; 2:7) and as Christ's obedient people (1:2, 22), they make an appeal from a good conscience,

---

[35] Noah is a "herald of righteousness" in 2 Pt. 2:5 where he and seven others saved from the Flood are presented as contrasts to the ungodly world destroyed by the deluge. Watson, *Invention,* 111–13, discusses the Flood in 2 Pt. 2:5 as one of three examples that serve as proof for the proposition "their condemnation . . . has not been idle, and their destruction is not asleep" (2:3b). Within the example Noah is "a type of the faithful Christian who will survive the judgment of the parousia" (112). Noah's role in 1 Pt. is less prominent, but he still serves as a type for the honored believer in his contrast to the disobedient spirits.

[36] The variety of interpretations of συνειδήσεως ἀγαθῆς ἐπερώτημα εἰς θεόν is reflected in the following sampling of translations: NRSV "an appeal to God for a good conscience;" Moffatt "the prayer for a clean conscience before God;" NIV "the pledge of a good conscience toward God;" RV "the interrogation of a good conscience toward God." For discussion of the options see Gervais T. D. Angel, "ἐρωτάω," *NIDNTT,* 2:880–81; BAGD, 285 (s.v. "ἐπερώτημα"); Michaels, *1 Peter,* 216–17.

confident that they have conformed themselves to the requirements of the household of God and will be accepted into it. Since in the dyadic culture of the Mediterranean world conscience is that set of norms, expectations, and dictates placed upon one by one's culture, συνείδησις may have such a reference in v. 21. The Christian resident alien or visiting stranger who is baptized can expect in that ritual a concomitant vindication by God since the requirements of the new sub-culture, the οἶκος τοῦ θεοῦ, have been adopted. Thus can Peter claim that baptism saves: it is the symbol for and the conferment of honored membership in the household of God, a status that is for alien peoples indeed salvation.[37]

Transition: "through the resurrection of Jesus Christ" (v. 21c)

The prepositional phrase δι' ἀναστάσεως Ἰησοῦ Χριστοῦ is a transition back to the hymn that was interrupted by the *digressiones* of vv. 19–21b. The phrase also serves to indicate that Christ himself, in whom God was active in the resurrection, is present in

---

[37] The social dimension of σώζω/σωτηρία is often overlooked in discussions of these words, but for the πάροικοι and παρεπίδημοι to whom Peter writes it very definitely has a social aspect since it involves a reversal vis-à-vis their culture, from shame to honor. "Salvation" undeniably has a spiritual and eschatological reference in the NT, but the socio-cultural aspect must not be ignored since σώζω in the OT can signify the vindication of the dishonored and oppressed (cf. LXX Ps. 71:4; 75:9). Suggesting a social dimension of σωτηρία in the NT is R. McL. Wilson, "*Soteria,*" *Scottish Journal of Theology* 6 (December 1953): 413–15, who maintains that salvation involves the whole person and brings present renewal in human relationships. In 1 Pt., σώζω and its cognates can refer to an eschatological salvation (1:5, 9), but it is deliverance that is at least partially experienced in the present (1:9), a fact expressed by the synonymous λυτρόω (1:18) and perhaps hinted at by διασώζω in 3:20 (saved, i.e., from the ungodly world).

σωτηρία is one of the three honors mentioned in the encomium 1:3–12, honors into which the readers were born (ἐλπὶς ζῶν, v. 3; κληρονομία ἄφθαρτος καὶ ἀμίαντος καὶ ἀμάραντος, v. 4; σωτηρία ἑτοίμη ἀποκαλυφθῆναι ἐν καιρῷ ἐσχάτῳ, v. 5). Cf. 1:9. For Peter the term extends beyond a designation of one's eternal destiny—it denotes one's present status of honor before and with God. Upon this status vv. 10–12 elaborate. In v. 10, salvation is equated with χάρις, a term that is one of the most significant positive words in the Petrine semantic field of honor-shame.

saving power in baptism[38] and thus baptism can be said to "save." It is a synecdoche in which a part, the ritual of passage and antitype, baptism, represents the whole, the regeneration and salvation of Christ.

The digressions have not been superfluous to Peter's purpose in his *exornatio*. Rather, the *digressiones* have had the function of arousing positive pathos among the audience through their identification with Noah. Furthermore, the author has reminded his readers of the appeal for divine vindication through baptism, an appeal that they have successfully made.

"Who has gone into heaven and is at the
right hand of God, with angels, authorities,
and powers made subject to him" (v. 22)

The climax[39] of the hymn is now reached: the supreme position of authority in the universe is Christ's: he is at the right hand of God, an anthropomorphous metonymy for God in his omnipotence.[40] After ascending into heaven, itself a common spatial metaphor for the sphere of the numinous,[41] Christ took his place of honor at God's side. There, the supernatural powers are prostrate in submission to Christ.

The genitive absolute clause v. 22c ὑποταγέντων αὐτῷ ἀγγέλων καὶ ἐξουσιῶν καὶ δυνάμεων features ὑποτάσσω, the same verb that Peter uses when enjoining submission by his audience to the political authorities (2:13–14), masters (2:18), and husbands (3:1, 5). Just as Christ experienced a reversal of status, from shame to honor (evinced by the submission of the

---

[38] Friedrich Schröger, *Gemeinde im 1. Petrusbrief: Untersuchungen zum Selbstverständnis einer christlichen Gemeinde an der Wende vom 1. zum 2. Jahrhundert*, Schriften der Universität Passau: Reihe katholische Theologie, vol. 1 (Passau: Passavia Universitätsverlag, 1981), 34.

[39] Heightening the dramatic effect of the passage, NRSV reverses the *cola* v. 22a and v. 22b in order to convey the logical temporal sequence that is reversed in the Gk.: ὅς ἐστιν ἐν δεξιᾷ [τοῦ] θεοῦ, πορευθεὶς εἰς οὐρανόν, ὑποταγέντων αὐτῷ ἀγγέλων καὶ ἐξουσιῶν καὶ δυνάμεων.

[40] See BAGD, 174–75 (s.v. "δεξιός").

[41] Ibid., 594–95 (s.v. "οὐρανός").

evil supernatural adversaries),[42] so too can the beleaguered Christians in Asia Minor anticipate such a reversal in their relationships with those to whom they must submit.[43] The accumulation of titles for the subjected spiritual beings accentuates the absoluteness of Christ's rule—further amplified by the *homoeoptoton*[44] in fourfold -ωv and *polysyndeton*[45] (καί twice). The entire v. 22 is a *demonstratio*, a vivid verbal description that positively stimulates audience imagination.[46]

Conplexio (4:1–11)

The presence of οὖν in 4:1 signifies the shift to another section. Here it is a minor shift, the major shift to a new rhetorical unit is indicated at 4:11 by the doxology that closes with ἀμήν. The section 1 Pt. 4:1–11 is a résumé for the argument that commences at 3:13. The *conplexio* sums up and draws together the rhetor's argument.[47] In 4:1–11, Peter returns to his previous emphases: suffering (4:1 → 3:14, 17–18), the reproaches of the pagans (4:4 → 3:16), and good conduct (4:7–11 → 3:13, 16).

---

[42] That the powers in 1 Pt. 3:22 are malevolent and opposed to Christ is not expressly stated there nor anywhere in the letter. I infer that they are so because of the correspondence throughout 1 Pt. between the readers and their Lord. If they face hostile spiritual forces (and they do, 5:8), Christ must have done so. The disobedient spirits of v. 19 may well be the angels, authorities, and powers of v. 22. Cf. also Eph. 6:12.

[43] Viz. those enumerated in 2:13–3:6 are examples of any human creature (ἀνθρωπίνη κτίσις, v. 13) to whom submission is due. The reversal of shame to honor would be necessary for πάροικοι and παρεπίδημοι in numerous kinds of social intercourse. The foreigner, with limited rights, was expected to defer to the native since the former was merely a guest of the latter, the host (cf. Martin, *Metaphor*, 196–98).

[44] *Her.* 4.20.28.

[45] Quint. *Inst. Or.* 9.3.50–52.

[46] See 136–39 above.

[47] *Her.* 2.18.28.

Exhortatio (4:1–2)

The Meaning of 4:1[48]

The notoriously difficult v. 1 has given rise to a variety of interpretations. Since space precludes a thorough consideration of them, I shall interact with them only on certain points as I present my own view.

"Since therefore Christ suffered in the flesh, arm yourselves also with the same intention"

The phraseology of v. 1a (Χριστοῦ οὖν παθόντος σαρκί) picks up the thought of 3:18 (Χριστὸς ἅπαξ περὶ ἁμαρτιῶν ἔπαθεν … θανατωθεὶς μέν σαρκί). In v. 1b, the notion of the Christian life as warfare for the resident aliens and visiting strangers in Asia Minor (2:11) reappears with the aorist middle imperative ὁπλίσασθε, a metaphorically used military term[49] meaning "arm yourselves." The weapon for spiritual warfare is the same intention that Christ embodied, his ἔννοια, his insight.[50]

"(For whoever has suffered in the flesh has ceased from sin)"

A maxim? The ὅτι clause could be generic, a maxim[51] that has been enlisted as a rationale for the command to the readers to arm themselves in v. 1b. Thus ὅτι ὁ παθὼν σαρκὶ πέπαυται ἁμαρτίας would stand in general reference to a Christian who either has died to the old life of sin in baptism, as in Rom. 6:7 (ὁ γὰρ ἀποθανὼν δεδικαίωται ἀπὸ τῆς ἁμαρτίας), or is purified of the evil influence of the flesh (sinful nature or mortal human existence) by way of suffering. The subject of the succeeding infinitives in v. 2 (βιῶται) and v. 3 (κατειργάσθαι) is that of the

---

[48] The following interpretation distills, refines, and builds upon the discussions in Goppelt, *Der erste Petrusbrief,* 264–71; Marshall, *1 Peter,* 132–34; Michaels, *1 Peter,* 225–29; and Millauer, *Leiden als Gnade,* 105–34.

[49] Michaels, *1 Peter,* 225.

[50] BAGD, 267 (s.v. "ἔννοια"). Cf. Phil. 2:5.

[51] See 177 above.

aorist gnomic participle ὁ παθών, "he who has suffered" (NIV),[52] unless the ὅτι clause is understood as parenthetical. If it is parenthetical, the second person plural subject of ὁπλίσασθε is the infinitival subject. The perfect πέπαυται is also gnomic if ὁ παθών is.

Arguments against 4:1c as a maxim. Despite 1 Pt. 3:21, a baptismal context is probably not the setting of 4:1. Rather, the context of the verse as the opening of a *conplexio* is a concern for honor and honorable conduct. Besides, Paul's ὁ ἀποθανών in Rom. 6:7 is not a convincing parallel to Peter's ὁ παθών, although a certain verbal similarity exists. πάσχω, when applied to Christians in 1 Peter, is not in reference to death either figurative or literal, but to the distress of slander from their opponents.[53]

As for the understanding of ὁ παθών σαρκὶ πέπαυται ἁμαρτίας as an affirmation of the refining power of suffering, 1:6–7 could be enlisted as support. The πειρασμοί there, however, serve to purify the faith of the believers that it may be found praiseworthy at the revelation of Jesus Christ. It is not purified "from sin." In 1 Pt. 4:1c, could the idea be not that of a refining process by means of suffering, but of an abandonment of a forbidden mode of conduct?

Christ as ὁ παθών. Michaels insists on the parenthetical nature of the ὅτι clause, but claims that is is in reference to Christ. (NRSV makes the clause parenthetical, but generic ["whoever has suffered"].) The parallel between Χριστοῦ . . . παθόντος σαρκί and ὁ παθών σαρκί indicates that both constructions are in

---

[52] REB makes clear this connection to the infin. βιῶσαι of v. 2 by inserting a full stop before the ὅτι clause. "Anyone" indicates a gnomic sense for ὁ παθών. The serial connection of κατειργάσθαι (v. 3a) with βιῶσαι is obscured in the REB, however, by the trans. in the 2nd pers. pl., "You have spent time enough in the past doing what pagans like to do" at v. 3a.

[53] This is evident from the contexts surrounding πάσχω at 2:19–23 (where undeserved physical beatings of slaves may also be involved), 3:14–17, and 4:14–16.

reference to Jesus.[54] Since he once (ἅπαξ) suffered for sins
(3:18), Christ was finished with sin, he was then through with it.
This is the meaning of πέπαυται in v. 1c. Peter wants every
believer to possess the same "intention" or "resolve" (ἔννοια) that
Christ had.

Although Michaels, in my opinion, is generally persuasive in
his suggestion, καὶ ὑμεῖς τὴν αὐτὴν ἔννοιαν ὁπλίσασθε is a
phrase that he leaves dangling without explanation. That Peter
wants his readers to resolve to be through with sins just as Christ
so resolved is inadequate since Christ's cessation with sin involved
his death and Peter is in no way advising his audience to literally
die. Complete parallelism in the ἔννοιαι of Christ and his
followers in 1 Peter does not exist.

A correspondence in the two experiences does reside,
however, in the correspondence of kind. There are references
both to Christ and his followers undergoing distresses of verbal
abuse in the letter. A comparison of 2:23 with 2:12; 3:9, 16 shows
this. The example of Christ in his distress is to be emulated by the
faithful whose non-retaliatory endurance in the face of unjust
suffering is adherence to their Lord's example. He endured
unjust maltreatment and so should they (2:20–21). The kind of
suffering and the nature of its endurance are identically shared by
Christ and his followers.

Michaels's argument would be more plausible if he were to
identify the common resolve between Christ and Peter's readers
as the commitment to endure verbal reproach. Christ has ceased
from sin (ἁμαρτία) in the sense that he has repudiated any
attempt to defend his honor by vengeful and retaliatory abuse,
the very point made in 2:22 where ἁμαρτία is defined by

---

[54] Michaels, *1 Peter*, 225–29. Marshall's view (*1 Peter*, 132–34) is that
Christians must show opposition to sinful living and thus be ready to suffer
for it, just as Christ showed his opposition to sinful living and suffered. The
connection that Marshall makes of the ὅτι clause to the Christians is
weakened (I think decisively) by the correspondence of the clause to
Χριστοῦ παθόντος σαρκί and, consequently, its reference to Christ, not the
believers.

δόλος—any kind of verbal malice or treachery.[55] I suggest that ὅτι ὁ παθὼν σαρκὶ πέπαυται ἁμαρτίας reverts primarily to Peter's thought in 2:20–23, not to 3:18 as Michaels suggests. The grammatical parallel of 3:18 with 4:1a remains, however. The infinitives of vv. 2–3 carry the exhoration ὁπλίσασθε forward.

Rhetorical features of v. 1. Rhetorically, then, 1 Pt. 4:1 stands as a recapitulation of earlier affirmations (viz. 2:21–23; 3:18) of Christ's suffering in his atonement, a typical feature of the *conplexio*. The ὅτι clause is a statement of precedent, a past fact that serves as a proof reasoning from the greater to the lesser.[56] It supports the instruction for believers to arm themselves with the same intention that Christ had. The proof is artificial in that the rhetor's application of it (to the non-retaliatory response of the audience) is not self-evident in the confessional tradition that solely recounts the Passion without ethical ramifications. The entire v. 1 is a *transitio*,[57] briefly recalling what Peter has already said ("since therefore Christ suffered in the flesh") and just as briefly presenting what is to follow ("arm yourselves also with the same intention").

Antithesis in v. 2

An antithesis[58] (indicated by ἀλλά) in v. 2 serves to distinguish precisely the desired life-style of the readership. The addressees are to live no longer by human desires (ἀνθρώπων ἐπιθυμίαις), but (ἀλλά) by the will of God (θελήματι θεοῦ). A pleasing alliteration subsists in θέλημα θεοῦ, a construction that has come to signify for Peter and his readers ἀγαθοποιεῖν: persistent well-doing that silences hostile critics (2:15) and that may lead to suffering (3:17).[59] Thus βιῶσαι is an *adjunctio*,[60] a figure in which

---

[55] At 1 Pt. 2:22, ἁμαρτία is defined by δόλος in synonymy. See 134 above. Of course, Christ endured more than slander! Slander, though, is the common element in his and his followers' suffering.

[56] Cf. Quint. *Inst. Or.* 5.10.8–14.

[57] *Her.* 4.26.35.

[58] A *contentio* of thought, *Her.* 4.45.58.

[59] Michaels, *1 Peter*, 230.

[60] *Her.* 4.27.38.

a single verb that holds the sentence is at either the beginning or, as here, the end.

Digressio (4:3–6)

Indignatio (vv. 3–4)

The opposite of the life that is lived according to God's will is a life described in a *digressio*,[61] a passage that digresses from the logical order of a speech for purposes of praise or blame, amplification or abridgement of a topic, emotional appeal, or enhancement of style.[62] In vv. 3–6, the author digresses from his forward focus in the *exhortatio* (ὁ ἐπίλοιπος χρόνος) in order for the audience to consider the time past (ὁ παρεληλυθὼς χρόνος, v. 3) which was sufficient for doing what the pagans like to do. The *digressio* is an important factor in Peter's *conplexio*, the part of his argument where he wants to stir his hearers emotions, including the emotion *indignatio* against persons or things.[63] Peter does not wish to enrage his listeners against the ἔθνη themselves, but against their practices that collectively constitute τὸ βούλημα τῶν ἐθνῶν.[64]

The commonplaces (*loci communes*) available to the rhetor in the amplification[65] of *indignatio* are numerous. Peter chooses the topic known as enumeration of attendant circumstances, a vivid, detailed description that brings a detestable act before the very

---

[61] Gk. παρέκβασις/Lat. *egressus, egressio*, or *excursus* (Quint. *Inst. Or.* 4.3.12), *digressio* (9.1.28=Cic. *De Or.* 3.53.203), and *digressus* (Quint. *Inst. Or.* 10.1.49). See Watson, *Invention*, 114–24, on this figure and the lengthy *digressio* in 2 Pt. 2:10b–22.

[62] Quint. *Inst. Or.* 4.3.14; Watson, *Invention*, 115.

[63] *Her.* 2.30.47–49 and Cic. *Inv.* 1.53.100–54.105 where the species of rhetoric under consideration is judicial, but the topics discussed may be adapted to deliberative oratory.

[64] πεπορευμένους, an acc. pl. ptc. of general reference in connection with the infin. κατειργάσθαι and, thus, taking the subject of the infin. ὑμεῖς (v. 1b), i.e., the readers, not the Gentiles (so NRSV and REB). Cf. 2 Pt. 2:10b–22 where the false prophets themselves are attacked.

[65] Amplification is an element of the conclusion of a speech, along with recapitulation and appeal to pity (*Her.* 2.30.47).

eyes of the audience.[66] He lists several vices[67] that are representative sins to be avoided by Christ's followers: "licentiousness, passions, drunkenness, revels, carousing, and lawless idolatry."

Yet another topic of amplification surfaces at the end of v. 4. "They are surprised," writes Peter, "that you no longer join them in the same excesses of dissipation,[68] and so they blaspheme." "Blaspheme" or "malign you" (NRSVmg), and "abusing you" (REB), all translate the present participle βλασφημοῦντες, the only appearance of the word or its cognates in 1 Peter. In these translations it is unclear whether βλασφημέω is directed toward God or toward people. The surprise of the pagans regarding the changed behavior of Christians (ἐν ᾧ ξενίζονται μὴ συντρεχόντων ὑμῶν εἰς τὴν αὐτὴν τῆς ἀσωτίας ἀνάχυσιν) suggests that the abuse is directed toward the converts from paganism, not God directly. The word family can have human persons as object, God and supernatural beings, or possibly both human and supernatural targets.[69] The fact that Peter chooses βλασφημέω in 4:4 as opposed to the already used καταλαλέω (2:12, 3:16), λοιδορέω (2:23*bis*; cf. 3:9 λοιδορία), ἐπηρεάζω (3:16), or a word yet to appear, ὀνειδίζω (4:14), is significant. βλασφημέω amplifies Peter's contention, heightening an accusation of the opponents' abuse to one of abuse with sacrilegious overtones.[70] To describe an action as nefarious and an outrage to piety is an effective way of stirring negative emotions of the hearers.[71] Peter, by using βλασφημέω, stresses the absolute incompatibility of the pagans' vices with new life in

---

[66] *Her.* 2.30.49; Cic. *Inv.* 1.54.104. Cf. *demonstratio* (see 136–39 and 186 above), and the figure *frequentatio*, *Her.* 4.40.52–53.

[67] Cf. Rom. 1:28–32; 1 Cor. 6:9–10; Gal. 5:19–21; Eph. 4:31, 5:3–5; Col. 3:5, 8–9; Selwyn, *St. Peter*, 210–12, 421.

[68] ἡ ἀνάχυσις τῆς ἀσωτίας, a hendiadys intensifying the abject corruption in the pagan life-style. On hendiadys see Bullinger, *Figures of Speech*, 657–72. The hendiadys in 1 Pt. 4:4 features an alliteration in α-.

[69] See BAGD, 142–43.

[70] Cf. Lk. 22:65, where βλασφημέω makes the verbal abuse of Jesus at the same time an outrage against God.

[71] *Her.* 2.30.49; Cic. *Inv.* 1.53.102.

the will of God. The author hopes to create in his audience a revulsion for those vices.[72]

"But They Will Have to Give an Accounting to Him . . ." (vv. 5–6)

The words λόγος and ἑτοίμως recall 3:15b (ἕτοιμοι ἀεὶ πρὸς ἀπολογίαν παντὶ τῷ αἰτοῦντι ὑμᾶς λόγον περὶ τῆς ἐν ὑμῖν ἐλπίδος) where the terms describe the manner in which the believers are to sanctify Christ in their hearts. Now the words are differently applied: λόγος means, not the reason of Christian hope, but the accounting of one's life at the last judgment.[73] He who will judge is ready (ἑτοίμως) to do so. The reversal in reference for λόγος signifies a reversal in honor status between the Christians, presently maligned and called into question for their belief, and their pagan opponents. The latter query and incriminate now, but will some day have to give an account to God[74] and, because of their blasphemy and dissipation (v. 4), will be found wanting.[75]

A well-constructed antithesis with precise verbal correspondence in its contrasting parts appears in v. 6b-c (κριθῶσι μὲν κατὰ ἀνθρώπους σαρκὶ ζῶσι δὲ κατὰ θεὸν πνεύματι). The *contentio* concludes the *digressio* and, as a maxim, serves to verify the assertion that a future judgment of all people ("the living and the dead") will transpire. The words following ἵνα have the

---

[72] This is a rare instance in 1 Pt. where Peter's words are capable of engendering ill will toward the Christians' pagan opponents themselves and not their wicked deeds alone.

[73] Cf. above on *antanaklasis*, a figure by which two different meanings of the same word arise.

[74] τῷ ἑτοίμως ἔχοντι κρῖναι is a *pronominatio* for God, like that in 1:17. See 65 above.

[75] Marshall, *1 Peter*, 137–39, reflects on the reversal of status, but not in terms of honor or shame. The judgment reverses the worldly estimates of who is right and who is wrong in the relationship of the world and the church.

antithetical cadence of hymnic or creedal material and could perhaps derive from some traditionally confessional source.[76]

The identity of the dead to whom the gospel has been preached is unspecified. Presumably they are certain human dead, for those were the νεκροί of v. 5. Marshall[77] helpfully reviews the basic options to the interpretation of v. 6 and concludes that "the reference is to Christians who are now dead but who heard and responded to the gospel before they died."[78] Regardless of the meaning of v. 6, Peter seems to believe in some sort of reversal: the dishonored believers who are called to account by the world will be exonerated and their opponents will themselves have to give an account to God.

Exhortationes (4:7–11)

Various Sententiae [79]

Peter concludes the deliberative *argumentatio* 3:13–4:11 with a series of recommendations that are maxims or *sententiae* like those in Gal. 5:25–6:10 which themselves conclude a major section of parenesis (5:1–6:10).[80] Probably intended as a heading to the collection is πάντων δὲ τὸ τέλος ἤγγικεν, itself a maxim with variations elsewhere in the New Testament.[81] In view of the imminent coming of the Lord, Peter instructs the believers to "be serious [σωφρονήσατε] and discipline yourselves [νήψατε] for the sake of your prayers." The two imperative verbs form a hendiadys, both used in order to give an emphasis that one verb

---

[76] Dalton, *Proclamation*, 101, notes the similarities between 3:18 and 4:6 and thus contends that these verses mark an *inclusio*. The phrases are not truly parallel, however, although similar in their hymnically oppositional style.

[77] Marshall, *1 Peter*, 136–39. See also Reicke, *Disobedient Spirits*, 206–8.

[78] Marshall, *1 Peter*, 137.

[79] *Her.* 4.17.24–25; Berger, "Gattungen," 1049–74.

[80] Betz, *Galatians*, 291–311, to whom I am indebted for the classifications that I use for the Petrine *sententiae.* Cf. Jewett, *The Thessalonian Correspondence*, 85 (outline), who assigns the heading *"exhortatio"* to 2 Thess. 3:6–15.

[81] Cf. Lk. 21:28, 31; Rom. 13:12; Phil 4:5(?); Heb. 10:25 (all with ἐγγ-words); Wolfgang Bauder and Hans-Georg Link, "ἐγγύς," *NIDNTT* 2:54–55.

alone could not.[82] The hendiadys forms a pithy kind of statement, a maxim in the imperative.

In vv. 8–10, *sententiae* with participles[83] (vv. 8, 10) or an adjective (v. 9) appear. Verse 8 itself is enthymematic; its syllogistic components are: you ought to cover others' sins (major premise), love covers a multitude of sins (minor premise), you ought to have love (conclusion). Peter's formula, closer to the Hebrew of Prov. 10:12b than to the LXX, is probably derived from a version of the saying circulating in that day.[84] The meaning is probably that ἀγάπη, since it always forgives the failings of others, must be persistently maintained.[85] ἐκτενῆ ἔχοντες is an intensifying alliteration. The *sententia* of v. 9, formed with the participial adjective φιλόξενοι,[86] has the highly onomatopoetic γογγυσμοῦ.[87] With the preceding ἄνευ, it forms an audile (but not visual) *homoeoptoton*.[88]

---

[82] The sense may be some thing like 'be serious—yes, serious and disciplined' or 'be clear-minded—clear-minded and sober!' On hendiadys, see Bullinger, *Figures of Speech*, 657–72.

[83] Here, I believe, one is on solid ground (with Daube, "Participle," 484) in ascribing imperatival value to the ptc. ἔχοντες in v. 8 as well as to the adj. φιλόξενοι in v. 9, and the ptc. διακονοῦντες in v. 10. The ptcs. and adj., embedded in maxims, have the character of rules of conduct just as their cousins in Tannaitic Hebrew do. See the discussion in Daube, "Participle," 467–88 passim.

[84] See Goppelt, *Der erste Petrusbrief*, 283–85, for a thorough discussion of the maxim and the entirety of v. 8. Goppelt identifies ὅτι ἀγάπη καλύπτει πλῆθος ἁμαρτιῶν as a maxim that circulated in early Christianity. The Heb. reads וְעַל כָּל־פְּשָׁעִים תְּכַסֶּה אַהֲבָה ("but love covers all offenses"), whereas the LXX renders it πάντας δὲ τοὺς μὴ φιλονεικοῦντας καλύπτει φιλία ("but affection covers all that do not love strife," Brenton trans.).

[85] Cranfield, *1 Peter*, 95–96. Cf. 1 Pt. 1:22.

[86] Martin, *Metaphor*, 196–98, discusses the notion of strangers as 'guests' within a 'host' country and the importance of hospitality to those guests in their unfamiliar environment.

[87] On the trope onomatopoeia, see *Her.* 4.31.42; Quint. *Inst. Or.* 8.6.31–33; Martin, *Antike Rhetorik*, 269.

[88] Although ἄνευ is indeclinable, the figure is present by virtue of the sound. Normally, *homoeoptoton* requires two or more words in the same case with like endings (*Her.* 4.20.28).

With verse 10, the apex of ethical instruction in the *argumentatio*, and perhaps in the entire letter, has been reached. The *sententia* resembles that of Gal. 6:10 (ἄρα οὖν ὡς καιρὸν ἔχομεν, ἐργαζώμεθα τὸ ἀγαθὸν πρὸς πάντας, μάλιστα δὲ πρὸς τοὺς οἰκείους τῆς πίστεως) without the universal scope of the Pauline maxim. Peter's εἰς ἑαυτοὺς αὐτὸ [sc. χάρισμα] διακονοῦντες is equivalent to Paul's ἐργαζώμεθα τὸ ἀγαθὸν πρὸς πάντας. Peter's ὡς καλοὶ οἰκονόμοι ποικίλης χάριτος θεοῦ and Paul's μάλιστα δὲ πρὸς τοὺς οἰκείους τῆς πίστεως both designate the *locus* of the service as the household of God: οἰκονόμοι means "household stewards"[89] and τοὺς οἰκείους τῆς πίστεως may be translated "those of the family of faith" (NRSV) or "members of the household of faith" (REB).

The participle διακονοῦντες (cf. διακονεῖ, v. 11) may very well have a household reference also, preserving the more original and literal sense of 'to wait at table.'[90] Elliott comments:

> The choice of terms in 4:10–11 also reflects the provenance of the household. Here the members of the community are told to "serve" (*diakountes* [*sic*], v. 10; cf. also v. 11) one another with the various gifts of grace which they have received. As conventional usage indicates, *diakonein* often denotes *domestic service* in particular, the daily round of household chores and menial tasks. By the time of 1 Peter, of course, *diakonein* and its paronyms could have become traditional terms for Christian ministrations in general. However, the specific identification of the agents of such service as "household stewards" makes the *domestic* dimension of this service here quite explicit. The service thus recommended would be the performance of practical tasks which were essential to the sustenance and growth of the household of faith.[91]

Only two examples of χαρίσματα appear in 1 Peter, contrary to the longer lists in 1 Corinthians 12, Romans 12, and Ephesians 4. The maxims of v. 11a and b[92] presuppose a third-person

---

[89] Elliott, *Home*, 162 n. 145. For the word οἰκονόμος in the NT, see Lk. 12:42, 16:1, 3, 8; Rom. 16:23; 1 Cor. 4:1, 2; Gal. 4:2; Tit. 1:7; 1 Pt. 4:10.

[90] BAGD, 184–85 (*sub* διακον- word-group).

[91] Elliott, *Home*, 203 (emphases Elliott's).

[92] v. 11a, εἴ τις λαλεῖ, ὡς λόγια θεοῦ. V. 11b, εἴ τις διακονεῖ, ὡς ἐξ ἰσχύος ἧς χορηγεῖ ὁ θεός.

present imperative (λαλεῖ → λαλείτω/διακονεῖ → διακονεί-τω).[93] Are λαλεῖν and διακονεῖν simply two examples of a longer list of χαρίσματα that Peter knows? One ought rather to assume that these are simply Peter's identification of the two basic functions of ministry within the primitive church: practical service and the teaching of the Word.[94]

The χάρισμα that each has received (v. 10) is a specific expression of God's χάρις that the believers not only await (1:13), but have already begun to experience (1:10).[95] Each member of the household has been honored with a χάρισμα. Now, just as s/he has been served in the things of salvific grace (1:12), so now each member is to serve others (4:10) as a good household steward of God's manifold grace (ποικίλης χάριτος θεοῦ). Peter has come full circle from his exordium (an epideictic discourse on the endowments of his readers) to the place where he urges them to be good stewards of those endowments in the οἶκος τοῦ θεοῦ. The purpose of good stewardship, exclaims Peter in the doxology that closes the *argumentatio*, is "so that God may be glorified in all things through Jesus Christ. To him belong the glory and the power forever and ever. Amen" (v. 11c-d).

With the doxology, Peter stirs the hearers' emotions.[96] The praise of God and Jesus Christ introduces objects which, by their divine nature, are of high importance and are most worthy of the weighty words that the author uses in relationship to them. Peter's ascription of glory[97] is evocative of the same impassioned response from the audience.[98]

---

[93] Gal. 6:4 (δοκιμαζέτω) and 6 (κοινωνείτω) are examples of maxims in the 3rd pers. sing. imper. identified by Betz, *Galatians*, 292, 302–6.

[94] Selwyn, *St. Peter*, 219. Cf. the distinction also in Acts 6:1–6.

[95] Cf. 1:9, κομιζόμενοι τὸ τέλος τῆς πίστεως [ὑμῶν] σωτηρίαν ψυχῶν, with v. 10, περὶ ἧς σωτηρίας ἐξεζήτησαν καὶ ἐξηραύνησαν προφῆται οἱ περὶ τῆς εἰς ὑμᾶς χάριτος προφητεύσαντες. σωτηρία and χάρις are virtually synonymous—the salvation that they now are receiving is that which the prophets foretold would come to the believers, i.e., grace.

[96] Cic. *Part Or.* 15.52–17.58.

[97] Michaels, *1 Peter*, 252–54, thoroughly discusses ᾧ ἐστιν ἡ δόξα κτλ and believes the rel. pron. refers to Jesus Christ. Little rhetorical difference is

made whether one accepts this view or that of, e.g., Goppelt, *Der erste Petrusbrief*, 291–92, which says God is the antecedent.

[98] Cic. *Part. Or.* 15.54, 16.56.

CHAPTER SEVEN

The *Peroratio*: 1 Peter 4:12–5:14

An *Expolitio* on Suffering (4:12–19)

The decisive break 4:11/12 signals the beginning of the *peroratio* for the entire letter; in 1 Pt. 4:12–5:14 Peter sums up the affirmations and arguments that he has put forth in 1:1–4:11. The exordium and his three *argumentationes* all find (1) their recapitulation in the last section of the letter along with (2) amplification of Peter's case and (3) appeals to pity. Thus 1 Pt. 4:12–5:14 fulfills the three functions of the conclusion according to classical rhetorical standards.[1]

Attempts to identify 4:12 as the commencement of a second correspondence[2] are unnecessary—they neglect the close verbal and conceptual connection to all that has gone before as well as the nature of 4:12–5:14 as a rhetorical *peroratio*. The striking recollections in 1 Pt. 4:12–5:14 of 1:1–4:11 argue for the integrity of the entire letter. Especially in 4:12–19, Peter picks up again and recapitulates what he has stated about suffering in the *argumentationes*, intensifying it by first returning to the notion of trial by fire, initially mentioned in 1:6–7.[3] Other reminiscences[4] to earlier ideas are suffering as slander (4:14 → 2:12; 3:16), just and unjust suffering (4:15–16 → 2:19–20; 3:14), suffering according to the will of God (4:19 → 3:17), the blessedness of the righteous sufferer (4:14 → 3:14), and joy in suffering (4:13 → 1:6, 8).

---

[1] *Her.* 2.18.28, 29.46–30.47 and Cic. *Inv.* 1.52.98 mention *enumeratio, amplificatio*, and *commiseratio/conquestio*. Arist. *Rh.* 3.19.1419b.10–1420b.5 identifies the first two, but includes two that are somewhat different: (1) to dispose a hearer favorably toward the rhetor and unfavorably toward the opponents and (2) to excite hearers' emotions. These seem to have been conflated by the Latin handbooks here cited into *commiseratio/conquestio*.

[2] See the discussion in Elliott, "Peter, First," 270–71.

[3] Feldmeier, *Die Christen als Fremde*, 148; Schelkle, *Die Petrusbriefe*, 122; Walls, "Introduction," in Stibbs and Walls, *1 Peter*, 58.

[4] Feldmeier, *Die Christen als Fremde*, 148 n. 63.

Moreover, Peter's major motif of the οἶκος τοῦ θεοῦ reappears in 4:17 → 2:5) as does the notion of the judgment of the disobedient (4:17 → 2:7–8, 3:19–20).

Although each verse in the section could independently stand as a proverb or maxim about the topic, the structure of 1 Pt. 4:12–19 is more that a string of concise and insightful *sententiae* on suffering. The frequency of πάθημα/πάσχω in the passage,[5] the ἵνα purpose clause as reason, the antithesis of vv. 15–16, an allusive example in v. 17, the scriptural quotation from Prov. 11:31, and the decisive conclusive statement (ὥστε) of v. 19 all intimate the rhetorical figure of *expolitio*,[6] the development of a thought or theme according to a generally accepted pattern in which the orator examines an idea from various angles. Restatement, synonymy, contrary, and example are common to this figure. Peter's arrangement of vv. 12–19 generally conforms to a standard *expolitio*.

Theme: The Fiery Ordeal (4:12)

The appearance of ἀγαπητοί makes forceful the discussion of vv. 12–13[7] (cf. 2:11). The verb ξενίζεσθε is the imperative of direct address (as opposed to the indirect participial and adjectival imperatives of 4:8–10). As a present-tense verb, it signifies here 'stop having the habit of being surprised,' counsel pertinent to the matter of afflictions that the readers have already begun to experience (1:6; 2:12; 3:16; 4:4).[8] In contrast to the libertine

---

[5] Three times, excluding the synonymous expressions πύρωσις πρὸς πειρασμόν, ὀνειδίζεσθε, αἰσχυνέσθω, κρίμα. A fourth usage of πάσχω is understood in v. 16.

[6] *Her.* 4.42.54–44.57.

[7] Feldmeier, *Die Christen als Fremde*, 148.

[8] The view (as in, e.g., Glenn W. Barker, William L. Lane, and J. Ramsey Michaels, *The New Testament Speaks*, [New York: Harper & Row, 1969], 342–43; and Hans Windisch and Herbert Preisker, *Die katholischen Briefe*, 3rd ed., Handbuch zum neuen Testament 15 [Tübingen: J. C. Mohr (Paul Siebeck), 1951], 160) that 1 Pt. 1:3–4:11 considers suffering only as a possibility and 4:12–5:11 considers it as fact is to be discounted on the basis of 1:6, 2:12, 3:16, and 4:4. The situation has not become more urgent in relation to the earlier parts of the letter, but the parenesis has (Schelkle, *Die Petrusbriefe*, 123 n. 1).

pagans whose surprise at the Christians' abstemiousness prompted a blasphemous outrage by the former toward the latter, no affliction, no verbal abuse should take Peter's audience by surprise.

The verb ξενίζω may indicate Peter's intention to relate the words of v. 12 to v. 4, indeed to the entire complex of slander and dishonorable treatment that so prominently concerns him in 2:11–4:11. The construction πύρωσις πρὸς πειρασμόν recalls 1:6–7 where ποικίλοι πειρασμοί have grieved the Christians in order that the genuine worth of their faith might pass the test of fire (πῦρ) like less precious gold.[9]

πύρωσις πρὸς πειρασμόν

The word πύρωσις is found only twice elsewhere in the New Testament. In Rev. 18:9 and 18 "the smoke of her burning" (ὁ καπνὸς τῆς πυρώσεως αὐτῆς) is witnessed by the kings and merchants who had dealings with Babylon which now is judged. In Did. 16:5, πύρωσις is qualified: ἡ πύρωσις τῆς δοκιμασίας, "the fiery test"[10] or "trial by fire."[11] In Justin *Dial.* 16.2, the devil and his minions harassingly try the believers with affliction and fiery trial (θλῖψις=πύρωσις) from which they are delivered.

The notion of refining by fire, a concept introduced in 1 Pt. 1:6–7, emerges in these passages (except in those from Revelation). In Prov. 27:21 LXX, πύρωσις appears as an equivalent of the Hebrew מַצְרֵף and כּוּר, words describing the process of refinement.[12] Thus the author affirms for his readers that the sufferings which they presently undergo are a test that

---

[9] Dalton, *Proclamation*, 96, notes the impressive inclusion of 1:6–7 with 4:12–13 which is marked by the common ideas of fire, trial/ordeal, suffering, the revelation of Christ/his glory. These similarities argue convincingly for the unity of the letter.

[10] BAGD, 731 (s.v. "πύρωσις").

[11] Ibid., 202 (s.v. "δοκιμασία").

[12] Prov. 27:21 LXX δοκίμιον ἀργυρίῳ καὶ χρυσῷ πύρωσις, ἀνὴρ δὲ δοκιμάζεται διὰ στόματος ἐγκωμιαζόντων αὐτόν. Cf. 17:3 ὥσπερ δοκιμάζεται ἐν καμίνῳ ἄργυρος καὶ χρυσός, οὕτως ἐκλεκταὶ καρδίαι παρὰ Κυρίῳ.

will serve to demonstrate the genuine worth of their faith and, because of its durability, the readers will be honored for it at the revelation of Jesus Christ (1:6–7; cf. 2:19–20).

Emilie T. Sander[13] denies that the process of refinement is connoted by πύρωσις at 1 Pt. 4:12. She maintains that the meaning of πύρωσις= מַצְרֵף has shifted from refinement/test (as in Prov. 27:21) to the ordeal of the end-time, the eschatological trial which the Hebrew מַצְרֵף had for the inhabitants of Qumran. For them, the מַצְרֵף was the final and decisive eschatological battle between the sons of light and the sons of darkness (allied with the angelic host and the host of Belial, respectively) or persecution, a time of apostasy, a cosmic cataclysm, indeed, any trial. This time of affliction was without refining capacity; after the ordeal had run its course, the righteous members of the sect would be found pure and thus vindicated and the wicked would be punished.[14]

This shift in meaning of מַצְרֵף (=πύρωσις) from refinement to its use as a Qumranian technical term for the end-time ordeal explains its function in 1 Pt. 4:12. The phrase πρὸς πειρασμόν is somewhat superfluous, but may be required to explain πύρωσις, whose meaning for Peter's audience was not so evident as מַצְרֵף was at Qumran.[15] The critical eschatological ordeal, with its various individual πειρασμοί (temptations or tests) has come, says Peter, and its endurance will bring vindication.

Although Sander appears to overlook a refining aspect of the eschatological ordeal in the Dead Sea Scrolls[16] and to exaggerate

---

[13] Emilie T. Sander, "ΠΥΡΩΣΙΣ and the First Epistle of Peter 4:12" (Th.D. thesis, Harvard Divinity School, 1966), 43–44, 49–50, 67, 85–86, 90–91, 93–94, 96, 103–4.

[14] The idea of מַצְרֵף as the end-time affliction is evident at 1QS 1.17; 8.4; 1QM 16.15; 17.1, 8–9; 1QH 4.16; 4QpPs.37 2.19; 4QFlor. 2.1; and CD 20.27. All instances are without the meaning of refining, but rather with that of the final ordeal, says Sander, "ΠΥΡΩΣΙΣ," 43–44, 49–50).

[15] In Did. 16:5, δοκιμασία may be epexegetical in relation to πύρωσις (Sander, "ΠΥΡΩΣΙΣ," 100, 104).

[16] Michaels, *1 Peter*, 260–61, maintains that מַצְרֵף "seems to have embraced both the testing of the righteous and the final punishment of the wicked" where the t.t. is clearest (e.g., 4QpPs. 37 2.19; 4QFlor. 2.1).

the relationship between Qumran and 1 Peter,[17] she does stress the vindication of the righteous at the end of the distress. The theme of vindication is prominent in 1 Peter and evidently is present in 4:12, linked closely with the eschatological joy of v. 13. First, however, the period of testing must take place in order that the purity of the believers' faith may be refined and its quality manifested (1:7).[18] Not only so, but the very fact of unjust suffering is a sign of election, of God's grace.[19]

When Peter repeats the pronoun ὑμῖν thrice in the passage, he is not being annoyingly redundant, but rhetorically skillful. The repetition itself is an instance of the figure reduplication (*conduplicatio*), the replication of one or more words for amplification or appeal to pity.[20] The threefold use of ὑμῖν arouses pity of the audience for itself, for the difficulties and distresses of its situation, and assures an attentive hearing to the *peroratio* since it so obviously concerns the suffering of its members.

Restatement of Theme (4:13a) and Reason (4:13b)[21]

The Restatement (v. 13a)

At the eschatological revelation of Christ's glory, those now severely tested (as it were, by fire) and rejoice (insofar as they

---

[17] The tone of the Qumran writings is more apocalyptic than 1 Pt. Although the latter does emphasize the revelation of Jesus Christ in glory (as apocalypticism stresses the coming of the Day of God in judgment and glory), Peter's tone ought to be described as eschatological rather than apocalyptic. Peter has an ethical concern like that of the prophets as opposed to apocalypticism which (with some exceptions: Dan., Rev., Test. XII, 1 En. 92–105) has abandoned ethical exhortation on account of the irremediability of the present evil age. Hope is altogether in the age to come (cf. 4 Ezr. 7:61, 18, 131; 8:6, 38, 56). For these points, see George Eldon Ladd, "Apocalyptic Literature," *ISBE*, 1:155–56.

[18] Millauer, *Leiden als Gnade*, 105–6, 138, 144.

[19] Ibid., 59–60, 102–3.

[20] *Her.* 4.28.38.

[21] For a tradition-critical examination of this verse, see Wolfgang Nauck, "Freude im Leiden: Zum Problem einer urchristlichen Verfolgungstradition," *Zeitschrift für die neutestamentliche Wissenschaft* 46 (1955): 68–80; and Selwyn, *St. Peter*, 442 (Table XIV), 450.

share his sufferings) will rejoice exceedingly. The orator asserts the certainty of his listeners' share in the eschatological joy by way of a maxim that restates the theme of the *expolitio* and affirms that the facts of the present ("insofar as you are sharing Christ's sufferings") ought to evoke a response of gladness now ("rejoice"). The purpose/reason for joy is that the hearers' gladness may be even greater in the eschaton ("so that you may also be glad and shout for joy when his glory is revealed"). Peter's thought is that the believer has joy in fellowship with the Christ whom the believer follows, even if that fellowship is one of suffering. Indeed, partnership with Christ in suffering is genuine and authentic discipleship, the basis of joy,[22] despite the fact that the sufferings are the Messianic woes that precede and give birth to the New Age.[23]

The Reason (v. 13b)

The two occurrences of χαίρω in 4:13 exhibit the rhetorical figure of transplacement[24] wherein the same word is reintroduced in a tasteful manner. Michaels identifies the fashion of reintroduction as that of a kind of "ascending parallelism"[25] in which χαίρετε refers to the act of rejoicing in the present, whereas χαρῆτε indicates the eschatological joy at Christ's glorious revelation. ἀγαλλιώμενοι intensifies the joy of χαίρω to a yet higher level. The utilization of ἀγαλλιώμενοι here creates a *gradatio*[26] of mild proportions compared to some other *gradationes*

---

[22] Millauer, *Leiden als Gnade*, 185.

[23] Note the discussion in Best, *1 Peter*, 162–63, 165–66. He believes that a view of the sufferings of Christ in v. 13 as the Messianic woes excludes a mystical sharing in those sufferings, but that does not necessarily follow. The Christians believe they enjoy genuine κοινωνία in the παθήματα τοῦ Χριστοῦ though they are the birthpangs of the end-time.

[24] *Traductio*, Her. 4.14.20.

[25] Michaels, *1 Peter*, 262.

[26] *Her.* 4.25.34. The next level in a series is attained only after the preceding one is mentioned then repeated. Here, the process is χαίρω/χαίρω → ἀγαλλιάω. As Michaels, *1 Peter*, 262, points out, the terms are synonyms in Mt. 5:12, but at 1 Pt. 4:13 they posssess different and ascending meanings. Cf. Lk. 6:23 χάρητε ἐν ἐκείνῃ τῇ ἡμέρᾳ καὶ

in the New Testament (cf. Rom. 5:3–5; 2 Pt. 1:5–7), but it is effective and pleasing nevertheless.

The time of the greater rejoicing is at the revelation of his glory (ἐν τῷ ἀποκαλύψει τῆς δόξης αὐτοῦ), a metonymy[27] for the appearance of Jesus Christ who is represented in the figure by his δόξα (cf. 1:7, 14). The readers already await their own δόξα at the parousia (1:7). Similarity in wording of 4:13 with 1:7 suggests to the reader that the glory of Christ will be the glory that they receive for their genuine faith:

ἵνα καὶ ἐν τῇ ἀποκαλύψει τῆς δόξης αὐτοῦ χαρῆτε ἀγαλλιώμενοι 4:13b

ἵνα τὸ δοκίμιον ὑμῶν τῆς πίστεως . . . εὑρεθῇ εἰς ἔπαινον καὶ δόξαν καὶ τιμὴν ἐν ἀποκαλύψει Ἰησοῦ Χριστοῦ 1:7

The eschatological joy of 4:13 stands in opposition to the present πύρωσις τὸν πειρασμόν (4:12) and the ποικίλοι πειρασμοί that have brought grief (1:6), that is to say, the shame of slanders and abuse from their unbelieving contemporaries (2:12; 3:16; 4:4). As Christ has received glory (3:22) and shall be revealed in it (1:7, 13; 4:13), so his people shall be given glory. As Christ suffered righteously and was vindicated, his people, too, shall be vindicated with glorious honor.[28]

σκιρτήσατε. Thus JB ". . . be glad, because you will enjoy a much greater gladness . . ."

Cognate terms appear also in 1 Pt. 1:8 (ἀγαλλιᾶσθε χαρᾷ ἀνεκλαλήτῳ καὶ δεδοξασμένῃ) in reverse order, but still with the sense of intensification of the former term by the latter.

[27] *Her.* 4.32.43.

[28] By the time of the emperors, the Roman concept of glory had differentiated between false and true glories. The *vera gloria* is the honor acquired from a good man (*bonus vir*); only his judgment counted. The opinion of the people or the community was not considered the true measure of *gloria* (A. J. Vermeulen, "Gloria," in *Reallexikon für Antike und Christentum*, ed. Theodor Klauser et al. [Stuttgart: Anton Hiersemann, 1950-], 11:201–2). Peter's intention in the letter is to persuade the audience that the falsely based ascriptions of honor and shame by the pagan world are inconsequential insofar as honor is concerned since the believers are honored by God himself. He stands in the place of the *bonus vir* for the subculture of the church. The estimations of non-believers, however, ought

The reason for the command not to be surprised in v. 12, but rather to rejoice in Christ's sufferings (v. 13a), is that a present joyful response leads to future glory and greater joy (v. 13b). In sum, the entire verse is a positive restatement ('rejoice') for what v. 12 states negatively ('do not be surprised').

Further Restatement (4:14a) and Reason (4:14b): Reproach for the Name of Christ

Words from the Jesus tradition contribute to the *sententia* of 1 Pt. 4:14, restating the theme of joyful acceptance of suffering and the reason for one to embrace it.[29] εἰ ὀνειδίζεσθε ἐν ὀνόματι Χριστοῦ, μακάριοι is a *makarism*, a *sententia* that pronounces a blessing upon those who behave in certain a way or exhibit a particular characteristic. Aristotle[30] mentions the *makarism* in relation to encomium, but the style preserved in the Beatitudes (Mt. 5:3–12; Lk. 6:20–23) and 1 Peter (3:14; 4:14) appears to derive from Jewish (and especially apocalyptic) prototypes.[31] The Petrine *makarism* in 4:14 displays syllogistic logic in an enthymeme, as do the dominical *makarisms*, but with a different

---

to be favorable in matters where pagans and Christians hold common notions of ἀγαθός and καλός. The believers are to do good and silence the unfounded and ignorant charges of wrongdoing that their opponents cast at them (2:15).

[29] Mt. 5:11 μακάριοί ἐστε ὅταν ὀνειδίσωσιν ὑμᾶς καὶ διώξωσιν καὶ εἴπωσιν πᾶν πονηρὸν καθ᾽ ὑμῶν [ψευδόμενοι] ἕνεκεν ἐμοῦ; Lk. 6:22 μακάριοί ἐστε ὅταν μισήσωσιν ὑμᾶς οἱ ἄνθρωποι, καὶ ὅταν ἀφορίσωσιν ὑμᾶς καὶ ὀνειδίσωσιν καὶ ἐκβάλωσιν τὸ ὄνομα ὑμῶν ὡς πονηρὸν ἕνεκα τοῦ υἱοῦ τοῦ ἀνθρώπου. Both passages are from Q.

[30] Arist. *Rh.* 1.9.1367b.33. 289

[31] See, e.g., Dan. 12:12; Tob. 13:14; Sir. 25:7–10; 1 En. 58:2; Ulrich Becker, "μακάριος," *NIDNTT*, 1:216–17; C. H. Dodd, "The Beatitudes: A Form-Critical Study," chap. in *More New Testament Studies* (Grand Rapids: William B. Eerdmans, 1968), 1–10; Klaus Koch, *The Growth of the Biblical Tradition: The Form-Critical Method*, trans. S. M. Cupitt (New York: Charles Scribner's Sons, 1969), 8, 17. A recently published fragment (4Q525) among the DSS incorporates *makarisms* that are sapiential rather than apocalyptic or eschatological as are Mt. and Lk's. For Eng. trans. and discussion, see Benedict T. Viviano, "Beatitudes Found among Dead Sea Scrolls," *Biblical Archaeology Review* 18 (November-December 1992): 53–55, 66.

syntax: μακάριος stands without a copula[32] (in contrast to the ἔστε of Matthew and Luke) and the blessing pronouncement (conclusion) stands, not first in the sentence, but in an apodosis after a conditional clause. The reasoning of Peter in the present syllogism is more elaborate than that of his other syllogisms: the latter have but three elements, whereas the *makarism* of 4:14 has five (sharing the enthymematic ὅτι with the Matthaean and Lukan *makarisms*):[33]

Major premise	Blessed are those on whom the Spirit is resting.
Proof	On those reviled for the name of Christ the Spirit is resting.
Minor Premise	You are reviled for the name of Christ.*
Proof	The Spirit is resting on you.
Conclusion	You are blessed.

(*The conditional εἰ introduces a first-class condition, assumed as true because of all that Peter has heretofore said about the reality of slander directed against his audience [2:12; 3:16]. See the discussion of this condition in Robertson, *Grammar*, 1004–12.)

The point of the *makarism* in 1 Pt. 4:14 is related to the affirmation of v. 13. There, the readers, certain of eschatological joy since they share Christ's sufferings, await the revelation of his glory (δόξα) that signifies the bestowal of glory on them, too. That divine glory, however, already rests upon them in the person of the Holy Spirit. They already, in the midst of suffering, partake in the honor whose consummative reception they anticipate in the future.[34] Dodd[35] observes that the Lukan *makarisms* express a

---

[32] See BAGD, 486 (s.v. "μακάριος") on the various constructions with μακάριος in the NT and elsewhere.

[33] An enthymeme, the rhetorical expression of syllogistic reasoning, could have as many as five logical parts behind it, but always at least three. However, the enthymeme suppresses one of the parts. A rhetorical epicheireme expresses three parts (major premise, minor premise, and conclusion) without suppression. An argument could take the form of major premise, proof, minor premise, proof, conclusion (Cic. *Inv.* 1.34.57, 37.67; Quint. *Inst. Or.* 5.10.1, 4; 14.5.9, 14; Kennedy, *NT Interpretation*, 17; Watson, *Invention*, 17–19).

[34] Schelkle, *Die Petrusbriefe*, 124.

[35] Dodd, "Beatitudes," 5–8.

περιπέτεια, a reversal of circumstances that accompanies the Kingdom of God. Dodd writes:

> There is to be a reversal of conditions and rôles, and even though it is a highly 'etherealized' kind of περιπέτεια, yet the poor, hungry, sorrowful and outcast will be such no longer, any more than the prosperous will retain their advantages.[36]

Peter's *makarism* demonstrates the same outlook as the Beatitudes of Luke. The descent of the Holy Spirit on Jesus at his baptism communicates to him that his is the honor of sonship and favor from God (Mt. 3:16–17; Mk. 1:10–11; Lk. 3:21–22; Jn. 1:32–34).[37] A similar honor now belongs to those who are reviled for the sake of Christ's name. The same Spirit rests upon them as upon Christ, as a sign of incomparable honor and eschatological glory.[38]

The structure of v. 14b, a reason for the statement in v. 14a, may read somewhat awkwardly ('for the of glory and the of God Spirit upon you rests'), but the attributes in the genitive are merely placed first for emphasis. τὸ τῆς δόξης καὶ τὸ τοῦ θεοῦ πνεῦμα is a hendiadys that may be translated as "that glorious Spirit which is the Spirit of God" (NEB) or "the glorious Spirit of God" (Goodspeed).

---

[36] Ibid., 7. Dodd believes Matthew is more ethically oriented than the socially-concerned Luke and, therefore, does not give expression to the idea of a περιπέτεια. I contend, however, that a genuine reversal of circumstances or status does exist in at least some of the Matthaean Beatitudes (Mt. 5:3, 4, 10) despite the fact that no woe pronouncements accompany them as in Luke.

[37] The Synoptics and John all use καταβαίνω (to come down) for the descent of the Spirit. Mt. adds ἔρχομαι (='the Spirit descended *and came* upon him') while Jn. adds μένω (to remain).

[38] Peter may not have the baptism of Jesus in mind at 4:14 since his verb is ἀναπαύομαι (to rest upon). However, the picture of the Spirit resting upon God's chosen one, honored by the Spirit, is present at Isa. 11:2 where a practically identical phraseology occurs: ἀναπαύσεται ἐπ᾽ αὐτὸν πνεῦμα τοῦ θεοῦ. Peter seems to allude in v. 14 to the wording of Isaiah with its ascription of honor.

A Contrary: Just and Unjust Suffering (4:15–16)

The contrary of the Petrine *expolitio* is artfully presented as an antithesis[39] of thought so that the original theme of joyful endurance in suffering is quickly rejoined. The negative pole is first stated, then the positive.

A. "But Let None of You Suffer as . . ." (v. 15)

Appearing in v. 15 is a vice list of perpetrators who are positioned in a descending order[40] insofar as gravity of social injury and disruption are concerned. No Christian is to suffer for being found a perpetrator of sin, that is, to justly suffer as an evil-doer (cf. 2:14, 20a). Deserved suffering could take the form of slander or conviction by the authorities for a misdeed and its corresponding penalty.

A murderer (φονεύς) is followed in the list by the thief (κλέπτης) and the κακοποιός, the very classification into which the Christians have been placed by their adversaries (2:12; cf. 2:14, 3:17). Peter may intend κακοποιός to be a general and summary term for any wrongdoer.[41] The final constituent of the list is ἀλλοτριεπίσκοπος, apparently set off from the rest of the transgressors by ἢ ὡς,[42] a phrase which may signal the identification of a malefactor whose type may be particularly numerous, prominent, troublesome, or odious in the church of Asia Minor.

---

[39] *Contentio, Her.* 4.45.48.

[40] Sander, "ΠΥΡΩΣΙΣ," xxxiv-xxxvii.

[41] Ibid. Cf. NIV "any other kind of criminal." NEB "sorcerer" follows Selwyn's suggestion (*St. Peter*, 225) that κακοποιός possibly refers to a "magician." This rendering has since been abandoned by REB in favor of a more general meaning ("any other crime"). In light of the imprecision of κακοποιέω in 1 Pt. 2:12, 14, and 3:17, the idea of κακοποιός=sorcerer ought to be discarded in favor of a generalization like that in NIV and REB.

[42] Cf. NRSV "But let none of you suffer as a murderer, a thief, a criminal, or even as a mischief maker." The segregation is noted by Brox, *Der erste Petrusbrief*, 218, and Selwyn, *St. Peter*, 225.

The actual sinful identity of the ἀλλοτριεπίσκοπος has been variously suggested as, for example,[43] a "revolutionary" (Moffatt), "busybody,"[44] "spy" (Phillips), "mischief maker" (NRSV), "meddler" (NIV), an embezzler,[45] or one guilty of "tampering with the slaves and the families of others."[46] Sander suggests that ἀλλοτριεπίσκοπος means a wrong/alien bishop, i.e., one who does not lead the flock in purity and innocence to Christ, but rather leads them to the Devil. The notion of the shepherd runs throughout 1 Peter and the sin of being an ἀλλοτριεπίσκοπος is the fundamental sin within it. The context for Peter's prohibition is not, however, an address to the elders or overseers, but the entire community (μὴ γάρ τις ὑμῶν πασχέτω). Furthermore, Sander overemphasizes the prominence of the church leaders in the epistle and the attention given to their conduct. Hence her interpretation must give way to another.[47]

Michaels effectively argues for the meaning "busybody," relating it to the word ἐπίσκοπος in 2:25:

> ἀλλοτριεπίσκοπος is set off from "murderer," "thief," and "criminal" by the repetition of ὡς simply because it does not refer to something potentially criminal but to an attitude or a pattern of behavior likely to bring reproach on Christians as a group. It is still possible that Peter chose ἀλλοτριεπίσκοπος instead of the more common περίεργος with the function of the Christian ἐπίσκοπος, or "overseer," in mind, so as to warn Christians to recognize the limits of their community and not try to legislate morality for others. Peter's conviction, after all, is that Christ alone is the real ἐπίσκοπος (2:25). Yet the term in no way suggests that

---

[43] For more thorough surveys of the options in translation see BAGD, 40 (s.v. "ἀλλοτριεπίσκοπος"); Best, *1 Peter*, 164–65; and Brox, *Der erste Petrusbrief*, 218–20.

[44] Michaels, *1 Peter*, 267–68; Selwyn, *St. Peter*, 225; AV "a busybody in other men's matters."

[45] Brox, *Der erste Petrusbrief*, 220.

[46] Ramsay, *The Church in the Roman Empire*, 293.

[47] Michaels, *1 Peter*, 267, judges Sander's ecclesiastical interpretation as unsuccessful, but for a different cause. "There is no reason," he maintains, "why false leaders of the Christian flock would necessarily 'suffer' for it [sic] at the hands of unbelievers." However, since suffering in Peter largely concerns slander, one can well imagine that a corrupt church leader could be slandered (and thus suffer) by hostile non-Christians eager to find grounds for accusation, especially if the charge of misconduct were true.

Peter's admonition is directed (like 5:1–3) to leaders of the congregations in distinction from the community as a whole (note the preceding μὴ . . . τις ὑμῶν, "none of you").[48]

Thus Peter is telling his audience, one and all, not to play Christ or God in others' lives. Ultimately, however, we must admit that ἀλλοτριεπίσκοπος is "a word whose meaning has not yet been determined with certainty."[49]

Could Peter really expect that the communities to which his letter is addressed might produce a murderer (φονεύς)? Probably not, but the term is rhetorically functional as a hyperbolic[50] first member of an accumulation[51] whose very presence in the rogues' catalogue would convey to the listeners that any sin that they commit, wherever ranked in the descending order, is akin to murder. The word φονεύς awakens revulsion, a negative pathos, for the sin of homicide and for all sins since they could conceivably be linked with it. The term ἀλλοτριεπίσκοπος could very well be a Petrine neologism[52] especially since this *hapax legomenon* does not appear elsewhere in classical, biblical, or patristic Greek until Epiphanius (fourth century CE, twice) and Dionysius the Areopagite (fifth century CE, once).[53]

---

[48] Ibid., 268.

[49] BAGD, 40 (s.v. "ἀλλοτριεπίσκοπος").

[50] Hyperbole (ὑπερβολή/*superlatio*) is a trope, "a manner of speech exaggerating the truth, whether for the sake of magnifying or minifying something" (*Her.* 4.33.44. Cf. Long. *Subl.* 38; Cic. *De Or.* 3.53.203; Quint. *Inst. Or.* 8.6.67; Watson, *Invention*, 76).

[51] Cf. *Her.* 4.40.52–41.53; Watson, *Invention*, 27. Whereas accumulation (*frequentatio*) appears to normally feature words which are identical in meaning or are presented in ascending rank, the accumulation in v. 15 apparently is in descending order.

[52] Demetr. *Eloc.* 2.91–98.

[53] Sander, "ΠΥΡΩΣΙΣ," xxx–xxxi; refs. to later writers in Michaels, *1 Peter*, 267, who, in disagreement with Sander, believes that the term is unlikely Peter's coinage since none of the later three usages of it is directly dependent on him. Sander believes Epiphanius reflects 1 Pt.

B. *"Yet if Any of You Suffers as a Christian . . ." (v. 16)*

The readers ought not to suffer justly for ignoble actions, but if they unjustly suffer for Christ, such suffering is honorable and the sufferer ought not to count it shame, but as an honor. The εἰ construction, a first class condition that is presumed as fact, omits the verb πάσχω[54] which here is understood. The omission constitutes the attractive figure of speech known as conjunction[55] by which two successive phrases are held by a verb between them (here, however, the two successive phrases are interrupted by the vice list). The affliction that Peter envisages in v. 16 is that encountered by a πάροικος/παρεπίδημος who, already socially outcast for her/his alien status, now endures cultural disdain for being a Χριστιανός, a 'Christ-lackey.'[56] The term, originating during the first century CE, is one of derision and ridicule coined by the believers' opponents.[57] 'To suffer as a Χριστιανός' does not denote an official persecution on any scale against believers. From the very earliest time, the followers of Christ were slandered for their allegiance to him in unofficial acts of hostility (cf. Acts 28:22). The possibility of Roman governmental intervention in such cases is possible, but not necessarily inferred by the term Χριστιανός.[58] Neither does the term necessarily signify suffering as a Christian was in the same kind or degree as the suffering encountered by the wrongdoers of v. 15. Those transgressors may have suffered actual judicial penalties, from some form of mob violence, or social opprobrium.[59]

---

[54] The form understood is πάσχει, 3rd. pers. sing., pres. act. ind., in agreement with τις in v. 15.

[55] Lat. *coniunctio*, *Her.* 4.27.38.

[56] Elliott, *Home*, 223–24.

[57] Ibid., 95–96. C. F. D. Moule, *The Birth of the New Testament*, Harper's New Testament Commentaries (New York: Harper & Row, 1962), 112.

[58] Elliott, *Home*, 81; C. F. D. Moule, "The Nature and Purpose of I Peter," *New Testament Studies* 3 (1956–57): 1–11; idem, *Birth of the NT*, 112–14. Suffering punishment for the name 'Christian' itself (*nomen ipsum*, cf. Pliny, *Ep.* 96.2) is not necessarily suggested by v. 16 (*pace* John Knox, "Pliny and I Peter: A Note on I Pet 4:14–16 and 3:15," *Journal of Biblical Literature* 72 [1953]: 187–89).

[59] Moule, *Birth of the NT*, 113–14.

The language of honor and shame comes to clear expression with the antithetical expressions μὴ αἰσχυνέσθω and δοξαζέτω δὲ τὸν θεὸν ἐν τῷ ὀνόματι τούτῳ. Infamy and humiliation for the sake of Christ and the name of Christian are marks of honor that can be recognized by the transfer of that honor to God (δοξαζέτω τὸν θεὸν), all by virtue of bearing the name of Christian, within the sphere of bearing that name.[60]

Comparison: Judgment within the Household of God (4:17–18)

For Peter, the crucial image of the church is the οἶκος τοῦ θεοῦ. Nevertheless, he feels at liberty to work with other images of the church, especially epithets that, once applicable to Israel, now apply to the Christian community as the new people of God (cf. 2:4–10). The theme of joyful endurance in suffering, rather than perplexity at it, is argued in v. 17 by the rhetor's allusion to the judgment of the Temple in the time of Ezekiel. That event serves as a historical precedent[61] for the fact that refining trials for God's people (his οἶκος) do occur. If such trials have come to them before, God's people ought not to be confused when they recur. Schutter classifies 4:17a as an explicit allusion to Ezek. 9:6 (καὶ ἀπὸ τῶν ἁγίων μου ἄρξασθε).[62]

---

[60] This understanding of ἐν as locative rather than instrumental is suggested by Moule, *Idiom Book*, 78–79; Selwyn, *St. Peter*, 225–26.

[61] An historical event to which the rhetor ascribes illustrative and persuasive properties in service of the argument at hand. Here an *auctoritas*/κρίσις, not merely a *praeiudicium*, is present because the *auctoritas* has no inherent relationship to the case at hand, but does so only by the rhetor's art (and thus is artificial). Folklore and poetry were sources for the proverbs that serve as the pronouncements of *auctoritates*. On this kind of argument see Arist. *Rh.* 1.2.1357b.25–1358a.1; Quint. *Inst. Or.* 5.11.1, 6, 36, 39; Lausberg, *Handbuch*, 410–26 (on *exempla* generally; 426 on *auctoritas*).

[62] Schutter, *Hermeneutic*, 37–38. The image of the Temple (LXX οἶκος) in Jerusalem permeates Ezek. 8–11 and it is in the Temple where judgment begins (9:6). Peter, of course, applies the image of the Temple/οἶκος to the communities of Asia Minor as a metaphor: they constitute the present-day οἶκος as a household of God, the οἶκος πνευματικός (1 Pt. 2:5), where the eschatological judgment begins.

What is Peter's reason for the introduction of the disobedient and their fate here (τί τὸ τέλος τῶν ἀπειθούντων τῷ τοῦ θεοῦ εὐαγγελίῳ;)? An unmistakable recollection of the disobedient who stumble at the Word (2:8) and to the disobedient imprisoned spirits (3:19–20) emerges here. The disobedient are placed in an inferior position in a piece of reasoning on the κρίμα that leads from the greater to the lesser:[63] "if it [i.e., the judgment] begins with us, what will be the end for those who do not obey the gospel of God?" By means of this rhetorical question,[64] the orator differentiates between his readers, whom he presumes will be saved (v. 18), and the disobedient. The hearers understand themselves to be on the opposite side of the impious who elsewhere in the letter represent those who are shamed in relation to others' triumphs.[65] Although they are grievously afflicted, the members of the οἶκος τοῦ θεοῦ are aligned finally against those who are shamed. God's people emerge from the πύρωσις πρὸς πειρασμόν purified and having passed the test (1:7) with honor. The quotation, another rhetorical question, from Prov. 11:31 LXX confirms Peter's point: "if it is hard for the righteous to be saved, what will become of the ungodly and the sinners?"

Conclusion: How to Live during Suffering (4:19)

Verse 19 is an apt summary that skillfully encapsulates themes of the entire letter heretofore presented. πάσχοντες (2:19, 20, 21, 23; 3:14, 17, 18; 4:1, 15[–16]; cf. 1:11; 4:13), τὸ θέλημα τοῦ θεοῦ (2:15; 3:17; 4:2), ἀγαθοποιΐα (2:14, 15, 20; 3:6, 11, 13, 16, 17; cf. 2:12) all recall prominent themes of the document. Whatever suffering the readers endure, Peter maintains, is according to the will of God. Since that will of God is to silence

---

[63] For this kind of reasoning in inductive argument with examples, see Quint. *Inst. Or.* 5.11.9.

[64] See the discussion on *erōtēsis*/interrogating in Bullinger, *Figures of Speech*, 943–56.

[65] In 2:7–8, those who believe have τιμή, whereas those who disbelieve (=disobey) stumble and are shamed. In 3:19 20 the unruly spirits hear the announcement of Christ's honor in his resurrection, ascension, and enthronement.

the ignorance of the foolish by well-doing (2:15) and God's will is
sometimes that one suffers for well-doing (3:17), Peter's readers
infer that their suffering for well-doing will silence their
antagonists to shame. Honor will be for Christ's people.[66] The
phrase πιστῷ κτίστῃ παρατιθέσθωσαν τὰς ψυχὰς αὐτῶν is
practically synonymous with παρεδίδου τῷ κρίνοντι δικαίως (in
reference to Christ) at 2:23. The legal aspect of παρατίθημι may
not be present as it is with παραδίδωμι, but if the verb alludes to
εἰς χεῖράς σου παρατίθεμαι τὸ πνεῦμά μου, Jesus' cry from the
cross recorded in Lk. 23:46,[67] the notion of one's resignation to
God for vindication may be present.[68] "A faithful Creator," a
pronominatio that differs from τῷ κρίνοντι δικαίως,[69] still
communicates the idea of justice since a faithful Creator can be
trusted to do what is just on behalf of those who entrust
themselves to him. The word ἀγαθοποιΐα, "continuing to do

---

[66] This deductive reasoning is not presented in the text, but represents the
logic that may be practiced by the implied or ideal reader/hearer of the the
text. See 237–38 below. Of course, Peter's readers may not have made the
deduction that I offer, but the premises (and thus the possibility) for the
conclusion are at hand.

The syllogism is 'If A=B and C=B, then A=C, where A=to silence foolish
ignorance by well-doing, B=God's will, and C=to suffer for well-doing. Or, to
express it differently, one may write,

Major premise	God's will is to silence foolish ignorance by well-doing.
Minor premise	God's will is [may be] to suffer for doing well.
Conclusion	Suffering for doing well is to silence foolish ignorance, for this is the will of God.

All three concepts intersect at v. 19 to create the syllogism for the implied
reader.

[67] Peter has adapted a saying of Jesus here according to Gundry, "'Verba
Christi,'" 343–44. Dissenting with Gundry are Goppelt, *Der erste Petrusbrief*,
316, and Michaels, *1 Peter*, 273.

[68] The Lukan expression is an allusion to Ps. 30:5 LXX which is a plea for
deliverance from shame, i.e., a hopeful request for honor (cf. v. 1a-b, ἐπὶ σοὶ
Κύριε ἤλπισα, μὴ καταισχυνθείην εἰς τὸν αἰῶνα; v. 17 κύριε, μὴ
καταισχυνθείην, ὅτι ἐπεκαλεσάμην σε· αἰσχυνθείησαν οἱ ἀσεβεῖς, καὶ
καταχθείησαν εἰς ᾅδου). The words ἐλπίζω and ἐπικαλέομαι may have
been extracted from this Psalm by Peter for his discussions about Christian
hope (1:3, 13, 21) and appeal to the Father for vindication (1:17; cf. 2:23).

[69] *Her.* 4.31.42.

good" (NRSV), or, "doing what is right" (NAS), is right behavior in society,[70] expressed in submission to political authorities, to masters, to husbands, in honorable treatment of wives (2:13–3:7), and generally in honor to all (2:17; 3:8–12).

A Farewell Speech of Exhoration (5:1–11)

A Pastoral Stratum or Second Letter?

The topic of judgment in the οἶκος τοῦ θεοῦ may have given rise to Peter's discussion of the πρεσβύτεροι within that house in 1 Pt. 5:1–4; they are the first mentioned in the listing of those on whom judgment falls in Ezek. 9:6 to which Peter alludes.[71] The possibility that Peter has that text in mind is strengthened by the appearance of νεώτεροι in v. 5, a term synonymous with Ezekiel's νεανίσκος (9:6).

The entire passage 5:1–11 resembles a farewell speech elsewhere found in ancient Jewish and Christian literature. The Petrine text embodies several features of the speech type. See Figure 4 for examples of the farewell speech and their common characteristics.[72] Winsome Munro's identification of 5:1–5a as part of a later pastoral (trito-Pauline) stratum that found its way into 1 Peter and the Pauline letters sometime between 90–140 CE[73] is unnecessary in light of the rhetorically intelligible relations

---

[70] Goppelt, *Der erste Petrusbrief,* 317–18.

[71] Schutter, *Hermeneutic,* 79. Ezek. 9:6 reads πρεσβύτερον καὶ νεανίσκον ... ἀποκτείνατε εἰς ἐξάλειψιν ... ἀπὸ τῶν ἁγίων μου ἄρξασθε. καὶ ἤρξαντο ἀπὸ τῶν ἀνδρῶν τῶν πρεσβυτέρων οἳ ἦσαν ἔσω ἐν τῷ οἴκῳ.

[72] For discussion on the farewell speech, see Kennedy, *NT Interpretation,* 73–85 (chap. on epideictic rhetoric and Jn. 13–17), et passim; Sander, "ΠΥΡΩΣΙΣ," viii, x, xlii, 89 (who regards 1 Pt. as, at least in part, a farewell/testament form); Stauffer, *NT Theology,* 344–47 ("Appendix VI: Valedictions and Farewell Speeches"); Watson, *Invention,* 96–101 (on the testament genre, related to the farewell-discourse form, that appears in 2 Pt. 1:3–15); idem, "Ephesian Elders," 184–208.

[73] Winsome Munro, *Authority in Paul and Peter: The Identification of a Pastoral Stratum in the Pauline Corpus and 1 Peter,* Society for New Testament Studies Monograph Series 45 (Cambridge: Cambridge University Press, 1983), 45, according to whom (38–49) the later pastoral stratum in 1 Pt. consists of Block A: 1:14–19, 22–23, 25b; 2:1–3, 8b; Block B: 2:11–20, 21c-d, 23–25; 3:1–9, 13–17, 19–22a; Block C: 4:1b, 2, 3 (οἰνοφλυγίαις ... πότοις),

between the material of the two alleged strata. In my estimation, even a skillful redactor could not have made such precise connections of thought and language between disparate blocks of material.

Figure 4: Examples of Farewell Discourse

Text	Features								
	A	**B**	**C**	**D**	**E**	**F**	**G**	**H**	**I**
1 Pt. 5:1–11		x	x	x	x	x	x	x	x
Acts 20:17–38	x	x	x	x	x	x	x	x	x
Jn. 13–17	x		x	x	x			x	x
Acts of Jn. 106–8	x		x	x		x	x	x	
Jn. 21:15–23		x			x				
4 Ezr. 14:28–36						x			x

A Prayer	D Self-vindication	G Warning of greed
B Tend the flock	E Prediction of suffering	H Love/humility
C The enemy	F Watch! Stand firm!	I Reward/judgment

Munro,[74] along with Friedrich Schröger,[75] perceives two types of ecclesiastical organization between 4:7–11 and 5:1–5. The allegedly later hierarchical structure of 5:1–5a Munro attributes to the pastoral stratum in contrast to the earlier charismatic and egalitarian church reflected in v. 11a. Schröger differentiates between two letters: 1:1–4:11, embodying a charismatically oriented church concept (as in Paul) that suggests escalating persecution, and 4:12–5:11 with its presbyterial outlook reflecting a later time when persecution had already spread.

These speculations, however, neglect the rhetorical bond between the sets of materials that they propose were originally disconnected. 1 Pt. 4:12–5:11, as a rhetorical *peroratio*, recapitulates

---

4–6, 8, 9; Block D: 4:11b, 16, 19; 5:1–5a. No textual witnesses support Munro's hypothesis which, in my opinion, unconvincingly renders 1 Pt. a complex puzzle ingeniously fit together by an unknown redactor.

[74] Ibid., 45, 50–51.

[75] Friedrich Schröger, "Die Verfassung der Gemeinde des ersten Petrusbriefes," in *Kirche im Werden: Studien zum Thema Amt und Gemeinde im neuen Testament*, ed. Josef Hainz (Munich: Verlag Ferdinand Schöningh, 1976), 239–52.

thoughts from previous sections and makes sense if it is regarded as originally linked to the preceding parts of the letter, especially to the household scheme of 2:13–3:7.[76] A more developed and centralized structure that supplants a looser 'charismatic' association is not required for a sectarian community (like the churches of Asia Minor) even if there were evidence for an intensification of persecution from without (and in 1 Peter there is no such evidence).[77] Elliott states:

> The presbyteral functions mentioned in 5:2–3 can hardly be taken as evidence of a centralization of function and authority. Leadership by presbyters reflects a still traditional and rudimentary division of responsibilities within the household or the Christian community identified as a household. The function of the content of 4:7–11 within the domestic pattern of instruction is to assure the readers that having leaders does not preclude the responsibilities which all members of the household have for serving and supporting one another. Thus 4:7–11 is similar in aim to the injunctions of 3:8–9 and 5:5b which conclude, respectively, the domestic exhortation of 2:18–3:7 and 5:1–5a. In sum, the responsibilities described in 4:7–11 and 5:1–5 are complementary rather than contradictory. The combination of these passages in 1 Peter represents at this stage the coalescence of traditions, development rather than displacement.[78]

The so-called charismatic church arrangement of 4:7–11 is not incongruous with a concurrent hierarchical structure. 1 Pt. 4:7–11 simply makes a general division between the two basic kinds of ministry in the primitive church (preaching/teaching and service, 4:11).[79] The elders of 5:1–4 are responsible for the preaching and teaching. From a very early time, elders exercised a shepherding function with the right and duty to execute these functions.[80]

---

[76] Elliott, *Home*, 163 n. 148.

[77] Ibid., 163–64 n. 148. The churches, as is evident in 4:11, still operate with a rudimentary division of labor.

[78] Ibid., 164 n. 148.

[79] Selwyn, *St. Peter*, 219.

[80] See David Wenham, "The Paulinism of Acts again: Two Historical Clues in 1 Thessalonians," *Themelios* 13 (January/February 1988): 54–55, who effectively argues for the presence of elders from the time of Paul's ministry in Thessalonica, Corinth, and Philippi. The epistolary evidence confirms the statement of Acts 14:23 that Paul very early appointed πρεσβύτεροι in his churches (sc. in Galatia). One may confidently assume Peter addresses

Rhetorical Design in 5:1–5a

Peter identifies himself as "a fellow-elder" (REB), ὁ συμπρεσβύτερος, a Petrine neologism[81] that conveys a humble sympathy for and partnership with the pastors whom he addresses. The author, already recognized as one with the eminence of an apostle of Jesus Christ (1:1), thus establishes further positive ethos for himself as one who can be trusted in what he says because he speaks from experience and understanding.[82] The συμ-compound, like others in the letter, promotes social solidarity between the readers and the writer.[83]

Furthermore, the self-appellations μάρτυς τῶν τοῦ Χριστοῦ παθημάτων ("a witness of the sufferings of Christ")[84] and ὁ καὶ

churches where church leaders have been duly appointed, especially since some of those communities, in Galatia and Asia, are probably of Pauline origin.

[81] Demetr. *Eloc.* 2.9.98. Michaels, *1 Peter*, 279, argues for the uniqueness of συμπρεσβύτερος in ancient literature. The word συνπρεσβευτών, from a 2nd cent. BCE inscription, is derived from a different word and means "co-ambassador." Likewise, the frequent συμπρεσβευτής originates differently (BAGD, 780 [s.v. "συμπρεσβύτερος"]).

[82] Hillyer, *1 and 2 Peter, Jude*, 138; Michaels, *1 Peter*, 280.

[83] Elliott, *Home*, 135–36 for a discussion of all the instances of συμ-composites in 1 Pt.

[84] The phrase μάρτυς τῶν τοῦ Χριστοῦ παθημάτων is a claim by the writer to have been an eyewitness of Christ's passion (Selwyn, *St. Peter*, 228). Thus he distinguishes himself from his fellow elders in the degree to which each party has known something of Christ's sufferings. Willi Marxsen ("Der Mitälteste und Zeuge der Leiden Christi: Eine martyrologische Begründung des 'Romprimats' im 1. Petrus-Brief?" in *Theologia Crucis—Signum Crucis*, Festschrift for Erich Dinkler, ed. Carl Andresen and Günter Klein [Tübingen: J. C. B. Mohr (Paul Siebeck), 1979], 377–93, passim) believes that 'Peter,' a pseudonym, is part of a fictive epistolary frame for 1:3–5:11, a text that itself is probably of two parts (1:3–4:11 and 4:12–5:11) that were joined at some time after the composition of the latter with the epistolary framework (1:1–2; 5:12–14). The συμπρεσβύτερος of 5:1 is not Peter the apostle, but a pastor in Asia Minor. His right to address the other pastors of the region is that he already has experienced what the others will experience: sufferings of persecution. His own person in its experience of suffering is a μάρτυς τῶν τοῦ παθημάτων Χριστοῦ. The writer, knowing a tradition that testifies to the apostle Peter's residence and martyrdom in

τῆς μελλούσης ἀποκαλύπτεσθαι δόξης κοινωνός ("one who shares in the glory to be revealed") in v. 1 bind the rhetor to the experiences of the auditors in other ways since these hearers are described with similar terms earlier in the letter.[85]

The job of tending the flock properly (ποιμάνατε τὸ ποίμνιον) is described by three sets of antitheses whose *cola*[86] are introduced by μή(δέ) and ἀλλά. The identical words at the commencement of each *colon* represents *epanaphora*[87] while a repetition of -ως on four adverbs is a pleasing *homoeoteleuton*.[88]

μή(δέ)	ἀλλά
ἀναγκαστῶς	ἑκουσίως κατὰ θεόν
αἰσχροκερδῶς	προθύμως
ὡς κατακυριεύοντες τῶν κλήρων	τύποι γινόμενοι τοῦ ποιμνίου[89]

Rome, understands himself and his addressees, churches and elders alike, as standing in that "*Leidens-Tradition*" of Peter himself, even though heretofore the suffering of the writer has been the suffering of persecution and not martyrdom. The martyrdom of Peter legitimates the pastor who speaks to the churches of Asia Minor. If one is to speak of a primacy of Peter, it is a primacy grounded in his exemplary martyrdom. In order to lend apostolic authority to the document, the redactor uses Peter's name at 1:1.

Marxsen's view is, however, strained and, in my opinion, harder to accept than the integrity of the letter including its epistolary framework. Since the συμπρεσβύτερος is nowhere identified, the most reasonable assumption is that he is identical with the apostle Peter of 1:1. Nothing in the text insures that the recipients would understand that the fellow elder (and not Peter) speaks at 5:1, or that his identity over the wide geographical area addressed is even known.

[85] The hearers await the ἀποκάλυψις of Christ (1:7, 13; cf.1:5) and his δόξα (4:13) while sharing (κοινωνέω) in his παθήματα (4:13).

[86] A κῶλον/*membrum* is a phrase that, although brief and complete, does not express an entire thought. It must be supplemented with one or two other *cola*. *Her.* 4.19.26.

[87] *Her.* 4.13.19, Lat. *repetitio.* In this figure, phrases in close succession, expressing like or different ideas, are begun with the same word. μηδέ is indistinguishable from μή.

[88] *Her.* 4.20.28, *similiter desinens*, a figure created when indeclinable words exhibit similar final terminations.

[89] Gabarrón, "El pastor," 331–51, who identifies the pastors as those who become examples of Christ's sufferings to which all are called for communion with him.

The entire exhortation to the elders resumes the metaphor of the shepherd and the flock from 2:25, a popular Christian topic.

The forbidden characteristics of the Petrine exhortation to pastors are associated with shameful behavior in the word αἰσχροκερδῶς in v. 2c ("not for sordid gain," "nicht aus schändlicher Gewinnsucht" [ZB]). Opposite the shame that attends undesirable pastoral behavior are the honorable qualities that lead to "the crown of glory [δόξα] that never fades away" (5:4b). Whether the metaphor στέφανος here represents the athlete's crown, the valiant soldier's wreath, the king's crown, the reward for service to the state, or the headpiece of a supernatural being,[90] the honor that is conferred by the ἀρχιποίμην when he appears is signified. Although his identity here is not clear, only alluded to by the *pronominatio*[91] "chief shepherd," the context of the whole letter strongly suggests Christ himself since it is he whose appearance in glory is forecast (1:7, 13; 4:13; cf. 2:25). Since the honorable qualities of vv. 2–3 constitute a picture of humble service by the elders, the young people (νεώτεροι) are to submit likewise (ὁμοίως) to the elders.[92]

Humility in the οἶκος τοῦ θεοῦ (5:5b–7)

Now the injunction for humility is extended to the entire community of believers. The inference from v. 4 is that humble service of one by another in the church will lead to the same honor that those who are the community's examples will receive. Although ὑποτάσσω in 1 Peter usually denotes the deference given by a subordinate to a superior in a social hierarchy (2:13; 18; 3:1, 5), the term can stand for a general attitude of deference that would include mutual submission within the Christian community irrespective of one's social standing *vis-à-vis* the other

---

[90] Grudem, *1 Peter*, 190–91. See discussions also in Best, *1 Peter*, 171, and Colin J. Hemer, "στέφανος," *NIDNTT*, 1:405–6.

[91] *Her.* 4.31.42.

[92] In Ezek. 9:6, the judgment that commences with the Temple touches first the πρεσβύτερος and the νεανίσκος (=νεώτερος) also who is listed immediately after in the list of those doomed to destruction.

(2:13a). Peter utilizes new submission terminology that is highly metaphorical[93] and vivid: πάντες ἀλλήλοις τὴν ταπεινοφρο-σύνην ἐγκομβώσασθε/"and all of you must clothe yourselves with humility in your dealings with one another" (5:5b). The proof for the simple Petrine argument on humility is an authoritative statement from Prov. 3:34 LXX, an inartificial proof since in its obvious relationship with the case presented it needs nothing from the rhetor's artifice to demonstrate its relevance.[94]

The quotation from Proverbs not only substantiates a command for mutual humility to one another, but toward God as well (v. 6). The clause ἵνα ὑμᾶς ὑψώσῃ ἐν καιρῷ refers to the exoneration of the harassed community to the place of public recognition and honor as God's specially favored οἶκος. Since that honor will come, the common cares of the community are to be cast on God as a concomitant of their humility before God (v. 7).[95]

Descriptio of the Devil (5:8–9)

The twin exhortations νήψατε, γρηγορήσατε, stemming from common traditional Christian parenesis, echo the Jesus sayings.[96] The terms, joined in asyndeton,[97] are an instance of synonymy,[98] a

---

[93] The phrase serves as a foil to ἀποθέμενοι κτλ ('putting off as a garment . . .') in 2:1.

[94] Cic. *Part. Or.* 2.6 states that oracles, prophecies, and the like are inartificial proofs. Quint. *Inst. Or.* 5.11.43–44 disputes this notion since an authoritative source is external to the case and requires the rhetor's art to apply it to the case. See also Watson, *Invention,* 16–17.

[95] πᾶσαν τὴν μέριμναν ὑμῶν ἐπιρίψαντες ἐπ' αὐτόν, 5:7a. The aor. ptc. ἐπιρίψαντες is thus not an independent impv. ptc. (JB, NEB, NRSV), but is to be taken with ταπεινώθητε (Robertson, *Grammar,* 946). Thus, 'humble yourselves . . . as you cast/having cast all your worry.'

[96] 1 Thess. 5:6 (both vbs. in 1st pers. pl. hort. subj.); cf. Mt. 24:42; 25:13; Mk. 13:33, 35, 37; Selwyn, *St. Peter,* 375–82.

[97] *Dissolutum,* the suppression of conjunctions. *Her.* 4.30.41.

[98] *Interpretatio,* the replacement of one word by another of the same meaning (*Her.* 4.28.38). Selwyn, *St. Peter,* 380, remarks on the verb νηφεῖν in 1 Thess. 5:6b (γρηγορῶμεν καὶ νήφωμεν) that it "represents a still further development of the same ethical idea" (i.e., of γρηγορεῖν=wakeful, alert). Since their order is reversed in 1 Pt. 5:8, one could say that γρηγορεῖν in turn develops νηφεῖν, but not necessarily so.

virtual replication of the same idea in different words. The imperative expressions introduce the figure *descriptio*,[99] a vivid description which, in judicial rhetoric, is a clear, lucid, and impressive exposition of the consequences of an act. In Peter's deliberative argument, the figure graphically portrays the Devil[100] with his predatory intentions. Whereas the farewell speech of Acts

---

[99] *Her.* 4.39.51, where an example amazingly similar in content (although longer) to the Petrine figure occurs: "But, men of the jury, if by your votes you free this defendant, immediately, like a lion released from his cage, or some foul beast loosed from his chains, he will slink [*volitabit*] and prowl [*vagabitur*] about in the forum, sharpening his teeth to attack every one's property, assaulting every man, friend and enemy, known to him or unknown, now despoiling a good name, now attacking a life, now bringing ruin upon a house and its entire household, shaking the republic from its foundations. Therefore, men of the jury, cast him out from the state, free every one from fear, and finally, think of yourselves. For if you release this creature without punishment, believe me, gentlemen, it is against yourselves that you will have let loose a wild and savage beast." The Lat. verbs above are equivalent to the Gk. περιπατέω. The intention of the "lion" to despoil a good name and bring ruin upon a household parallels the intention of the διάβολος and the Gentiles aligned with him in 1 Pt.

[100] Luther's treatment of 1 Pt. 5:8 itself contains a lively *descriptio* of the Devil as a prowling lion (Martin Luther, "Sermons on the First Epistle of St. Peter," trans. Martin H. Bertram, in *Luther's Works*, ed. Jaroslav Pelikan, vol. 30, *The Catholic Epistles* (Saint Louis: Concordia Publishing House, 1967), 141 [WA 394–95].

For general discussions of διάβολος/Σατανᾶς in the NT, see Hans Bietenhard and Colin Brown, "Satan, Beelzebul, Devil, Exorcism: διάβολος," *NIDNTT*, 3:468–73; Rudolf Bultmann, *Theology of the New Testament*, trans. Kendrick Grobel (New York: Charles Scribner's Sons, 1951–55), 1:257–59; 2:15–17, 24–25, 147–54; G. B. Caird, *Principalities and Powers: A Study in Pauline Theology* (Oxford: Clarendon Press, 1956); Werner Foerster and K. Schäferdiek, "σατανᾶς," *TDNT*, 7:151–65; Werner Foerster and Gerhard von Rad, "διαβάλλω, διάβολος," *TDNT*, 2:71–81; Richard H. Hiers, "Satan, Demons, and the Kingdom of God," *Scottish Journal of Theology* 27 (February 1974): 35–47; Ladd, *TNT*, 65–69, 227–28, 400–403, 595–96, 619–32; Edward Langton, *Essentials of Demonology: A Study of Jewish and Christian Doctrine: Its Origin and Development* (London: Epworth Press, 1949), Trevor Ling, *The Significance of Satan: New Testament Demonology and Its Contemporary Relevance,* S. P. C. K. Biblical Monographs no. 3 (London: S. P. C. K., 1961); Heinrich Schlier, *Principalities and Powers in the New Testament* (New York: Herder and Herder, 1961); Roy Yates, "The Powers of Evil in the New Testament," *The Evangelical Quarterly* 52 (April-June 1980): 97–111.

20 features "savage wolves" (v. 29) which threaten the flock, in 1 Pt. 5:8 a lion (sc. the Devil) jeopardizes God's flock. The foe in John 13–17 is "Satan" (13:27) who is "the evil one" (17:15). In Acts of John 108 the enemy is "our adversary." The spiritual opponent of the believers is foremost a slanderer (διάβολος).[101] Peter significantly uses the epithet for Satan in order to identify him as the ultimate source behind the slander flung at his readers. The striking simile[102] of the lion (ὡς λέων) colorfully depicts a beast who not only walks about,[103] but does so in order to seek someone to devour (ζητῶν [τινα] καταπιεῖν). His wanderings are accompanied by roaring (ὠρυόμενος), an onomatopoetic[104] word that blends an audile vibrancy with the visual detail about stalking prey. The image captures for the audience the ferocity of its adversary and fosters self-pity for the hearers' plight. Their misery is to be matched by the graciousness of God in v. 10.

In v. 8, the Devil is "your adversary" (ὁ ἀντίδικος ὑμῶν), a legal term[105] that indicates Peter's imagery lies within the concerns of slander and vindication, of accusation and exoneration.[106] Already Peter has confirmed that his readers appeal to God for vindication (ἐπικαλέομαι, 1:17) and ought to entrust themselves to their faithful Creator as they do good, thereby following Christ's example (2:23). When the accusations, which have their ultimate source in the Devil, come, the maligned are to resist him firm in faith (v. 9).

---

[101] BAGD, 182 (s.v. "διάβολος").

[102] *Imago*/εἰκών, *Her.* 4.49.62; Arist. *Rh.* 3.4.1406b.20; Lausberg, *Handbuch*, 558.

[103] Cf. Job 2:2 τότε εἶπεν ὁ διάβολος ἐνώπιον τοῦ Κυρίου, διαπορευθεὶς τὴν ὑπ᾽ οὐρανὸν, καὶ ἐμπεριπατήσας τὴν σύμπασαν, πάρειμι.

[104] See 196 n. 87 above.

[105] Caird, *Principalities*, 33, who observes a legal sense at 1 Tim. 3:6 μὴ νεόφυτον, ἵνα μὴ τυφωθεὶς εἰς κρίμα ἐμπέσῃ τοῦ διαβόλου (hence κρίμα τοῦ διαβόλου is a subjective gen.: the condemnation that the devil hurls at the believer).

[106] Cf. Rev. 12:9–10 for the confluence of several traditions/images of the Devil: ὁ δράκων ὁ μέγας, ὁ ὄφις ὁ ἀρχαῖος, διάβολος, ὁ Σατανᾶς, ὁ πλανῶν τὴν οἰκουμένην ὅλην, ὁ κατήγωρ τῶν ἀδελφῶν ἡμῶν.

The non-believing outsiders, the Gentiles, are those who malign, criticize, and slander the members of the community, the οἶκος τοῦ θεοῦ. Thus the opponents, in standing against God's household of faith, are in league with the Devil who is the great accuser. In the *descriptio*, Peter portrays the danger to the churches, therefore, as more than injurious accusations from unbelievers; it is hostility from the infernal power of Satan himself. The author hopes, by magnifying the peril as a supernatural one, to promote group unity and identity in the community.[107] The attribution of the community's struggles to the antagonism of a malevolent supernatural being assures the flock that it does not suffer as κακοποιοῦντες (2:12, 14; 4:15), but as the opposite, ἀγαθοποιοῦντες (2:14) and Χριστιανοί (4:16).

Hence in the Petrine dualistic cosmology, the believers' sufferings assume a cosmic dimension. In the battle between Christ and Satan,[108] the beleaguered πάροικοι and παρεπίδημοι are front-line troops against the foes of darkness. When vv. 8–9 are viewed in conjunction with vv. 10–11, the reversal of suffering to glory, of shame to honor, of slander to vindication within Peter's cosmology becomes evident. The nature of his universe allows for, and even requires, the reversal of status for the unjust sufferer. Christ, the righteous sufferer par excellence, has enjoyed such a reversal and is established by the author as a paradigm for the way God works with his people (see 2:21–25; 3:18–22).[109] The divine power guarantees the process (v. 11).

In that the slanders of the outsiders are the expressions of the Devil's own malignity, the readers and their just behavior are starkly contrasted to the diabolical conduct of those who do not

---

[107] Elliott, *Home*, 81, 108, 114–15, 144–45.

[108] Cf. Neyrey, *Paul, in Other Words*, 15–17, 168–78, for discussion of the symbolic universe and the component of evil/misfortune that, in Paul, gives way to honor for the suffering apostles in an attack-victory scheme (1 Cor. 4:8–13; 2 Cor. 4:7–12, 6:3–10, 11:23–32).

[109] Pearson, "Hymnic Pattern," 10, declares regarding the suffering-glories pattern: "That scheme declares that, in God's plan, righteous suffering is followed by vindication, exaltation, and 'glories.'"

believe. The hearers' pity for their own cause is extended, not in terms of a miserable deploring of their own luckless fate, but of an assurance that their affliction is a participation in that of Christ (4:13) and the normal experience of God's people—after all, the addressees realize that all their fellow members of God's household world-wide undergo the same sufferings (εἰδότες τὰ αὐτὰ τῶν παθημάτων τῇ ἐν [τῷ] κόσμῳ ὑμῶν ἀδελφότητι ἐπιτελεῖσθαι, v. 9b).[110] The phrase ἐν [τῷ] κόσμῳ need not refer to a persecution of universal/imperial proportions, but is a hyperbole[111] intended to stress the fact that suffering as a Χριστιανός is typical for one who adopts that name.

Accumulation and Doxology (5:10–11)

God is the final arbiter in the honor contest. His grand function is to bestow his grace (χάρις) and glory (δόξα). In fact, Peter asserts that God is the God of all grace (πάσης χάριτος)—every true favor and distinction of honor is from him alone, for which reason the calumniation of the Gentiles against his elect is insignificant and a gross distortion of the true eternal verdict of the honor contest waged between the believing community and the antagonistic world. All the members of the οἶκος τοῦ θεοῦ are called into his eternal glory in Christ Jesus—they are destined for honor and vindication that will be recognized by the entire cosmos.

However, a time of testing and suffering must precede that glory. "And after you have suffered for a little while" (ὀλίγον παθόντας) is reminiscent of ὀλίγον ἄρτι εἰ δέον [ἐστὶν] λυπηθέντες ἐν ποικίλοις πειρασμοῖς (1:6), and, with the duplication of δόξα (1:7), forms a definite *inclusio* for the letter.[112] The stylistic

---

[110] "The same sufferings are laid upon the brotherhood or are accomplished in the case of the brotherhood," BAGD, 302 (s.v. "ἐπιτελέω").

[111] *Her.* 4.33.44. Cf. Rom. 1:8b ἡ πίστις ὑμῶν καταγγέλλεται ἐν ὅλῳ τῷ κόσμῳ.

[112] Dalton, *Proclamation*, 95–96.

device of accumulation,[113] featuring four future-tense verbs[114] (καταρτίσει, στηρίξει, σθενώσει, θεμελιώσει) represents the effort by the writer to emphasize absolutely the incontestable intention of God to vindicate the presently harassed readers. The device is particularly useful here, at the end of the Petrine *peroratio*.[115] The verbs are practically identical in meaning, although some progression may exist between the first three verbs and the fourth: only after God has restored, supported, and strengthened someone can s/he be established or put on a firm foundation (θεμελιόω). Power belongs to God (v. 11), the one who promises a glorious vindication which is certain to come.

Closing Remarks and Greetings (5:12–14)

The issues of authorship and provenance surrounding "Silvanus" and "Babylon" in this passage have been addressed in the introduction above and warrant no further discussion here. The section 5:12–14 is actually not part of the *peroratio*, nor is it technically a rhetorical unit, but it is appended to the *peroratio* in order to provide (with 1:1–2) the discourses of 1:3–5:11 with a suitable epistolary frame. However, since verses 12–14 include characteristics of summation and positive pathos, it may be classified as a "quasi-peroratio."[116]

Verse 12 is rhetorically important in that it contains the author's own statement in regard to his rhetorical strategy. In other words, he states the purpose that he has had in writing: ἔγραψα παρακαλῶν καὶ ἐπιμαρτυρῶν ταύτην εἶναι ἀληθῆ χάριν τοῦ θεοῦ· εἰς ἣν στῆτε. In 1 Peter, χάρις has signified the favor and honor of God (1:2, 11, 13; 2:19–20; 3:7; 4:10; 5:10),

---

[113] Lat. *congeries*. Long. *Subl.* 12; Quint. *Inst. Or.* 8.4.26–27; Watson, *Invention*, 27; 115 (on 2 Pt. 2:12–14). On the particular instance of the figure in 1 Pt. 5:10, see Davids, *1 Peter*, 195–96.

[114] The verbs are not in the optative mood, which is present in most closing blessings (e.g., 1 Thess. 5:23; 2 Thess. 3:16), but in the ind., signifying more certainty about God's future action. Davids, *1 Peter*, 195.

[115] Cic. *Or.* 36.127; Watson, *Invention*, 27–28.

[116] Watson, *Invention*, 76–77, so classifies the doxology of Jude 24–25.

virtually synonymous with δόξα and τιμή (1:7; 5:10). Now, at 5:12, Peter reminds his readers that what he has instructed them about their identity as chosen and beloved members of God's household, in addition to what he has said about their future vindication to honor, is true and to be held firmly in hope. The short sentence εἰς ἥν στῆτε summarizes well all of Peter's exhortations for endurance and well-doing to those who seek God's vindicating honor (χάρις, the antecedent of ἥν).

The greetings of the church in Babylon (Rome) and of Mark confirm to the readers the honor that God has appointed for them; the salutations of prominent members of the ἀδελφότης ἐν κόσμῳ (v. 9) demonstrate the high esteem and honor in which the churches of Asia Minor are held. Mark, the "son" of an apostle, would possess extraordinary ethos with Peter's audience. So, too, would the Roman church. It already ranks as one of the world's pre-eminent Christian communities since it is the church of the imperial capital and the apostle Peter's own church.

In order for the community to have a tangible expression of the divine honor, Peter enjoins the sharing of the kiss of love (v. 14). That greeting is a witness to the church and to the world that it has a distinct and honorable identity and boundaries to mark it off from the world. Rather than attempting to erase the stigmata of themselves as πάροικοι and παρεπίδημοι, the believers are to celebrate them with the φίλημα ἀγάπης.[117] Once again (cf. 1:2d) the author wishes his audience to know the peace that the knowledge of their honor from God can bring (v. 14b).

---

[117] The φίλημα ἀγάπης (cf. the φίλημα ἅγιον in Rom. 16:16; 1 Cor. 16:20; 2 Cor. 13:12; 1 Thess 5:26) is public evidence that the holy people of God experience the honor and love of God in interaction with each other. Furthermore, the kiss demonstrates that they wish to publicly express the reconciliation with one another that is provided by the cross. See William Klassen, "The Sacred Kiss in the New Testament: An Example of Social Boundary Lines," *New Testament Studies* 39 (1993): 135.

CHAPTER EIGHT

A Review of the Analysis of 1 Peter

Summary of the Findings

Exordium: 1 Pt. 1:3–12

After an address that serves as a quasi-exordium (1:1 2), Peter praises his audience for the benefits that they have received as children of God and for their virtuous qualities of joy, faith, and love for Christ. The prophets themselves have prophesied of the grace to come to Peter's audience (v. 10) who, indeed, have been served by the prophets as well as the preachers of the good news who have brought the gospel to Asia Minor. Angels themselves keenly seek to understand matters relating to the salvation of Peter's hearers (vv. 10–12).

The entire passage is an encomium on the Christians of Asia Minor. The short discourse, a typical piece of epideictic rhetoric, recognizes the genealogy, endowments, and virtues of its subjects. Furthermore, the prophets, preachers, and angels all constitute an attestation, like that of a memorial, to the privileged and honored status of the audience. The effect of the encomium on the addressees is to arouse positive pathos—not only toward themselves, but also toward the arguments to come. The rhetor has established his ethos by his self-identification as an apostle of Jesus Christ (1:1) and augments that ethos by creating for himself the capability of an omniscient observer, who can authoritatively praise, denounce, and argue because of his insight into the thoughts, desires, and understandings of God's human and angelic emissaries (vv. 10–12).

First *Argumentatio*: 1 Pt. 1:13–2:10

In the Latin rhetorical handbook *Rhetorica ad Herennium* is a pattern of argumentation that Peter copies in each of his three *argumentationes*, whose species is deliberative in each case. Although the same general pattern of discourse is present in each *argumentatio*, Peter develops all three with different creative touches. His artistry notwithstanding, each argument basically consists of a proposition, reason, confirmation of the reason, an embellishment, and a résumé.

The proposition (1:13–15) enjoins the readers, to set their hope completely upon the grace to be brought to them at Christ's revelation. The issue is really one of the mind: the διάνοια is to be ready for action by directing its focus toward the future. Such a mental outlook is antithetical to the ἄγνοια of the readers' pagan past, oriented as it was to selfish desires. Why should the readers develop a new mental focus, one toward the future and its coming χάρις? As his *ratio* (v. 16), Peter maintains that the holiness of God requires it. A hopeful eschatological orientation is an expression of holiness.

In order to confirm the reason that he has given for hope to be placed on the grace to come, Peter introduces corroboration (vv. 17–21). The fact that the readers hope for their vindication from God (=hope for the coming grace) means that they ought to conduct themselves during their παροικία with reverence. The redemption from their past futility has been effected for the believers, not by perishable silver or gold, but with Christ's precious blood. God has raised and glorified Jesus in order that their faith and hope might be in God.

Peter embellishes his argument by means of a command for mutual love and by a *iudicatio* (a divine pronouncement) from Isaiah on the imperishable word of God that contrasts with the perishable glory and honor of humankind. The author's most extensive scriptural interpretation of the entire letter emerges in 2:4–10. The entire passage, another Petrine *iudicatio*, represents the recipients of the letter as the honored new people of God, an οἶκος πνευματικός.

In conjunction with the encomium of 1:3–12, the first *argumentatio* confirms the identity of the harassed Christian communities in Asia Minor. They, despite being culturally and politically estranged πάροικοι and παρεπίδημοι (1:1; 2:12; cf. 1:17), are the honored people of God. Having established the audience's distinguished new identity, Peter has prepared them for the second *argumentatio* of 2:11–3:12 with its stronger hortatory tone.

Second *Argumentatio*: 1 Pt. 2:11–3:12

In retrospect the section 2:11–3:12 emerges as the core of the letter. The first and third *argumentationes* revolve around it: the first further establishes, after the encomium of 1:3–12, the identity of the recipients as the honored people of God. The audience is then in a frame of mind that is receptive to the rhetor's case since he has won their goodwill and interest. The third *argumentatio* attempts to address the hypothetical objector who maintains that, despite a commitment to upright behavior as described in 2:11–3:12, the Christian will doubtlessly suffer harm. Peter says that no one will harm his readers who are zealous for the good, but, even if someone does mistreat them, the sufferer is blessed (3:13–14).

Characteristics of the second *argumentatio* that speak for its centrality in the letter are (1) the use of the endearing term ἀγαπητοί (also occurring in the *peroratio* at 4:12); (2) the conjunction of πάροικος and παρεπίδημος for the only time in the document; (3) the οἰκέται (themselves following the supreme example, Christ), paradigmatic for the entire οἶκος τοῦ θεοῦ, appear in the section; (4) the most comprehensive and concrete parenesis (for each member of the οἶκος τοῦ θεοῦ) is in this section; and (5) for the first time a detailed account of the challenge-response pattern in 1 Peter appears. The scheme, found in 2:11–12, is the basis for all that Peter has to say on the honor contest.

In 1 Pt. 2:12b, ἐν ᾧ καταλαλοῦσιν ὑμῶν ὡς κακοποιῶν refers to that public challenge of the Christians by the unbelievers in which the cultural value of honor is at stake. As a limited good in Mediterranean society, public esteem is only conferred either on the party that successfully challenges, or that successfully answers a challenge. The πάροικοι and παρεπίδημοι of Asia Minor have experienced cultural and political estrangement there. That sense of alienation has been exacerbated among those who have embraced the Christian faith. Pagan society has issued a challenge to the sect of 'Christ-lackeys' that it believes is a danger to its cultural equilibrium.

The sectarians' response to the challenge, a riposte in attitude, action, and/or word, will shape social opinion about the Christians and lead to a public verdict that either sustains the challenging culture and its threatened welfare/honor, or deprives the society of it and grants honor to the challenged church. In 1 Peter, challenger and public are indistinguishable. The sect perceives itself as threatened by a public that is unbelieving and antagonistic. Peter is confident that, despite the slanders against the believers, by their good conduct they will gain honor. Their adversaries will render a verdict that grants glory to God and to those who represent him (2:12d), political authorities will praise those who do good (v. 14), thus silencing the ignorance of the foolish (v. 15). Furthermore, God himself bestows honor. The household slaves who unjustly suffer and endure with due submission have God's χάρις (2:19-20), whereas wives who defer to their husbands can expect to win their unbelieving partners and to become the children of Sarah (3:1-6). The entire community of believers has been called to bless others in order to receive the distinction of a εὐλογία themselves.

The resident aliens and visiting strangers are exhorted to abstain from fleshly lusts and to maintain a good conduct among the Gentiles, negative and positive expressions of the one propostion (vv. 11-12a). The *ratio* is a missionary one; Peter's expectation is that those who presently slander the believers will one day, at the day of visitation, glorify God (v. 12b-d). In order to restrain ungodly impulses and maintain good behavior among the unbelievers, the addressees are to submit, to show deference of honor, to every human creature (v. 13). The remaining part of the *argumentatio* Peter devotes to specific kinds of people who are to receive that honor: civic rulers (v. 13b-14), masters (v. 18), husbands (3:1), and wives (v. 7).

The sub-sections in the Petrine household code dealing with submission to political authorities, slave owners, and husbands are examples of a particular kind of rhetorical discourse, the thesis, a unit that characteristically consists of a proposition (thesis), a reason, an opposite, an analogy, an example, an authoritative citation, and a conclusion. The deference that a husband ought to display to his wife is described in a rhetorical *expolitio* (v. 7) that gives way to a summary of the *argumentatio* enumerating a list of required Christian qualities (vv. 8–12). The entire *argumentatio* closes with a lengthy passage from Psalm 34.

Third *Argumentatio*: 1 Pt. 3:13–4:11

"Now who will harm you," asks Peter," if you are eager to do what is good?" That rhetorical question of 3:13 probably answers some of his hearers who are convinced that Christians are always doomed to suffer for their faith. Peter is not as sceptical, though he does rhetorically concede in v. 14 the possibility of suffering for righteousness' sake (an experience that his audience has already encountered [1:6; 2:12, 19, 20]). In case of suffering, Peter's argument contains the necessary prescription for it. Again, the *argumentatio* has as its oratorical end the honor of the audience. Peter seeks to persuade his hearers that they are honored and that they ought to pursue a course of action commensurate with their privileged position.

The proposition (vv. 14b–16b) is fourfold: (1) do not fear the unbelievers, but rather (2) sanctify Christ as Lord in your hearts, (3) being ready always to give an answer for your hope, (4) having a good conscience. The phraseology of the reason, like that of the proposition, resembles that of 2:12. The reasons 2:12b-d and 3:16c are the positive and negative sides of the defamers' future verdict that reverses their present opinion of the community. To glorify God (2:12d) is the positive aspect of what it means to be ashamed (3:16)—both responses represent a reversal of the opponents' judgments of the Christians.

In order to confirm the reason of the argument, Peter brings forth a maxim, a *Besser-Spruch* (v. 17), about suffering ("for it is better to suffer for doing good, if suffering should be God's will, than to suffer for doing evil") and a lengthy *exemplum* (3:18–22) on the suffering and glorified Christ, whose experience of affliction and vindication becomes paradigmatic for the suffering Christian community (cf. 2:21–25). The *exemplum* incorporates hymnic/confessional and catechetical material that Peter skillfully blends for rhetorical effect.

In a *conplexio* (summary) for the argument, Peter presents a series of hortatory *sententiae* in 4:7–11 that follow an *exhortatio* on Christian resolve (vv. 1–2) and a *digressio* on the excesses of the wicked and future judgment (vv. 3–6). The *sententiae* basically concern life within the community and are headed by the maxim "the end of all things is near." A doxology concludes the entire argument.

Peroratio: 1 Pt. 4:12–5:14

Since many reminiscences and links to previous parts of 1 Peter exist in 4:12–5:11, the likelihood that the section is a rhetorical *peroratio* (and not a literary entity originally distinct from 1:1–4:11), is very great. In my rhetorical analysis, I have argued that the features of a standard argumentative *peroratio* appear in 1 Pt. 4:12–5:14. Recapitulation, amplification, and appeals to the auditors' pity all are evident. An admonition to church leaders (5:1–5) and a vivid *descriptio* on the Devil (v. 8) are present in the section. An *expolitio* on suffering (4:12–19) develops the theme of the ordeal by fire that the Christians of Asia Minor face, examining it from different angles throughout the section. The standard epistolary conclusion to the document is in 5:12–14, a "quasi-exordium."

Throughout 1 Pt. 4:12–5:14, concerns for honor and shame continue to emerge in the text. Peter, in his summation, urges his readers, on whom the glorious dignity of the Holy Spirit already rests (4:14), to avoid the ignominy of the criminal (v. 15), but consider suffering as a Christian to be honorable (v. 16). Unimaginable as it may seem, an end in suffering is in view, a time when God will establish with honor those who now undergo afflictions for Christ's sake (5:10).

Final Considerations

The analysis of 1 Peter which I have undertaken has presented many insights from the text of the letter that may not have been readily observable in other types of approaches. The interpreter who employs classical-rhetorical criticism is sensitive to rhetorical patterns and stylistic devices that the form critic, for example, might overlook. The social-scientific exegete experiments with different sociological and anthropological lenses in order to understand more clearly social and cultural forces at work in the letter. Those lenses may not come to recognition in other types of study. My attempt has been to combine classical-rhetorical criticism and social-scientific analysis in order to clarify the rhetorical ends and means of the author of 1 Peter. I encourage my reader to engage in criticism, extension, and improvement of my work wherever they are needed.

The Legitimacy of the Classical-Rhetorical Approach to 1 Peter

Throughout the dissertation, I have maintained that Peter operates according to definite principles concerning the invention, arrangement, and style of discourse as these principles found expression in the theoretical treatises on Greco-Roman rhetoric. In his significant *Metaphor and Composition in 1 Peter*,[1] Troy W. Martin calls for a compositional analysis of 1 Peter which satisfactorily provides the following features: (1) a construction that arises from the text itself and is not an importation of an external one, (2) an explanation of the relationship of 1:3–12 to the remainder of the letter, (3) a precise number of clearly marked sections in the letter, and (4) an identification of the controlling theme(s) of each section.

The classical-rhetorical analysis that I have undertaken adequately furnishes the four properties that Martin advocates for any explanation of composition in 1 Peter. (1) A similar rhetorical pattern of argumentation arises throughout 1 Peter,

---

[1] Martin, *Metaphor*, 39.

not just in isolated instances. The arrangement that Peter adopts reflects one found in *Rhetorica ad Herennium*. (2) A classical-rhetorical approach is alert to the encomiastic nature of 1 Pt. 1:3–12 and its function to win the favor of its hearers. The rhetorical function of the passage as an encomium is typically neglected by interpreters who tend to regard 1 Pt. 1:3–12 as a praise or blessing of God. (3) My study identifies the quantity of sections in the letter and provides means to determine their boundaries. A decisively imperatival tone distinguishes each *propositio* from a preceding indicative section (at 1:12/13), or a long scriptural reference (at 2:10/11 and 3:12/13). (4) The controlling themes of each section are discernible in its *propositio*. A terminal *peroratio* in a section can be identified by long scriptural commentary (2:4–10), a major scriptural citation (3:10–12), or doxology (4:11).

The Legitimacy of the Social-Scientific Approach to 1 Peter

The cultural value of honor appears to govern Peter's language and strategy as a theoretical persepective. Derived from that perspective (i.e., that the Mediterranean cultural milieu of 1 Peter is agonistic), is the model of the honor contest which features challenge and response. In order to test the model's validity, I examined the semantic field of honor/shame in 1 Peter and found it to be well represented. An extraordinary number of terms associated with public esteem and public disgrace in the text strongly suggests that Peter's concern is predominantly with honor, the primary cultural value of the ancient Mediterranean world.

The pattern of challenge and riposte in the contest for honor makes sense of the data in 1 Peter. The acridity in relations between the Christian community and the pagans has arisen from a perceived threat to societal welfare. In 1 Peter, the unbelievers have unjustly slandered the believers as evildoers. In the minds of the non-Christians, the Christians endanger the equilibrium of Greco-Roman culture. The undeserved suffering of the believing community is the rhetorical exigence of 1 Peter and it demands that Peter argue for the readers' honor.

According to the author's argument, the harassed household of God stands in a divinely honored position and can look forward to a reversal in the honor contest presently occurring. In that reversal, the Christians will be vindicated with honor and their opponents will be put to shame. However, the community must adopt or maintain certain behaviors that Peter sets forth in his *propositiones*. His rhetorical arguments develop the propositions and reasons for their execution. By a careful cataloging of honor/shame language and a cautious plotting of challenge and riposte in the letter, I have endeavored to minimize the chances of incommensurability.

The Implied Hearer and the Influence of 1 Peter

The imposition of rhetorical patterns on a text where those patterns do not really exist is another danger of which I have been aware and have hopefully avoided. Still, even if one can establish convincingly that certain rhetorical patterns and attendant oratorical devices are present in discourse, one cannot know absolutely the effects that they had upon the original audience without ancient testimony about those effects. We have no such testimony regarding the influence that 1 Peter exercised among the Christian communities of Asia Minor. Hence I have worked with an "implied hearer" whose ideal responses to Peter's rhetorical art I have sought to determine.[2]

---

[2] In suggesting an "implied hearer" for the rhetoric of 1 Peter, I borrow from narrative criticism and its concept of an "implied reader." An implied reader is a hypothetical figure, "an imaginary reader with the ideal responses implied or suggested by the narrative, experiencing suspense or feeling amazement or sympathizing with a character at the appropriate times" (David Rhoads and Donald Michie, *Mark as Story: An Introduction to the Narrative of a Gospel* [Philadelphia: Fortress Press, 1982], 137). The implied hearer of 1 Peter embodies the ideal responses that the rhetorical features of the letter are intended to produce. I designate the ideal recipient of rhetoric as a hearer since oratory was primarily auditory in the first century CE. Even when NT epistles convey a rhetorical argument, most recipients of the argument would hear it rather than read it (cf. Col. 4:16). In the dissertation

Naturally, no hearer responds ideally to a discourse. My assumption is, therefore, that at least some of the hearers responded some of the time to some of the discourse as I have analyzed it. In all probability, a number of Christians in communities throughout the Roman provinces of Pontus-Bithynia, Galatia, Cappadocia, and Asia found comfort and help in Peter's letter. Many of those believers were likely encouraged to stand fast in the true grace of God (5:12), confident that honor was (and would be in increased measure) theirs.

I have used 'hearer' and 'reader' interchangeably since the epistle is a literary text that was (and continues to be) both heard and read. (Hence I have alternated between 'speaker' and 'writer' also since Peter's rhetorical art is accessible both auditorily and visually.)

The Semantic Field of Honor and Shame in 1 Peter

HONOR

Nouns: grace, mercy, inheritance, praise, glory, honor, reverent fear, head of the corner, deference, credit, reverence, lord, Sarah's daughters, heirs, blessing, right hand (of God), gift, strength, crown of glory, power, kiss of love

Verbs: to glorify, to accept the authority of, to do right, to conduct oneself honorably, to honor, to fear, to win over, to obey, to do what is good, to pay honor to, to do good, to live in the spirit, to exalt, to restore, to support, to strengthen, to establish

Adjectives: chosen, blessed, glorious, precious, without defect or blemish, good, acceptable, royal, holy, honorable, very precious, better, hospitable, chosen together

SHAME

Nouns: exiles, sufferings, evildoers, slander, ignorance, griefs, cross, humble mind, evil, abuse, deceit, disgrace, murderer, thief, criminal, mischief maker, sordid gain

Verbs: to be put to shame, to reject, to stumble, to fall, to malign, to do wrong, to suffer unjustly, to be beaten, to suffer, to abuse, to return abuse, to threaten, to hinder prayers, to do evil, to harm, to blaspheme, to be reviled, to be clothed with humility, to oppose the proud, to humble oneself

Adjectives: foolish, humble

CHALLENGE, COUNTER-CHALLENGE, VERDICT

Nouns: judgment, adversary, devil

Verbs: to judge impartially, to punish, to judge justly, the face to be against, to give an accounting, to judge, to be judged

Adjectives: kind, gentle, harsh, righteous, unrighteous

Based on NRSV

APPENDIX 2

The Rhetorical Handbooks: A Brief Introduction[1]

Aristotle (384–322 BCE): *On the "Art" of Rhetoric* (Arist. *Rh.*) originated c. 360–365 BCE. The work is important in that it provides the basis of later discussion on rhetoric. Aristotle identifies the three species of rhetoric (judicial, deliberative, epideictic). Book 3 of *Rhetoric* having to do with style is perhaps the most interesting as well as the most influential part of the work (especially in its discussion on virtues of style and metaphor).

Cicero (106–43 BCE): Marcus Tullius Cicero was well-known as an orator and statesman as well as a theorist. Among his many works, I have utilized *De inventione* (*Inv.*), a work of Cicero's youth (c. 85 BCE?) that deals with issues/*stases* and the appropriate arguments for them; *De oratore* (*De Or.*), written some thirty years after *Inv.* (c. 55 BCE) on general principles of oratory; the perfect orator is described in *Orator* (*Or.*), a work in which Cicero employs a dialogic form. *Topica* (*Top.*), is an amplification of Aristotle's thought on types of argument and dates from c. 44 BCE. The most systematic of Cicero's works on rhetorical theory that have survived is *De partitione*, (c. 50–45 BCE) a response to his young son's queries on the art of oratory.

Quintilian (fl. 1st cent. CE) produced the monumental *Institutio oratoria* (c. 95 CE), a work of rhetorical theory that discusses the training of the orator from infancy to adulthood. His summaries of earlier writers' rhetorical theories give insight into how those theories were understood during the time of the composition of the New Testament.

Rhetorica ad Herennium (*Her.*, c. 86–82 BCE), author unknown. The work is valuable for its presentation of the five divisions of

---

[1] Clark, *Rhetoric*, 68–77; N. G. L. Hammond and H. H. Scullard, *The Oxford Classical Dictionary*, 2nd ed. (Oxford: Clarendon Press, 1970), 114–18, 234–38, 326, 505, 619, 907–8, 920–22; Kennedy, *NT Interpretation*, 12–13.

rhetoric: invention, arrangement, style, delivery, and memory. Implicit in Aristotle, with *Her.* they are obviously well established in the first century BCE. Furthermore, *Her.* constitutes the oldest extant Latin treatment of rhetorical style. The section in *Her.* on style is abundant with illustrations of stylistic matters.

Other significant works are Aristotle, *Poetica*; Demetrius, *On Style* (late Hellenistic/early Roman period); Hermogenes, *Progymnasmata* (2nd cent. CE?); Longinus, *On the Sublime* (1st cent. CE); and *Rhetorica ad Alexandrum* (author unknown, c. 200 BCE).

SOURCES CONSULTED

Primary Sources

Aristotle. "On the Art of Poetry." In *Classical Literary Criticism*, 29–75. Translated by T. S. Dorsch. Penguin Classics. Harmondsworth, England: Penguin Books, 1965.

———. *The "Art" of Rhetoric*. Translated by John Henry Freese. The Loeb Classical Library. Cambridge, MA: Harvard University Press, 1947; London: William Heinemann, 1947.

———. "Topica." In *The Basic Works of Aristotle*, ed. Richard McKeon, 187–206. Translated by W. A. Pickard. New York: Random House, 1941.

Cicero. *De Inventione*. Translated by H. M. Hubbell. The Loeb Classical Library. London: William Heinemann, 1960; Cambridge, MA: Harvard University Press, 1960. (In the LCL volume with Cicero, *Topica*.)

———. *Orator*. Translated by H. M. Hubbell. The Loeb Classical Library. Cambridge, MA: Harvard University Press, 1952; London: William Heineman, 1952.

———. *De Oratore* (Books 1–3). Translated by E. W. Sutton and H. Rackham. 2 vols. The Loeb Classical Library. London: William Heinemann, 1948; Cambridge, MA: Harvard University Press, 1948.

———. *De Partitione Oratoria*. Translated by H. Rackham. The Loeb Classical Library. London: William Heinemann, 1948; Cambridge, MA: Harvard University Press, 1948. (In the LCL volume with Cicero, *De Oratore*, Book 3.)

———. *Selected Letters*. Translated by D. R. Shackleton Bailey. Penguin Classics. New York: Penguin Books, n.d.

———. *Topica*. Translated by H. M. Hubbell. The Loeb Classical Library. London: William Heinemann, 1960; Cambridge, MA: Harvard University Press, 1960. (In the LCL volume with Cicero, *De Inventione*.)

Clement of Alexandria. "The Instructor." In *The Ante-Nicene Fathers*, ed. Alexander Roberts and James Donaldson, 2:207–98. Grand Rapids: William B. Eerdmans, 1951.

Demetrius. *On Style*. Translated by W. Rhys Roberts. The Loeb Classical Library. Cambridge: Harvard University Press, 1932; London: William Heinemann, 1932. (In the LCL volume with Longinus, *On the Sublime*.)

Hermogenes. "Elementary Exercises." In *Medieval Rhetoric and Poetic (to 1400): Interpreted from Representative Works*, by Charles Sears Baldwin, 23–38. N.p.: Macmillan Co., 1928; reprint, Gloucester, MA: Peter Smith, 1959.

Homer. *The Odyssey*. Translated by E. V. Rieu. Penguin Classics. Harmondsworth, England: Penguin Books, 1946.

Longinus. *On the Sublime*. Translated by Hamilton Fyfe. The Loeb Classical Library. Cambridge: Harvard University Press, 1932; London: William Heinemann, 1932. (In the LCL volume with Demetrius, *On Style*.)

———. "On the Sublime." In *Classical Literary Criticism*, 97–158. Translated by T. S. Dorsch. Penguin Classics. Harmondsworth, England: Penguin Books, 1965.

Pliny. *Letters and Panegyricus*. 2 vols. The Loeb Classical Library. Cambridge, MA: Harvard University Press, 1969; London: William Heinemann, 1969.

Plutarch. "On The Avoidance of Anger" [excerpt of *Moralia*]. Chap. in *Essays*. Translated by Robin Waterfield. Penguin Classics. London: Penguin Books, 1992.

———. *Plutarch's Lives*. Translated by Bernadotte Perrin. 10 vols. The Loeb Classical Library. Cambridge: Harvard University Press, 1914–26.; London: William Heinemann, 1914–26.

Quintilian. *The Institutio Oratoria*. Translated by H. E. Butler. 4 vols. The Loeb Classical Library. Cambridge, MA: Harvard University Press, 1953; London: William Heinemann, 1953.

Rhetorica ad Alexandrum. Translated by H. Rackham. The Loeb Classical Library. Cambridge, MA: Harvard University Press, 1957; London: William Heinemann, 1957.

Rhetorica ad Herennium. Translated by Harry Caplan. The Loeb Classical Library. Cambridge, MA: Harvard University Press, 1954; London: William Heinemann, 1954.

Suetonius. *The Twelve Caesars*. Translated by Robert Graves. Penguin Classics. Baltimore: Penguin Books, 1957.

Tacitus. *The Annals of Imperial Rome*. Translated by Michael Grant. Penguin Classics. Baltimore: Penguin Books, 1956.

Theophylact, *Expositio in Epistolam Primam S. Petri*. In Patrologiae Cursus Completus: Patrologiae Graecae [vol. 125, 1189–1252], ed. J. P. Migne, vol. 125. Paris: J. P. Migne, 1864; reprint, n.p.: Turnhout, Belgium, 1979.

Virgil. *The Aeneid*. Translated by W. F. Jackson Knight. Penguin Classics. Harmondsworth, England: Penguin Books, 1956.

Secondary Sources
1 Peter

Books and Commentaries

Balch, David L. *Let Wives Be Submissive: The Domestic Code in 1 Peter*. Society of Biblical Literature Monograph Series 26. Atlanta: Scholars Press, 1981.

Beare, Francis Wright. *The First Epistle of Peter: The Greek Text with Introduction and Notes*. 3rd ed. Oxford: Basil Blackwell, 1970.

Best, Ernest. *1 Peter*. New Century Bible Commentary. Grand Rapids: William B. Eerdmans, 1971.

Bigg, Charles. *A Critical and Exegetical Commentary on the Epistles of St. Peter and St. Jude*. International Critical Commentary. Edinburgh: T. & T. Clark, n.d.

Brox, Norbert. *Der erste Petrusbrief*. 2nd ed. Evangelisch katholischer Kommentar über das neue Testament 21. Zürich: Benziger Verlag, 1986; Neukirchen-Vluyn: Neukirchener Verlag, 1986.

Cranfield, C. E. B. *The First Epistle of Peter*. London: SCM Press, 1950.

Dalton, William J. *Christ's Proclamation to the Spirits: A Study of 1 Peter 3:18–4:6*. 2nd ed. Analecta Biblica 23. Rome: Editrice Pontificio Istituto Biblico, 1989.

Davids, Peter H. *The First Epistle of Peter.* New International Commentary on the New Testament. Grand Rapids: William B. Eerdmans, 1990.

Elliott, John Hall. *The Elect and the Holy: An Exegetical Examination of I Peter 2:4–10 and the Phrase* βασίλειον ἱεράτευμα. Supplements to *Novum Testamentum* 12. Leiden: E. J. Brill, 1966.

———. *A Home for the Homeless: A Social-Scientific Criticism of 1 Peter, Its Situation and Strategy.* Minneapolis: Fortress Press, 1981, 1990.

Feldmeier, Reinhard. *Die Christen als Fremde: Die Metapher der Fremde in der antiken Welt, im Urchristentum und im 1. Petrusbrief.* Wissenschaftliche Untersuchungen zum neuen Testament 64. Tübingen: J. C. B. Mohr (Paul Siebeck), 1992.

Gielen, Marlis. *Tradition und Theologie neutestamentlicher Haustafelethik: Ein Beitrag zur Frage einer christlichen Auseinandersetzung mit gesellschaftlichen Normen.* Athenäums Monografien Theologie. Bonner biblische Beiträge 75. Frankfurt on Main: Hain, 1990.

Goppelt, Leonhard. *A Commentary on 1 Peter.* Translated and edited by John E. Alsup. Grand Rapids: William B. Eerdmans, 1993.

———. *Der erste Petrusbrief.* Kritisch-exegetischer Komentar über das neue Testament 12/1. 8th ed. Göttingen: Vandenhoeck & Ruprecht, 1978.

Grudem, Wayne A. *The First Epistle of Peter: An Introduction and Commentary.* Tyndale New Testament Commentaries. Leicester: InterVarsity Press, 1988; Grand Rapids: William B. Eerdmans, 1988.

Hillyer, Norman. *1 and 2 Peter, Jude.* New International Biblical Commentary. Peabody, MA: Hendrickson, 1992.

Kelly, J. N. D. *A Commentary on the Epistles of Peter and of Jude.* Harper's New Testament Commentaries. New York: Harper & Row, 1969.

Luther, Martin. "Sermons on the First Epistle of St. Peter." Translated by Martin H. Bertram. In *Luther's Works,* ed.

Jaroslav Pelikan. Vol. 30, *The Catholic Epistles*. Saint Louis: Concordia Publishing House, 1967.

Marshall, I. Howard. *1 Peter*. IVP New Testament Commentary Series. Downers Grove, IL, and Leicester: InterVarsity Press, 1991.

Martin, Troy W. *Metaphor and Composition in 1 Peter*. Society of Biblical Literature Dissertation Series 131. Atlanta: Scholars Press, 1992.

Michaels, J. Ramsey. *1 Peter*. Word Biblical Commentary 49. Waco, TX: Word Books, 1988.

Millauer, Helmut. *Leiden als Gnade: Eine traditionsgeschichtliche Untersuchung zur Leidenstheologie des ersten Petrusbriefes*. Europäische Hochschulschriften 23. Theologie 56. Bern: Herbert Lang, 1976; Frankfurt on Main: Peter Lang, 1976.

Perdelwitz, Richard. *Die Mysterienreligion und das Problem des I. Petrusbriefes: Ein literarischer und religionsgeschichtlicher Versuch*. Giessen: Alfred Töpelmann, 1911.

Prostmeier, Ferdinand-Rupert. *Handlungsmodelle im ersten Petrusbrief*. FB 63. Würzburg: Echter, 1990.

Reichert, Angelika. *Eine urchristliche praeparatio ad martyrium: Studien zur Komposition, Traditionsgeschichte und Theologie des 1. Petrusbriefes*. Beiträge zur biblischen Exegese und Theologie 22. Frankfurt on Main: Peter Lang, 1989.

Reicke, Bo. *The Disobedient Spirits and Christian Baptism: A Study of 1 Pet. III. 19 and Its Context*. Acta Seminarii Neotestamentici Upsaliensis Edenda Curavit A. Fridrichsen. Copenhagen: Ejnar Munksgaard, 1946.

———. *The Epistles of James, Peter, and Jude*. The Anchor Bible. Garden City, NY: Doubleday, 1964.

Robertson, Archibald Thomas. *Word Pictures in the New Testament*. Vol. 6, *The General Epistles and the Revelation of John*. Nashville: Broadman Press, 1933.

Schelkle, Karl Hermann. *Die Petrusbriefe, der Judasbrief*. Herders theologischer Kommentar zum neuen Testament. Freiburg: Herder, 1961.

Schröger, Friedrich. *Gemeinde im 1. Petrusbrief: Untersuchungen zum Selbstverständnis einer christlichen Gemeinde an der Wende vom 1. zum 2. Jahrhundert*. Schriften der Universität Passau. Vol. 1,

Reihe katholische Theologie. Passau: Passavia Universitäts-verlag, 1981.

Schutter, William L. *Hermeneutic and Composition in I Peter.* Wissenschaftliche Untersuchungen zum neuen Testament. 2nd Series no. 30. Tübingen: J. C. B. Mohr (Paul Siebeck), 1989.

Selwyn, Edward Gordon. *The First Epistle of St. Peter: The Greek Text with Introduction, Notes and Essays.* London: Macmillan & Co., 1949.

Stibbs, Alan M. and Andrew F. Walls. *The First Epistle General of Peter.* Tyndale New Testament Commentaries. Grand Rapids: William B. Eerdmans, 1959.

Thurén, Lauri. *The Rhetorical Strategy of 1 Peter: With Special Regard to Ambiguous Expressions.* Åbo, Finland: Åbo Academy Press, 1990.

Windisch, Hans, and Herbert Preisker. *Die katholischen Briefe.* 3rd rev. ed. Handbuch zum neuen Testament 15. Tübingen: J. C. B. Mohr (Paul Siebeck), 1951.

Articles, Dissertations, and Unpublished Sources

Achtemeier, Paul J. "Newborn Babes and Living Stones: Literal and Figurative in 1 Peter." In *To Touch the Text: Biblical and Related Studies in Honor of Joseph A. Fitzmyer, S. J.*, ed. Maurya P. Horgan and Paul J. Kobelski, 207–36. New York: Crossroad, 1989.

Balch, David L. "The First Letter of Peter" [introduction and annotations]. In *The HarperCollins Study Bible*, ed. Wayne A. Meeks, 2277–85. New York: HarperCollins Publishers, 1993.

———. "Hellenization/Acculturation in 1 Peter." In *Perspectives on First Peter*, ed. Charles H. Talbert, 79–101. NABPR Special Studies Series no. 9. Macon, GA: Mercer University Press, 1986.

Bammel, F. "The Commands in I Peter II.17." *New Testament Studies* 11 (1964–65): 279–81.

Best, Ernest. "1 Peter." In *The Oxford Companion to the Bible*, ed. Bruce M. Metzger and Michael D. Coogan, 583–86. New York and Oxford: Oxford University Press, 1993.

Bultmann, Rudolf. "Bekenntnis- und Liedfragmente im ersten Petrusbrief." *Coniectanea Neotestamentica* 11 (1947): 1–14.

Carrez, Maurice. "L'esclavage dans la première epître de Pierre." In *Études sur la première lettre de Pierre*, 207–17. Lectio Divina 102. Paris: Cerf, 1980.

Combrink, H. J. B. "The Structure of 1 Peter." *Neotestamentica* 9 (1975, 1980²): 34–63.

Cothenet, Édouard. "Les orientations actuelles de l'exégèse de la première lettre de Pierre." In *Études sur la première lettre de Pierre*, 13–42. Lectio Divina 102. Paris: Cerf, 1980.

Dalton, William J. "1 Peter 3:19 Reconsidered." In *The New Testament Age: Essays in Honor of Bo Reicke*, ed. William C. Weinrich, 1:95–105. Macon, GA: Mercer University Press, 1984.

Daube, David. "Appended Note: Participle and Imperative in I Peter." In *The First Epistle of St. Peter: The Greek Text with Introduction, Notes and Essays*, by Edward Gordon Selwyn, 467–88. London: Macmillan & Co., 1949.

du Toit, A. B. "The Significance of Discourse Analysis for New Testament Interpretation and Translation: Introductory Remarks with Special Reference to 1 Peter 1:3–13." *Neotestamentica* 8 (1974): 54–79.

Elliott, John H. "Backward and Forward 'In His Steps': Following Jesus from Rome to Raymond and Beyond. The Tradition, Redaction, and Reception of 1 Peter 2:18–25." In *Discipleship in the New Testament*, ed. Fernando F. Segovia, 184–208. Philadelphia: Fortress Press, 1985.

———. "1 Peter, Its Situation and Strategy: A Discussion with David Balch." In *Perspectives on First Peter*, ed. Charles H. Talbert, 61–78. NABPR Special Studies Series no. 9. Macon, GA: Mercer University Press, 1986.

———. "Peter, First Epistle of." In *The Anchor Bible Dictionary*, ed. David Noel Freedman et al., 5:269–78. New York: Doubleday, 1992.

———. "The Rehabilitation of an Exegetical Step Child: 1 Peter in Recent Research." *Journal of Biblical Literature* 95 (1976): 243–54. [Reprint in *Perspectives on First Peter*, ed. Charles H.

Talbert, 3–16. NABPR Special Studies Series no. 9. Macon, GA: Mercer University Press, 1986.]

Ellul, Danielle. "Un exemple de cheminement rhétorique: 1 Pierre." *Revue d'histoire et de philosophie religieuses* 70 (1990/1): 17–34.

France, R. T. "Exegesis in Practice: Two Samples." In *New Testament Interpretation: Essays on Principles and Methods*, ed. I. Howard Marshall, 264–81. Grand Rapids: William B. Eerdmans, 1977.

Gabarrón, Jose Cervantes. "El Pastor en la teologia de 1 Pe." *Estudios Biblicos* 49 (1991): 331–51.

Gundry, Robert H. "Further *Verba* on *Verba Christi* in First Peter." *Biblica* 55 (1974): 211–32.

————. "'Verba Christi' in 1 Peter: Their Implications concerning the Authorship of 1 Peter and the Authenticity of the Gospel Tradition." *New Testament Studies* 13 (1966–67): 336–50.

Kendall, David W. "The Literary and Theological Function of 1 Peter 1:3–12." In *Perspectives on First Peter*, ed. Charles H. Talbert, 103–20. NABPR Special Studies Series no. 9. Macon, GA: Mercer University Press, 1986.

Knox, John. "Pliny and I Peter: A Note on I Pet 4:14–16 and 3:15." *Journal of Biblical Literature* 72 (1953): 187–89.

Lohse, Eduard. "Parenesis and Kerygma in 1 Peter." Translated by John Steely. In *Perspectives on First Peter*, ed. Charles H. Talbert, 37–59. NABPR Special Studies Series no. 9. Macon, GA: Mercer University Press, 1986.

Martin, Ralph P. "The Composition of 1 Peter in Recent Study." *Vox Evangelica* 1 (1962): 29–42.

————. "Peter, First." In *The International Standard Bible Encyclopedia*, ed. Geoffrey W. Bromiley et al., 3:807–15. Grand Rapids: William B. Eerdmans, 1986.

Marxsen, Willi. "Der Mitälteste und Zeuge der Leiden Christi: Eine martyrologische Begründung des 'Romprimats' im 1. Petrus-Brief?" In *Theologia Crucis—Signum Crucis*. Festschrift for Erich Dinkler, ed. Carl Andresen and Günter Klein, 377–93. Tübingen: J. C. B. Mohr (Paul Siebeck), 1979.

Moule, C. F. D. "The Nature and Purpose of I Peter." *New Testament Studies* 3 (1956–57): 1–11.

Nauck, Wolfgang. "Freude im Leiden: Zum Problem einer urchristlichen Verfolgungstradition." *Zeitschrift für die neutestamentliche Wissenschaft* 46 (1955): 68–80.

Pearson, Birger A. "James, 1–2 Peter, Jude." In *The New Testament and Its Modern Interpreters*, ed. Eldon Jay Epp and George W. MacRae, 371–406. Atlanta: Scholars Press, 1989.

Pearson, Sharon Clark. "The Christological Hymnic Pattern of 1 Peter." Ph.D. diss., Fuller Theological Seminary, 1993.

Prigent, Pierre. "1 Pierre 2, 4–10." *Revue d'histoire et de philosophie religieuses* 72 (1992): 53–60.

Sander, Emilie T. "ΠΥΡΩΣΙΣ and the First Epistle of Peter 4:12." Th.D. thesis, Harvard Divinity School, 1966.

Schierse, F. J. "Ein Hirtenbrief und viele Bücher." *Bibel und Kirche* 31 (1976): 86–88.

Schröger, Friedrich. "Die Verfassung der Gemeinde des ersten Petrusbriefes." In *Kirche im Werden: Studien zum Thema Amt und Gemeinde im neuen Testament*, ed. Josef Hainz, 239–52. Munich: Verlag Ferdinand Schöningh, 1976.

Snyder, Scot. "1 Peter 2:17: A Reconsideration." *Filologia Neotestamentaria* 4 (November 1991): 211–16.

Sylva, Dennis. "A 1 Peter Bibliography." *Journal of the Evangelical Theological Society* 25 (March 1982): 75–89. [Reprint in *Perspectives on First Peter*, ed. Charles H. Talbert, 17–36, as "The Critical Exploration of 1 Peter." NABPR Special Studies Series no. 9. Macon, GA: Mercer University Press, 1986.]

———. "1 Peter Studies: The State of the Discipline." *Biblical Theology Bulletin* 10 (October 1980): 155–63.

Unnik, W. C. van. "A Classical Parallel to 1 Peter II 14 and 20." Chap. in *Sparsa Collecta: The Collected Essays of W. C. van Unnik*. Part 2, *1 Peter, Canon, Corpus Hellenisticum, Generalia*. Supplements to *Novum Testamentum* vol. 30. Leiden: E. J. Brill, 1980.

———. "The Teaching of Good Works in 1 Peter." Chap. in *Sparsa Collecta: The Collected Essays of W. C. van Unnik*. Part 2,

1 Peter, Canon, Corpus Hellenisticum, Generalia. Supplements to *Novum Testamentum* vol. 30. Leiden: E. J. Brill, 1980.

Watson, Duane F. [Letter] to Barth Campbell, 10 February 1992. Barth Campbell's personal files.

————. Review of *The Rhetorical Strategy of 1 Peter: With Special Regard to Ambiguous Expressions,* by Lauri Thurén. In *Journal of Biblical Literature* 10 (Winter 1991): 746–48

Classical Rhetoric and CRCNT

Books and Commentaries

Baldwin, Charles Sears. *Ancient Rhetoric and Poetic: Interpreted from Representative Works.* N.p.: Macmillan Co., 1924; reprint, Gloucester, MA: Peter Smith, 1959.

————. *Medieval Rhetoric and Poetic (to 1400): Interpreted from Representative Works.* N.p.: Macmillan Co., 1928; reprint, Gloucester, MA: Peter Smith, 1959.

Berger, Klaus. *Formgeschichte des neuen Testaments.* Heidelberg: Quelle & Meyer, 1984.

Betz, Hans Dieter. *Galatians: A Commentary on Paul's Letter to the Churches in Galatia.* Hermeneia—A Critical and Historical Commentary on the Bible. Philadelphia: Fortress Press, 1979.

Bloomquist, L. Gregory. *The Function of Suffering in Philippians.* JSNT Supplement Series 78. Sheffield: JSOT Press, 1993.

Bullinger, Ernest W. *Figures of Speech Used in the Bible Explained and Illustrated.* London: Eyre & Spottiswoode, 1898.

Bultmann, Rudolf. *Der Stil der paulinischen Predigt und die kynisch-stoische Diatribe.* Forschungen zur Religion und Literatur des alten und neuen Testaments 13. Göttingen: Vandenhoeck & Ruprecht, 1910.

Campbell, Douglas A. *The Rhetoric of Righteousness in Romans 3:21–26.* JSNT Supplement Series 65. Sheffield: JSOT Press, 1992.

Chadwick, Henry. *The Sentences of Sextus: A Contribution to the History of Early Christian Ethics.* Cambridge: Cambridge University Press, 1959.

Clark, Donald Lemen. *Rhetoric in Greco-Roman Education.* Morningside Heights, NY: Columbia University Press, 1957.

Cole, Thomas. *The Origins of Rhetoric in Ancient Greece.* Ancient Society and History. Baltimore and London: Johns Hopkins University Press, 1991.

Donfried, Karl P. *The Romans Debate: Revised and Expanded Edition.* Peabody, MA: Hendrickson, 1991.

Elliott, Neil. *The Rhetoric of Romans: Argumentative Constraint and Strategy and Paul's Dialogue with Judaism.* JSNT Supplement Series 45. Sheffield: JSOT Press, 1990.

Hammond, N. G. L., and H. H. Scullard. *The Oxford Classical Dictionary.* 2nd ed. Oxford: Clarendon Press, 1970.

Highet, Gilbert. *The Classical Tradition: Greek and Roman Influences on Western Literature.* New York and London: Oxford University Press, 1949.

Hock, Ronald F., and Edward N. O'Neil. *The Chreia in Ancient Rhetoric: Volume I. The Progymnasmata.* Texts and Translations 27. Graeco-Roman Religion Series, ed. Hans Dieter Betz and Edward N. O'Neil, no. 9. Atlanta: Scholars Press, 1986.

Jewett, Robert. *The Thessalonian Correspondence: Pauline Rhetoric and Millenarian Piety.* Foundations and Facets. Philadelphia: Fortress Press, 1986.

Kennedy, George A. *The Art of Rhetoric in the Roman World 300 B.C.-A.D. 300.* Princeton: Princeton University Press, 1972.

———. *Classical Rhetoric and Its Christian and Secular Traditon from Ancient to Modern Times.* Chapel Hill: University of North Carolina Press, 1980.

———. *New Testament Interpretation through Rhetorical Criticism.* Chapel Hill: University of North Carolina Press, 1984.

Lausberg, Heinrich. *Handbuch der literarischen Rhetorik: Eine Grundlegung der Literaturwissenschaft.* 2 vols. Munich: Max Hueber, 1960.

Longenecker, Richard N. *Galatians.* Word Biblical Commentary 41. Dallas: Word Books, 1990.

Lund, Nils Wilhelm. *Chiasmus in the New Testament: A Study in Formgeschichte.* Chapel Hill: University of North Carolina Press, 1942.

Mack, Burton L. *Rhetoric and the New Testament*. Guides to Biblical Scholarship, New Testament Series, ed. Dan O. Via, Jr. Minneapolis: Fortress Press, 1990.

Martin, Josef. *Antike Rhetorik: Technik und Methode*. Handbuch der Altertumswissenschaft 2.3. Munich: C. H. Beck, 1974.

Mitchell, Margaret M. *Paul and the Rhetoric of Reconciliation: An Exegetical Investigation of the Language and Composition of 1 Corinthians*. Hermeneutische Untersuchungen zur Theologie 28. Tübingen: J. C. B. Mohr (Paul Siebeck), 1991.

Perelman, C., and L. Olbrechts-Tyteca. *The New Rhetoric: A Treatise on Argumentation*. Translated by John Wilkinson and Purcell Weaver. Notre Dame: University of Notre Dame Press, 1969.

Pokorny, Petr. *Colossians: A Commentary*. Translated by Siegfried S. Schatzmann. Peabody, MA: Hendrickson, 1991.

Rau, Eckard. *Reden in Vollmacht: Hintergrund, Form, und Anliegen der Gleichnisse Jesu*. Forschungen zum Religion und Literatur des alten und neuen Testaments 149. Göttingen: Vandenhoeck & Ruprecht, 1990.

Robbins, Vernon K. *Jesus the Teacher: A Socio-Rhetorical Interpretation of Mark*. Philadelphia: Fortress Press, 1984.

van der Horst, P. W. *The Sentences of Pseudo-Phocylides: With Introduction and Commentary*. Studia in Veteris Testamenti Pseudepigrapha 4. Leiden: E. J. Brill, 1979.

Wanamaker, Charles A. *The Epistles to the Thessalonians: A Commentary on the Greek Text*. The New International Greek Testament Commentary, ed. I. Howard Marshall and W. Ward Gasque. Grand Rapids: William B. Eerdmans, 1990.

Watson, Duane Frederick. *Invention, Arrangement, and Style: Rhetorical Criticism of Jude and 2 Peter*. Society of Biblical Literature Dissertation Series 104. Atlanta: Scholars Press, 1988.

———. *Persuasive Artistry: Studies in New Testament Rhetoric in Honor of George A. Kennedy*. JSNT Supplement 50. Sheffield: JSOT Press, 1991.

Witherington, Ben III. *Conflict and Community in Corinth: A Socio-Rhetorical Commentary on 1 & 2 Corinthians.* Grand Rapids: William B. Eerdmans, 1993.

Articles and Unpublished Sources

Berger, Klaus. "Hellenistische Gattungen im neuen Testament." In *Aufstieg und Niedergang der römischen Welt,* ed. Hildegard Temporini, Wolfgang Haase, and W. Haace, 2.25.2: 1031–1432, 1831–35. Berlin and New York: Walter De Gruyter, 1984.

Betz, Hans Dieter. "The Literary Composition and Function of Paul's Letter to the Galatians." *New Testament Studies* 21 (1975): 353–79.

Bitzer, Lloyd F. "The Rhetorical Situation." *Philosophy & Rhetoric* 1 (Winter 1968): 1–14.

Black, C. Clifton II. "Keeping up with Recent Studies XVI: Rhetorical Criticism and Biblical Interpretation." *The Expository Times* 100 (April 1989): 252–58.

———. "Rhetorical Questions: The New Testament, Classical Rhetoric, and Current Interpretation." *Dialog* 29 (Winter 1990): 62–63, 66, 68–70.

Campbell, Barth. "Flesh and Spirit in 1 Cor 5:5: An Exercise in Rhetorical Criticism of the NT." *Journal of the Evangelical Theological Society* 36 (September 1993): 331–42.

Fesenmayer, G. "Rhetorik." In *Lexikon für Theologie und Kirche,* ed. Josef Höfer and Karl Rahner, 8:1276–78. 2nd ed. Freiburg: Herder, 1963.

Hansen, G. Walter. "Rhetorical Criticism." In *Dictionary of Paul and His Letters,* ed. Gerald F. Hawthorne, Ralph P. Martin, and Daniel G. Reid, 622–26. Downers Grove, IL, and Leicester: InterVarsity Press, 1993.

Kennedy, George A. "'Truth' and 'Rhetoric' in the Pauline Epistles." In *The Bible as Rhetoric: Studies in Biblical Persuasion and Credibility,* ed. Martin Warner, 195–202. London and New York: Routledge, 1990.

Kroll, Wilhelm. "Rhetorik." In *Paulys Realencyclopädie des classischen Altertumswissenschaft,* ed. Wilhelm Kroll et al., supplemental vol. 7, cols. 1039–1138. Stuttgart: J. B. Metzler, 1940.

Majercik, Ruth, Thomas B. Dozeman, and Benjamin Fiore. "Rhetoric and Rhetorical Criticism." In *The Anchor Bible Dictionary*, ed. David Noel Freedman, et al., 5:717–19. New York: Doubleday, 1992.

Matera, Frank J. "The Culmination of Paul's Argument to the Galatians: Gal. 5.1–6.17." *Journal for the Study of the New Testament* 32 (February 1988): 79–91.

Muilenburg, James. "Form Criticism and Beyond." *Journal of Biblical Literature* 88 (1969): 1–18.

Myers, Charles D., Jr. "Chiastic Inversion in the Argument of Romans 3–8." *Novum Testamentum* 35 (1993): 30–47.

Robbins, Vernon K. "Rhetorical Argument about Lamps and Light in Early Christian Gospels." In *Context: Festskrift til Peder Johan Borgen/Essays in Honour of Peder Johan Borgen*, ed. Peter Wilhelm Bøckman and Roald E. Kristiansen, 177–95. Relieff 24. Trondheim: Tapir, 1987.

———. "Using a Socio-Rhetorical Poetics to Develop a Unified Method: The Woman Who Anointed Jesus as a Test Case." Paper presented at the annual meeting of the Society of Biblical Literature, San Francisco, CA, 21–24 November 1992.

———. "Writing as a Rhetorical Act in Plutarch and the Gospels." in *Persuasive Artistry: Studies in New Testament Rhetoric in Honor of George A. Kennedy*, ed. Duane F. Watson, 142–68. JSNT Supplement 50. Sheffield: JSOT Press, 1991.

Smit, J. "The Genre of 1 Corinthians 13 in the Light of Classical Rhetoric." *Novum Testamentum* 33 (1991): 193–216.

Watson, Duane F. "James 2 in Light of Greco-Roman Schemes of Argumentation." *New Testament Studies* 39 (1993): 94–121.

———. "The New Testament and Greco-Roman Rhetoric: A Bibliographical Update." *Journal of the Evangelical Theological Society* 33 (December 1990): 513–24.

———. "The New Testament and Greco-Roman Rhetoric: A Bibliography." *Journal of the Evangelical Theological Society* 31 (December 1988): 465–72.

———. "Paul's Speech to the Ephesian Elders (Acts 20:17 38): Epideictic Rhetoric of Farewell." In *Persuasive Artistry: Studies* in *New Testament Rhetoric in Honor of George A. Kennedy*, JSNT Supplement 50, ed. Duane F. Watson, 184–208.

————. "Rhetorical Criticism." In *Dictionary of Jesus and the Gospels*, ed. Joel B. Green, Scot McKnight, and I. Howard Marshall, 698–701. Downers Grove, IL, and Leicester: InterVarsity Press, 1992.

————. "Rhetorical Criticism." In *The International Standard Bible Encyclopedia*, ed. Geoffrey Bromiley, et al., 4:181–82. Grand Rapids: William B. Eerdmans, 1988.

————. "The Rhetoric of James 3:1–12 and a Classical Pattern of Argumentation." *Novum Testamentum* 35 (1993): 48–64.

Wuellner, Wilhelm. "Rhetorical Criticism and Its Theory in Culture-Critical Perspective: The Narrative Rhetoric of John 11." In *Text and Interpretation: New Approaches in the Criticism of the New Testament*, ed. P. J. Hartin and J. H. Petzer, 171–85. New Testament Tools and Studies 15. Leiden: E. J. Brill, 1991.

————. "Where Is Rhetorical Criticism Taking Us?" *Catholic Biblical Quarterly* 49 (1987): 448–63.

Zeilinger, Franz. "Die Echtheit von 2 Cor. 6:14–7:1." *Journal of Biblical Literature* 12 (Spring 1993): 71–80.

The Social Sciences and SSCNT

Books

Elliott, John H., ed. *Social-Scientific Criticism of the New Testament and Its Social World.* Semeia 35. Decatur, GA: Scholars Press, 1986.

————. *What Is Social-Scientific Criticism?* Guides to Biblical Scholarship, New Testament Series, ed. Dan O. Via, Jr. Minneapolis: Fortress Press, 1993.

Gowler, David B. *Host, Guest, Enemy and Friend: Portraits of the Pharisees in Luke and Acts.* Emory Studies in Early Christianity 2. New York: Peter Lang, 1991.

Holmberg, Bengt. *Sociology and the New Testament: An Appraisal.* Minneapolis: Fortress Press, 1990.

Kee, Howard Clark. *Knowing the Truth: A Sociological Approach to New Testament Interpretation.* Minneapolis: Fortress Press, 1989.

Malina, Bruce J. *Christian Origins and Cultural Anthropology: Practical Models for Biblical Interpretation.* Atlanta: John Knox Press, 1986.

———. *The New Testament World: Insights from Cultural Anthropology.* Louisville: John Knox Press, 1981.

Malina, Bruce J., and Richard L. Rohrbaugh. *Social Science Commentary on the Synoptic Gospels.* Minneapolis: Fortress Press, 1992.

Stambaugh, John E., and David L. Balch. *The New Testament in Its Social Environment.* Library of Early Christianity 2. Philadelphia: Westminster Press, 1986.

Articles and Unpublished Sources

Abou, A. M. Zeid. "Honour and Shame among the Bedouins of Egypt." In *Honour and Shame: The Values of Mediterranean Society,* ed. J. G. Peristiany, 243–59. The Nature of Human Society Series. Chicago: University of Chicago Press, 1966; London: Weidenfeld & Nicolson, Midway Reprint, 1974.

Campbell, J. K. "Honour and the Devil." In *Honour and Shame: The Values of Mediterranean Society,* ed. J. G. Peristiany, 139–70. The Nature of Human Society Series. Chicago: University of Chicago Press, 1966; London: Weidenfeld & Nicolson, Midway Reprint, 1974.

Delaney, Carol. "Seeds of Honor, Fields of Shame." In *Honor and Shame and the Unity of the Mediterranean,* ed. David D. Gilmore, 38–41. A Special Publication of the American Anthropological Association no. 22. Washington: American Anthropological Association, 1987.

Edwards, O. C. "Sociology as a Tool for Interpreting the New Testament." *Anglican Theological Review* 65 (October 1983): 431–48.

Elliott, John H. "The Epistle of James in Rhetorical and Social-Scientific Perspective: Holiness-Wholeness and Patterns of Replication." *Biblical Theology Bulletin* 23 (Summer 1993): 71–81.

———. Personal communication to Barth Campbell, 1992.

————. "On Wooing Crocodiles for Fun and Profit: Exegesis and the Social Sciences; Confessions of an Intact Admirer." Paper presented at the annual meeting of the Society of Biblical Literature, San Francisco, CA, 21–24 November, 1992.

Garrett, Susan R. "Sociology of Early Christianity." In *The Anchor Bible Dictionary*, ed. David Noel Freedman et al., 6:89–99. New York: Doubleday, 1992.

Gilmore, David D. "Anthropology of the Mediterranean Area." *Annual Review of Anthropology* 11 (1982): 175–205.

————. "The Shame of Dishonor." In *Honor and Shame and the Unity of the Mediterranean*, ed. David D. Gilmore, 1–9. A Special Publication of the American Anthropological Association no. 22. Washington: American Anthropological Association, 1987.

Judge, E. A. "Slave, Slavery. II. In the New Testament." In *New Bible Dictionary*, ed. J. D. Douglas and N. Hillyer, 124–25. 2nd ed. Leicester: InterVarsity Press, 1982; Wheaton, IL: Tyndale House, 1982.

Klassen, William. "The Sacred Kiss in the New Testament: An Example of Social Boundary Lines." *New Testament Studies* 39 (1993): 122–35.

Love, Stuart L. "A Macrosociological View: The Household: A Major Social Component for Gender Analysis in the Gospel of Matthew." *Biblical Theology Bulletin* 23 (Spring 1993): 21–31.

Malina, Bruce J., and Jerome H. Neyrey. "Honor and Shame in Luke-Acts: Pivotal Values of the Mediterranean World." In *The Social World of Luke-Acts: Models for Interpretation*, ed. Jerome H. Neyrey, 25–65. Peabody, MA: Hendrickson, 1991.

Moxnes, Halvor. "Honour and Righteousness in Romans." *Journal for the Study of the New Testament* 32 (1988): 61–77.

Peristiany, J. G. "Honour and Shame in a Cypriot Highland Village." In *Honour and Shame: The Values of Mediterranean Society*, ed. J. G. Peristiany, 171–90. The Nature of Human Society Series. Chicago: University of Chicago Press, 1966; London: Weidenfeld & Nicolson, Midway Reprint, 1974.

———. "Introduction." In *Honour and Shame: The Values of Mediterranean Society*, ed. J. G. Peristiany, 1–18. The Nature of Human Society Series. Chicago: University of Chicago Press, 1966; London: Weidenfeld & Nicolson, Midway Reprint, 1974.

Pitt-Rivers, Julian. "Honour and Social Status." In *Honour and Shame: The Values of Mediterranean Society*, ed. J. G. Peristiany, 19–77. The Nature of Human Society Series. Chicago: University of Chicago Press, 1966; London: Weidenfeld & Nicolson, Midway Reprint, 1974.

Rollins, Wayne Gilbert. "Slavery in the NT." In *The Interpreter's Dictionary of the Bible*, ed. Keith Crim, supplementary vol., 830–32. Nashville: Abingdon, 1976.

Schneider, Jane. "Of Vigilance and Virgins: Honor, Shame and Access to Resources in Mediterranean Societies." *Ethnology* 10 (1971): 1–24.

Scroggs, Robin. "The Sociological Interpretation of the New Testament: The Present State of Research." *New Testament Studies* 26 (1980): 164–79.

Smith, Jonathan Z. "The Social Description of Early Christianity." *Religious Studies Review* 1 (September 1975): 19–25.

Vermeulen, A. J. "Gloria." In *Reallexikon für Antike und Christentum*, ed. Theodor Klauser et al., 11:196–225. Stuttgart: Anton Hiersemann, 1950- .

Veyne, Paul. "The Roman Empire." Chap. in *A History of Private Life: I. From Pagan Rome to Byzantium*. Translated by Arthur Goldhammer. A History of Private Life, ed. Philipe Aries and Georges Duby, no. 1. Cambridge, MA: Harvard University Press, Belknap Press, 1987.

Miscellaneous Subjects

Books

Barker, Glenn W., William L. Lane, and J. Ramsey Michaels. *The New Testament Speaks.* New York: Harper & Row, 1969.

Bauer, Walter. *A Greek-English Lexicon of the New Testament and Other Early Christian Literature.* 2nd ed. Translated and edited by William F. Arndt, F. Wilbur Gingrich, and Frederick W. Danker. Chicago: University of Chicago Press, 1979.

Benko, Stephen. *Pagan Rome and the Early Christians.* Bloomington and Indianapolis: Indiana University Press, 1984.

Blass, F., and A. Debrunner. *A Greek Grammar of the New Testament and Other Early Christian Literature.* Translated and revised by Robert W. Funk. Chicago and London: University of Chicago Press, 1961.

Brown, Francis, S. R. Driver, and Charles A. Briggs. *A Hebrew and English Lexicon of the Old Testament.* Oxford: Clarendon Press, n.d.

Bultmann, Rudolf. *Theology of the New Testament.* Translated by Kendrick Grobel. 2 vols. New York: Charles Scribner's Sons, 1951–55.

Caird, G. B. *Principalities and Powers: A Study in Pauline Theology.* Oxford: Clarendon Press, 1956.

Carrington, Philip. *The Primitive Christian Catechism: A Study in the Epistles.* Cambridge: Cambridge University Press, 1940.

Carson, D. A., ed. *Studies in Biblical Greek.* Vol. 1, *Verbal Aspect in the Greek of the New Testament, with Reference to Tense and Mood,* by Stanley E. Porter. New York: Peter Lang, 1989.

Culpepper, R. Alan. *Anatomy of the Fourth Gospel: A Study in Literary Design.* New Testament Foundations and Facets. Philadelphia: Fortress Press, 1983.

Dana, H. E., and Julius R. Mantey. *A Manual Grammar of the Greek New Testament.* N.p.: Macmillan, 1955.

Esler, Philip Francis. *Community and Gospel in Luke-Acts: The Social and Political Motivations of Lucan Theology.* Society for New Testament Studies Monograph Series 57. Cambridge: Cambridge University Press, 1987.

Fee, Gordon D. *The First Epistle to the Corinthians.* The New International Commentary on the New Testament. Grand Rapids: William B. Eerdmans, 1987.

Fowler, H. W. *A Dictionary of Modern English Usage.* 2nd ed. Revised by Sir Ernest Gowers. New York and Oxford: Oxford University Press, 1965.

Guthrie, *New Testament Theology*. Leicester and Downers Grove, IL: InterVarsity Press, 1981.

Hengel, Martin. *Crucifixion in the Ancient World and the Folly of the Message of the Cross*. Translated by John Bowden. Philadelphia: Fortress Press, 1977.

Koch, Klaus. *The Growth of the Biblical Tradition*. Philadelphia: Fortress Press, 1969.

Ladd, George Eldon. *A Theology of the New Testament*. Grand Rapids: William B. Eerdmans, 1974.

Langton, Edward. *Essentials of Demonology: A Study of Jewish and Christian Doctrine: Its Origin and Development*. London: Epworth Press, 1949.

Ling, Trevor. *The Significance of Satan: New Testament Demonology and Its Contemporary Relevance*. S.P.C.K. Biblical Monographs no. 3. London: S.P.C.K., 1961.

Liversidge, Joan. *Everyday Life in the Roman Empire*. London: B. T. Batsford, 1976; New York: G. P. Putnam's Sons, 1976.

Metzger, Bruce M. *A Textual Commentary on the Greek New Testament*. N.p.: United Bible Societies, 1971.

Morris, Leon. *The Apostolic Preaching of the Cross*. Grand Rapids: William B. Eerdmans, 1955.

Moule, C. F. D. *An Idiom Book of New Testament Greek*. 2nd ed. Cambridge: Cambridge University Press, 1959.

———. *The Birth of the New Testament*. Harper's New Testament Commentaries. New York: Harper & Row, 1962.

Munro, Winsome. *Authority in Paul and Peter: The Identification of a Pastoral Stratum in the Pauline Corpus and 1 Peter*. Society for New Testament Studies Monograph Series 45. Cambridge: Cambridge University Press, 1983.

Neyrey, Jerome H. *Paul, in Other Words: A Cultural Reading of His Letters*. Louisville: Westminster/John Knox Press, 1990.

Porter, Stanley E. *Idioms of the Greek New Testament*. Biblical Languages: Greek 2. Sheffield: JSOT Press, 1992.

Ramsay, W. M. *The Church in the Roman Empire before A.D. 170*. New York and London: G. P. Putnam's Sons, Knickerbocker Press, 1919.

Rhoads, David, and Donald Michie. *Mark as Story: An Introduction to the Narrative of a Gospel.* Philadelphia: Fortress Press, 1982.

Robertson, A. T. *A Grammar of the Greek New Testament in the Light of Historical Research.* Nashville: Broadman Press, 1934.

————. *Word Pictures in the New Testament.* Vol. 3, *The Acts of the Apostles.* Nashville: Broadman Press, 1930.

Robinson, John A. T. *Redating the New Testament.* Philadelphia: Westminster Press, 1976.

Schlier, Heinrich. *Principalities and Powers in the New Testament.* New York: Herder and Herder, 1961.

Soulen, Richard N. *Handbook of Biblical Criticism.* 2nd ed. Atlanta: John Knox Press, 1981.

Stauffer, Ethelbert. *New Testament Theology.* Translated by John Marsh. New York: Macmillan, 1955.

Theissen, Gerd. "Social Stratification in the Corinthian Community: A Contribution to the Sociology of Early Hellenistic Christianity." Chap. in *The Social Setting of Pauline Christianity: Essays on Corinth.* Translated and edited by John H. Schütz. Philadelphia: Fortress Press, 1982.

Articles

Angel, Gervais T. D. "ἐρωτάω." In *The New International Dictionary of New Testament Theology,* ed. Colin Brown, 2:879–81. Grand Rapids: Zondervan, 1976.

Barclay, William. "*Lutron, Lutroun* and *Apolutrōsis*: The Debt and Its Payment." Chap. in *New Testament Words.* Philadelphia: Westminster Press, 1964.

Bauder, Wolfgang, and Hans-Georg Link. "ἐγγύς." In *The New International Dictionary of New Testament Theology,* ed. Colin Brown, 2:53–55. Grand Rapids: Zondervan, 1976.

Beasley-Murray, G. R. "Ezekiel." In *The New Bible Commentary: Revised,* ed. D[onald] Guthrie and J. A. Motyer, 664–87. Grand Rapids: William B. Eerdmans, 1970.

Becker, Ulrich. "μακάριος." In *The New International Dictionary of New Testament Theology,* ed. Colin Brown, 1:215–17. Grand Rapids: Zondervan, 1975.

Beyreuther, Erich. "Good, Beautiful, Kind: ἀγαθός, καλός, χρηστός." In *The New International Dictionary of New*

Testament Theology, ed. Colin Brown, 2:98–107. Grand Rapids: Zondervan, 1976.

———. "Shepherd: ποιμήν." In *The New International Dictionary of New Testament Theology*, ed. Colin Brown, 3:564–69. Grand Rapids: Zondervan, 1978.

Bietenhard, Hans, Colin Brown, and Burghard Siede. "Heaven, Ascend, Above." In *The New International Dictionary of New Testament Theology*, ed. Colin Brown, 2:184–96. Grand Rapids: Zondervan, 1976.

Bietenhard, Hans, and Colin Brown. "Satan, Beelzebul, Devil, Exorcism: διάβολος." In *The New International Dictionary of New Testament Theology*, ed. Colin Brown, 3:468–73. Grand Rapids: Zondervan, 1978.

Bruce, F. F. "ὑπογραμμός." In *The New International Dictionary of New Testament Theology*, ed. Colin Brown, 2:291. Grand Rapids: Zondervan, 1976.

Büchsel, F., and O. Proksch. "λύω, κτλ." In *Theological Dictionary of the New Testament*, ed. Gerhard Kittel and Gerhard Friedrich, trans. and ed. Geoffrey Bromiley, 4:329–59. Grand Rapids: William B. Eerdmans, 1967.

Coenen, Lothar. "Call: καλέω." In *The New International Dictionary of New Testament Theology*, ed. Colin Brown, 1:271–76. Grand Rapids: Zondervan, 1975.

Daube, David. "κερδαίνω as a Missionary Term." *Harvard Theological Review* 40 (1947): 109–20.

Dockery, David S. "New Testament Interpretation: A Historical Survey." In *New Testament Criticism and Interpretation*, ed. David Alan Black and David S. Dockery, 39–69. Grand Rapids: Zondervan, 1991.

Dodd, C. H. "The Beatitudes: A Form-Critical Study." Chap. in *More New Testament Studies*. Grand Rapids: William B. Eerdmans, 1968.

Esser, H. H. "Grace, Spiritual Gifts." In *The New International Dictionary of New Testament Theology*, ed. Colin Brown, 2:115–24. Grand Rapids: Zondervan, 1976.

Foerster, Werner, and Gerhard von Rad. "διαβάλλω, διάβολος." In *Theological Dictionary of the New Testament*, ed. Gerhard

Kittel and Gerhard Friedrich, trans. and ed. Geoffrey Bromiley, 2:71–81. Grand Rapids: William B. Eerdmans, 1964.

Foerster, Werner, and K. Schäferdiek. "σατανᾶς." In *Theological Dictionary of the New Testament*, ed. Gerhard Kittel and Gerhard Friedrich, trans. and ed. Geoffrey Bromiley, 7:151–65. Grand Rapids: William B. Eerdmans, 1971.

France, R. T. "Servant of the Lord." In *New Bible Dictionary*, ed. J. D. Douglas and N. Hillyer, 1092–94. 2nd ed. Leicester: InterVarsity Press, 1982; Wheaton, IL: Tyndale House, 1982.

Haarbeck, Hermann, and Hans-Georg Link. "λυπέω." In *The New International Dictionary of New Testament Theology*, ed. Colin Brown, 2:419–21. Grand Rapids: Zondervan, 1976.

Harris, Murray J. "Appendix: Prepositions and Theology in the Greek New Testament." In *The New International Dictionary of New Testament Theology*, ed. Colin Brown, 3:1171–1215. Grand Rapids: Zondervan, 1978.

Hemer, Colin J. "στέφανος." In *The New International Dictionary of New Testament Theology*, ed. Colin Brown, 1:405–6. Grand Rapids: Zondervan, 1975.

Hengel, Martin. "Hymns and Christology." Chap. in *Between Jesus and Paul: Studies in the Earliest History of Christianity*. N.p.: Fortress Press, 1983.

Hiers, Richard H. "Satan, Demons, and the Kingdom of God." *Scottish Journal of Theology* 27 (February 1974): 35–47.

Jeremias, Joachim. "ἀμνός, ἀρήν, ἀρνίον." In *Theological Dictionary of the New Testament*, ed. Gerhard Kittel and Gerhard Friedrich, trans. and ed. Geoffrey Bromiley, 1:338–41. Grand Rapids: William B. Eerdmans, 1964.

———. "γωνία, ἀκρογωνιαῖος, κεφαλὴ γωνίας." In *Theological Dictionary of the New Testament*, ed. Gerhard Kittel and Gerhard Friedrich, trans. and ed. Geoffrey Bromiley, 1:791–93. Grand Rapids: William B. Eerdmans, 1964.

———. "λίθος, λίθινος." In *Theological Dictionary of the New Testament*, ed. Gerhard Kittel and Gerhard Friedrich, trans. and ed. Geoffrey Bromiley, 4:268–80. Grand Rapids: William B. Eerdmans, 1967.

————. "πάσχα." In *Theological Dictionary of the New Testament*, ed. Gerhard Kittel and Gerhard Friedrich, trans. and ed. Geoffrey Bromiley, 5:896–904. Grand Rapids: William B. Eerdmans, 1970.

Ladd, George Eldon. "Apocalyptic Literature." In *The International Standard Bible Encyclopedia*, ed. Geoffrey Bromiley et al., 1:151–61. Grand Rapids: William B. Eerdmans, 1988.

Link, Hans-Georg. "Blessing, Blessed, Happy: εὐλογία." In *The New International Dictionary of New Testament Theology*, ed. Colin Brown 1:206–15. Grand Rapids: Zondervan, 1975.

Maurer, Christian. "σκεῦος." In *Theological Dictionary of the New Testament*, ed. Gerhard Kittel and Gerhard Friedrich, trans. and ed. Geoffrey Bromiley, 7:358–67. Grand Rapids: William B. Eerdmans, 1971.

Morris, Leon. "Redeemer, Redemption." In *New Bible Dictionary*, ed. J. D. Douglas and N. Hillyer, 1013–14. 2nd ed. Leicester: InterVarsity Press, 1982; Wheaton: Tyndale House, 1982.

Mundle, Wilhelm. "Rock, Stone, Corner-Stone, Pearl, Precious Stones: γωνία." In *The New International Dictionary of New Testament Theology*, ed. Colin Brown, 3:388–90. Grand Rapids: Zondervan, 1978.

Peisker, Carl Heinz, and Colin Brown. "Parable, Allegory, Proverb: παραβολή, παροιμία." In *The New International Dictionary of New Testament Theology*, ed. Colin Brown, 2:743–60. Grand Rapids: Zondervan, 1976.

Schmidt, Karl Ludwig. "καλέω, κτλ." In *Theological Dictionary of the New Testament*, ed. Gerhard Kittel and Gerhard Friedrich, trans. and ed. Geoffrey Bromiley, 3:487–536. Grand Rapids: William B. Eerdmans, 1965.

Siede, Burghard. "κέρδος." In *The New International Dictionary of New Testament Theology*, ed. Colin Brown, 3:136–38. Grand Rapids: Zondervan, 1978.

Siede, Burghard, Egon Brandenburger, and Colin Brown. "Cross, Wood, Tree." In *The New International Dictionary of New Testament Theology*, ed. Colin Brown, 1:389–405. Grand Rapids: Zondervan, 1975.

Stewart, R. A. "Passover." In *New Bible Dictionary*, ed. J. D. Douglas and N. Hillyer, 881–83. 2nd ed. Leicester: InterVarsity Press, 1982; Wheaton, IL: Tyndale House, 1982.

Tiedtke, Erich. "Face: πρόσωπον." In *The New International Dictionary of New Testament Theology*, ed. Colin Brown, 1:585–87. Grand Rapids: Zondervan, 1975.

Viviano, Benedict T. "Beatitudes Found among Dead Sea Scrolls." *Biblical Archaeology Review* 18 (November-December 1992): 53–55, 66.

Walls, A. F. "Erastus." In *New Bible Dictionary*, ed. J. D. Douglas and N. Hillyer, 341. 2nd ed. Leicester: InterVarsity Press, 1982; Wheaton, IL: Tyndale House, 1982.

Wenham, David. "The Paulinism of Acts again: Two Historical Clues in 1 Thessalonians." *Themelios* 13 (January/February 1988): 53–55.

Wheaton, D. H. "Pilate." In *New Bible Dictionary*, ed. J. D. Douglas and N. Hillyer, 939–40. 2nd ed. Leicester: InterVarsity Press, 1982; Wheaton, IL: Tyndale House, 1982.

Wilson, R. McL. "*Soteria*." *Scottish Journal of Theology* 6 (December 1953): 406–16.

Yates, Roy. "The Powers of Evil in the New Testament." *The Evangelical Quarterly* 52 (April-June 1980): 97–111.

CPSIA information can be obtained
at www.ICGtesting.com
Printed in the USA
LVOW07s2327270717
542802LV00002BA/264/P